WARRIORS OF THE NIGHT

By the same author

A LEGACY OF HATE (1982)

WARRIORS OF THE NIGHT

SPIES, SOLDIERS, AND AMERICAN INTELLIGENCE

ERNEST VOLKMAN

WILLIAM MORROW AND COMPANY, INC.

NEW YORK

Library of Congress Cataloging in Publication Data

Volkman, Ernest.
  Warriors of the night.

  Bibliography: p.
  Includes index.
  1. Intelligence service—United States. 2. United
States—Military policy. I. Title
UB251.U5V65 1985   327.1'2'0973   84-20551
ISBN 0-688-04177-9

Printed in the United States of America

First Edition

1 2 3 4 5 6 7 8 9 10

BOOK DESIGN BY BERNARD SCHLEIFER

For The Toad

Tecum vivere amem, tecum obeam libens

acknowledgments

IT WOULD BE IMPOSSIBLE to list all the people to whom I owe a debt of gratitude in the making of this book, although I do want to pay special tribute to several who contributed more than a reasonable share of their time: David Kahn, William Corson, L. J. Davis, Knut Royce, John Cummings, Vladimir Sakharov, Sam Greenberg, Duane Yorke, and Dr. Cornelius Savin. Special thanks are also due Leon Shuro (for Russian translations) and to Eric Goldstein and Karen Schwarz (for invaluable research assistance). I am particularly indebted to Peter Bloch, executive editor of *Penthouse* magazine, for his encouragement and advice, and Bob Guccione, publisher of *Omni* and *Penthouse* magazines, for his many kindnesses toward me, along with his unflagging support.

A number of other people, whose aid was of inestimable value, cannot be publicly acknowledged. They know who they are; I am very grateful to them. However, they are in no way responsible for the opinions, interpretations, and statements of fact in this book, and any errors are solely my own.

—ERNEST VOLKMAN

New York
July 1984

contents

introduction

GOD AND ICE WATER: THE AMERICAN INTELLIGENCE PROCESS

> It ain't what a man doesn't know that
> makes him a fool, but what he knows
> that ain't so.
>
> —JOSH BILLINGS

PRESSED ONE DAY to succinctly define the quality of American intelligence, Lieutenant General Samuel V. Wilson, former deputy director of the Central Intelligence Agency, replied: "We can't tell you what God is going to do on Tuesday of next week. But we probably can tell you when He's getting mad."

It remains one of the better definitions around, yet there is cause to wonder about that formula. True, no one expects that any intelligence service, least of all the American one, can read God's mind. But, more important, does American intelligence—as Wilson claimed metaphorically—have a fairly sound idea of what's going on out there in the rest of the world?

Generally speaking, no. Judged in overall terms, the record of American intelligence since the birth of its modern form in the post-World War I era has been a poor one. Indeed, it is possible to recite a history of American intelligence solely in terms of a long litany of failure, from revolutionary Russia to Vietnam, from Pearl Harbor to Lebanon. That would amount to a certain amount of oversimplification, yet the fact remains: Beginning with Woodrow Wilson, every President in this century has experienced at least one major foreign-policy disaster that was directly attributable either to a lack of adequate intelligence or to an outright failure to understand the intelligence at hand.

And failure continues to dominate American intelligence, despite the fact that the United States has a vast intelligence apparatus at work, which now employs more than 150,000 people and spends over $15 billion annually. Yet the more we spend, the less we seem to know, judging by a recurring series of foreign-policy disasters, an astonishingly high percentage of them involving intelligence failure.

How this came to be is a matter of some import, for fundamentally, all intelligence is about warning. Is danger imminent? What are the significant trends? Is the other side about to move? These are vital questions that define national security, and it is intelligence—effective, timely, rational— that must provide the answers. Without good intelligence in a dangerous world, nations tend to operate blind, often with fateful consequences. The United States has not been exempt from that hard lesson of history—witness the bitter example of its intelligence failure at Pearl Harbor, or in a more recent occurrence, what happened when it placed military forces into the middle of a Lebanese political madhouse, which American intelligence did not even begin to comprehend.

The overall failure of American intelligence results in equal measure from politics, some uniquely American cultural characteristics, and the very nature of intelligence itself. To understand how this combination works, a few words about the intelligence process are in order.

To begin with, it is important to remember that there is a difference between *information* and *intelligence,* which can be broadly defined as *processed information.* The process is roughly similar to the one that goes on each day inside a newspaper office—a large amount of information of varying reliability flows in, there to be checked, digested, analyzed, and processed into a package that the editors believe is a reasonably complete report on the important events of the day. In intelligence, the same process is often called "intellection," by which is meant the processing of information (sometimes termed "raw intelligence") into judgments. These judgments are given to policymakers (sometimes known as "users" or "customers" in intelligence jargon), who are then supposed to make decisions based on them.

But that, in turn, rests on the confidence of the customers in the intelligence agency providing the judgments and, often more significantly, on the quality of the intelligence itself. It is this intellection process, involving important questions of confidence and reliability, that is the tricky part. The process is constantly affected by the biases of the people who make the judgments, the predilections of the customers, and, more often than not, sheer inability to make solid deductions because of a lack of information. In this last case, one of the more dangerous atmospheres in which intelligence agencies can operate, judgments tend to become hedged and indefinite, inducing either overcaution or simply wrongheaded conclusions.

Of course, there is rarely an intelligence agency conclusion that is infallible, unless there is an unparalleled, unimpeachable source. Even Ultra, the famous British code-breaking operation of World War II, which allowed the Allies to read virtually all the German High Command's secret radio signals, was not an intelligence paragon. Despite the vast advantage Ultra gave American and British strategists, it is sometimes forgotten that the operation could read only the German decisions and orders that were dispatched in radio form. It could not detect verbal orders, nor could it detect information sent by telephone over secure land lines. And most important, it could not detect the thought processes inside the heads of Germany's military leadership. (It did not detect, for example, Hitler's plan to fall upon a thinly defended area of the Western front in 1944, a plan conducted under radio silence. Thus, when the Germans struck at the

INTRODUCTION

Battle of the Bulge, among the more shocked witnesses were the American and British intelligence officers who had believed that ULTRA would always give them advance notice of significant German military moves.)

The intelligence failure at the Bulge—and many others —offer convincing proof of the error of overreliance on a single technical source. But American intelligence has continued to be obsessed with finding the one intelligence paragon that will answer all questions. That search has centered on technology, a quest in which there emerges the first important theme in the development of American intelligence: as an institution totally smitten with technology.

In large measure, the reason for that technical infatuation stems from a peculiar bias of American culture, which is dominated by an ethos that most, if not all, problems are soluble by systems. The result is that modern American intelligence tends to distrust raw intelligence produced by human beings (called HUMINT in American intelligence slang), the traditional cloak-and-dagger spy.

Instead, the sprawling U.S. apparatus has concentrated its efforts on ever more complicated technical systems to collect the raw intelligence, leaving humans the job of interpreting this huge amount of data. The data is regarded as unbiased (in the human sense), since it is collected by photo-reconnaissance satellites (PHOTINT), electronic eavesdropping (SIGINT), and communications intercepts (COMMINT), all of them dutiful machines that will produce only the images and electronic blips they are told to collect, without interpretation. (Slightly less than 20 percent of all American intelligence is collected by human beings, the bulk of them CIA agents attached to U.S. embassies abroad and military-intelligence personnel.)

The operating theory is that the more intelligence is produced by machine, the less likely it is to be subject to the fallacies of human error. In fact, however, no technical solution is possible, no matter how many billions the United

States pours into more and more technical sophistication.

The problem is twofold: First, the human beings who interpret the supposedly immutable "facts" produced by technical collection systems are just that, human. What a spy-satellite picture might mean is subject to a whole range of human biases, the most important being political ones. Second, there is no intelligence system, even the massive American apparatus, that collects *everything*. What it collects is determined by a system of collection priorities, which in turn immediately involves questions of bias, since human beings decide what is important to collect, and what is not. (For example, a number of experts in 1972 tried to persuade U.S. intelligence agencies, notably the CIA, to pay more attention to the growing economic power of the petroleum-exporting countries and its possible implications for U.S. national security. Their arguments went unheeded, and the 1973 OPEC oil boycott came as a complete shock, catching this country totally unprepared.)

At the same time, a prevailing belief exists that there is some sort of correlation between quantity and quality of intelligence—the greater the amount of raw intelligence collected, the more likely that the "truth" will be unearthed. Again, this is a reflection of an American cultural bias; in a country where the microcircuit and the resulting information explosion were born, there is an abiding faith that much intelligence work is a simple function of collection. For that reason, U.S. intelligence officials do not dwell on the quality of whatever human sources they might control, or on the incisiveness of an intelligence analysis. Instead, there is much delight in recounting the wonders of their technical collection systems—how the latest spy satellite can spot a golf ball from hundreds of miles up in space, and so on.

But quantity is no guarantee of anything save quantity; the most detailed raw intelligence is only a pile of filmstrips and paper unless there is somebody around who understands what it all means. And if resources are concentrated on the technical systems themselves (and they do swallow up the lion's share of American intelligence budgets), then there is relatively little left to buy the kind of human resources needed to make sense out of all that raw intelligence. What has happened is that intelligence has been outrun by technology; American intelligence, especially, is flooded by the mountains of data it so assiduously and ingeniously collects. In the process, the humans who are supposed to be interpreting this ocean are often overwhelmed. The tail is wagging the dog; an increasing percentage of human resources in U.S. intelligence agencies are expended in organizing and directing the technical collection systems. (Or, as Lady Astor was reputed to have said during that fateful night aboard the *Titanic:* "I asked for a glass of ice water, but this is ridiculous.")

This might be called the "Lady Astor Factor," and it runs in tandem with another consistent theme in the development of modern American intelligence—the peculiar characteristics of this country's politics. The central problem is that intelligence is a highly politicized item, for it often carries with it immense political implications. To cite another Vietnam example, consider the billions of dollars appropriated by Congress for that war on the basis of an intelligence statistic: How many Viet Cong and North Vietnamese troops were in combat? A low figure would indicate "progress," while a higher figure would show the American attrition strategy a failure.

Intelligence judgments do not take place in a political vacuum, least of all in the complex American political system. For that reason, intelligence tends to be subject to a whole series of political pressures, the most important of them from the executive branch, which has a bad habit of wanting to hear only the intelligence that it wants to hear. American policymakers are often the product of a catechism of assumptions and political beliefs (and, often, shibboleths) that no amount of information will shake. As Vietnam demonstrated, policymakers locked into a policy of their own devising tend to be annoyed by intelligence that suggests that they may have made a mistake.

This process has been called "the pleasures of self-deception," an accurate phrase that illustrates an interesting statistic: Of nine major strategic "surprise" attacks throughout the world since 1940, not one was truly a surprise. In each case, leaders of the nations about to be attacked knew such a strike was imminent and were often in possession of detailed intelligence. Yet the leaders simply did not believe, so they discounted any intelligence that ran counter to what they knew to be "fact." Not even a series of aggressive moves before the attack, unmistakably tipping the attacker's hand, could dissuade them. And so Joseph Stalin in 1941 refused to believe that a German invasion was imminent—"British provocation" he contemptuously scrawled across one intelligence report giving the precise day of the Nazi attack.

It is tempting to believe that such myopia is a a symptom of totalitarian societies, where rigidly enforced belief systems tend to spawn narrow thinking imposed from above, or no thinking at all. But consider that only nine years after this monumental intelligence blunder, the representative of a democracy—U.S. Assistant Secretary of State Dean Rusk—solemnly assured a congressional committee that there was no possibility that the North Koreans would launch an invasion southward. (Only a few days later, the North Koreans did precisely that.) And just eighteen years after *that* blunder, the uniformed representatives of the democracies included in NATO went off on leave one day after discounting what they considered "impossible" intelligence reports warning of an imminent Soviet invasion of Czechoslovakia. Several hours after reaching their vacation spots, they heard on the radio that the impossible invasion had just taken place.

At root, of course, intelligence is an inexact science. And it is especially inexact when it operates, as does the American intelligence community, in the context of what is an extremely complex and often troublesome political system. Which is to say that American intelligence has been operating in a flawed democracy, and one of the costs of that democracy may be that its intelligence is equally flawed.

It has always been that way, seemingly, from the very moment of the birth of modern American intelligence, a difficult birth that began not in the United States, but in Moscow.

WARRIORS
OF THE
NIGHT

one

OUR MAN IN MOSCOW

> The history of old Russia was the
> continual beatings she suffered for
> falling behind. She was beaten by the
> Turkish beys. She was beaten by the
> Polish and Lithuanian gentry. She was
> beaten by the British and French
> capitalists. All beat her—for her
> backwardness. . . . That is why we
> must no longer lag behind.
>
> —JOSEPH STALIN, 1931

ON THE RAINY NIGHT of September 15, 1918, the man who
represented what remained of American intelligence in
Russia stood in the darkened doorway of a house just across
the street from the Norwegian Legation building in Moscow.

Xenophon Dmitrevich Kalamatiano carefully watched as
a contingent of Red Guards paced in front of the high wall
surrounding the legation building. As the rain poured
down, Kalamatiano, somewhat incongruously grasping his
fancy walking stick, peered through the storm, seeking the
opening that would allow him to dash across the street
unobserved and clamber up the wall, then into the diplomatic sanctuary of the legation grounds. When he gauged
that that moment had come, Kalamatiano ran across the
street and began climbing.

But he had miscalculated. The wall, slippery from the
rain, resisted his effort to scale it. As he struggled, somehow
trying to climb while still holding on to his walking stick, he
suddenly felt one of the Red Guards seize him by the ankle.
There was a cry for help, and then other Red Guards ran up
to aid in pulling the struggling Kalamatiano to the ground.

23

WARRIORS OF THE NIGHT

Taken to the headquarters of the Cheka,* the secret police and internal-security force of the young Bolshevik government, Kalamatiano was indignant. Why, he demanded to know, was he being held? He insisted he was merely a trade representative in Russia for a New York-based import-export company known as Pankivel; he knew nothing about any espionage.

Jacov Peters, head of the Moscow Cheka, regarded all this with a bemused tolerance, for he knew better. For one thing, he knew that Kalamatiano was in fact the chief American intelligence agent in revolutionary Russia, the man for whom his agents had been scouring the country for weeks. For another, he knew that Kalamatiano, however much the American looked liked a prosperous trader, was nothing of the sort; the trading operation was actually cover for an extensive operation to gather intelligence on the revolutionary regime's military and economic strength. As for circumstantial evidence, Peters had only to unscrew the top of the fancy walking stick the elegantly attired Kalamatiano invariably carried. Concealed inside the hollow top was a rolled-up piece of paper listing the names of a dozen Russian assets, with annotations on how much they had been paid for providing information.

And Peters and the Cheka knew a great deal more. Most important, they knew that American intelligence in the person of Kalamatiano had made a serious blunder. The blunder had everything to do with the very nature of American intelligence itself at this early point in its existence, which makes some of the events surrounding the Kalamatiano spy case worthy of examination, for there is much to heed in that all but forgotten incident.

The case was a subplot to the most dramatic and consequential historic event of this century, the Russian Revolu-

*So called from Russian initials of the All-Russian Extraordinary Commission for Combating Counterrevolution and Sabotage. Formed on December 20, 1917, the Cheka underwent a number of organizational and acronymic transformations, ultimately emerging as the modern Commissariat for State Security, known more familiarly by its initials, KGB.

tion. It came at a time when the United States, already involved in the First World War, suddenly found itself thrust for the first time in its history onto the world stage. And it also came at a time when the United States was singularly unprepared for that role: In a word, it was blind.

In intelligence terms, the Americans knew nothing, except whatever their allies told them. The American armies, then battling the Germans on the Western Front, had a nascent intelligence service that had built a modest capability for low-level reconnaissance and other such operations, but it was a capability that rested on a foundation constructed by British and French military intelligence. And in broader terms, for the kind of high-level intelligence needed by President Woodrow Wilson as he presided over this first American foray into world politics, the Americans had only something called U1, a State Department bureau that functioned as an informal centralized intelligence agency, collecting and collating reports from various U.S. representatives abroad. It also ran some amateur intelligence-collection operations, recruiting ordinary American citizens who were willing to do espionage on the side.

Kalamatiano was among a group of several such Americans who had been thus recruited, on this occasion for the purpose of finding out what was happening in revolutionary Russia. The question was of some priority, for what happened in Moscow, it was believed, would determine the course of the war.

The United States had entered the war only three weeks after the czar had been overthrown, but there was the problem of several million German troops preoccupied on the Eastern Front. Should the revolutionary government in Russia sign a separate peace with Germany, then all those troops would be released to fall upon the Allies in the west. All of which amounted to a critical foreign-policy consensus among the Americans and the Allies: Somehow, Russia must stay in the war.

And it also created an intelligence priority: determining if Russia had the capacity and will to remain in that war. The first attempt to answer that question was mounted by British intelligence in the person of the writer Somerset Maugham, who was dispatched to Russia in the spring of 1917 and, operating under the cover of researching a book, told to divine if the new revolutionary government under Aleksandr Kerenski had the wherewithal to continue in the war.

Maugham's recruitment is worthy of note, because it was carried out by an old friend, Sir William Wiseman, head of British intelligence in the United States. Officially, Wiseman was head of the British Purchasing Mission to the United States, but he was in fact busily engaged in running a large-scale intelligence, propaganda, and counterespionage operation against the Germans—with the even more important subsidiary assignment of getting the Americans into the war. An influential figure in the American establishment, Wiseman had a direct pipeline to the White House, and in the absence of any effective American intelligence presence, it was thus British intelligence that shaped most of Wilson's perceptions about the European conflagration.

Those perceptions turned out to be quite wrong. Maugham had reported that the Kerenski government in Russia had no hope of continuing the war without massive Allied support and, more important, was in danger of coming apart in the face of the growing power of the Bolsheviks—who had vowed to take Russia out of the war when they took power.

The subsequent Bolshevik coup proved Maugham right, but Wilson then agreed to a number of drastic steps the British (and, later, the French) proposed to solve the "Bolshevik problem": landing of Allied forces in Russia, first ostensibly to bolster the Russian war effort, but actually to help destroy the Bolshevik regime; approval of a covert-action program to disrupt and destroy the new government, and direct support for the anti-Bolshevik forces in the Russian civil war.

The perceptions on which Wilson based these drastic steps were badly out of touch with reality. Wilson not only misunderstood the power and influence of the Bolsheviks but, in trying to prop up Kerenski, believed that a divided Russia somehow could continue a war when its economy was a shambles and its politics a madhouse, and when the rank-and-file of its soldiers no longer heeded their officers. Furthermore, Wilson shared the conviction, largely fostered by the British, that the Bolsheviks were transitory and therefore vulnerable to outside pressure.

It was a belief that rested on the dubious assumption that the Bolsheviks enjoyed no real popular support in Russia; hence, pressure by the Allies would cause the government to collapse, and its presumably more moderate replacement would then rejoin the war. The belief resulted in a foreign-policy disaster of the first magnitude. Wilson sent thirteen thousand American troops to Russia, a force that achieved little except to earn the undying hatred of the Bolsheviks, who never forgave the Americans. At the same time, the other key component of the Allied plan, support of the so-called "White" forces in the Russian civil war, also turned out to be a fiasco. Led by a motley lot of corrupt incompetents, the Whites failed against the more energetic efforts of the new Red Army under Leon Trotsky.

The less overt aspects of the plan to get rid of the Bolsheviks, including sabotage actions, Allied-fostered uprisings by Russian military units, and an assassination plot against Lenin himself, also failed. And the failure in this case had everything to do with the character of American intelligence, summarized in the case of Xenophon Kalamatiano.

As noted earlier, Kalamatiano was among a group of amateurs recruited by the State Department for espionage in Russia. A professor of languages, Kalamatiano was in fact a good intelligence agent. Operating under his cover of trade representative, he had formed a ring of more than thirty agents who penetrated every level of the Bolshevik government, including the Red Army high command.

But Kalamatiano's effectiveness depended on his keeping his cover, and that effectiveness was destroyed when his superiors got the idea of involving him in the covert-action operations against the Bolsheviks. That was a fundamental error, for Kalamatiano, meeting openly with dissidents, soon became known to Cheka. And he became known because the "dissidents" were actually Cheka agents who had let the assorted plots run their course until all the Allied intelligence operatives involved were identified. Then the Cheka struck. Nearly three hundred Russian citizens were arrested (most were later shot), and the Allied intelligence agents and diplomats involved in the plots had to flee for their lives. But Kalamatiano had been trapped out of range of a friendly embassy in which to gain sanctuary and, after barely eluding a Cheka dragnet for several weeks, finally took the desperate step of attempting to scale the wall around the Norwegian Legation. (Convicted of espionage, Kalamatiano was to spend nearly a year in prison before being released as part of an American-Soviet bargain over U.S. food shipments.)

All this amounted to a very troubled birth for modern American intelligence, all the more so because from that first moment, it acquired a number of bad habits. One was the reliance on "friendly" intelligence services, an especially dangerous practice that has the advantage of providing intelligence resources otherwise unavailable, but has the singular disadvantage of source: Friendly services tend to provide intelligence that is carefully screened to provide whatever the recipient is supposed to hear, rather than what they should hear. The second was the error of mixing intelligence and covert-action operations, a mistake, as we shall see, that would be repeated later and often.

The overreliance on friendly intelligence services was the central theme of American intelligence in its infancy following the end of World War I. Much of the reason was lack of resources. In 1922, the Army's Military Intelligence Division had a grand total of ninety people, and the Navy's Office of Naval Intelligence had forty-two. All this for a world that was in convulsion politically, including the rise of the Soviet Communist state and the resurgence of fascism, two of the more important political hurricanes that would eventually involve the United States.

Yet American intelligence had no real inkling of the forces and developments that were tearing the world's political fabric apart. It saw the world through the eyes, for the most part, of friendly services, most notably the British Secret Intelligence Service (SIS, later MI6). But SIS at that point was more an unruly fraternity house than an intelligence service. Under the command of Captain Sir Mansfield Cumming, a wild character who once amputated his own leg after it was shattered in an automobile accident (he later had the disconcerting habit of striking matches on the wooden replacement), SIS specialized in freebooting. The more "active" a scheme seemed, especially in operations directed against the Soviet Union, the more likely it was to be set in operation.

Such schemes—including the one to smuggle millions of moths into the Soviet Union to chew up movie screens and wreck the government's extensive movie propaganda operation—might have provided the British with some way of striking back at the hated Bolsheviks, but they had little to do with intelligence. The Americans, however, failed to recognize that fact, much as they failed to recognize that the aid provided in the interwar years by another friendly service—the Chinese Kuomintang secret police under Colonel Tai Li—was equally valueless. Li was supposed to be telling the Americans what was happening in China and what the Japanese and Russians were up to in Manchuria. Unfortunately, most of the Americans who dealt with Colonel Li failed to understand that he was spending most of his time in his real avocation—gunrunning and operating a stable of fifty-seven White Russian prostitutes in his famed brothel, known as the "House of One Thousand Assholes."

Such intelligence blindness led to a terrible confusion in the formulation of American military policy. Consider, for example, that in 1928, at a time when the Soviet Union and Germany were already deeply engaged on a secret military collaboration,* the U.S. War Department's War Plans Division—responsible for formulating American strategic plans for future wars—arrived at the odd conclusion that America's most probable future enemy was Great Britain. The division prepared a complex plan for that future conflict, during which the United States would seize Canada and British possessions in the Western Atlantic, then invade Great Britain itself from Ireland. (This fantasy was not formally scrapped until 1939, when, in a masterful understatement, the Secretary of War pronounced it "wholly inapplicable to present conditions.")

The American intelligence vacuum had other consequences for the American military, notably in the Army Air Force, youngest and most aggressive component of America's creaky military machine. The AAF was dominated before World War II by a mafia of big-bomber advocates who believed that the next war could be won almost exclusively by fleets of such bombers that would pulverize an enemy into terrorized submission. Their strategic vision was fixed on the great cities of Europe, where, according to their calculus, the nerve centers of governments lay vulnerable to air power.

This vision finally resulted in the unique American idea of a heavily armed, long-range bomber able to carry out high-precision daylight missions against strategic objectives while unescorted by fighter cover; the bombers' gun defenses would shoot their way out of any enemy fighter defenses. The result was the B-17 "Flying Fortress," first introduced in 1938. It looked impressive enough, but there was not the slightest shred of intelligence to support its operating assumption; instead, the plane was developed from a series of assumptions that had become shibboleths.

And they were shibboleths that had ignored incontrovertible evidence that what the AAF believed to be truth was

---

*The collaboration was born in the 1922 Rapallo Pact between the two countries, which included secret addenda for military cooperation. Despite the large scale of the program, the British and Americans missed it. The U.S. Army MID discounted newspaper reports of the secret agreement, and a British intelligence report of 1931, when the program was in full swing, concluded that it didn't exist.

actually dangerous fantasy. The man who provided that evidence, Captain Claire Chennault (later a general and head of the famed Flying Tigers, American volunteer pilots in China), had insisted throughout the 1930s that AAF calculations about bomber survivability in the face of fighter defenses were all wrong. Finally, in 1940, after World War II had already started and Spitfires were decimating German bombers over England, Chennault was permitted a test of his thesis. In the skies over a California desert, Chennault's fighters, using his innovative tactics of fighters "scrambled" by extensive warning networks, took on a squadron of B-17s. It was a slaughter. The fighters, firing gun cameras instead of bullets, showed they could shoot down the bombers with ease. As Chennault had argued, the gun crews aboard the B-17s could take on only one target at a time, meaning that the fighters simply overwhelmed the guns guarding one side of the aircraft. AAF generals, alarmed at how the B-17 formations had been chopped to pieces, ruled Chennault's tactics "dangerous" and invalidated the results of the test.

But Chennault wasn't finished. A year later, Chennault set up an alert network for his Flying Tigers fighters, and on the first day of operation, they shot down twenty-six unescorted Japanese bombers before they even came close to their target. It was a lesson lost on the AAF, which persisted in sending unescorted B-17s over Germany in daylight raids until 1944, when terrible losses finally convinced them that Chennault had been right all along. New long-range fighters were developed to keep the Messerschmidts away from the vulnerable bombers.

Chennault had reached his conclusions on the basis of careful analysis of after-action reports from air battles, the kind of intelligence function his service hadn't bothered to carry out. Nor had army intelligence bothered to analyze the tactical and technological developments that were revolutionizing land warfare. As late as 1940—when German air-armor teams had already smashed three of the world's most powerful armies—Major General John K. Herr, the army's chief of cavalry, argued before a congressional committee that "modernized" horse cavalry would lead the United States to victory in any future war. Defined as horses moved in trucks up to the front lines, backed by antitank guns, Herr's modernized cavalry was supposed to defeat the German panzer divisions. Asked about Poland, where the German armor made short work of the brave but hopelessly outgunned Polish cavalry, Herr blandly replied that the Poles had not had good cavalry; if they had had, he insisted, the Germans would have been defeated.

Herr's monumental stupidity was important, for he was then in the forefront of a fight to give his branch control over all American mechanized units, a fight that had blocked development of American armor for years. A confirmed horse soldier, Herr worked in a military service whose intelligence never confronted him with any evidence that his assumptions were wrong. Likewise, the big-bomber officers of the AAF and the battleship admirals of the navy could doze on in ignorance, content that their benign belief of the next war to be fought with the tactics and weapons of the last was established truth. And it took the shock of tragic events to awaken them from their torpor: battleships, lined up like sitting ducks at Pearl Harbor for the new queen of naval warfare, the airplane; inadequately armored American tanks incinerated by superior German armor; and formations of B-17s overwhelmed by fighters.

This dark picture of intelligence myopia was only partly relieved by a single bright spot: the brilliant American success in code breaking, but even there, the piecemeal nature of American intelligence militated against the most effective use of that precious raw intelligence. The problem was apparent to President Franklin D. Roosevelt long before Pearl Harbor, but it was not until just a few months before that event that he decided to do anything about it.

His solution was a cautious attempt to create America's first real centralized intelligence service. He appointed one of his unofficial ambassadors-at-large (and informal intelligence agent), well-connected Republican lawyer William O. Donovan, to the innocuous-sounding title of coordinator of information (later changed to Office of Strategic Services, or OSS).

"You will have to begin with nothing," Roosevelt told Donovan upon appointing him to the job. "We have *no* intelligence service." That was not strictly true, of course, for the United States at that point in fact had several intelligence services. Besides the various military-intelligence agencies, there was also the FBI, which in those days also had foreign-intelligence-collection duties, and at least a dozen other federal agencies with varying intelligence functions. The problem was that none of them seemed to talk to the other, and all jealously guarded their respective turfs, protected by assorted congressional allies.

Roosevelt was aware of that political fact of life, which is why he trod cautiously in the intelligence domain. He was not quite certain exactly what kind of new intelligence agency he wanted, but it is clear that what he had in mind was something along the lines of the intelligence service he admired the most, the British SIS. But Roosevelt's uncritical admiration, which failed to perceive some of the real decay behind the flashy facade of a service that had seen better days, was to lead to a fatal mistake in his conception of the OSS.

The problem was that Roosevelt was attempting to create an SIS clone for a very different set of circumstances. Unlike Great Britain, which had a long history of centralized intelligence, the United States not only had military intelligence agencies of long standing, but a very powerful federal law enforcement agency under a politically unassailable director —J. Edgar Hoover's FBI. And Roosevelt failed to recognize that none of those agencies would happily submerge its interests to a centralized intelligence service.

And so, from the very beginning of OSS, the military intelligence agencies and the FBI sought to clip its wings. In the process, OSS was ultimately transformed into an intelligence agency that was not very much of an intelligence agency at all. Barred from code-breaking operations, the crowning achievement of American intelligence at that point (and guarded like a jewel by the military-intelligence agencies), OSS became something of a large-scale commando organization. That became the only real role left to it, considering the outright hostility of the FBI and the refusal of the military intelligence agencies to cooperate (General Douglas MacArthur totally banned OSS from his command in the Pacific).

The OSS record, judged in action terms, is well known, but it is worthwhile asking what any of the work with resistance organizations, extensive propaganda operations, and sabotage missions had to do with intelligence. Not much, and it is here that the seed of what was to be a very nettlesome problem was planted. For when the OSS later served as a model for the new postwar centralized American intelligence apparatus, that model was precisely wrong: OSS had blurred the distinction between intelligence and paramilitary action. Furthermore, it was an agency in which action always reigned paramount over intelligence collection, a heritage carried over into postwar American intelligence, notably the CIA.

From an intelligence standpoint, the overall record of the OSS was appalling, although it should be noted that the record of the rest of American intelligence was equally poor—best demonstrated in the case of how the war's most important decision, the construction and use of the atomic bomb, came about.

The original rationale for the Manhattan Project was the conviction that German development of an atomic bomb was surely imminent. This amounted to an intelligence judgment by induction: The first fission of uranium had occurred in Germany in 1938, Germany was preeminent in science, Hitler had talked publicly about "wonder weapons," and so on—all of this seemingly pointing to a viable German atomic weapons program. Yet where were the vast processing plants necessary to manufacture weapons-grade uranium? Where were the large testing facilities needed to perfect such a weapon? In short, where was the hard evidence that the Germans were in fact building what we thought they were building?

There wasn't any. American intelligence, especially the OSS, had no topflight sources inside Germany—or anyplace else inside Europe, for that matter—to reveal the extent or lack of it of the German program. All the Americans had to go on were *indications* that the Germans were rushing pellmell to build an atomic bomb, not hard intelligence. Nevertheless, a curious intelligence deduction was formulated: No evidence of the German program could be seen, which meant that such a program was indeed under way. How so? Because the program was so secret, obviously the Germans had taken extraordinary measures to conceal it.

However curious, the judgment was taken quite seriously by the men who formulated it, a special U.S. Army intelligence unit assigned to the Manhattan Project with the specific mission of discovering the extent of the German atomic program. Without any sources or means of gathering intelligence from within Germany itself, the unit was reduced to a form of intelligence ouija board, extrapolating critically important deductions from a series of what may or may not have been important clues while at the same time filtering them through the prism of the American experience. In other words, if the Americans had been in the same position as the Germans, then there was no doubt they would have tried to develop an atomic weapon. Therefore, the Germans were definitely trying to build one, and were undoubtedly well advanced.

It was not until 1945, when special intelligence teams fanned out over Germany to track down the small band of German atomic scientists, that the realization dawned that the Germans were nowhere near to building an atomic bomb. Germany had gone as far as construction that year of a small, crude nuclear pile in a tiny southern German village. There, while the German scientists waited for the pile to reach the critical stage, the brilliant physicist Werner Heisenberg, director of the program, sat in a nearby church and played mournful Bach fugues on an organ.

In effect, then, the American atomic bomb had been constructed primarily out of intelligence failure; all along, it had been intended as the answer to what American intelligence had deemed the certitude of a Nazi atomic bomb.

The people of Hiroshima wound up paying the price for that failure. On the morning of August 6, 1945, the air-raid sirens in the Japanese city went off at 7:08 A.M., the third such alarm in twenty-four hours. The alarm this time had been triggered by the appearance of a single American B-29 bomber, a weather-reconnaissance plane called by its crew *Straight Flush,* and decorated by a cartoon of a Japanese soldier being flushed down a toilet. *Straight Flush* reported clear weather to another B-29 trailing some miles behind—the *Enola Gay.* At 8:15 A.M. plus 17 seconds, *Enola Gay* dropped a nine-thousand-pound atomic bomb over the city. It exploded 660 yards above the ground in a fireball that stretched out 110 yards in every direction.

Combined with another atomic bomb that devastated the city of Nagasaki, the new weapon ended the war. It rendered academic the argument that preceded its use—whether the Americans would suffer a million casualties if they invaded Japan without it or whether, as intelligence had predicted, the Japanese would fight to the death for every square inch of homeland. No one will ever know for sure, but however final the atomic horror made all such disputes, it did not, as some predicted, promise to make all forms of international conflict obsolete.

Indeed, even before the death of Hiroshima, a new series of international tensions was arising. And they were tensions that would impose urgent requirements on a newly resurgent American intelligence, for how well it could function in a newly disordered world would determine much of the course of history.

For the 1,350 American fliers held in the prisons of Germany's wartime ally Romania, deliverance came on the morning of August 29, 1944, when twenty-one members of an outfit calling itself the United States Air Crew Rescue Unit landed at Popecti Airport in Bucharest. Six days earlier, Romania had suddenly left the war, and the Romanian government, eager to curry favor among the Allies—the Red Army spearheads were only days away—had allowed the American unit to land and arrange for the immediate evacuation of the U.S. prisoners.

The American team landed in a time of total confusion. The Germans were evacuating as fast as they could, the Romanian government was in a shambles, and nobody knew when the first Russian soldiers would come pouring into Bucharest. The team evacuated the prisoners quickly, then surveyed the utter chaos of the Romanian capital: government offices unstaffed, German offices and billets vacant, with a general sense that nobody was in charge.

Which was just fine with Frank Wisner, head of the American team. For the Air Crew Rescue Unit was a fiction. In fact, all its members were actually OSS agents. They were engaged only coincidentally in rescuing American prisoners; their real function was to carry out the first important Cold War intelligence mission against the Soviet Union. It was called Operation Bughouse.

Wisner, head of OSS operations in southeastern Europe, was mainly interested in paper: documents and records left undestroyed by the hastily fleeing Germans and their Romanian allies, especially any material that would show what the Germans and the Romanians had managed to learn about the Soviet Union. Wisner did not know how much time he had before the Russians arrived, so the Americans set to work quickly, prowling through the German and Romanian military headquarters and intelligence offices.

To their surprise, they discovered that the Germans, in their haste to evacuate, had taken very few papers of value with them and had not bothered to destroy the rest. Wisner's men struck an intelligence mother lode: stacks of German intelligence files, including the dossiers of more than four thousand German intelligence agents and assets.

WARRIORS OF THE NIGHT

Taken out of Bucharest one step ahead of the Russians, the captured paper provided two important pieces of information. One was data German intelligence had managed to collect on the Soviet Union from the Romanian listening post; the second, of even greater importance, was a collection of names—names of agents who had operated against the Russians in the past, and who might be useful for similar operations in the future; names of Romanians who had collaborated with the Nazis (and who might be willing to collaborate again, this time for a different cause); and names of informants who had given information to the Germans.

A number of dossiers struck Wisner as he pored through this trove, among them that of Otto Albrecht von Bolschwing. The name indicated a man of the German nobility, a Prussian aristocrat who had joined the Nazi party in 1932. More interesting, he had become a member of the S.D., Germany's Nazi intelligence service, largely because of certain unique qualifications: a university education, fluency in four languages, and important contacts everywhere. The dossier revealed that von Bolschwing had headed up an important S.D. operation in 1941 to overthrow the government of Romania in a plot organized by Heinrich Himmler as a means of establishing a more pro-Nazi government. Von Bolschwing organized the coup on schedule, but it failed; he fled to Germany, there to face a wrathful Adolf Hitler, who was furious at the failure. Von Bolschwing's S.D. career was in shadow for a while, until he managed to work himself back into Nazi good graces by running an S.S. bank that handled the expropriated property of Jews who had been shipped to extermination camps.

The name of von Bolschwing was filed away, along with many others. In a short time, the paths of the Nazi and the American intelligence operative were to cross.

The Bughouse operation that had uncovered von Bolschwing's name was the direct result of a dramatic shift in the perceptions of American intelligence; events in Poland and elsewhere during 1944 had reoriented their vision toward the Soviet Union and Eastern Europe. Even before the war's end, it was clear to a small but growing group of American policymakers and some OSS officials that there was going to be serious trouble with the Russians. Already, American-Soviet relations were tense: nasty arguments over U.S. Lend Lease supplies, ominous rumbles from Moscow about post-war political settlements in Europe, and a general sense that the central Russian objective after the defeat of Germany was to dominate the European continent.

But the Soviet Union represented a blank wall to American intelligence. There were no intelligence sources behind the Iron Curtain that was soon to drop across the middle of Europe, there was no idea of Soviet intentions, there was no comprehensive intelligence on Russia's scientific and technological capabilities, and there was not even the most rudimentary intelligence on the location, size, and strength of the vast Soviet armies that Stalin apparently had no intention of demobilizing.

In sum, it was an intelligence gap of truly monumental proportions, and there had been only modest attempts at that point to fill it. Wisner had carried out Operation Bughouse, and other OSS officials in Europe—especially Richard Helms in Germany and Allen Dulles in Switzerland—ran small-scale agent-infiltration operations eastward, trying to get some idea about the Soviet military presence overshadowing Eastern Europe. The operations failed, and a 1945 OSS intelligence report, one of the more extensive the agency ever attempted to compile about the Soviet Union, admitted candidly that it did not have even the slightest clue to what was going on there.

But with the onset of the Cold War, the necessity for real intelligence on Soviet capabilities and intentions became urgent. There appeared to be no time for the patient building of networks and support organizations, the time-consuming process that might ultimately puzzle out the new enemy, for the fear was that the Russians might strike for the English Channel *now*.

The result was an attempt to fill the intelligence gap on the Soviet Union as quickly as possible. And since American assets with the requisite background and experience on the Soviet Union did not exist, American intelligence reached out for assets already in place, for whatever preassembled pieces of machinery could be put to work immediately. And among the assets thus discovered was Otto Albrecht von Bolschwing.

Like most of his ex-S.D. or Gestapo colleagues, von Bolschwing was lying low in Austria just after the war, waiting to see how the political winds would blow. His future looked bleak—the victorious Allies had declared the S.D. and Gestapo "criminal organizations" whose members were subject to prosecution—and von Bolschwing's name was among a list of eighty thousand suspected Nazi war criminals.

But what von Bolschwing did not know was that the list, drawn up by a U.S. Army organization called CROWCASS (Central Registry of War Criminals and Security Suspects), was already being regarded more as an intelligence asset than as a guide to prosecuting Nazi war criminals. Primarily, the list was used by army intelligence to locate intelligence assets who would be used in a crash program to gather intelligence on Soviet forces in Germany, Austria, and Eastern Europe.

Von Bolschwing was among the assets selected from that list, but in the process, the Americans betrayed the first evidence of several blind spots, chief among them a moral one. The United States was trying to have it both ways, on the one hand vowing it would bring Nazi war criminals to justice before the International Military Tribunal at Nuremberg, while on the other quietly recruiting some of them for intelligence work. In von Bolschwing's case, his record included work for Adolf Eichmann, during which he formulated plans to strip Jews of their assets and civil rights. He was, in fact, one of the architects of the Final Solution—the extermination of Jews— the crime that formed the crux of the indictments against the Nazis at the Nuremberg trials. In addition, there was the matter of that uprising von Bolschwing had fomented in Romania in 1941. The chosen instrument for the uprising was the Iron Guard, Romania's domestic Nazis, and under von Bolschwing's aegis, during the coup they embarked on a pogrom, slaughtering Jews in the streets. (Jewish children were murdered and hung up on meathooks in slaughterhouses, the word *kosher* carved into their bodies.)

Despite this bloody history, von Bolschwing's record was expunged—army intelligence managed to get him cleared by a denazification court in 1948—and he was soon in business as an American intelligence agent. His first task, rounding up other ex-S.D. officers and officials, went easily enough, but then he was confronted with a much more difficult assignment: to obtain intelligence on Soviet forces in Romania. This was no simple task, for Romania from the time of its liberation by Soviet troops in 1944 had been the subject of an effort to impose a Communist government. American concern over the course of events in Romania was strong, but the question of what to do was complicated by a lack of intelligence on what was going on inside the country. It was this gap that von Bolschwing was supposed to fill.

But nobody had stopped to think about the kind of resources he would be using to create, almost overnight, an intelligence network inside Romania. Overlooked was the fact that von Bolschwing's World War II connections in Romania centered on the Iron Guard, a group of fascist fanatics who lacked any kind of popular support in their own country. Its leaders, in hiding all over Europe, were unearthed by American intelligence with von Bolschwing's help and enlisted for the American operation. They were useless for such an enterprise, for as a group they had spent most of their time before and during the war plotting against the government and attacking Jews. It was highly improbable that they had any grasp of the political realities in Romania.

Predictably, the Guardists turned out to be something less than stellar agents, a deficiency compounded by an amateurish American operation to foster the democratic opposition to Romanian Communists. The operation quickly came to the attention of the Soviet MVD, mostly because the Americans not only met too openly with opposition leaders but also made the unforgivable mistake of keeping detailed records, with names and addresses of Romanians who had expressed a willingness to combat the Russians. The inevitable happened when the Russians cracked down. The records were seized, and the democratic opposition was rolled up in one blow.

Similarly, other American intelligence operations using ex-Nazis in Eastern Europe came to grief. The Americans simply did not realize that the Nazi S.D. and Gestapo had never been much in the way of intelligence services, especially on the subject of the Soviet Union, and the boasting of the former Nazis on how much help they would be able to render U.S. intelligence was largely a sham.

In a seller's market, however, the Nazis had the edge. To a gullible and increasingly desperate American intelligence, they offered a quick fix for a pressing intelligence problem— in return for what amounted to an amnesty for genocide. It was quite some time before the Americans realized that they had been hoodwinked, but by then, the matter was mostly academic, for history imposed more urgent priorities.

The failed effort to construct an intelligence presence in Europe overnight proved, once and for all, that the fragmented American intelligence setup did not work. But the question was: What would replace it?

The emerging consensus was that the United States needed some sort of centralized intelligence apparatus that would end, finally, the overlapping jurisdictions and squabbling among the various components of American intelligence. OSS, which might be roughly described as a central intelligence organization, had been disbanded by President Harry S Truman almost coincidentally with the end of World War II, and several months later he replaced it with a tentative step toward a new centralized American intelligence. It was called the Central Intelligence Group, an organization that was supposed to coordinate the intelligence operations of twenty-five different federal agencies. But it was doomed from the start, for without sufficient organizational clout, the new agency soon fell victim to the attempts by military intelligence agencies to throttle it.

The military's hostility centered on the fact that the CIG was run by civilians, a fact that threatened the long history of independence by military intelligence agencies, who operated in a narrow world bounded by their respective services' interests. But the squabble between the civilians and the military, fought largely in closed congressional hearings on the state of American intelligence, illustrated the problem. More important, the military's arguments against centralized intelligence were handicapped by memories, still fresh in congressmen's minds, of Pearl Harbor.

Truman himself, never an advocate of centralized intelligence, was gradually becoming a convert. He was confronted with an ever more menacing Soviet threat, while what passed for intelligence agencies could tell him almost nothing about the dimensions and implications of that threat. His mood could not have been improved by some of the drivel that passed across his desk, much of it from J. Edgar Hoover, who had ambitions to become czar of American intelligence. To demonstrate the FBI's foreign-intelligence skills, Hoover bombarded Truman with "intelligence reports," among them the news that the Soviet Union had developed an atomic bomb aboard a submarine in 1940, and that Joseph Stalin had been deposed in 1945.

The ultimate result was the National Security Act of 1947, a sweeping reorganization of the American military-intelligence structure, including creation of the post of Secretary of Defense, a unified annual defense budget, the National Security Council, and the Central Intelligence Agency. The new CIA was of a piece with an overall conviction that some sort of armed clash between the United States and the Soviet Union was inevitable. Thus the CIA was intended as an agency that would collect and analyze all intelligence coming into the government. The finished intelligence would be provided to the National Security Council, which would then direct all diplomatic, military, and industrial planning consistent with the threat enunciated by the CIA.

The problem, of course, was that this structural plan included a number of major assumptions. One was that the CIA in fact would be able to deliver accurate, timely intelligence. Another was that no matter what the organization chart said, the rest of the American intelligence community would be content with its new subordinate role. Neither of these assumptions proved correct, and the problem was worsened by some serious mishandling of America's first real centralized intelligence agency.

The mishandling began with a decision to take the offensive against the Soviet domination of Eastern Europe. The idea was questionable, at best, and it was an even more dubious proposition, given the decision on how it would be handled. Because it was supposed to be a secret operation, the plan to contain and then roll back the Soviet monolith was entrusted to the CIA.

The central reason for this decision was the realization that the CIA's initial strength of around two thousand people included a third who had served in the OSS. These OSS veterans had the requisite experience in running underground and resistance operations, but what was the relevance of that experience to the changed circumstances of postwar Europe? Not much. To begin with, there was a big difference between the German military occupation (and its Gestapo and S.D. internal-security adjuncts) and the much more pervasive Soviet secret-police organization. Despite the Gestapo's reputation for brutal thoroughness, it never even began to compare in sheer size and efficiency with its Soviet counterpart. Moreover, despite the wondrous deeds ascribed by mythmakers to World War II resistance movements, in fact, most of them were failures.

Yet, the United States was convinced it could repeat that World War II "success" with a three-pronged plan. First, anti-Communist elements in Western Europe would be covertly organized and funded, establishing something of a political Maginot Line against further Communist encroachments. Second, discontent among the oppressed peoples of Eastern Europe would be covertly organized and supported, to the point where they would rise up and overthrow their Communist masters. Third, guerrilla armies-in-being, large forces of armed anti-Communists in Western and Eastern Europe, backed by hidden arms caches, would be organized and ready to rise up in the event of a Soviet invasion of Western Europe.

The entire operation was run by Frank Wisner, who had led that American intelligence team into Romania before the end of the war. A wealthy Mississippi lawyer for whom civilian life had palled after his OSS experiences—a not uncommon symptom among the ex-OSS people who drifted into the CIA upon its creation—Wisner was dynamic, brimming over with ideas for the great covert offensive that would roll back the Iron Curtain.

But like the government for which he worked, Wisner was also a man in a hurry, and in the rush to create his grand apparatus, he made a number of serious mistakes. One of them was Otto Albrecht von Bolschwing, the ex-Nazi who had failed so ignominiously in creating an American intelligence network in Romania. Now, along with hundreds of other ex-Nazis, von Bolschwing was enlisted in the new operation.

His task was to create an anti-Communist alternative to the Communist government in Romania, a job for which he was totally unsuited. Again, von Bolschwing tapped into his old fascist allies, the ex–Iron Guard members, this time to become the vanguard of what was expected to be a vast anti-Communist Romanian army with guerrilla forces-in-being inside the country. They had no hope of doing any such thing, and their failure was representative of what happened to all of Wisner's plans. He combed the displaced persons camps for Nazi collaborators from the Baltic and Eastern European countries—all of whom were despised in their own countries for their involvement with the hated Nazis. He mined the old lode of White Russian and other such émigré groups—none of whom had the slightest idea of what was going on in the Soviet Union. He enlisted the help of the Ukrainian anti-

Communist underground—permanently tainted among the Russian people for its involvement with the brutalities of the Nazi occupation forces. He enrolled virtually the entire Byelorussian (White Russian) collaborationist government that had fled West with the retreating Germans—heartily disliked in its homeland as a "government" that killed Jews and rounded up forced labor for Germany.

In short, Wisner's operation was a disastrous mistake. Its intelligence implications were also disastrous, for it began to swallow up a disproportionate chunk of the CIA's resources, which were supposed to be used for intelligence collection not for putting old Nazis on the payroll. By 1949, Wisner had an American force of 302 people to run his vast operation and a $4.7 million annual budget; three years later, he had 2,812 Americans working directly for him and $82 million—nearly half the CIA's entire budget.

Wisner was getting very little for his money. There had been some success in Western Europe, especially covert American aid to anti-Communist forces in the 1948 Italian election, but otherwise, it was a bleak picture of failure. Von Bolschwing had not ignited an anti-Communist revolt in Romania, the teams of exiles sent behind the Iron Curtain were being picked up almost as soon as they crossed the border, and the "guerrilla armies" did not seem to be toppling anybody. The dimensions of the failure were made glaringly apparent in 1956, when stay-behind guerrilla forces in Hungary proved useless when Soviet forces crushed the Hungarian revolution. The guerrilla forces, organized under a Wisner operation known as Red Sox/Red Cap, were never unleashed; as President Eisenhower noted, with two hundred thousand Soviet troops in Hungary, and the United States firmly against any military intervention, there was no hope that any Red Sox/Red Cap guerrillas would make a difference, except to get a lot of people killed needlessly.*

---

*The Hungarian tragedy caused Wisner's mind to snap. The following year, he suffered a nervous breakdown. Seemingly recovered after a six-month hospital stay,

The failure of Red Sox/Red Cap marked the end of the scheme to roll back the Iron Curtain, and in its wreckage could also be found American intelligence's modest assets on Eastern Europe and the Soviet Union. How badly their loss blinded the American view of that part of the continent was not realized until the failure of another, even more important, American intelligence resource.

It was called, simply, The Org, a German intelligence apparatus conceived and directed by one of the more interesting figures in postwar intelligence, Reinhard Gehlen. The chief American intelligence resource in Europe after the war, Gehlen had been the last World War II head of the FHO, Germany's main military intelligence agency responsible for the Soviet Union. Gehlen, a German Army staff officer with a passion for detail, took over FHO after it had been humiliated by its serious underestimation of Russian military strength in 1941.

Then a colonel, Gehlen succeeded brilliantly, building what was to become one of the most efficient and best-organized military intelligence agencies in the world, in the process winning promotion to general. But he became a victim of his own success. The more accurate his reports on growing Soviet military capabilities, the more disliked he was by Hitler. On January 9, 1945, when a Soviet offensive that Gehlen had predicted exactly broke through the last German defenses in the east—Hitler had dismissed the prediction as "rubbish"—Gehlen was finished.

Ever a man to predict the future accurately, Gehlen after the war offered his services to the Americans. For the United

---

he returned to work, but amid signs of another imminent breakdown, left the agency in 1961. In 1965, he blew his brains out with a shotgun. As for von Bolschwing, he was brought to this country by the CIA in 1959 and given a series of jobs with companies whose executives were ex-CIA officials. In 1981, by then a prosperous business executive, his luck suddenly ran out: The Justice Department moved to deport him as a former Nazi war criminal. The CIA managed to get a court hearing closed to prevent revelation of his connections with the agency. However, von Bolschwing, seriously ill, died in 1982.

States, the deal he offered was irresistible: In exchange for financial support, he would create an intelligence agency in Germany that, using his old FHO staff, would become an unparalleled resource on intelligence about the Soviet Union and Eastern Europe. As Gehlen shrewdly realized, the Americans were desperate. They had stood open-mouthed as Gehlen's men unearthed vast quantities of FHO files Gehlen had foresightedly hidden away. "Here are the secrets of the Kremlin," he said rather melodramatically. "If you use them properly, Stalin is doomed."

Stalin was in no grave danger, of course, from the piles of paper Gehlen proffered, but he was in danger from the kind of intelligence apparatus Gehlen planned to weave across every square foot of Communist territory. The threat lay in the combination of Gehlen's thoroughness with the money the Americans were willing to provide. The Org, as Gehlen's organization was known, was interested not in the sort of political covert action and guerrilla armies so beloved by Wisner but in pure intelligence collection. Most of Gehlen's people worked as *tiefe Aufklärung*, "line-crossers," men who infiltrated behind the Iron Curtain, patiently observing, listening and collecting, gathering up every scrap of information, no matter how trivial it seemed. Back at headquarters, the reports were collated into a vast file system that slowly became a veritable encyclopedia on all aspects of life behind the Iron Curtain.

Like thousands of rivulets merging into a single stream, the intelligence sent back by battalions of agents dispatched by Gehlen began to form a mosaic.* His objective was a slow and patient building of his networks ever eastward, until he

*One of The Org's intelligence tidbits had far-reaching consequences in the Korean war. In 1949, a Gehlen operative in East Germany photographed a new Soviet jet fighter undergoing tests. U.S. Air Force intelligence analysts, poring over the pictures, noticed that the Soviet jet, the MiG-15, had a fixed horizontal stabilizer on the tail, reducing maneuverability at high speed. The American F-86 was therefore redesigned to include a movable stabilizer, and in subsequent air battles in Korea, the more maneuverable F-86s slaughtered the MiG-15s in high-speed dogfights.

was ready to begin large-scale operations inside the Soviet Union itself.

But American intelligence was characteristically impatient for more immediate results, and in the summer of 1948, Gehlen began to feel intense CIA pressure to accelerate his operations. The American pressure also stemmed from the ominous direction of world events. In that year, the Berlin crisis had erupted and, combined with the Communist takeover in Czechoslovakia, made it seem that the Soviet Union was about to make a precipitate move westward. (Indeed, the alarm was so great, army intelligence said flatly that war with the Soviet Union was imminent, perhaps only a matter of days.)

The American pressure led directly to a serious mistake, the dropping of hundreds of émigré volunteers by parachute into the Soviet Union on spying missions. But the hastily organized missions made the error of overreliance on Russian émigré organizations for the volunteers, and all the organizations had been extensively penetrated by the Russians. That error was compounded by another: a CIA demand that Gehlen's organization become involved in the covert-action program. The covert-action operations had no hope of toppling any Communist government and had the added disadvantage of exposing undercover agents who should have been collecting intelligence, not organizing secret arms caches in Eastern Europe.

American intelligence bears the major portion of the blame for the subsequent decline in The Org's capability as an intelligence organization. But Gehlen exacerbated the situation by his worst fault, an abiding faith in the allegiance of the many former S.S., Gestapo, and S.D. men he had recruited for the top levels of his organization. Gehlen believed, fatuously, that the former Nazis were so rabidly anti-Communist that there was no possibility that they would ever betray The Org to the Soviets. Thus there was no background or security check on Gehlen's recruits.

But it was discovered in 1961 that two of The Org's top

officials—including the chief of its counterintelligence efforts against Eastern Europe and the Soviet Union—had been Soviet agents for ten years. The disaster was total: For a decade, the most important American intelligence resource on Eastern Europe and the Soviet Union was an open book to the Russians, who had an inside view on virtually every operation eastward. It is no wonder that by the mid-1950s, American intelligence on its most abiding concern, the Soviet Union, amounted to a view that was almost opaque.*

The ultimate result was a military policy that rested almost entirely on ignorance of the main opponent. From that dynamic flowed a decision to construct a mighty U.S. strategic arsenal against a threat looming ever larger. But it was a threat constructed from fear, for no one seemed to have any real idea of the size and power of the Soviet arsenal—or, more important, of what Moscow intended to do with it. And the less known about the dimensions of that threat, the more fear it seemed to engender among American policymakers, who most often opted for what is still known as the "worst case scenario." In other words, when nothing or little is known about a threat from the other side, always assume the worst, just to be on the safe side.

How problematical that process can be is illustrated by two major intelligence controversies of the 1950s era, controversies that remain the most notorious in the history of American intelligence.

They became known as the bomber and missile gaps.

The first of these episodes, the "bomber gap," was born just after World War II, when the Central Intelligence Group and air-force intelligence disputed whether the Soviet Union would develop a strategic bomber force. Over air-force objections, the CIG concluded that the Russians, intent on developing nuclear weapons, obviously would need strategic

---

*Among the more important results of that ignorance was the underestimation by American intelligence of the Soviet atomic weapons program, resulting in a major shock: detonation of the first Russian atomic bomb in 1949, nearly twenty years before the United States had thought that event would occur.

bombers to deliver the bombs against the United States; otherwise, what good would such weapons do them? A special commission appointed by Truman in 1947 went even further, asserting that the Soviets would have an atomic strike capability against the United States by 1952, deliverable by strategic bombers.

What strategic bombers? There were no such planes in the Soviet inventory, and American intelligence, lacking insight into the Soviet armaments industry, had no clue as to whether the Russians might be trying to develop any. But in 1948, a plum dropped into the American laps. A Red Air Force technical expert defected and revealed that the Russians were embarked on an urgent program to develop a "long-range air force." The program, the defector revealed, centered on making a Russian copy of the American B-29 bomber.

In May of that year, U.S. military attachés at the annual May Day parade in Moscow noticed a new Russian bomber—nicknamed Bull by air-force intelligence—flying publicly for the first time. The bomber, the TU-4, bore a strong family resemblance to the B-29, but the air force was not especially flattered by this imitation. Instead, it was alarmed, for if the Russians had managed to develop an equivalent to the B-29 in so short a time, the air force concluded, then it was possible that the Russian bomber program was very far advanced. It was at this point that the air force began to see the Soviet bomber "threat" in increasingly starker terms, no small influence being that service's battle for bigger budgets.

In fact, however, the TU-4 looked formidable, but it lacked sufficient range to attack the U.S. mainland and return. Furthermore, Russian aircraft engines were badly underpowered; it was not until 1953 that the Soviet technicians were able to develop engines of 15,000-pound thrust, the minimum considered necessary to power high-performance aircraft. Besides, the Russians had not yet developed in-flight refueling techniques, which the American Air Force had first begun using in 1949.

American intelligence knew nothing of these real problems. It was reduced to watching the new bomber in flight, then trying to make a series of deductions based on what had been observed, a process that tends not to be very useful for technical intelligence. Merely observing a piece of machinery is only part of the puzzle; the real intelligence comes when it is discovered how efficiently the machinery works, its level of technical sophistication, and so on.

Possibly aware of this observation gap, the Russians made strong efforts to conceal the serious faults that made its growing bomber fleet, while impressive to look at, a useless pile of junk in military terms. In 1949, at another May Day parade, the Russians flew squadrons of TU-4s in formations that spelled out SLAVA STALINU, "glory to Stalin," and five years later, their bomber program still not off the ground technologically, they put on a show that was to have dramatic consequences for American intelligence.

The occasion was again the event that at the time was the chief American intelligence resource on Soviet military technology: the annual May Day parade, traditionally used by the Russians to display their military might—including the latest weapons developments. The 1954 May Day parade was especially auspicious for the Soviets, for it was the first one to be held since the death of Stalin. It was a very bellicose parade, including an extensive flyby of Soviet military aircraft, apparently meant to demonstrate that the Soviet Union remained a powerful nation militarily, despite the jockeying for power among its leadership.

Among the more attentive people in the audience that day was the U.S. Air Force attaché at the Moscow embassy, Colonel Charles E. Taylor. As the flyby began, Taylor was startled to see a new Soviet bomber in formation, its large size suggesting intercontinental range. Later dubbed the M-4 (or Bison to air-force intelligence), it precipitated deep concern on the part of Taylor—and the air force, which spun out a whole series of deductions.

Chief among these were that the Soviets had probably built a prototype of the plane in 1952, and that full-scale production could be anticipated somewhere in 1956. There was no intelligence behind these deductions; they were formulated on estimates that used American aircraft production standards as a guide. They were alarming enough, but a year later, at the next May Day flyby, Taylor caused even more consternation by reporting the sight of *an entire squadron* of M-4 Bisons flying overhead.

Taylor's new report set air-force intelligence abuzz—obviously, the Russians must be building Bisons much faster than had been estimated only a year previously. All the assumed dates of development and deployment for the plane were revised, and a new intelligence estimate concluded that the Soviets would have a force of seven hundred long-range Bison bombers by 1959. But even that estimate paled when Taylor subsequently reported seeing twenty-eight Bisons at a Soviet air show, leading to still another revised intelligence estimate, this one concluding that the Russians would have more than one thousand bombers by the end of 1959, a truly massive and threatening force.

Regrettably, Taylor did not know that he had been hoodwinked. At the time, the Russians had only eight Bisons. To convince Taylor and other interested observers that there was a huge Soviet bomber force in development, the Russians circled their minuscule bomber fleet out of sight for repeated flybys, thus leading to the impression of a much larger force. The Russians succeeded in convincing the rest of the world that this bomber "Potemkin Village" was real, but they could not have anticipated that it would also set off a full-fledged panic in the United States, where leaked stories from the air force (coincidental with sharply increased budget requests) portrayed a formidable Soviet bomber force poised to wipe the United States off the map. The Soviet force was contrasted with the more modest American bomber fleet; hence, the bomber gap.

In the end, the air force used this gap to achieve a major buildup in its bomber forces, especially the new B-52, but the price included what still remains an estrangement from its sister services, and a persistent legacy of distrust of air-force intelligence estimates.

The distrust was most pronounced in the young CIA, whose strong point at that time was economic analysis. The agency, joined in a rare alliance with the army and navy, began poking significant holes in the bomber gap. CIA analysts were able to demonstrate that the Soviet industrial base, including numbers of aluminum forges, extent of production lines, and other important factors, could not possibly produce the vast numbers of bombers the air force was claiming. To buttress its argument, the CIA contrived to steal several wire coat hangers from the closet of a plane belonging to Aeroflot, the Soviet Union's national airline. Metallurgical analysis of the coat hangers—usually made out of scrap metal from a plane's manufacturing process—revealed that Soviet metallurgy was not yet advanced enough to build high-performance intercontinental-range bombers.

The real death knell of the bomber gap, however, did not come until 1956, when some of the first U-2 photos from overflights of the Soviet Union revealed no large fleets of bombers. Those pictures led, finally, to a 1957 intelligence estimate that concluded that the total Soviet strategic bomber force was actually somewhere between 90 and 150 planes, with only "modest" increases planned in that force. (The Russians never did build a big bomber fleet, although there are periodic predictions that they plan to develop a bomber similar to the American B-1.)

The dust had hardly settled over the bomber gap when the Soviet Union made an electrifying announcement on October 4, 1957: the launching of an 184-pound *iskusstvennyy sputnik zemli,* "artificial earth satellite," into orbit.

Intelligence interest in *Sputnik*—as the satellite came to be known—focused not on the satellite but on the rocket the Russians used to launch it, the SS-6. Two months before *Sputnik*'s launch, the Russians had announced the successful test of the SS-6, which they advertised as their first operational intercontinental ballistic missile (ICBM). The administration of Dwight D. Eisenhower was not especially concerned about this development, for the SS-6 was distinctly inferior to its American equivalent. The SS-6 had lofted *Sputnik I* and then, in November 1957, sent up *Sputnik II*, a one-thousand-pound satellite with a live dog aboard. However, the American Atlas, the U.S. ICBM, could launch a one-ton payload into orbit and the first American satellite being readied for launching was far superior technologically to the *Sputnik*.

True, but however primitive, the Soviets had launched their satellite *first*, using a rocket that had sufficient range to reach the United States. The public was much less sanguine than the administration about these developments, and the humiliating explosion that December of the American Vanguard rocket with the first U.S. space satellite aboard contributed to the uneasiness.

The stage was set for the "missile gap" episode.

Among other things, *Sputnik* triggered that most dangerous of all elements in intelligence, politics. And it was politics that dominated the discussion about *Sputnik:* fears of declining American technological supremacy, the Russians far ahead in space, Soviet rockets ready to rain down upon the United States, and on and on, a full-fledged political controversy framed in terms of the United States falling behind a resurgent Soviet Union.

Alarm was everywhere. In June 1957, Soviet Premier Nikita Khrushchev had made his famous "we will bury you" speech, and taken in conjunction with continued Soviet space spectaculars, it contributed to a general state of deep disquiet among the American public. However, among those not disquieted was Eisenhower himself, who was aware that although the Russians had concentrated their resources on carrying out a few flashy space spectaculars, that did not mean that the Soviet Union had achieved the large-scale technological breakthroughs and vast resources needed to build an ICBM force capable of threatening the United States.

Only a few people were aware that Eisenhower was holding an intelligence ace he could not reveal publicly: The high-altitude U-2 spy plane had begun flying missions over the Soviet Union in 1956, and although the results of the first flights were not definitive, they nevertheless showed no evidence of any large-scale Soviet ICBM deployment. As Eisenhower correctly deduced, the few Soviet ICBMs were being used exclusively to propel Russians into space. There were none of the obvious signs that the Russians were embarked on a full-scale ICBM development program or had managed to overcome the considerable technological hurdles that the Americans at that point were just beginning to cross: small, compact warheads for thermonuclear weapons, sophisticated guidance systems, and extensive "fields" of missile silos to protect them from retaliatory strikes. Unless the Russians had managed to develop operational ICBMs in secret without complicated (and easily spotted) tests, and were hiding the rockets in the Kremlin basement, the alarm over Soviet missiles was unwarranted.

But alarm there was, underscored by a proposal lying on Eisenhower's desk that the United States spend $40 billion on fallout shelters, presumably as protection against the imminent rain of Soviet warheads. Eisenhower named a special blue-ribbon panel of prominent defense experts, engineers, and scientists to study the proposal with a recommendation for approval or disapproval.

The panel had a broad mandate, since its examination of the proposal inevitably led it into questions about the extent of the Russian threat. In other words, something of an intelligence judgment. To Eisenhower's dismay, the panel wound up concluding that the Soviet Union was far ahead of the United States in development of ICBMs.

How was this alarming conclusion reached? By extrapolation, mostly, a process that grew out of the very inadequacy of American intelligence on the subject. The plain fact was that despite the U-2, the Americans knew next to nothing about the Soviet ICBMs, especially how many there were and the level of their technology. The panel's solution to this dearth of information was to view the Soviet rockets through the prism of American experience. The process went something like this: The launch of *Sputnik* indicated development of a rocket of a certain size that was capable of firing into orbit a payload of a certain weight. Therefore, such a rocket would probably have been developed at a particular point, almost definitely as part of a program to develop long-range missiles. And since the Russians were undoubtedly embarked on a crash program to develop such missiles, it could be deduced that large-scale deployment was imminent. How imminent? Based on American experience—the length of time between development and deployment of missile technology—it could be deduced that the Russians would have a certain number of rockets deployed by such and such a date.

The intelligence deductions thus formulated had all the solidity of a spider web, but in the absence of hard intelligence, the panel members really had no choice. They were reduced to taking a few crumbs of evidence and constructing a conclusion on what they assumed the Russians would do. The intelligence problem was complicated further by squabbling between the CIA and the air force; the military people were upset at the attempt by the "civilian" CIA to encroach on an intelligence preserve—military technology— that the air force felt belonged only to military intelligence agencies.

The CIA and the military had been arguing over Soviet rockets for several years, a rivalry that became serious in 1954 when the agency estimated that the Russians would need about five years to fully develop an operational ICBM. The military, particularly the air force, vigorously dissented, the first major exchange of fire in a disagreement that has lasted for years. The initial battle was fought out in public to a certain extent because the air force began to leak alarmist stories about vast numbers of powerful Soviet ICBMs. The leaks accelerated after *Sputnik,* fuel for the fire of a raging political controversy.

Eisenhower must have felt like a man besieged. Not only did there seem to be new allegations each day about a missile gap opening up between the Soviet Union and the United States, but the phrase surfaced continually later, in the 1960 presidential campaign, as part of an overall claim by the Democratic opposition about American "unpreparedness" in the face of a dangerous threat. At the same time, Eisenhower discovered that the alarm was beginning to creep into intelligence estimates. In 1958 these claimed that the Russians were a full year ahead of this country in ICBM development; a year later, an estimate predicted that the Russians would have the incredible total of fifteen hundred ICBMs by 1963—more than double the projected American deployment.

In other words, a critical missile gap, but by the time of the 1960 campaign, there were unmistakable signs that the intelligence projections of Soviet missile power were perhaps due for revision. For one thing, the CIA noted that there was a significant number of failures of Soviet rockets; if the Russians were supposedly so advanced in rocket technology, why so many failures? Moreover, there had been a pronounced slowdown in the Soviet rocket-development program—mostly in numbers of tests—a clear indication that the Russians were encountering severe technical problems.

The growing body of evidence, however, did not end the CIA-military squabble on the issue, and a 1960 intelligence estimate included the judgment of both sides on where the Soviet ICBM program would be by 1963. The CIA said the Russians would have two hundred rockets, while the military said seven hundred—a disparity so wide that the estimate was useless. (The U-2 was of limited help at this important juncture, for all flights over the Soviet Union had been suspended following the shooting down of Gary Powers's plane in May 1960.)

Eisenhower could have used something more definite, for he was facing a major decision: How many U.S. ICBMs should be built and deployed? Eisenhower had tentatively decided on a rough figure of one thousand—which should allow enough missiles to survive a Soviet first strike and carry out a retaliatory second strike. The Joint Chiefs of Staff argued that the number was too low, and sought sixteen hundred. (The air force, whose Strategic Air Command (SAC) was assigned the job of actually firing those missiles in event of war, wanted ten thousand—a number, Eisenhower noted with some irritation, that would bankrupt the country.)

In the end, the United States decided to deploy eight hundred missiles, a decision made by the incoming administration of John F. Kennedy. And the man who made it was the new Secretary of Defense, Robert Strange McNamara. Former president of the Ford Motor Company, McNamara was a man committed to systems analysis and hard facts, and the wildly disparate intelligence estimates on Russian ICBMs seemed to have little to do with any kind of precision. McNamara took the trouble to carefully examine all the evidence for the conclusion that the Russians were indeed building all those missiles. As he must have suspected, there was precious little of it. For the most part, the estimates of Soviet ICBM strength were constructed of flimsy extrapolations, glued together with the institutional and other biases of the people making those estimates.

McNamara ruled that the United States would build eight hundred ICBMs—more than enough, he argued, to handle any potential Soviet ICBM threat. As for the missile gap, he quietly disposed of it by noting that he could find "no signs" of a Russian crash program to build and deploy ICBMs. (He was right. The Russians had fewer than a dozen ICBMs at the time, none of which worked properly.)

And so the great bomber and missile gaps, the most contentious issues dividing American intelligence up to that point, ended. So too ended—for a while, at least—the infighting among the military and CIA over Soviet strategic forces. In fact, intelligence concern over the whole range of Soviet military power was receding.

The reason was not a lack of interest in Soviet power, but because the attention of American intelligence was being diverted elsewhere—southward, toward the South American continent, where a dramatic series of events was shortly to preoccupy all of American intelligence.

It was a preoccupation that became an obsession.

two

HOMAGE TO DUMB LUCK

The world is kept warm by people
who believe.

—Old Russian proverb

SLOWLY DROPPING to 3,000 feet, the Aero Commander cruised
near the bend of the river, its pilot searching in the gathering
twilight for a patch of white—an old bed sheet—that would
mark an improvised landing strip cut out of the thick tropical
forest. Nervously chewing an entire pack of gum, pilot Charley Carter* tried to find the landing strip while at the same
time checking the sky around him for enemy fighters.

Just as he spotted the landing strip and its white signal,
he caught out of the corner of one eye the unmistakable glint
of the sun's last rays on the silver wing of another plane,
closing very fast just above and behind his tail. Instantly,
Carter went to full throttle, heading for a bank of heavy clouds
nearby as the fighter plane bored in for the kill. Once he was
in the clouds, the odds were equalized, for Carter, drawing on
the experience of several years of bush hopping all over Latin
America, played out his bag of tricks. After a while, the pursuing fighter plane left for home, apparently tired of the cat-
and-mouse game—or perhaps running low on fuel.

*A pseudonym

Safe now, Carter again headed for his rendezvous: Alto Cedro, a small town in the southern part of Cuba. He set the plane down on the landing strip just outside of town and was warmly greeted by a group of *barbudos,* "bearded ones." They unloaded the treasure in Carter's plane—several crates of new M-1 rifles, a machine gun, boxes of ammunition, and a bazooka. Once the plane was unloaded and safely under a pile of branches as camouflage against the incessant government air patrols, Carter had time to relax with an old acquaintance, the leader of the *barbudos*—a young, restless man with narrow eyes who sharply ordered around other *barbudos* at least twice his age.

Carter and the young man spoke with the respectful familiarity of two men who had shared much danger—the brash young American, a contract agent for the CIA, smuggling in arms on hair-raising hops across the water from Florida; the other man, a battle-scarred revolutionary trying to overthrow a dictatorial government with a small group of like-minded guerrillas.

Aside from the mutual respect of shared danger, there was not much else similar about the two men in that year of 1958. Carter was a knockabout adventurer, virtually uninterested in politics; for him, the $1,000 a month he received from a small air service in Miami (a CIA front) was justification enough for the missions he was to discuss with no one. He had only mild curiosity about the *barbudos* and their military leader, the man to whom he delivered his arms shipments—Raúl Castro. It was a curiosity piqued only more slightly about the *barbudos'* overall leader, Raúl's brother, Fidel (who amused Carter by invariably wearing a wristwatch on each hand—so he would never have to move his hand to tell the time while hiding in the bush, Fidel explained).

There was no doubt in Carter's mind, however, about what the Castros wanted to achieve: the overthrow of the Cuban dictator Fulgencio Batista by an armed struggle in which they were prepared to fight for years, if necessary. They were grateful for the support provided (unofficially) by the U.S. government via the CIA, but, as they continually told an uninterested Carter and a handful of other American adventurers who worked for the CIA helping the Cuban revolutionary movement, it would be a *Cuban* revolution. They would not fight in the bush for years only to become another in the long collection of Latin American puppets of the United States. And, they warned, no "interference" by the United States would be permitted in the "political goals" of the revolution—goals that remained somewhat obscure.

Carter's flight into Cuba that day in the late fall of 1958 was to be his last face-to-face meeting with the Castros. Within a few months, the *barbudos* shattered Batista's plodding army and took over Cuba. Carter went on to fly hundreds of missions all over Latin America—some of them for the CIA and others on behalf of assorted shadowy smuggling operations—and much later, in the spring of 1982, by then an aging and tired bush pilot who had spent his money as fast as he earned it, he was flying new missions for the CIA, this time in the jungles of Honduras, just north of the border with Nicaragua.

The near quarter century spanning those two events amounts to the most curious chapter in the history of American intelligence. It is a chapter filled for the most part with misjudgments, misplaced priorities, serious errors—and a series of events that at one point brought the world to the brink of World War III. In sum, it is the account of a magnificent obsession, an obsession about a small group of men who managed the impossible feat of creating a Communist revolution on the island of Cuba just ninety miles off Florida. This obsession has gripped the American intelligence community in varying degrees for nearly three decades. For want of a better term, we might call it Castrophobia—the unswerving conviction that Fidel Castro and the Cuban revolution have amounted to a Trojan horse for the Soviet Union in the Western Hemisphere, whose central aim is the submersion of the entire region in Marxism in an attempt to attack the United States from its soft Latin American underbelly.

The Cuban preoccupation has proved a dangerous atmosphere in which to conduct intelligence. Alarums like Cuba induce in intelligence agencies not only a tendency to collect facts that support the prevailing wisdom of policymakers, but also to expend a disproportionate share of resources on what is perceived as the chief "problem" of the moment. The greater the perceived problem, the more pressure intelligence agencies feel to produce greater and greater amounts of information on the subject. In the case of Cuba (and Latin America), American intelligence has moved from crisis to crisis, each time under the most severe pressure to produce "facts" that will fit the preconceptions of the currently prevailing orthodoxy.

And in Cuba, that pressure was felt right at the beginning, when Fidel Castro and his band of guerrillas were fighting for their lives in the Sierra Maestra, their exploits the subject of countless admiring accounts in the American media.

At the very moment Charley Carter was delivering his arms to Raúl Castro in the fall of 1958, a more significant drama was unfolding in Havana, some miles away. The key figure in the drama was Lyman G. Kirkpatrick, Jr., Inspector General of the CIA. Kirkpatrick, despite a crippling attack of polio several years before that had confined him to a wheelchair, was a no-nonsense, energetic man who had made the difficult trip from Washington to Havana to personally check out disturbing reports about one of the CIA's favorite creations.

The pet project—originally conceived by Kirkpatrick—was BRAC (Bureau to Repress Communism), a Cuban intelligence agency created, funded, and trained by the CIA in 1956. Its mission was to find out all there was to know about Communists in Cuba. Of special concern were recurring rumbles about Communists in Castro's July 26th Movement, a leftist group fighting against Batista in the Cuban countryside (although Castro himself was not considered to be a Communist). But as Kirkpatrick discovered, the problem was that

BRAC was out of control; Batista had staffed it with a collection of criminals who spent their time torturing and murdering anyone who dared to utter a word of criticism against the Batista government. Bodies, horribly mutilated, were found regularly in the streets of Havana, and BRAC's odious reputation was further enhanced by its habit of publicly hanging "Communist sympathizers" from trees. BRAC agents became known as *cortacuellos*, "throat-cutters," among Cubans.

This would not do, Kirkpatrick informed Colonel Mariano Paget, the CIA's hand-picked chief of BRAC. Aside from the terrible publicity the Cuban agency's activities were causing (along with a pronounced drop in official American support), BRAC did not even seem to be performing its basic mission, collecting intelligence on the Communist movement and its influence. Paget shrugged his shoulders. Shrugs were about the only reaction Kirkpatrick got among Batista's minions as he tried to make some sense out of the Cuban turmoil, while at the same time attempting to determine how long Batista could reasonably expect to remain in power. Not much longer, Kirkpatrick finally concluded, and sent a controversial cable to CIA headquarters predicting flatly that Batista would be out by the end of the year.*

Kirkpatrick's cable caused controversy because it came at a moment when American intelligence was bitterly divided over the broad issue of what to do about Cuba and the more specific issue of Castro's movement. The CIA station at the American Embassy was of two minds, some arguing that Castro was a secret Communist who would turn Cuba into a Communist state if he should take power, while others argued

---

*Kirkpatrick turned out to be right. Just before dawn on December 31, 1958, Batista and a small entourage secretly flew out of Havana to exile in the United States, carrying with them suitcases stuffed with an estimated $300 million in cash Batista had reaped in the form of bribes from U.S. corporations and Mafia-run gambling casinos. Batista's departure came as a surprise to Americans in Havana— except to David Atlee Phillips, a young CIA agent working under deep cover as a public-relations executive. Phillips noticed an unscheduled airliner leaving Havana airport at 4 A.M., and reasoned that Batista must be aboard; only Batista, he correctly deduced, had the power to order up a flight all for himself.

that Castro—despite the presence in his movement of such notorious Communist leaders as his brother Raúl and Che Guevara—was a leftist reformer who would present no danger to the United States if properly handled. The debate was regarded as nothing short of treasonous by conservative Eisenhower administration types, among them Earl T. Smith, the American ambassador to Cuba, who was a fervid supporter of Batista as an anti-Communist. Smith's feelings about Batista ran so deep, he openly accused CIA officials in Havana of Communist sympathies for the mere mentioning of Fidel Castro as a possible successor to Batista.

The arguments underscored the deep divisions within the American government itself over the Cuban mess. Clearly, Batista had become a liability, yet there was the argument about the cure—Castro—being worse than the disease. The central problem was that American intelligence was badly out of touch with the Latin American revolutionary movements then beginning to percolate throughout the continent; for too many years it had depended on a motley assortment of Latin American "security services" and secret-police forces for information on what was happening out in the countryside. As the BRAC incident demonstrated, those groups usually were more preoccupied with stamping out all forms of dissent than gathering intelligence—for which they had no real ability, anyway.

Another reason why American intelligence by 1958 was so far out of touch was the slapdash nature of American policy. Ever since the 1920s, when the United States had sent military forces to "restore stability" in several Latin American countries, American policymakers had regarded the entire area—especially Central America and the Caribbean—as firmly within the U.S. sphere of influence. And within that sphere, the United States felt it could control or shape political destinies at whim. Beginning in 1948, a further Cold War element was added to that policy: No form of Communism would be permitted in the Western Hemisphere; the continent would in effect become a political isolation ward into which the Marxist germ would never enter.

To that end, the United States began to prop up a collection of right-wing or military juntas, their sole justification a strong anti-Communism that qualified them for American military and economic aid. For those oligarchs whose excesses made them political liabilities in the eyes of the United States, there were certain measures—they were either shunted aside or, in extreme cases, simply done away with. (Such a fate befell the recalcitrant Generalissimo Rafael Trujillo of the Dominican Republic, whose barbarities embarrassed his American patrons. The political problem of the generalissimo was duly eliminated by a CIA-arranged assassination in 1961.)

Batista's Cuba was a classic illustration of the dilemma of American policy. Shrewd and completely ruthless, Batista had been a Cuban Army sergeant who befriended influential Americans, especially those with extensive commercial interests in the country. He ran a relatively mild (by Latin American standards, anyway) dictatorship for eleven years up to 1944, when he made way for a popularly elected government. In 1952, however, Batista again seized power and unleashed a brutal regime whose tastes for corruption, vice, and repression had within a few short years turned Cuba into a charnel house. Despite early official American support, Batista—who had deservedly earned the sobriquet "Caligula of the Caribbean"—soon became a distinct liability. This was a recurring problem for the United States in Latin America—the more actively it associated itself with right-wing regimes, the more it shared the blame when those regimes became unbearably repressive. The only way out was to find "moderate" (for which read pro-American) alternatives, but that in turn created another dilemma: Since the repression was aimed at eliminating that "moderate" opposition in the first place, as a practical matter, such an alternative often did not exist. It did not exist in Batista's 1958 Cuba, so when the United States began to withdraw support from him, the Americans faced the stark alternative of Fidel Castro's July 26th Movement, the only really broad-based opposition group remaining in the entire country.

WARRIORS OF THE NIGHT

The CIA station in Havana might have shed some light on the situation, but it was not one of the agency's more efficient outposts. Its confusion over Castro's political allegiances reflected the fact that most of its personnel were not very good. Few CIA agents had ever bothered to spend time out in the countryside—where the political future of Cuba was being decided—and the information they gained, mainly from Cuban coffeehouse gossip and Batista's secret police machinery, was nearly useless. One problem, as Captain Charles R. Clark, Jr., discovered upon being assigned as naval attaché to the U.S. Embassy in 1957, was that the CIA group there was regarded as an open joke among Cubans. Everybody in Havana, Clark later recounted, knew who the CIA men were, especially Batista's secret policemen, who kept them all under close surveillance and told them only what Batista wanted them to hear.

The U.S. Embassy and its CIA contingent remained in operation for more than a year after Castro triumphantly entered Havana (diplomatic relations were severed in January 1961), but by then, the agency had already made a number of serious mistakes. Chief among them was the matter of BRAC, the CIA-created organization that was left high and dry on New Year's Eve of 1958 when Batista suddenly fled the country. Castro and the guerrillas did not arrive in Havana for another two days, yet in that intervening time, nobody in the CIA station thought to take control of either the BRAC agents or BRAC files—loaded with highly damaging data about relations with the American agency, not to mention the identities of CIA operatives and their Cuban assets. Consequently, upon Castro's arrival in Havana, the first thing his aides did was to seize the BRAC building, gather up the files, arrest whatever BRAC agents they could get their hands on, and then cart the lot over to the old Spanish fortress that guards the entrance to Havana Harbor.

Too late, the CIA realized it was in trouble, for among other prizes, Castro's men had seized Captain José Castaño Quevedo, BRAC's American-trained liaison officer with the CIA station. Between the material in the files and what was inside Castaño's head, Castro would soon have a complete picture of the CIA in Cuba.* A CIA emissary was dispatched on an urgent mission to the rebels in an attempt to save Castaño from certain death at the hands of a revolutionary firing squad. An appeal was made directly to Che Guevara, who dismissed it, replying that he would have Castaño shot either as a *Batistiano verdugo,* "Batista thug," or as a CIA agent, whichever the CIA preferred—but Castaño would be shot, in any event.

In the bloodbath that followed Castro's accession to power, the death of Castaño was simply another statistic. But it had important intelligence implications, for Castaño and his henchmen, however modest their abilities as agents, nevertheless represented the last remaining CIA assets in Cuba. With those assets gone, and the CIA station increasingly isolated as Castro's revolutionary government consolidated its power, American intelligence became badly out of touch with Cuban realities. (So badly that CIA Director Allen Dulles on January 16, 1959, only fourteen days after Castro had taken power, told a closed session of the Senate Foreign Relations Committee that Castro had "no Communist leanings," although he said the CIA was "suspicious" about Raúl Castro and Che Guevara.)† This simple lack of facts about what was happening inside Cuba led to the first of several extremely serious misjudgments about that island nation and its leader, the man who would come to preoccupy, as no other individual human being ever has, the concerns of American intelligence.

The first error the CIA made about Castro was that he was fundamentally weak and could be overthrown relatively

*The CIA did manage to spirit BRAC's chief, Colonel Paget, out of the country. Later, he was given an agency job spotting Castro infiltrators among the Cuban refugees arriving in Miami. Unfortunately, Paget was hopeless at the job; he managed to detect not one of the nearly one hundred Castro agents who entered the United States among the refugees from 1959 to 1961.

†Vice-President Richard Nixon found Dulles's judgment fatuous. During a face-to-face meeting with Castro the following April, Nixon listened carefully to one of Fidel's lengthy monologues, following which he told Eisenhower flatly that Castro was a Communist.

easily. This conclusion stemmed directly from the CIA's historic experience in Latin America, where political developments—and leaders—seemed remarkably susceptible to covert-action operations. The CIA considered its experience in Guatemala a model for getting rid of an embarrassing or dangerous political problem. There, a CIA operation in 1954 had deposed a vaguely leftist government and replaced it with a right-wing one. The operation had gone off virtually without a hitch and helped to enhance the CIA's reputation as a worker of political and paramilitary miracles.

In Cuba, the CIA sought to repeat the scenario: A small group of men (twenty-five in the first operation against Castro) would be lavishly equipped with arms and equipment and infiltrated into the country, where they would rally other anti-Castro Cubans to their cause, proclaim a new government (which the United States would instantly recognize), and finally sweep through the rest of the island, toppling Castro. Simple.

But there existed a world of difference between Guatemala and Cuba. For one thing, Guatemala's professional army sat on its hands in 1954, unwilling to help the government then in power against CIA-sponsored rebels. For another, the Guatemalan government enjoyed no broad support among the country's people. In Cuba, however, Castro had the loyalty not only of his rebel army but also of the large numbers of militia forces he had created just after the Cuban revolution. More important, despite loss of support from the middle class and other segments of Cuban society, he still enjoyed widespread backing among most of the Cuban people. Moreover, Castro was that rarity among Latin American leaders, a charismatic revolutionary with a genius for leadership.

How a group of twenty-five exiles was supposed to topple Castro remains a monument to naïveté. It also stands as a monument to intelligence stupidity, for there was absolutely no intelligence on the Cuban situation that would have justified this pipe dream. The fact is that the CIA had no idea whatsoever about Castro's popular support (or the absence of it), the status of his military forces, the efficiency of his counterintelligence units—or indeed, anything else relating to Cuba. The CIA's chief lack was an underground intelligence network inside Cuba; without it, the agency operated blind.

Predictably, the first teams of infiltrators failed ignominiously. Castro regarded them as annoying pinpricks that deterred him not in the slightest from pursuing the collision course that was enraging his North American neighbor: seizure of U.S. property, admission of his Marxist-Leninist convictions, and finally, the decision to buy arms from the Soviet Union.

Clearly, a serious conflict of some sort was inevitable between Castro and the United States. But no one suspected that it would take the form of the worst American intelligence failure in the postwar period: Operation Zapata as it was known to the men who planned and tried to execute it—or as the operation was more popularly called, the Bay of Pigs.

In its basic form, Operation Zapata amounted to a slight expansion of the tried and true covert paramilitary action that had worked so well on a number of other problems, notably Guatemala and Iran. Exiles would be collected clandestinely and armed and trained by the Americans, who would then "sponsor" their invasion of the homeland. There, they would coalesce with the underground opposition and go on to overthrow the ruling regime. Aside from logistical support, the United States would provide an extensive propaganda barrage and, even more important, official recognition once the rebels had taken power.

The difficulty, of course, was that any such plan required the most detailed intelligence from inside the homeland. The invaders would have to know the precise location, size, and fighting efficiency of the regime's forces, the extent of opposition to the regime, the size and organization of the underground resistance movement, and the exact amount of military pressure required before the regime would collapse.

In the case of the Cuban invasion, there was no real intelligence whatsoever; instead, a series of assumptions was constructed into an elaborate justification. These were some of the assumptions:

- Discontent with the Castro regime was widespread throughout Cuba, and the discontented people would rise up in a spontaneous revolt once they saw the invaders.
- Despite Soviet military aid, Castro's armed forces were weak, incapable of halting a paramilitary invasion.
- A force of only fourteen hundred exiles, with extensive American support, could overthrow Castro's rickety regime.
- A few planes of the rebel air force could destroy Castro's small air force on the ground and eliminate it as a factor in the invasion.
- Preparations for the invasion, including large-scale training programs, could be kept a secret from the Cuban government, which would be totally surprised when the invasion took place.

Not one of these assumptions was true. Why did the men planning Operation Zapata believe them? Partly because the planners—especially Allen Dulles and one of his key deputies, Richard Bissell—were in effect arbiters of their own plan. Tightly compartmentalized, the planners performed two functions at once: evaluating intelligence about Cuba, and using that intelligence to formulate the Zapata plan. This was a serious error, for it meant that the men planning the invasion were also evaluating the chances for its success. Dulles and the small staff of planners involved in Zapata were under strong pressure from the White House to hurry the plan along, to "do something" about Castro before the growing influx of Soviet support made him impervious to pressure from the outside. In that atmosphere, the CIA planners tended to focus on any scrap of intelligence that would buttress their conviction that the plan would work.

For the most part, the intelligence came from the stream of Cuban exiles pouring into Miami. Bitterly anti-Castro, they were largely middle-class or upper-class people for whom Communism, especially in their own homeland, was anathema. In CIA debriefing centers in Florida, they angrily told stories of expropriation of property and harsh repressive measures against Cubans thought to be "counterrevolutionary elements"—apparently all those perceived as nonenthusiastic supporters of Castro's revolution. The exiles burned with a white-hot hatred, and in their view, revulsion against Castro inside Cuba was so great, there was no question but that an uprising against him was imminent. Their genuine hatred for Castro and his revolution tended to color a great many of the exiles' judgments and perceptions of what they had seen in Cuba, and they in turn colored the CIA's perceptions.

The perceptions, however, had come from a limited source. Very few lower-class Cubans or peasants, who constituted the bulk of the Cuban population, were among the exiles fleeing northward, and it was among those groups that Castro's political strength was the strongest. However much the middle and upper classes detested Castro, for the people on the lower rungs of the economic ladder, Castro was regarded as a genuine savior. It was an important distinction that was overlooked by the CIA. To sum up, the intelligence amounted to the belief that fourteen hundred exiles could defeat an army of two hundred thousand men who were led by a weak "hysterical" leader (how he had managed to lead a revolution in that condition was not explained). Further, a powerful underground (so powerful as to forestall any Castro move) would join the exiles in a march on Havana—all of this under an American cover story so clever that it would defy any attempt to expose it.

Even a modest outside review would have raised serious objections to the intelligence supporting this fantasy, but Zapata, unfortunately, lacked this contact with reality. The military had only a limited role in reviewing the plan, and that review was cautious. The caution was induced by politics: The CIA's established reputation at that point for successful paramilitary operations, made the military tread carefully on the subject of CIA covert-action plans, even when they involved direct military action. The Joint Chiefs of Staff dispatched a three-man team to review the Zapata plan, which wound up with a carefully phrased verdict that the operation stood a "likelihood of achieving military success"—provided that "political factors" were successful (referring to the belief that the invasion would touch off a popular uprising against Castro), and that full surprise was achieved.

In the process of being politically cautious, the JCS experts somehow missed several basic military deficiencies in the Zapata plan, deficiencies so glaring a West Point plebe would have spotted them in an instant. One was the decision to place all the invasion's communications equipment aboard one ship, an elementary error that raised the danger of a complete communications blackout if the ship was sunk (which is exactly what happened at the Bay of Pigs). Furthermore, there clearly was not enough air power to knock out the Cuban Air Force even under the best of circumstances, and the CIA had missed a large shipment of heavy-caliber Russian artillery Castro received just before the invasion—artillery that helped tip the battle in his favor.

The disaster at the Bay of Pigs in April 1961 was total, and underscored the dimensions of the intelligence failure that had made it inevitable. Clearly every single intelligence judgment on which the success of the operation rested turned out to be not only wrong but colossally wrong. There was no hope of any popular uprising against Castro, invasion or not. Castro's air force was much stronger than believed. The Cuban military had better weapons than the CIA thought they had. The Bay of Pigs site was about the worst possible choice for an amphibious landing. The entire operation had become a matter of common knowledge in the Cuban exile community—and, presumably, to Castro.

The list goes on and on, and it is no wonder that an angry President John F. Kennedy vowed to "splinter the CIA into a thousand pieces" over the failure. Kennedy did not carry out the threat, but he did form a secret commission under his military guru, General Maxwell Taylor, to study the invasion and determine what went wrong. In a moment of subtle revenge, Kennedy appointed Allen Dulles to the commission, and for several months Dulles had to sit there, day after day, as Taylor mercilessly exposed the CIA's bungling and incompetence. This humiliation infuriated Dulles and his aides, who suspected—rightly—that Taylor's central mission was to exonerate the military from as much responsibility for the fiasco as possible. (Dulles resigned his CIA post shortly after this episode.)

Not surprisingly, Taylor's final report to Kennedy concluded that there ought to be somebody around to hold the CIA's hand on the next occasion it mounted a covert paramilitary operation. At the same time, Taylor raised many questions about the quality of the CIA's intelligence on Cuba, which he did not find very impressive. Taylor was right, but despite the obvious necessity for the CIA to improve its intelligence on Cuba, the agency was diverted instead to a new mission that repeated some old errors. And they were errors that came to have grave consequences, not the least of them bringing the world to the brink of nuclear holocaust.

It was one of those code names that seemed to fit perfectly: Operation Mongoose, which represented a plan ordered by President Kennedy following the Bay of Pigs to solve the Cuban problem once and for all. There was nothing very subtle about the operation—using every means short of another Bay of Pigs-type invasion, the CIA was to get rid of Fidel Castro.

As a covert political destabilization operation—indeed, a prototypical example of such an operation—Mongoose is technically outside our study of intelligence operations. However, Mongoose involved American intelligence assumptions about Cuba that are worth examining, for they were assumptions that guaranteed the failure of the operation from the very start.

At root, the assumptions were the same ones that had gotten the United States involved in Zapata: The overwhelming mass of the Cuban people were against Castro, and they would revolt if given the chance—meaning if Castro's organizational and economic structures were weakened enough. Incredibly, despite the failure of the Bay of Pigs, the CIA had learned nothing; the agency persisted in portraying Castro and his revolution as some sort of anomaly imposed by deceit and trickery on the Cuban people. The CIA saw no solid ground under Castro's feet; his regime was perceived as so shaky, merely the smallest push would cause it to collapse. The assumptions reflected a lack of real intelligence from inside Cuba, and they also reflected a mind-set about Cuba in the Kennedy administration, a mind-set that originated at the very top.

Nothing in the entire United States government had a higher priority than getting rid of Fidel Castro, as President Kennedy and his brother Robert, the U.S. Attorney General, demonstrated by personally involving themselves in every possible aspect of Mongoose. Robert Kennedy, especially, made it clear that the White House wanted results—and it wanted results *immediately.* He popped in unannounced on meetings of the Special Group Augmented—a high-level White House/military/CIA group that planned and directed operations against Castro—to goad them to more and faster action, and even took to calling shocked CIA officials directly involved in Mongoose, asking them about their operations. Obviously, Kennedy was not in a mood to hear either that the intelligence assumptions behind Mongoose might be wrong or that a destabilization effort on the scale of the one against Cuba would take a lot more time than the Kennedys assumed.

Plainly, Cuba had become an obsession to the Kennedys, and the climate they created of high-level pressure for results had a number of disturbing effects, one of which was conformity. In such an atmosphere, there are few officials who do not feel compelled to "get on the team," to agree with the higher-level wisdom that has pronounced an operation do-able. Mongoose was a perfect example of the phenomenon: Nobody bothered to tell the Kennedys forcefully that if a paramilitary invasion with the full support of the United States had not succeeded in toppling Castro, then a lower-level campaign of harassment, plus economic and political pressure, stood no hope of succeeding either.

Conformity in such circumstances tends to spawn career-ism, a dangerous development in intelligence officers who begin to understand that the route to promotion lies in telling the policymaker what he wants to hear. Thus, when the CIA brought a thirty-four-year-old operative named Theodore Shackley in from Berlin to head up Task Force W (the CIA operational unit that was to carry out Mongoose), Shackley's first assigned task was to produce a "vulnerability and feasibil-ity" study. A standard exercise in covert political operations, such studies are supposed to determine whether the plan for such an operation is feasible, based on all available intelli-gence. In the case of Mongoose, Shackley concluded that the plan was feasible. It is difficult to imagine that Shackley ar-rived at this conclusion on the basis of purely objective rea-sons; a protégé of such important CIA figures as William Colby (later a director of the agency), Shackley had already gained experience in covert political operations while serving in the hot spots of Laos, Vietnam, and Berlin. Given that experience, Shackley was perfectly aware of the complexity and time required for such operations and that the relatively minor harassment actions designed for use against the Castro regime stood no real chance of success.

But Shackley was no different from other CIA officers, from the director on down, who eagerly endorsed an opera-tion already pronounced feasible by those above. In the presi-dential doghouse since the Bay of Pigs, the CIA was eager to demonstrate that it was worthy of presidential favor, that it could rectify the disaster of Zapata with a glittering success in Mongoose. And what the CIA wound up with was a plan strikingly reminiscent of the prototype for all such covert destabilization operations—the attempt by American intelligence in 1919 to overthrow the infant Communist regime in Russia: sabotage and hit-and-run missions using anti-Communist elements, along with economic and political pressure from the outside. (As in 1919, it also included an assassination plan, in the case of Mongoose a series of comic-opera attempts on the life of Fidel Castro.)

The important difference between the two schemes was size: Mongoose was eventually to create a vast CIA paramilitary empire, involving more than three hundred CIA agents, more than twenty-five hundred Cuban-exile contract agents, and a $50 million annual budget. As these statistics indicate, Cuba had become the central preoccupation of the CIA, to the virtual exclusion of just about anything else. Initially, at least, the key element of the Mongoose plan was the building of large underground networks inside Cuba, which were to perform the dual functions of obtaining detailed intelligence about the island and carrying out an extensive program of sabotage. (It is astonishing how often this fundamental error of trying to combine intelligence and paramilitary action has been repeated.)

But the pressure from the White House for immediate results was so strong that the idea of building such underground networks was soon abandoned. In its place was substituted a program of hit-and-run raids by Cuban exiles. Beginning in the summer of 1961, there were raids against sugar mills, oil refineries, and other installations, establishing a pattern that became familiar over the next several years: CIA-trained exiles would be taken in a CIA mother ship to within fifty miles of the Cuban coast, where they would be offloaded into rubber boats powered by motors equipped with special silencers. The exiles would land, carry out their attack, then flee back to the mother ship before the Cuban military had time to react.* All very daring, but such

*Some of the exiles were to carry out such raids for years. Among them was Rolando Martínez, an exile who was involved in 354 missions against Cuba on behalf of the CIA for five years without suffering so much as a scratch—only to be arrested in 1972 during the Watergate breakin.

attacks had no hope of overthrowing Castro. So what was the point?

Virtually nothing of any merit, for Mongoose, which was to continue for another six years until President Lyndon Johnson, preoccupied with events in Vietnam, ordered it closed down, was a total failure. As a paramilitary operation, it was a disaster; the United States eventually spent nearly $500 million for a series of pinpricks that served only to strengthen a regime that used the raids as a rationale for a large-scale buildup of military and internal-security forces that eventually turned Cuba into a fortress. From an intelligence standpoint, Mongoose was an even greater disaster, because sabotage teams flitting in and out of Cuba may have had enough time to wreck a sugar refinery, but they surely weren't in any position to collect intelligence.

Another, and even more important, result was that Mongoose badly distorted CIA priorities. So much money, time, effort, and personnel were poured into the operation that the agency's intelligence-collection efforts became very much a second string on the fiddle. As in any other government bureaucracy, power at the CIA—and in the rest of American intelligence—tends to flow in directions set by policymakers. Thus Mongoose set the career ground rules: Money, promotion, and prestige went to those involved in boom and bang operations. The paramilitary and covert-action types came to rule the agency roost, a development that was to prove very damaging to American intelligence, for it not only made the less glamorous function of intelligence collection and analysis something of a second-class job, it also tended to create two very distinct cultures in American intelligence: those who collected intelligence, and those who really made things happen.

The primary emphasis of the CIA began to shift from intelligence toward something very different, in the process creating a Cold War version of the OSS. One look at some of the men running Mongoose illustrated the transformation. For example, Shackley (who later went on to run CIA operations in South Vietnam during the height of the Vietnam War) was succeeded as chief of Task Force W by another covert-action specialist, William Harvey, a former FBI agent who had joined the CIA in 1947. Harvey, a rough-talking, squat man who had the unmistakable demeanor of cop about him, always carried a gun—which he had the alarming habit of pointing toward anyone with whom he was arguing, slowly releasing the safety catch. A heavy drinker, Harvey was the prototypical CIA "cowboy" (agency slang for covert-action operator) whose sinister flamboyance fit right in with some of the other cowboys in Mongoose.

Among them was William "Rip" Robertson, a CIA legend who had started his agency career by running boom and bang operations behind Communist lines in Korea. By the time of Mongoose, everybody in the agency had heard about his feats of derring-do in a dozen other countries. He was not a man the agency liked to have around headquarters: He preferred to stay in the field, dressed in old work clothes, his glasses tied with a string behind his head, and a pulp novel invariably stuck in his back pocket. Robertson had become a near deity among the Cuban exiles for his courage and had openly ignored CIA orders forbidding him to land on the beach during the Bay of Pigs, only narrowly avoiding capture by Castro.

But the grand legends of such CIA cowboys obscured an important fact: These ostensible "intelligence agents" were not really intelligence agents at all. They collected almost no intelligence, preferring to leave that task to a vague group of people who operated in a wholly different division someplace else in the agency—people to whom the cowboys hardly spoke. Nor were they paying much attention to the counterintelligence aspects of their job, notably the bona fides of the small army of Cuban exiles recruited for Mongoose. The exiles had been enrolled in the CIA's secret war willy-nilly; many of them had been signed up almost as soon as they stepped off refugee flights arriving in Miami from Havana. There was only a modicum of screening, mostly by incompetent ex–Batista secret police, and the prevailing presumption was that any exile professing a hatred for Castro and a willingness to fight possessed sufficient credentials.

The lack of caution in the recruitment of exiles made Mongoose vulnerable to penetration by the DGI, Castro's Soviet-trained intelligence service, whose task was considerably eased by the very openness of Task Force W operations in southern Florida. The DGI penetrations, which mainly took the form of infiltrating DGI agents among the refugees and then waiting for a CIA recruitment approach, reached very high levels. Carlos Rivero Collado, for example, had fled to the United States in 1959 and was one of the original founders of the White Rose exile group, among the first exile organizations supported by the CIA on U.S. soil. Son of the last elected president of Cuba, Rivero had been captured at the Bay of Pigs, and upon his release in December 1962, returned to Miami, where he was again enlisted by the CIA, this time for a high-level job in Mongoose. Twelve years later, however, Rivero suddenly fled to Cuba and revealed that he had been a DGI agent all along.*

CIA intelligence analysts had long suspected such DGI penetration, and combined with the distinct lack of good intelligence from the exiles before the Bay of Pigs, it made the exiles extremely unreliable in the analysts' view. Indeed, whatever the exiles had to say upon their arrival in this country came to be regarded as useless by the analysts, who felt that the exiles' highly prejudiced political views and tendency to exaggerate pretty well outweighed whatever intelligence they might have. The analysts did not know it, but their distaste for the exiles would lead to what was eventually re-

*In 1976, Castro revealed publicly that the DGI had managed to infiltrate all of the one hundred Cuban exile groups in the United States, a claim the CIA does not dispute. Castro also revealed several abortive CIA attempts to recruit Cuban government officials, including Nicolás Sirgado Ros, general director for supplies in the Cuban Ministry of Construction. In 1966, Sirgado, while on a trip to London, was recruited by the CIA. Sirgado played along on behalf of the DGI, and was told by the CIA to bug his boss's office with a device hidden inside a rock. Sirgado complied, but the DGI controlled the transmissions. Sirgado was given a gold Rolex watch by the CIA for his work, and managed to pass three CIA lie-detector tests that pronounced him "genuine."

garded as American intelligence's finest hour—although, in truth, it was more nearly its worst.

Like the unmistakable signals of an approaching storm, the clues began to accumulate early in 1962. The first hints were detected in Cheltenham, England, by experts at the British Government Communications Headquarters, the chief British code-breaking operation. The experts who kept round-the-clock surveillance on radio transmissions emanating from inside the Soviet Union began to detect some strange goings-on during the month of March: an unusual jump in radio traffic between Cuba and Moscow. There were also unusual ship movements in southern Russia near the port of Odessa, origination point for shipments to Cuba, and the fact that the Russians apparently were concentrating lumber-carrying merchant ships at the port made the movements even more unusual.

Nothing about the movements made sense. Cuba has plenty of forests, so it was unlikely that the Russians were about to ship lumber to Havana. Therefore, the ships were being readied to take a different sort of cargo—something similar to lumber in its high volume and low weight. What could it be?

The CIA's analysts thought they knew the answer: IL-28 jet bombers, whose operating radius of five hundred miles would put them within reach of U.S. targets. The CIA had become progressively more alarmed about Soviet military shipments into Cuba since the Bay of Pigs, shipments that included forty MiG fighters. The MiGs, interceptor models, were clearly designed for air defense—a not unnatural concern for Castro in view of the rebel air-force attacks preceding the Bay of Pigs—but the IL-28s would be a far different matter. Only one purpose for those planes was possible: attacks against the United States.

Despite the CIA's suspicion that the bombers were being shipped into Cuba, however, there was no firm evidence that the Russians had done so. Indeed, the evidence pointed the other way: No large new airfields were being constructed, there were no new radar-control facilities being built, and there was no sign of any of the extensive facilities needed to support bomber operations. At the same time, though, there was a great deal of activity on the island. Beginning in late July 1962, aerial reconnaissance detected at least eight large military shipments from the Soviet Union into Cuba, the arrival of fifteen hundred Soviet military personnel under tight security (bringing total Soviet forces in Cuba to more than five thousand men), the off-loading of large amounts of what appeared to be electronic equipment, and the closing to Cubans of Mariel, a largely unused small port on the northern coast of Cuba, while the Russians unloaded their ships. If the Russians weren't shipping bombers, then what *were* they shipping?

The CIA was paying the price for its lack of good intelligence sources inside Cuba; aerial reconnaissance could tell the analysts that there was plenty of Soviet military equipment being funneled into Cuba, but the pictures could not tell them exactly what Castro (or the Russians) intended to do with it. The CIA's only human-intelligence sources were the Cuban refugees still flowing into Miami, all of whom were processed through something called the Caribbean Admissions Center, ostensibly a U.S. government operation to help the refugees get resettled. In reality, the center was a CIA front designed to debrief the refugees about events inside Cuba. However, as noted earlier, the CIA analysts had become skeptical of refugee reports, a skepticism that increased when some of the refugees arriving in Miami during the summer of 1962 began to tell wild stories about seeing large Russian rockets being transported on long trailers into the countryside.

In the analysts' view, the reports were preposterous. Obviously, it was reasoned, the refugees were spreading the same sort of alarmist prattle that had convinced the CIA only a year before that Castro was teetering on the brink of ruin. Besides, none of the refugees were trained military observers; most probably, they had encountered ordinary Russian surface-to-air defense missiles and, having never seen any before, believed them to be intermediate- or intercontinental-range rockets.

What was happening amounted to one of the more invidious processes in intelligence: trying to fit the facts to a preconception. In the case of events in Cuba during that summer of 1962, the CIA analysts had already rejected the possibility that the Russians would install long-range missiles on the island. The agency's preconception, summarized in an intelligence estimate prepared for the White House, concluded that there was no possibility of the Soviet Union's installing such missiles in Cuba. In the CIA's view, such a deployment was unthinkable because the Russians would not want to upset the delicate strategic balance with the United States, would not risk a confrontation involving strategic weapons, would not emplace missiles nine thousand miles from the Soviet Union (no Soviet missile up to that point had ever been stationed outside Soviet territory), and would not risk such valuable weapons in an exposed forward position, especially considering the certainty of a strong American reaction.

The estimate found favor in the White House, which shared the analysts' conviction that the Russians would never be so foolish as to risk emplacement of long-range missiles in Cuba. To a certain extent, the estimate was welcome reassurance for the Kennedy administration, which was beginning to feel real political heat about the missile situation. The heat had been generated by New York Senator Kenneth Keating, who was making widely publicized charges that the Russians were installing long-range missiles in Cuba—and that the Kennedy administration wasn't doing anything about it.

In addition, the missile question was generating even more heat within the U.S. intelligence community. The Pentagon's newly created Defense Intelligence Agency (DIA) reacted furiously to the CIA estimate, arguing that the agency had missed the Russian rockets in Cuba because it considered only the evidence that supported a predetermined conclusion that the Russians would never install the missiles. Among other pieces of evidence ignored by the CIA, the DIA noted, the Russians had begun work on several mysterious construction sites in the Cuban countryside, far from any known military installations. Furthermore, the DIA military analysts pointed out, the construction sites were being guarded by surface-to-air missiles arranged in a trapezoidal pattern—the very same pattern the Russians invariably used inside the Soviet Union to guard their long-range missile sites. And for a clincher, the DIA argued that the reports from refugees about large rockets being trundled through the streets of port towns at night were too persistent and extensive to be entirely dismissed.

But the CIA's conclusion had an even more significant critic—the director of the CIA himself. John A. McCone, a wealthy Republican businessman, had been appointed by Kennedy as successor to Allen Dulles, a choice that involved a shrewd political calculation by the President. The choice protected Kennedy's right flank from congressional conservatives, although in fact Kennedy and Secretary of Defense Robert S. McNamara both personally detested McCone, an overbearing and arrogant man who had spent a lifetime getting his way. McCone irritated Kennedy further by insisting that Keating—whom Kennedy regarded as a deadly political enemy—was right about Cuba.

McCone admitted he had no hard evidence for his conviction—just an instinct, as he put it—and he was infuriated when the CIA's Board of National Estimates, responsible for preparing the intelligence community's official verdict on events in Cuba, concluded that the Russians were not installing (and probably would never install) long-range missiles on the island. McCone was not a trained intelligence agent, but he did have a strong streak of common sense honed to a native shrewdness by the many years he had spent in the very down-to-earth world of the construction business. And what McCone knew about the construction business told him that even the Russians would never be so foolhardy as to spend all that money using expensive surface-to-air missiles to guard ordinary construction sites. No, McCone insisted, obviously the Russians intended those surface-to-air missiles to guard something very important to be built at those sites—almost certainly long-range rockets.

But the analysts refused to budge, counterarguing that such renowned Kremlinologists as Charles Bohlen and Llewelyn Thompson, a former ambassador to the Soviet Union, both concurred in the analysts' estimate. The analysts were unimpressed with any evidence to the contrary, including some human intelligence that had caught McCone's eye. This was a debriefing report on a Cuban refugee known as "the accountant." The refugee was an extremely fastidious man devoted to precision not only in his work but in all aspects of his everyday life. It was a fastidiousness that made him a prime intelligence source.

The accountant—whose name has never been revealed —arrived in Miami on September 15. Six days before leaving Cuba, he told the CIA debriefers at the reception center, he had noticed a very strange sight near his home. He was awakened one night by the rumble of a convoy of Russian vehicles, among them long trailers covered with tarpaulins. Taking care not to be discovered, he watched as the trailers moved slowly through the town; each trailer, he noted, was about seventy feet long, and whatever was underneath the tarpaulin appeared to be cylinder-shaped. And although care had been taken to conceal whatever the trailers were carrying, he added, the cylindrical objects appeared to be too long for the trailers, and part of them stuck out of the back. What part? Something that looked like the bottom end of a rocket, the accountant replied, because it had large fins.

Judging by the excited reaction, the accountant might as well have told them of seeing Nikita Khrushchev himself that night. He was asked to go over his account repeatedly. Was he sure about what he had seen? Was he certain about its dimensions and appearance? The accountant was positive; he had taken very careful mental measurements of all that he had seen, then committed them to memory. There was absolutely no doubt. Finally convinced that the accountant was telling the truth, the CIA debriefers now faced a stark reality: He had described almost exactly the measurements for the Soviet SS-4 "Shyster" missile—which had a range of one thousand miles. According to the CIA's own official judgment, the missile wasn't supposed to be anywhere near Cuba, yet here was highly reliable eyewitness evidence that an *entire convoy* of them had been in the country only six days before. Obviously, something was seriously amiss; either the accountant was completely wrong (which seemed unlikely) or the CIA had made a gross intelligence error (which seemed at the time to be equally unlikely).

Despite the debriefers' excitement, the accountant's revelations had no impact on the analysts, who continued to insist that his story represented still another example of an overexcited Cuban refugee misestimating what was probably just another Soviet surface-to-air missile. So the official judgment stood: There were no Soviet long-range missiles in Cuba. It was a judgment that made McCone increasingly restive, although his unease was communicated by long distance; he had remarried that month and was honeymooning in the south of France. How he was spending his honeymoon became the subject of some amused speculation at CIA headquarters, which was bombarded by a steady stream of cables at all hours of the day and night from McCone demanding that further analysis and study be carried out on the question of missiles in Cuba.

The blizzard of cables from McCone had the fortunate effect of spurring the CIA into a maximum effort to determine, once and for all, the truth about the missile controversy. The effort was concentrated in American intelligence's greatest strength, its technology. Virtually the entire power of American intelligence's considerable technical resources was turned on the island, the most important being the U-2 spy planes. Beginning in early September, U-2s crisscrossed the island, their cameras seeking the positive proof (or lack of it) of Russian long-range missiles. The flights were so common, Castro later complained, that Cuban women were afraid to go out naked onto their balconies, fearful they would be ogled by American pilots.

But the last thing on any U-2 pilot's mind was nude Cuban sunbathers; the pilots were under considerable pressure to get results, to snap the one picture that would prove conclusively that there were or were not long-range missiles someplace on the island. To a large extent, the pilots were taking a long shot. Parts of Cuba are honeycombed with large caves, perfectly suitable for hiding missiles from prying eyes during the day. In addition, long-range Russian missiles were transportable, which meant they could be in one place at four o'clock in the afternoon, and somewhere miles away the next day. At the same time, the pilots were battling weather; that time of year is the hurricane season in the Caribbean, with thick cloud cover and weather often bad enough to keep spy planes grounded (especially planes that depend on clear weather to take pictures). Then too, the Russians were known to be adept at camouflage; it was probable that they had taken great pains to hide the missiles.

Meanwhile, the CIA's Office of Current Intelligence—the branch most directly concerned with breaking intelligence, especially on Cuba—supplemented the U-2 effort with a new twist in intelligence collection. It was called "craterology," basically a subspecialty of photo interpretation, itself the highly arcane art of poring over reconnaissance pictures and picking out even the smallest item of significance. The craterologists, as they called themselves, were a small group of trained analysts who had gone a step further; through careful study of how the Russians crated their weapons for shipment, they were able to identify what weapons were being shipped just by observing pictures of the crates. A jet fighter-bomber, for example, was packed into three large crates of distinctive size and shape. And so, when the analysts looked at a picture of crates awaiting shipment on a dock in Cuba, they were able to determine, with great accuracy, which crates contained radar parts, which contained jet fighters, or which contained artillery pieces.

The craterologists provided the first hard indication that

the Russians were shipping missiles into Cuba. Some Soviet merchant ships in the Caribbean, buzzed incessantly by low-flying U.S. Navy patrol planes equipped with cameras, made the mistake of carrying above deck some distinctive crates containing missile components, making the analysts' job that much easier. Other ships, the analysts noted, had large covered hatches and decks loaded with vehicles, but the ships were riding too high in the water for such bulk cargo, which meant that they were carrying high-volume, low-weight cargo —such as missiles—belowdecks.

Still, there was no firm evidence from Cuba itself that the missiles had actually been deployed. Day after day, the U-2s roared across Cuba from all points of the compass, unsuccessfully seeking a missile installation. The planes spotted several Russian surface-to-air missiles (one shot down a U-2), but no long-range missiles. At this point, the DIA took a bold step. Its analysts asked themselves a simple question: If they were Russian and were installing long-range missiles in Cuba, where would be the best site for them? After some debate involving ranges and firing angles of missiles, it was decided that the San Cristóbal area in western Cuba would be just about ideal. A U-2 was ordered to overfly the area, and after several delays caused by bad weather, it crossed over San Cristóbal on the morning of October 14, 1962. Several hours later, the developed U-2 pictures showed Soviet medium-range missiles being installed at San Cristóbal. And at almost the same moment, Kennedy's national security adviser, McGeorge Bundy, was saying in an interview that there was "no present likelihood" of the Russians installing such missiles in Cuba.

Bundy's remark was the last gasp of the shared wisdom that had dominated the Kennedy administration's thinking about what the Russians were doing in Cuba. Six days later, President Kennedy made his dramatic speech that brought the world to the brink of nuclear war.

To a large extent, the Cuban missile crisis has passed into American mythology as a great success of "crisis management," of "measured response," and a whole series of other triumphs, not the least of them intelligence. It is a dangerous myth, for the fact is that the Cuban missile crisis, especially in intelligence terms, was a horrendous botch right from the beginning. Former Secretary of State Dean Acheson was right when he later called this American triumph not really a success at all but a "homage to dumb luck."

Certainly, it was purely a matter of luck that despite a series of intelligence fumblings, the United States finally managed to find out whether there were long-range missiles only ninety miles from its shores. It was also a matter of pure dumb luck that however inept the American intelligence community's performance in Cuba, the Russians were even more inept. Their ineptitude, as a matter of fact, was astonishing. They had not only seriously (and almost tragically) misread the reaction of the United States to the presence of nuclear missiles virtually in the American backyard, they had also failed to take even the most elementary measures to conceal those missiles. There was no attempt at any time to camouflage the missile sites, and American military-reconnaissance pilots were astounded to discover that Soviet units in Cuba had the habit of affixing their regimental colors to their barracks and installations, making identification of Soviet units in Cuba almost elementary.

The missile crisis demonstrated clearly how dangerous intelligence failures can be in the age of missiles and thermonuclear weapons. Each side's intelligence failure was total —the United States underestimated Khrushchev's willingness to take an "impossible" gamble, and the Russians gravely underestimated American determination. It would seem, then, that both sides would resolve never again to be caught in the position of trying to settle questions of war and peace in an atmosphere of little or no information about the other side, much like two blind men stumbling at each other with drawn swords. But neither side seemed to learn anything from the crisis. They signed a vague "understanding" about Cuba that left plenty of room to continue the sort of dangerous actions that had led to the crisis in the first place. The United States pledged, in return for the Soviet withdrawal of missiles, never to invade Cuba—but Mongoose and its hit-and-run raids against Castro were allowed to continue. The Russians agreed never to base "strategic offensive weapons" in Cuba—but the massive buildup of Cuba's conventional armed forces went on.

The ink was hardly dry on the understanding when the old mutual suspicions again began to take hold. On the American side, Kennedy was pressed by his conservative opponents to take even more drastic action against the Russians; how did he know, the critics charged, that the Russians had indeed removed all those missiles from Cuba? Actually, Kennedy didn't know for sure. He had all the wonders of modern intelligence technology at his command—U-2, the craterologists, communications intercepts, and so on—but American intelligence still lacked good human sources inside Cuba, so there was always that slight element of doubt. But it was a doubt that Kennedy kept private; publicly, he offered assurances that there was no possibility—thanks to American surveillance—of Soviet cheating on the withdrawal. To underscore that reassurance, Kennedy in February 1963 had the Pentagon conduct what still ranks as the most extraordinary public discussion about American intelligence ever held, a televised briefing on what intelligence knew about Cuba and the Russian missiles. For two hours, a fascinated group of reporters and a large television viewing audience watched as blowups of U-2 pictures were analyzed by CIA photo interpreters.

This extraordinary insight into the dark world of espionage was convincing to most of the American public, but there were some people who remained unimpressed. These formed an odd coalition of some of the more rabid elements of the Cuban exile community, assorted bitter opponents of Kennedy, and several wealthy right-wingers determined to "show up" Kennedy for failing to take advantage of the missile crisis and destroy Castro. They were to take part in what became the darkest episode in the history of American intelligence's involvement with Cuba, for this coalition received direct help from CIA operatives connected with Mongoose, plus tacit support from the CIA itself. What resulted was a dangerous enterprise known as Operation Red Cross.

The original sparks for Red Cross were the most fanatical anti-Castro exiles, for whom the accolades heaped upon Kennedy for his handling of the missile crisis were obscene. In their view, Kennedy had failed again; first, he had betrayed them at the Bay of Pigs, and just when he had the opportunity to set off the conflagration to destroy Castro, he backed down, compromising with the Russians. They were convinced Kennedy had been tricked; not only was Castro in power, stronger than ever, but the Russians hadn't really removed all those missiles. The missiles were probably hidden in caves, and besides, there were still several thousand Russian soldiers on the island.

The belief was shared by some of the CIA's Mongoose case officers, cowboys who felt, as did the exiles, that Kennedy had failed to eliminate Castro when he had the chance. This volatile mix of people now received what seemed to be a stroke of incredible fortune: One of the Cuban exiles who worked for the CIA showed a letter he claimed to have received from a guerrilla unit inside Cuba. According to the letter, two Soviet Army colonels stationed in Cuba, both missile officers, wanted to defect to the United States, and—even more sensational—had already revealed that Khrushchev had ordered them to hide the missiles in caves.

The exile who claimed to have received the letter was Eduardo Pérez (known in the exile community as Bayo), a fanatic who had once served as military aide to Raúl Castro during the guerrilla war against Batista. He later broke with the Castros and ultimately wound up working for the CIA in Mongoose, for which he ran an old converted subchaser on raids into Cuba. Pérez claimed to be in contact with a group of anti-Castro guerrillas deep in the Cuban interior, and on behalf of Commando L, among the more fanatic exile groups, went on regular gun-running trips to Cuba, delivering arms to what was supposed to be Castro's biggest nemesis.

Pérez illustrated how far out of control Mongoose and its anti-Castro army had become. No one but Pérez had ever made contact with the alleged group of guerrillas fighting Castro, and for all the CIA knew, the guerrillas existed only in his imagination. On top of that, Pérez had now come up with this extraordinary letter. Worse, he proposed a bizarre plan to the CIA: The agency would support a foray by a ten-man handpicked team of exiles (including himself), who would go into Cuba, kidnap the two Russian colonels, then bring them to the United States. Once there, the colonels would reveal publicly how Kennedy had been hoodwinked, thus completely destroying the President's credibility. And that, Pérez informed his CIA contacts, inevitably would lead to the election of Barry Goldwater in 1964—a man who in Pérez's view almost certainly would carry out an American military invasion of Cuba.

These were dangerous political waters, and by rights, the CIA should have told Pérez not even to mention the crack-brained proposal. But at least three Mongoose case officers encouraged it, even to the extent of formally proposing Operation Red Cross to CIA headquarters. Cooler heads there called the idea a "plant" by Castro and the Russians, possibly to lure CIA-sponsored exiles into a trap—but then tacitly okayed the idea by saying Pérez could go ahead, although the agency would not provide any money. That was no problem; the Mongoose case officers easily arranged financing from several wealthy southern right-wingers.

On the night of June 7, 1963, Pérez and his team of exiles were ready to go. A CIA-provided PBY seaplane flew them near the Cuban coast, where they off-loaded into a speedboat and headed for a prearranged rendezvous with the guerrillas inside the country.

And that was the last anybody (at least outside Cuba) ever saw of Pérez and his team. CIA men and exiles from Pérez's organization waited and searched for the next six days, but there was no sign of him. Finally, everybody gave up and went home, leaving open the question of what happened to Pérez and Operation Red Cross. It remains a mystery to this day. The Cubans themselves have never mentioned anything about the incident, which would seem to remove the possibility that Pérez was a DGI double agent all along. On the other hand, there was no announcement by the Cuban government about a group of exiles being intercepted, so that raises the possibility that Pérez is still alive, fighting his holy crusade someplace in the mountains.

The bizarre Red Cross episode was symptomatic of the decline of Mongoose. Its CIA control officers clearly had been in the field for too long and had begun to share some of the more brainless flights of fancy that often afflicted the Cuban exiles, men for whom hope and illusion served as justification for the terrible risks they took running raids into Cuba. But time had passed the exiles by; they had failed, and it was clear that no matter how many sugar refineries were wrecked or how many Cuban ships were sunk, Castro was not about to be driven out of Cuba. Not, that is, with the Soviet Union providing $10 million a day in aid.

The exiles would be cast aside a few years later, having served their purpose. But despite the death of Mongoose, the American obsession over Cuba remained, and there would be continued American-Cuban clashes in the years to come. The exiles, however, no longer had any role to play. As the missile crisis showed, Cuba more than ever had become a focal point of the tension between the two great superpowers, and what happened in Cuba began to be seen strictly in terms of East-West conflict. In an important sense, Cuba had become the Berlin of the Western Hemisphere. The United States and the Soviet Union in effect staked their prestige in that small island nation, the Americans vowing that Castroism would be quarantined in Cuba, the Russians vowing that they would never permit Castro to be pushed around by the U.S. bullies.

The implications of this face-off would prove enormous, for it signaled the real beginning of an unparalleled American-Soviet competition for prestige and power, a competition that the United States took some time to recognize. It cannot be said that the Americans weren't warned early. In October 1962, Soviet diplomat Vasily Kuznetsov met with U.S. negotiator John J. McCloy at McCloy's Connecticut home to hammer out details of the understanding under which Soviet missiles would be withdrawn from Cuba. Fearful that the McCloy house was bugged, Kuznetsov took the American outside to talk. They sat on a rail fence as they spoke of the agreement, but then Kuznetsov suddenly said, "We shall live up to this agreement, but we shall never be in this position again."

McCloy later dutifully reported his Soviet counterpart's words to Washington, but nobody there seemed to quite understand their meaning. It was not long before the Russians began to demonstrate what Kuznetsov meant.

three

A FLY IN SPACE

> But when a man's fancy gets astride
> his reason . . . the first proselyte he
> makes, is himself. . . .
>
> —Jonathan Swift,
> "The Tale of a Tub"

In the spring of 1961, the unflappable staff of the Mount
Royal Hotel in London ushered into a suite of its best rooms
the unmistakably Slavic group of six men whose air of grim
determination and unusual cohesiveness—they moved almost
as a monolithic entity, each man seemingly watching the other
—marked them as Russians. Or so thought the hotel staff,
long experienced in the art of sorting out ethnic identities
from the mere appearance of its international clientele.

They were quite correct; the men were indeed Russians,
a delegation of senior Soviet Trade Ministry officials, in England to discuss future trade relations between the two countries. The sensitive antennae of the hotel staff detected a few
anomalies in this little group. For one thing, one of its members did not seem to quite fit in; he was much more voluble
than the rest, an engaging short man with thinning hair who
seemed (unlike the usual run of Soviet officials) to have a
genuine sense of humor. For another, the Russian group
seemed to have attracted an inordinate amount of attention;
there were all sorts of men around the hotel before and during the Russians' arrival, and even more intriguing, one

group of businessmen had rented a suite that they insisted had to be directly above the one where the Russians were staying. It all seemed a little out of the . . . ordinary.

It certainly was. The staff did not realize that they were in the middle of one of the more significant incidents in Cold War espionage, an incident that should have had enormous ramifications. That it did not makes the incident all the more extraordinary.

At first glance, the Soviet delegation seemed typical enough. As was the case with all such groups, at least some of them were not trade officials at all, but Soviet intelligence operatives. Of the six men who arrived in London, two were actually representatives of the GRU, the Soviet military intelligence agency. One of the two was an ordinary GRU functionary, but the other was a much more interesting figure, the engaging man whose uncharacteristic vivacity struck the hotel staff—Oleg Vladimirovich Penkovsky. A colonel in the GRU, Penkovsky was not only an expert on foreign trade, he was also one of the Soviet Union's leading experts on missiles, privy to virtually all the technical aspects of Moscow's deepest military secrets.

He was also a British spy.

Penkovsky had initially come to the attention of British intelligence six years before, when he was first spotted as a GRU operative while posted as an assistant Soviet military attaché at the Soviet Embassy in Ankara, Turkey. This standard intelligence agency exercise in ferreting out the intelligence operatives working under cover of various diplomatic jobs at an embassy—sometimes called "spot the spook"—includes an implication: Can the operative be "turned" into working for the other side? What are his political sympathies? What weaknesses—liquor, money, women, drugs—can be exploited?

Penkovsky was potentially exploitable because of his deep disaffection with Soviet Communism, concluded the man who first spotted him—Greville Wynne, ostensibly a British businessman deeply involved in East-West trade, but in fact a senior agent of MI6 who had been running British intelligence's most productive operation against the Soviet Union. The operation was simple enough: Wynne had recruited a small group of British businessmen who regularly visited the Soviet Union during the thaw in East-West trade relations following Stalin's death in 1953. Wynne elaborately prepared the businessmen before their visits, assigning specific items they were to look for—locations of major industries, types of machine tools, serial numbers on planes parked at airfields, and a thousand and one other small, but significant, details. Upon their return, Wynne subjected them to exhaustive debriefing sessions during which they would recount everything they had managed to see, no matter how trivial.

At the same time, Wynne had branched out into an intelligence sideline: running operations to "turn" high-ranking Soviet intelligence and military officials who might be persuaded to work for the other side. It was much more dangerous work than the intelligence-gathering operation, but Wynne, blessed with nimble wits and apparently unlimited fearlessness, had managed to escape the vigilance of the KGB. Indeed, the KGB seemed to have no inkling that the slightly bumbling Englishman—a moderately plump, mustached man in tweeds who looked for all the world like a typical British businessman—was involved in any significant intelligence work. (They did not know, for example, that the mysterious man who jumped from the deck of a ship in Odessa one night just a few steps ahead of KGB agents searching for someone who had tried unsuccessfully to recruit a Soviet naval officer was the very same Greville Wynne.)

Certainly, the KGB did not know that in 1960 Wynne, while on a trip to Moscow, had managed to establish contact with Colonel Oleg Penkovsky of the GRU. Penkovsky, by then reassigned back to the Soviet capital in the Foreign Trade Ministry as a cover for his intelligence activities, had been

turned by Wynne. The turning was total: Penkovsky, saying
he was very upset at what he perceived to be the Soviet
Union's danger to world peace because of its decision for a
large-scale military buildup program, told Wynne he would
provide to MI6 whatever information came across his desk.

Transferring such high-grade information in Moscow,
with its pervasive KGB surveillance of foreigners, would have
been dangerous, so an elaborate plan was worked out: Penkovsky was scheduled to accompany a Soviet trade delegation
on a trip to London the following year, and it was there that
he would unburden himself. The plan called for some tricky
logistics, but by the time Penkovsky and the Soviet delegation
arrived in London in April 1961, all the components were in
place. In the suite above the rooms where the Russians were
staying, MI6 had set up what amounted to a temporary spy
headquarters, equipped with all sorts of elaborate electronics.
Dozens of agents from MI6 and MI5 (the British counterintelligence service) were involved in the operation designed to
glean whatever intelligence gems would be forthcoming from
Penkovsky, by now known within MI6 by the code name Alex.

The CIA was also involved, for the very nature of what
Penkovsky was promising to deliver—information on the Soviet Union's strategic rocket forces—made it essential that the
"cousins" (as British intelligence slang called their American
counterparts) be called in. The CIA responded somewhat
reluctantly, an attitude directly related to its increasing fascination with technical collection systems. The men who dominated the CIA's intelligence-collection efforts at that point
were openly contemptuous of human-intelligence sources—
as Richard Bissell, chief deputy to Allen Dulles, never tired of
pointing out, human agents were far more trouble than they
were worth. In the view of Bissell and such other leading tech-
nologists at the agency as Herbert Scoville, Jr. (directly responsible for the growing sophistication of satellite and
similar technical-intelligence systems), machines solved the
central problem connected with human-intelligence operations: How could you ever be 100 percent certain that the

intelligence being provided was free of human bias or, in the case of a turned agent from the other side, that it was not cooked?

Penkovsky seemed too good to be true. Here was a senior officer at the GRU, a man with an impeccable Communist party record, a brilliant technician with not the slightest blemish on his record of service to the Soviet state, now offering to betray his country for what appeared to be vague political reasons. It reeked of a clumsy KGB plant, although Wynne and most of his MI6 colleagues were convinced that Alex was the genuine article.

Despite the CIA's reluctance, the operation connected with Alex moved forward. It went off like clockwork. The Soviet delegation, to its surprise, found that its British hosts had laid on an exhausting schedule of visits to industrial sites all over the British Isles. And to the delight of the GRU man in the delegation, the British appeared to be quite careless; unaccountably, they had included in the tour a number of normally off-limits defense installations, and what's more, the British escorts seemed remarkably lax. The GRU man, who had brought along a miniature camera, was soon busily snapping away while the British escorts (actually MI5 agents under orders to act careless) seemed to be paying practically no attention.

The Russians were so preoccupied they did not notice that Penkovsky, who was supposed to be leading the delegation, always seemed to be busy elsewhere. He was. In debriefing sessions, he poured out the Soviet Union's most vital military secrets. By happy coincidence, the CIA representative in these debriefing sessions was George Kisvalter, who had been assigned the job because he was already in England working on another case. Known as Teddy Bear within the agency, Kisvalter was a roly-poly Russian expatriate who had built a reputation as the agency's best evaluator and handler of Soviet defectors. Kisvalter established an early rapport with Alex, and was quickly convinced that the MI6's enthusiasm for the Soviet officer was fully justified.

Despite the CIA's uneasiness, Kisvalter concluded that the Russians would never provide so much high-grade information simply to bolster the bona fides of a plant, if that was the idea behind Penkovsky's apparent willingness to commit high treason. What Penkovsky provided in those debriefing sessions was a veritable intelligence gold mine: microfilms with thousands of pages of highly sensitive Soviet military documents—including information on the status and reliability of its ICBM rockets—plus information on dozens of GRU officers stationed around the world and, most important, cryptonyms of key GRU officers posted overseas, priceless intelligence that allowed the U.S. National Security Agency to begin tapping into Soviet intelligence codes. Clearly, Alex was genuine.

Proof of Penkovsky's genuineness, however, presented American intelligence with something of a shock: Among other sensational revelations, Penkovsky was able to demonstrate that the American estimates on Soviet missile strength were almost totally wrong. Instead of the estimated one hundred–plus missiles the Russians were supposed to have, Penkovsky revealed that Soviet ICBM strength at that point was a grand total of four—and none of them worked properly. In fact, Penkovsky pointed out, the Soviet ICBM was a white elephant, plagued by technical problems so severe that missile technicians were under enormous pressure from the Soviet leadership to get the problems straightened out before the American buildup in missiles prevented the Soviet Union from ever catching up.*

Clearly, this kind of unparalleled intelligence should have caused a fundamental reevaluation of how the United States perceived the question of Soviet ICBMs. And, more broadly, how it perceived its own military posture. After all, there was now incontrovertible evidence that the strategic

---

*This firsthand evidence of Soviet weakness was of some help to the United States during the Cuban missile crisis a year later, but by then Penkovsky had been caught by the KGB, along with Wynne. For the circumstances surrounding their arrests—and Penkovsky's ultimate execution—see Chapter Six.

balance between the two superpowers, believed at the beginning of the Kennedy administration to be just barely in favor of the United States and extremely precarious because of what was assumed to be a massive Russian buildup, was in fact a huge American lead. So huge, in fact, that there seemed no rationale whatsoever for demands by the military services, especially the air force, that the United States embark on a large-scale strategic weapons program in order to overcome an imminent Soviet advantage.

Yet, as things turned out, Penkovsky's sensational revelations had a minimal impact upon American intelligence. There was some rethinking at the CIA, which in September 1961 concluded that previous estimates that the Soviets would have fifty to one hundred operational ICBMs by the end of 1961 were clearly wrong, and that the entire Soviet strategic threat was not of much concern. However, the revisionism, a clear reflection of Penkovsky, was not unanimous; air-force intelligence insisted that there would be three hundred Soviet ICBMs by the end of 1961 and vigorously dissented from the CIA's revised estimates of Soviet missile strength. How this conviction persisted in the face of Penkovsky's evidence—and the further evidence provided by early satellite reconnaissance, which indicated no such large deployment—is another demonstration of how firmly held beliefs can survive in the face of even the most conclusive evidence.

In the case of air-force intelligence, the belief began to generate phantoms. Pressed to explain why there was no evidence at hand for the alleged massive Soviet ICBM deployment, the air force devised what may be called the "hidden rocket theory." According to the air force, the Soviets had managed to hide most of their ICBMs. In one briefing, air-force intelligence officers pointed to spy-satellite pictures of the Soviet Union, showing a Crimean War monument and a medieval tower, both of which, the air force suggested grimly, could be camouflaged ICBM sites. The air force went on to claim that probably there were at least one thousand Soviet

ICBMs in service, with two hundred actually emplaced and the remainder cleverly hidden at innocent-appearing sites all over the Soviet Union.

How the Soviets had managed this stupendous feat was not explained, since they had not yet overcome some other very real technical problems that had been outlined by Penkovsky and were already showing up on early satellite photographs of Russian missile sites. From these early indications, it was clear that the Soviets had not yet developed solid-fuel techniques for their rockets (easy to store, solid fuel allows rockets to be fired quickly), and had not yet hardened their missile emplacements (as the United States had already done to protect them from enemy missile strikes). Early photographs of the Soviet SS-7, the main Russian ICBM, showed the rockets clustered in crude bin-type shelters. Besides, the rockets had first to be raised to an upright position, then fueled, a process that could take hours—hardly the kind of technology useful for fighting a nuclear war against a country armed with quick-firing rockets encased in underground concrete silos invulnerable to attack.

The question of Soviet ICBMs was not an arcane intelligence argument, for it went to the very heart of the military balance between the two superpowers. The arrival of the Kennedy administration and its promises for new approaches to world problems, coinciding with the often heretical policies of the new Soviet leadership under Nikita Khrushchev, suggested that a real watershed had been reached in the Cold War. Was it possible that both sides, seemingly free of the policies of the past, could now draw back from the arms race and perhaps work out some sort of major understanding?

There were clues that the Soviets, at least, may have found the time propitious. A month before the Kennedy administration took office, two senior advisers to Kennedy—Jerome B. Wiesner and Walt W. Rostow—attended a disarmament conference in Moscow, during which they were taken aside by a Soviet Foreign Ministry official. Talk of large-scale

Soviet deployment of missiles was absurd, the Soviet official said, warning that his country would not remain "passive" if the United States followed through with Kennedy's vow of an extensive buildup in U.S. strategic forces. (Some time later, another American, physicist Freeman Dyson, an adviser on disarmament to the government, was buttonholed by Russian delegates at a conference in London and urgently told of "big decisions" that would be made soon in Moscow concerning military forces. Dyson was told that it was "now or never" on disarmament, that both sides had the opportunity at that point to come up with a disarmament plan before the military buildups got out of hand.)

However slender, these were significant intelligence clues suggesting some hope that the arms race might be stopped. But it was not, one of the chief reasons being that very few people believed the Russians were really interested in disarmament. In addition, the signals from the Soviet Union were ambiguous. On one hand, there were senior Soviet officials privately hinting of a deal to stop the arms race, while on the other hand, the Soviets spent a great deal of time publicly boasting about the extent, size, and power of their weapons. Khrushchev was the most prominent braggart, talking publicly of antimissile missiles that could "hit a fly in space," or how his powerful ICBMs could annihilate any "aggressor" (for which read the United States).* However, as Khrushchev was fully aware, the United States had overwhelming military strength—and was getting stronger almost with each passing hour. At the very time when the Soviet leader was bragging that his weapons made the Soviet Union

---

*It is now clear that the Russian boasting, designed to conceal the very real weaknesses in the Soviet ICBMs, was probably the result of a high-level KGB spy inside the U.S. Joint Chiefs of Staff. The spy was Lieutenant Colonel William H. Whalen, a liaison officer who had access to the CIA estimates of Soviet missile strength. Beginning in 1960 and until his arrest in 1966, Whalen sold copies of those documents to the KGB, which apparently ran a deception operation to convince the Americans that the exaggerated forecasts of Soviet missile strength were actually correct.

invulnerable, the American arsenal was capable of absorbing a full strategic nuclear strike, then retaliating with a force that could kill one hundred million Russians and destroy more than 80 percent of all Soviet industry. Indeed, the United States had so many strategic weapons that 2,657 American nuclear warheads were on constant alert, able to strike the Soviet Union at a minute's notice.

Yet there were recurring American fears about Soviet strength. One of the important results of this fear was the new Polaris submarine-launched nuclear missile. The missile grew out of an intelligence alarm in the late 1950s over a huge projected force of Soviet nuclear-powered submarines. The American reply to this projected threat was a plan to divert Soviet naval expenditures into antisubmarine warfare and away from nuclear-submarine development. To that end, the Polaris was born: a nuclear-submarine system capable of firing an ICBM missile, representing a strategic threat so powerful the Russians would be compelled to spend most of their naval resources trying to counter it. (It didn't work out that way: To this day, the Russians have not been able to develop technology capable of tracking and locating U.S. nuclear submarines hiding in oceans all around the Soviet Union. And contrary to American expectations, the Russians went ahead and developed their own nuclear-submarine force, regardless of cost.)

As the incoming Kennedy administration discovered in 1960, the vast size of the American strategic arsenal was, to a large extent, in direct proportion to the fears of American policymakers about Soviet strength. And those fears, in turn, stemmed from some very serious intelligence gaps on Russian military power.

Several months before he took office, Kennedy's Secretary of Defense, Robert S. McNamara, was shown one of the Eisenhower administration's final contributions to national security, the nation's first Single Integrated Operational Plan (SIOP). It amounted to the top-secret strategic-target list to be used in the event of all-out nuclear war, specifying how the

3,500 American bomber-, missile-, and submarine-launched nuclear weapons would be used against 2,600 targets in the Soviet Union, China, and Eastern Europe. Behind the dry bureaucratic language of the SIOP and its rows of numbers and coded launch orders lay an Armageddon that seemed unimaginable: a nuclear holocaust that would virtually end civilization on earth.

How, then, had these targets been selected? What intelligence convinced the planners who made up the SIOP that it was necessary to incinerate 2,600 targets—including the 151 largest population centers in the Soviet Union—in order to "win" World War III?

There wasn't any intelligence; the planners had no idea of what was worth hitting with a nuclear warhead, so they targeted virtually everything standing. What to hit was under the control of air-force intelligence's Air Targets Division, which year after year piled up targets in its computers. Its conclusions were only rarely challenged, and the few who did get to see the basis on which targets had been selected were horrified by the lack of intelligence for the decisions. One of the few was George B. Kistiakowsky, the physicist who was one of President Eisenhower's science advisers. At one point, he took a detailed look at the targeting information on the Strategic Air Command's first large computers and pronounced it "pure bull." Some targets, Kistiakowsky discovered, had been targeted to be hit four or five times with nuclear warheads, simply because there were so many American warheads they had to be expended somehow.*

This was massive retaliation with a vengeance, and McNamara was appalled. At that point, the United States already had a stockpile of eighteen thousand nuclear weapons, and was building more just as fast as the factories could churn

---

*Another serious intelligence failing was lack of adequate maps of the Soviet Union and China. Before advanced U-2 and satellite photography, which eventually were able to provide detailed photographs that were used to make accurate maps of both countries, nuclear-war planners had to rely on czarist-era or pre–World War II maps of the Soviet Union. The maps were seriously outdated, and one reason for all those warheads was to blast a large enough area to ensure hitting a target that might or might not be there.

them out. As McNamara realized, the size of this arsenal meant that nuclear weapons had become the weapons of first resort, a clear implication that the United States had developed not a retaliatory capability but a first-strike capability. That was precisely the problem. What could possibly justify thirty-five hundred nuclear warheads destroying civilization on earth? Certainly, an all-out strategic attack against the United States or, much less likely, perhaps a Soviet invasion of Western Europe, but any threat below that would not justify such a holocaust. Nuclear weapons had not been used in Korea—despite the clear example of invasion by Communist forces—and there was no real reason to believe that any American President would unleash Armageddon when, as Eisenhower phrased it, "we find out that Russian troops are on the move."

American military policy was bankrupt, McNamara realized, a realization underscored when he learned that the tiny Communist nation of Albania was targeted to be wiped off the face of the earth by virtue of the fact that it contained a single Soviet air-defense radar installation. In March 1961 an extensive review ordered by McNamara of American military plans for all-out war revealed that there was no clear strategic rationale for the horrendous fallout and destruction by America's massive-retaliation forces. The entire policy was riddled with monumental intelligence blindness, especially on the question of Soviet strategic nuclear forces. Those forces, the top priority for American weapons, nevertheless were something of a mystery to American planners; they had no real idea where the Soviet weapons were located, how many there were, and how much American strength would be required to put them out of commission. The planners had assumed a "worse case" scenario—vastly exaggerated numbers of Soviet nuclear weapons justifying even larger numbers of American warheads to knock them out.

What began to emerge in this review was a fundamental revolution in American military policy. Its father was

McNamara, an unlikely man to play such a vital role. He was reputed during a lifetime in business to have read only one book on military strategy, and as an increasingly restive Joint Chiefs of Staff discovered to its annoyance, the new Secretary of Defense did not have much regard for expert military opinions. Nor did he appear to have much regard for the product of intelligence agencies.

McNamara did have high regard for the kinds of things that had made him famous during his tenure as president of the Ford Motor Company—systems analysis, data, facts, figures, and statistics. McNamara was a monument to rationality; his outlook was circumscribed by a world that was subject to reasoned, dispassionate analysis, which identified a problem and pointed to the "correct" solution. It was a rationality that was brought to bear on the problems of military policy, summed up in his recurring question "How much is enough?" Exactly how many weapons would the United States need to guarantee deterrence of nuclear attack by the other side? Exactly how many and what types of ships would be necessary to maintain American naval supremacy? And so on and so on.

This "new look," as McNamara came to call it, resulted in a wholesale change not only in the way the United States regarded its military forces but also in how it looked at the world in which those forces, especially its nuclear arsenal, stood poised on the brink of war. In the McNamara view:

- Military force could be fine-tuned, using precisely the amount of force necessary to defeat a threat of whatever dimension—no more, no less.
- War could be limited to specific geographic and political circumstances, with each side deciding beforehand to risk only a certain proportion of its military and political capital.
- It was inevitable that the Soviet Union would build its strategic forces to a level roughly equal to that of the United States, in which case both sides would work out

> arms control measures to keep strategic forces at mini-
> mum levels and ensure deterrence.
> - The interests of the United States and the Soviet Union
>   were converging, and each side would come to see the
>   "rationality" of certain "mutually beneficial" policies,
>   including arms control.

None of this was original with McNamara; it all came
from a group of men who were soon to dominate American
thinking about military policy. They amounted to a mafia of
civilian strategists, most of them economists or specialists in
other academic disciplines who had almost no military experience. Located primarily in such think tanks as the RAND
Corporation in California, they had first come to notice during the Eisenhower administration, when they began to question some of the military assumptions behind the vast
American overkill nuclear arsenal. Supreme rationalists like
McNamara, they began to formulate complex theories about
the use of nuclear weapons, in the process devising what they
considered near-immutable "laws" about the circumstances
under which nuclear weapons would be used, and how they
would be used.

Many of them were brought into McNamara's Office of
Systems Analysis in the Pentagon, where they developed the
arcane theories of nuclear and conventional war that not only
formed the basis of American thinking about military force for
decades to come but also marked the end of the military's
dominance in the formulation of American military strategy.

This was not all to the good, as we shall see, but for the
moment it is interesting to consider what role intelligence
played in the intricate formulations of these strategies. The
answer is hardly any; the strategists built their conceptions on
a series of intricate calculations and assumptions about what
the United States would do in a given situation—and, more
important, what the other side would do. There was no intelligence, for example, that suggested that the Russians agreed
in the slightest with such favorite McNamara touchstones as

the "mutual-deterrence theory"—the idea that each side would construct strategic weapons only to the degree necessary to inflict "unacceptable damage" on the other side. Nor was there any intelligence to show that the Russians shared such grand American strategic visions as "escalation," or "flexible response," or "counterforce," or "countervalue," or indeed any other strategic panacea formulated during those years.

A wide gulf was beginning to open up between the people who formulated American military policy and the people who were collecting the intelligence on which that policy was supposedly based. The formulators were operating in an informational vacuum, largely because they distrusted both the military and the intelligence agencies, whom they regarded as little more than bean counters, collectors of minutiae that could have no practical effect on the great theories of war and peace.

The gulf was best illustrated by the career of Bernard Brodie, who was perhaps America's premier civilian strategist. The inventor of deterrence theory (he coined the very phrase), Brodie had served a brief stint in U.S. Navy Intelligence during World War II, where he developed an abiding distrust of the people who collect intelligence, a process he found not especially stimulating intellectually. Later, he studied for his Ph.D. at the University of Chicago, and it was while working on his doctoral thesis—"Major Naval Inventions and Their Consequences in International Politics, 1814–1918"— that Brodie arrived at an insight that provided the spark for the entire civilian-strategist movement. The insight grew out of Brodie's analysis of the pre–World War I naval construction race, when each major power sought to build bigger and bigger dreadnoughts (huge, heavily armored battleships) in order to gain an advantage on the other side. Regarded as the ultimate weapon, they were intended as great deterrents, but the ships were too big and too frightening to be used in anything short of all-out war. As a result, the British and German navies tentatively poked at each other during the

Battle of Jutland, then hurriedly retreated to their respective anchorages. Neither side could afford the risk of losing any dreadnoughts.

Brodie drew a parallel between the dreadnoughts and nuclear weapons. Nations with dreadnoughts before World War I had made the most detailed calculations showing how the nations with the largest number of dreadnoughts equipped with the heaviest firepower would automatically "win" without ever firing a shot, since no one would dare challenge them. The calculations were easy to formulate, since dreadnoughts and their capabilities—given their size— were impossible to conceal and were thus generally known.

Unlike military men, who tended to see an atomic bomb as just another weapon with a bigger bang, Brodie understood instantly the revolutionary potential of the new nuclear weapon. Distressed by some of the loose talk surrounding nuclear bombs—philosopher Bertrand Russell, who should have known better, openly advocated using atomic weapons to "discipline" the Soviet Union—Brodie set about formulating new strategies to govern their use. In 1950 he joined RAND, where he wrestled with such problems as: Can atomic weapons ever be used? How is it possible to ensure that they will not be? How can the American nuclear arsenal be kept invulnerable from attack by nuclear weapons from the other side? In the process, he formulated the deterrence theory, which he summed up in what the military regarded as a heresey: "Thus far, the chief purpose of our military establishment has been to win wars. From now on, its chief purpose must be to avert them. It can have almost no other useful purpose."

Like all such strategic theories formulated in that period, deterrence (sometimes called "mutual hostage") was neat and plausible and seemed perfectly workable. Its intelligence implications were also neat. In McNamara's view, intelligence was fundamentally a quantifiable matter, ideally restricted to a careful compilation of the numbers of new weapons and equipment on each side. He tended to distrust intelligence that went beyond that basic task to such functions as judging the efficiency of those forces or predicting probable courses of action. Intelligence of that sort included too much guess-work for McNamara's taste. Then too, his perception of the intelligence function was overshadowed by his basic prejudice about American intelligence's central preoccupation, the Soviet-American rivalry. To McNamara, much of the resulting information was too loaded with political implications, since it always seemed to play a role in the arguments over the size of the American military establishment. McNamara saw the Soviet-American rivalry in terms of what he liked to call the "action-reaction phenomenon." In other words, each side planned its forces on the basis of the most menacing intelligence about the forces of the other side. This phenomenon, in McNamara's view, meant that each side had built an arsenal out of all proportion to its legitimate defense needs, in order to cope with the "worse possible case."

McNamara was despairing of the internecine arguments within the American intelligence community, especially the running dispute between the CIA and the military-intelligence agencies. He was everlastingly coming up with organizational schemes to solve at least the Pentagon end of the problem (he had no control over the CIA), and emerged with a new Pentagon entity, the Defense Intelligence Agency (DIA). The idea was that the disparate military-intelligence agencies would be centralized under one umbrella organization and speak with one voice on intelligence matters. The new agency would concentrate on collecting detailed intelligence about foreign military developments, with emphasis on specific weapons systems. In that way, McNamara believed, military intelligence would be kept away from the most prominent bone of contention with the CIA, political interpretation.

There was no hope that this scheme would work. For one thing, McNamara had somehow overlooked the fact that military officers assigned to the DIA from their respective services were not about to submerge their services' interests in the

113

name of the umbrella organization; their promotions and careers rested not with the DIA but with their own services, and that is where their institutional loyalties remained. Moreover, no organizational chart had any hope of ending the military-CIA intelligence disputes, since those disputes involved some critical budgetary implications for the military services. Realistically, the military was in no mood to quietly accept a CIA intelligence judgment that might have a serious impact on their budgetary requests. The military had always operated on the worst-case basis, for that was where the money was.

Despite McNamara's best efforts, the intelligence disputes, especially the CIA-military arguments, grew sharper. They would coalesce in one of those raging battles that consume American intelligence from time to time. The spark in this case was the antiballistic missile (ABM).

It began in the summer of 1958, when one of the pictures from a U-2 overflight of the Soviet Union showed something very curious going on at Sary-Shagan, the main Soviet nuclear test site in Central Asia. The picture revealed construction of what appeared to be a huge radar system, about three football fields in size. Dubbed Hen House by intelligence analysts, it precipitated the first arguments in what would come to be a furious intelligence controversy.

The background for the controversy was the abiding concern of American intelligence with the question of Soviet missiles, a concern that became especially sharpened in the wake of the Cuban missile crisis. As intelligence was aware, the Soviets were betting more and more of their strategic chips on rockets, a strategy that implied that the Russians would seek to protect their valuable missile assets by developing an antiballistic-missile system. That, in turn, raised even more significant implications, for if the Russians succeeded in developing such defensive missiles, their ICBMs would be invulnerable to American counterstrikes. In simple terms, that would mean a Soviet first-strike capability; the Russians could launch a strike against the United States without fear of retaliation. The Russians would win World War III.

The United States had been working on ABMs since the mid-1950s, but the considerable technical problems of such systems—once described as the feat of "hitting one bullet in space with another bullet"—made American confidence that any feasible system could be developed something less than total. In 1959, the U.S. Army, which under a complex inter-service agreement had responsibility for antiballistic missiles, tested the Nike-Zeus ABM system, but Eisenhower decided not to deploy it. Eisenhower argued that the system could be countered easily: As a point-defense system—meaning that it defended one particular point on the map—it could always be overwhelmed by a large number of incoming warheads.

American intelligence, notably the CIA, had for quite some time assumed that the Russians had reached the same conclusion. But the first faint ring of an intelligence alarm sounded in 1957, when the Russians began openly to discuss the feasibility of ABM systems—although the CIA estimated that because of the many technological hurdles, the Soviets would not develop an operational ABM before 1962.

However, the discovery of Hen House in 1958 began to undercut that confidence, and it was further undercut when Vice-President Richard Nixon a year later, during a trip to Moscow, reported seeing very large radars near the Soviet capital, which he deduced were some sort of space-tracking radars. Nixon considered this sighting an important clue, and he was right. The critical parts of any ABM system are the radars, which must be able to detect ICBM warheads high up in space, track them and then guide ABM missiles to destroy them. Furthermore, the radars must separate out decoy warheads, overcome penetration aids, evade electronic jamming, and work quickly enough for the ABM warheads to destroy the ICBMs high in space before they do any damage. Such radars are much larger than conventional air-defense radars.

The ABM alarm grew even more distinct in 1960, when Soviet leaders began to boast publicly of their ability to "intercept offensive pilotless devices at high altitude." It was an astounding claim, but was buttressed with the evidence of a special series of Russian nuclear tests that year, during which the Soviets detonated a nuclear charge at high altitude over a radar installation. The CIA immediately concluded that the Russians were testing their ABM radar's ability to function during a phenomenon known as EMP (electromagnetic pulse), the tendency of a nuclear explosion to completely black out all electromagnetic transmissions over a wide area. Overcoming this phenomenon was fundamental to all ABM systems. Obviously, any effective ABM radar would have to operate in an environment of strong EMP. Had the Russians managed to solve this very critical problem?

According to Khrushchev and Soviet military leaders, they had. There were public pronouncements in September 1961 that the Soviet Union had solved the problem of intercepting and destroying ICBMs in flight. American intelligence took these assertions at face value—as the argument ran, why would the Russians lie?—and a full-fledged intelligence panic was under way, very similar to the missile-gap episode of only a few years before. And the evidence kept piling up: Shortly after the Soviet pronouncement, spy satellites detected thirty large military construction sites near Leningrad. Pictures of these sites were subjected to the most minute analysis by CIA photo interpreters, who concentrated on the shape and size of the concrete foundation work. They concluded that the foundations were very similar to the foundations that had been built at Sary-Shagan. Further, the CIA noted, the construction sites were located across the flight corridors of American ICBMs flying polar orbits targeted on sites in European Russia.

McNamara was displeased by the increasing controversy over the Soviet ABM, which not only threatened his carefully constructed mutual-deterrence strategy, but also threatened to ignite a massive spasm of spending on weapons systems of dubious value. Most especially, McNamara did not want to be forced into the position of spending money on ABM, whose technical feasibility, he was persuaded by his "whiz kids" group of systems analysts, was so far from reality that there was grave doubt it would ever work. He was also persuaded that there was something not quite right with the intelligence alarms about the Soviet ABM; if the vaunted American technology had not been able to overcome the very real hurdles on the ABM, was there any reasonable expectation that the Russians had somehow managed the feat?

There wasn't, McNamara concluded, but he was gradually being boxed in, largely because politics began to exert a strong influence. It came in the form of the Senate debate over the 1963 nuclear-test-ban treaty between the United States and the Soviet Union. The conservatives were adamantly against ratification, insisting that the Soviet Union would violate the treaty and increase its military lead over the United States—a lead they believed existed in fact. To the distress of McNamara and President Kennedy, CIA Director John McCone strongly supported the conservatives' position, arguing that American cessation of open-air nuclear tests would allow the Russians—who wouldn't observe the treaty anyway—to make great improvements in their nuclear weapons.

McCone, already disliked by McNamara and the White House, now became persona non grata, and he was put further into the doghouse when Kennedy discovered that he had assigned a CIA analyst to the staff of Senator Strom Thurmond of South Carolina, leader of the conservative opposition to the test-ban treaty. Kennedy was even more enraged when Thurmond and the conservatives, during an extraordinary secret Senate session to debate the treaty, began to discuss CIA intelligence about the Leningrad construction sites. The sites were proof positive, Thurmond claimed, that the Russians had developed a workable ABM system, which meant that they were far ahead of the United States in that area. And a nuclear-test ban, he further argued, would freeze the Soviet lead while the United States would not be able to carry out open-air tests of ABM warheads.

McCone's deliberate leaking to Thurmond of highly sensitive intelligence about the Soviet ABM question guaranteed that it would become a public intelligence controversy. Very soon, McNamara found himself embroiled in an acrimonious debate that put him in the position of defending the administration's lack of alarm over the Soviet ABM threat. But the question was: Did the threat really exist? The intelligence community was uncertain. The evidence of the Leningrad site was subjected to the most arcane and intricate arguments over whether it constituted a real ABM site or just a testing area, whether it was actually a crude air-defense system against American supersonic bombers, or whether it was a gigantic Soviet charade (although nobody could quite answer why the Soviets would go to such trouble).

Kennedy tried to defuse the controversy by first telling McCone in effect to shut up about ABMs, then convening a special task force of experts to thoroughly examine the question. The group concluded that it was not too impressed with Soviet ABM technology, and went on to tell Kennedy that even if the Russian ABMs were any good, the United States could restart its own ABM test program easily and quickly. For his part, McNamara told a hostile Senate Armed Services Committee that American ICBM warheads, equipped with the newest penetration aids—primarily electronic jamming devices and special shields to confuse radar beams—could easily penetrate any existing Soviet defense. Besides, McNamara said, the Soviets could not yet have a "full-scale, high altitude" ABM ready because there was no evidence that they had tested it. The two different Soviet ABMs under development, McNamara added, were almost certainly designed not as defense against American ICBMs, but against U.S. short-range missiles that would be launched from Western Europe. At the outside, McNamara insisted, the Soviets could not have a real ABM system operational until 1968, if then.

McNamara was relying heavily on CIA conclusions about the Soviet ABM, but they were conclusions that the military-intelligence agencies regarded as hopelessly optimistic. In their view, the CIA had consistently underestimated the Soviet ABM threat, mostly because the CIA itself was dominated by analysts committed to arms control, who therefore saw Soviet weapons developments in the most sanguine light possible.

Military intelligence in 1963 had pointed to new information on the subject of Soviet ABMs—still another large military construction site, this one near Tallinn in Estonia. The satellites detected the same kind of foundations as at Sary-Shagan and Leningrad, but there was an additional mystery: The Soviets had moved aircraft-tracking radars to the site. That seemed to make no sense; the foundation work clearly indicated construction for an ABM, yet what were the aircraft-tracking radars doing there? Meanwhile, two new large radars —the type needed for ABM tracking—were detected north of Moscow, and to really complicate things, a military parade in Moscow during November of that year excited the attention of American military attachés, who noticed a large new missile being displayed. The missile was deduced to be a high-altitude ABM rocket, which American intelligence dubbed the SA-5 Griffon. Another Soviet ABM rocket, displayed in a similar parade a year later, was dubbed Galosh.

All this evidence, the military agencies insisted, meant that Tallinn was definitely an ABM site, and what was more, the Russians were proceeding at a very high rate of development in ABM technology. Not only had they built the sites and radars, but they had developed at least two actual ABM rockets. It was, they concluded darkly, just a matter of time before the American ICBMs would be checkmated.

As McNamara had feared, the alarm caused all sorts of complications in the military budget process, with the army demanding more money to develop its Nike ABM system, the air force demanding more money for new Minuteman ICBMs, and the navy demanding more money to increase the numbers of its Polaris missiles. Each service used the Soviet ABM as justification for more and bigger missiles to overcome the threat.

The military's belief in the threat flourished despite some odd developments in the Soviet Union. The Russians suddenly abandoned their Leningrad site, and a close look by the CIA at the radars being installed at Tallinn revealed that the scanners for them were mechanically operated—meaning that they could track only one target at a time and were absolutely useless against a large-scale American ICBM attack, with large numbers of warheads approaching at very high speed. The DIA and the military services disagreed with that conclusion, claiming that the Russians had abandoned the Leningrad site only because they had "found something better" at Tallinn. And as for the mechanically operated scanners, that was just a "temporary expedient" pending arrival of much more sophisticated radars. The DIA also pounced on the evidence of a public announcement by one of the Soviet Union's top experts on ABM technology, General Nikolai Talensky of the Soviet Academy of Sciences, who claimed that a high-altitude ABM system was "technically feasible." Talensky had also claimed in his announcement that ABMs, overall, were "good things," seemingly an unmistakable clue that the Soviet leadership had decided to commit whatever resources necessary to build a workable ABM system.

By 1966, Tallinn had assumed, in the view of the DIA and the military, the status of major threat. There were twenty-three sites there, and it seemed conclusive evidence that they amounted to an ABM Maginot Line, designed to block the northwest approaches to the Soviet Union to American ICBM warheads. At this point, the argument between DIA and CIA had become quite bitter, because the CIA insisted on regarding the Tallinn sites as defense against bombers, not ICBMs. And such a defense, the CIA argued, was laughable; the Russians had made the colossal error of spending millions of rubles to defend against an American bomber threat that was the least of their worries. Obviously, the CIA pointed out, the Russians had become alarmed over such projected U.S. bomber developments as the high-speed B-58 Hustler (never actually deployed), and had been taking measures to defend against them. There was, in the CIA view, overwhelming evidence to indicate that the Griffon and Galosh missiles were primarily intended against high-altitude, supersonic-speed American bombers.

The military was infuriated by these arguments, and the Joint Chiefs of Staff at one point in 1964 flatly told President Johnson that the very future of the United States depended on his immediately deploying Nike-X missiles (the most advanced American ABMs in development) around twenty-five American cities. The request alarmed McNamara, who actually impounded a good portion of the money Congress had appropriated to start building the Nike-X system. To McNamara, the military's arguments were ludicrous; they conceded that the CIA might be right that Griffon and Galosh were primarily antiaircraft weapons, but they then went on to claim that the missiles could be "upgraded" at any time for use against ICBMs. The same empty argument was made about all the other components of what the Russians had shown so far: They all could be upgraded (apparently at a minute's notice) to a much more sophisticated system.

In the end, McNamara and the CIA were proven right. Accumulating evidence from overflights of Tallinn and other sites showed no nuclear facilities of any kind, including nuclear warheads—which meant that the missiles deployed there were not real ABMs (such missiles detonate nuclear warheads in space near incoming warheads to destroy them). All along, the Russians had been trying to accomplish two things: to develop a defense system against what they perceived to be an imminent threat of supersonic American bombers; and at the same time to develop a workable ABM system. They never could get the system to work, and some years later, they would in effect trade it away as part of the first Strategic Arms Limitation Talks agreement.

But in intelligence terms, the entire ABM alarm had been a confusing argument from beginning to end. Once again, the American intelligence process had demonstrated how susceptible it was to politics and the exigencies of military budgets. Clearly, it had been an intelligence mess of the first order, and some of the components that caused the problem would play an important role in another intelligence controversy during the same period, this one also involving Soviet missiles. The consequences in that case, however, were to prove much more damaging.

McNamara failed to heed an important lesson of the ABM intelligence controversy. He (and virtually every American expert on such technology) had assumed all along that the Russians would never expend a lot of resources trying to build an ABM system, chiefly on the grounds that such an expenditure would not be "rational." In other words, since a practical ABM system was beyond the prevailing technology, and since the United States had not been able to overcome the technological hurdles, then it was reasonable to expect that the Soviet Union would reach the same conclusion and not build one either. But in fact the Russians had gone ahead and tried to build it anyway, and that should have provided a significant lesson in trying to divine Soviet intentions—however rational McNamara thought a particular course of action, there was no guarantee that the Russians shared his view. The Russians expended a prodigious amount of effort trying to build an ABM system because they thought it was a good idea and had shown themselves unimpressed with what McNamara considered commonly shared visions of logical strategies.

McNamara repeated this error in the case of another important piece of military technology, ICBM rockets. He took great comfort in U.S. intelligence predictions that the Soviet Union would have somewhere around two hundred "soft" ICBMs (not deployed in hardened underground silos) by 1967. It made sense. In McNamara's view, the Russians would be rational on the question of ICBMs, and therefore would not embark on an all-out program to build large numbers of such rockets. Such a task, McNamara was convinced, was clearly irrational, since the American lead in such technology—both quantitatively and qualitatively—was so large that there was no real hope of the Russians catching up in the foreseeable future. And why would they even try? After all, McNamara argued, the Russians already had a sufficient number of deliverable nuclear warheads for a "minimum deterrence," so there would be little to gain by investing so many billions of rubles in a strategic arms race with the United States they could not possibly win.

There was no intelligence that suggested that these assumptions were in the least correct: McNamara was in effect deducing what was inside the heads of the Kremlin leadership by the risky method of assuming that they thought as we thought. And the problem extended further. This sort of deductive reasoning began to find its way into the thought processes of CIA intelligence analysts assigned the task of estimating the probable future course of Soviet strategic-weapons development. In the case of ICBMs, the analysts increasingly formulated their estimates on the basis of anticipated Soviet courses of action, a process that became, in effect, a form of intelligence tea-leaf reading. The Russians, according to the analysts, shared American theories about nuclear weapons, so they would construct a minimum deterrent and sometime during the 1970s would achieve a very rough parity (but far inferior technologically) with the American nuclear arsenal.

There were seductive reasons for these assumptions. One was the very size of the awesome American nuclear arsenal; the Strategic Air Command had added more than 400 Minuteman missiles to its ICBM force in 1963 alone, and during the 1960s, the United States increased its ICBM arsenal from 18 to 1,054. It was a force of unrivaled power and represented the high point of postwar American strategic muscle. Its cost, more than $100 billion, had contributed the lion's share to soaring American defense budgets, and it seemed a perfectly reasonable presumption that a much more constricted Soviet economy would not withstand the demands of a similar arsenal. Then too, the memory of the old missile-gap episode induced powerful caution among CIA analysts about any alarmist estimates on Soviet missiles. (Although the military-intelligence agencies continued to insist that the CIA was consistently underestimating Soviet strength.)

However reasonable these convictions about Soviet intentions seemed, the Russians would reveal that they played by their own set of rules. At the very time when McNamara and the CIA were predicting a relatively modest Soviet effort in ICBMs, the Russians embarked on a military buildup, missiles included, that dwarfed anything in their history. In the process, they undercut every American intelligence assumption and extrapolation about their intentions; they demonstrated that they were committed to a military machine designed to back up their own convictions about the Soviet Union's place in the world, not to accommodate what some American strategists thought they ought to be doing. Somehow, despite all their economic troubles, the Russians found the resources to build a strategic arsenal that by 1970 roughly equaled that of the United States. (In that year, the Soviet Union deployed the extraordinary total of 271 new ICBMs.)

It was not until that year that the CIA realized the extent of its error on Soviet missiles. As one later study showed, of fifty-one intelligence analyses on Russian ICBMs during the period 1961 to 1970, forty-two of them underestimated the size of the Soviet nuclear arsenal, sometimes grossly so. The consistent underestimate seems surprising, for it coincided with a vast improvement in technical intelligence-collection systems, especially spy satellites.

But despite this growing sophistication, the results still had to be interpreted by human beings—and what human beings saw in reconnaissance photographs, spy-satellite pictures, telemetry readings, and radar signals depended, to a great extent, on what prejudices (institutional, political, and otherwise) they brought with them. There was virtually no satellite picture of the Soviet Union that was not regarded with some alarm by people who worked for military-intelligence agencies—"every flyspeck on a piece of a film is a goddam missile to them," as one CIA analyst phrased it—but CIA analysts often demonstrated a disturbing tendency to reject evidence that did not fit their own preconceptions.

CIA personnel responsible for preparing National Intelligence Estimates (NIEs, known as "nees"), or Special National Intelligence Estimates (SNIEs, called "snees") were in an especially difficult position, since their products represented—or were supposed to represent—the consensus judgment of the American intelligence community. That subjected them to considerable political pressure from all sides, since there was seldom an estimate that pleased everybody. The solution, increasingly, was to formulate estimates that were masterpieces of obfuscation, loaded with hedges, qualifications, and on-the-one-hand-this-on-the-other-hand-that statements that became as inoffensive as possible.

They also became virtually useless, a far cry from the original idea of national intelligence estimates born during the OSS days: a totally objective judgment on what could be deduced from all available intelligence. The process had been refined and expanded in 1950, when the CIA, surprised by the invasion of South Korea, decided on a renewed and centralized office to coordinate intelligence judgments. Then called the Office of National Estimates, it was first headed by the man who created the OSS Research and Analysis Branch, William Langer, a university professor. Langer, whose real passion was the American duck—on which he was regarded as the country's leading expert—set the academic and highly objective style that marked the CIA's initial estimating process.

The estimators, like Langer and his successor, Princeton professor Sherman Kent, were largely academic types who shared their mentors' view of their function. That was defined by Kent as the power of evaluation and "reasoned extrapolation," a process to be separated from "basic descriptive" and "current reportorial," which were defined as functions to be handled by other parts of the CIA. The estimators, who came to form a distinct "culture" at the CIA, most often dealt with ambiguity. For security reasons, they were not told the specific identity of sources of intelligence—the job of judging the worthiness of raw intelligence was the task of analysts—so they often had no idea of the quality of the data base on which they were to formulate their estimates.

Besides technical intelligence—undoubtedly the most important American intelligence resource during the 1960s—the data base also included low-scale human-intelligence resources and intense analysis of open sources. There were problems with all three of these. In technical collection, there was the recurring difficulty of the biases of the people interpreting the material, plus an additional problem: Since the satellites and other systems could not see *everything* in the Soviet Union, there was always the question of whether there was sufficient coverage to make real deductions. Human-intelligence resources were much more meager. Aside from Penkovsky, there had been no high-level human sources developed inside the Soviet Union or China, and American intelligence was reduced to utilizing part of the wave of tourists and businessmen who entered the Soviet Union during the Khrushchev thaw following the death of Stalin. Some of the efforts could be ingenious—at one point, the CIA had some tourists taking pictures of the smoke emanating out of the smokestacks of factories. Subjected to later analysis on such things as the color of the smoke, the pictures could reveal important clues about manufacturing processes.

There were critical limitations to this sort of program, for there was always the danger that amateur spies would be caught (a dozen of them were), collect the wrong information, or encounter a number of other possible hitches. There were also limitations on the analysis of open sources from such closed societies as the Soviet Union (and, to an even greater extent, China).* In the absence of top-level intelligence from

*The extent to which the Soviets tried to complicate the job of American intelligence can be seen in the case of the Soviet space center. For some years during the 1960s, all Russian space launchings were announced from what was described as the main Soviet space center at Biakonur. CIA analysts, who had difficulty spotting

inside those countries, analysts took to microanalysis of all their published writings and broadcasts, with special emphasis on military and political pronouncements. But these writings were (and still are) often ambiguous, sometimes reflecting intense inner-party struggles for one particular political view or the other. Thus, as with the results of technical-intelligence collection, such analysis had a tendency to descend into Talmudism. The analysts ultimately became split between two factions. One faction believed that the essentials of Soviet or Chinese thought were abundantly evident in the body of official writings, the implication being that the Russians or Chinese say what they mean and mean what they say. All such writings, therefore, can be used as an intelligence resource, providing important clues to the thinking of military and political leaders. The second faction believed that such writings should not be taken at face value; they were most often wishful thinking, especially those authored by military writers, and not very valuable clues about what the other side was thinking.

The stark fact was that although more and more resources were being expended to obtain intelligence, there was nevertheless a climate of growing uncertainty; there were recurring errors, and despite constant reorganization and bureaucratic shuffling, it was clear that the proliferating American intelligence community knew less and less about what was going on. Aside from the Soviet Union, where intelligence had been marked by gross failures,* there were also

---

Biakonur on satellite photographs, double-checked the trajectories of the orbits of Russian rockets, and realized the real launch site was Tyuratam, 150 miles to the southwest of Biakonur.

*One of the worst failures did not come to light until 1976, when American intelligence discovered it had missed a colossal nuclear accident in 1957 at Kyshtym, near the city of Sverdlovsk. Kyshtym, site of the main Soviet complex that produced plutonium for nuclear weapons, virtually disappeared in a huge nuclear explosion caused by nuclear waste carelessly dumped in a lake bed. The blast, which devasted four hundred square miles, was kept secret by the Soviets, but in 1976, émigré Soviet geneticist Zhores Medvedev, then living in London, painstakingly put together clues from obscure Russian scientific publications and concluded that a nuclear accident

lapses in the Middle East (where, despite close relations with its Israeli intelligence counterpart, the CIA somehow was completely surprised by the Israeli invasion of Sinai in 1956), and in China, where the unmistakable early clues pointing to the Sino-Soviet split were completely misread.

China had been an American intelligence preoccupation second only to the Soviet Union since at least the end of World War II, when the United States decided to support the Nationalists under Chiang Kai-shek against the Communist forces led by Mao Tse-tung. In that decision lay the seeds of a disaster, for it had been made on the basis of poor intelligence, namely, the conviction that Mao was merely a tool of Moscow and that the Chinese civil war amounted to an effort by the Soviet Union to take over China.

The only real intelligence coming out of China in that period was the material produced by a small group of State Department Far East experts, many of whom had been born and raised in that country. Their reports on the actual complexities of the Chinese situation had no impact on the policy-makers in Washington, who wanted to believe that events in China were simply part of the Soviet-American conflict. They wound up betting everything on Chiang, and his defeat— regarded as inevitable by the State Department officers on the scene—came to have a severe impact on American intelligence. The root cause was politics. Caught up in the McCarthy hysteria about "Who lost China?," the State Department was purged of its Chinese experts, and the CIA (which only narrowly avoided an investigation by McCarthy), began to tread very carefully in the area of intelligence on China. The only acceptable intelligence amounted to simplis-

---

had occurred. American intelligence and nuclear-weapons experts initially pronounced Medvedev's conclusions wrong—missing a nuclear blast that size was considered impossible—but further checking showed that he was right. Final proof came some years later, when the CIA discovered that new Soviet maps of the area omitted the names of thirty villages (all of them irradiated by the blast), and that a vast new canal system had been built to bypass waters contaminated by the explosion's fallout.

tic versions of events in Asia—the Chinese were under the direct control of Moscow, which planned to take over all of Asia by the use of Communist surrogates such as Ho Chi Minh in Indochina.

This sort of intelligence myopia has a habit of ultimately boomeranging, and in the case of China, it took the immediate form of the Korean War. The United States was surprised when the North Koreans suddenly moved across the 38th parallel on June 25, 1950, mostly because its intelligence services had no idea of what was happening on the Chinese mainland—key to all events in Asia—nor did it have any conception of what was happening in the peripheral countries. The CIA had been spending its meager Asian resources, since the triumph of Chinese Communist guerrilla forces in 1949, running boom and bang operations. Among its more notorious (and useless) operations was a twelve-hundred-man guerrilla "army" composed mostly of ex–Nationalist Chinese soldiers who carried out raids into China and North Korea.* (In one of the few operations that produced any intelligence, they managed to tap into the cable under the Yellow Sea used by the Chinese military for communication between Peking and its Manchurian commands.)

There was also the ten-thousand-man Chinese Nationalist army the CIA supported in Burma, to which the soldiers had fled in the wake of Mao's victory in 1949. According to the CIA, these forces would help tie down the Chinese Communist army, although how ten thousand men would tie down an eight-million-man army remains a puzzle. The Nationalists invaded China in 1952, were promptly and predictably routed, then retreated back into Burma, where they went into the more profitable business of opium growing.

---

*The Pentagon had grave doubts about these pinpricks, and with good reason. At one CIA briefing, Hans Tofte, a CIA cowboy who ran the guerrilla operations, showed a movie of one of his teams disembarking from rubber rafts on the Chinese coast. One army officer, incredulous, asked if Tofte dispatched his teams on such landings in *daylight.* Tofte was compelled to admit that the movie was of a "simulated" landing.

The outbreak of the Korean War compelled the CIA to embark on a crash program of developing intelligence assets overnight, especially in China. To that end, it ran Operation Bluebell, which involved the hasty recruitment of thousands of Korean refugees who were sent behind Communist lines with vague instructions to collect what intelligence they could, then make their way back to American lines somehow. The operation was a failure, only slightly less disastrous than another operation, this one involving the dropping of CIA agents and Chinese Nationalists by parachute into China, there to link up with anti-Communist Chinese elements and produce intelligence. (Most of the Americans who were dropped came out of the 1950 Yale University graduating class, which was heavily recruited by the CIA.) Like Bluebell, the operation reflected slapdash and overhasty arrangements; it too ended in disaster, with most of the parachuted agents either killed or captured.

The failures had severe repercussions. In the winter of 1950, the Chinese Communists struck the badly overextended American forces in North Korea and decisively routed them. An extensive series of subtle Chinese warnings that they were about to strike went unheeded by the United States, which lacked the intelligence resources to understand them.

The disasters of the Korean War, the inability to fathom what was going on inside China, and the continuing failure to get any kind of grasp on Soviet capabilities and intentions—all represented a defeat for intelligence. It was a commonly acknowledged problem within the intelligence community, but the question was how could it be solved. One obvious answer, of course, was that American intelligence needed more Oleg Penkovskys; it needed to develop high-level sources who could deliver firsthand and reliable intelligence.

But in the dangerous world perceived by the United States in the decades of the 1950s and 1960s, there seemed to be a new crisis every day. One day it was Berlin, the next day Quemoy and Matsu, the next day Cuba, and the next day

the Middle East. Human-intelligence sources were too difficult to develop and nourish in this pellmell crisis atmosphere;
besides, the very nature of human sources meant some ambiguity, which would only worsen the highly charged political
atmosphere of American intelligence.

The solution was machines—unambiguous technical collection systems of the greatest possible sophistication that
would perform the tasks individual spies had been trying to
perform for centuries. Why go through all the trouble of
trying to get a spy to obtain, say, the plans of the latest Russian missile when a piece of machinery could do the job much
more easily and quickly with much less fuss and bother? Why
not make maximum use of the American advantage in technology and use that advantage to create the most elaborate
and thorough technical-intelligence collection system the
world had ever seen? Wouldn't that solve the problem?

To the increasingly technically minded American intelligence, the answer was clear. Yet, had they been able to consult their greatest human-intelligence source, he might have
provided a different perspective.

Sometime during the spring of 1963, Colonel Oleg Penkovsky stood before a Red Army firing squad and was shot.
His death brought to an end the only major human-intelligence resource of American intelligence to be developed behind the Iron Curtain since the end of World War II. As a man
who was both an experienced intelligence officer and a technical expert, Penkovsky (had he been asked) might have been
able to tell the Americans that however seductive the wonders
of modern technology, it was no panacea; he might have told
them that however sophisticated the American intelligence
technology, there was much it could never do.

Most especially, it could not provide all the answers the
United States was seeking about his homeland.

four

"NATIONAL TECHNICAL MEANS"

Marshal de Soubise is always followed
by a hundred cooks. I am always
preceded by a hundred spies.

—FREDERICK THE GREAT

AMONG THE THOUSANDS of visitors who troop each day
through the halls of the National Air and Space Museum in
Washington, D.C., there are probably few who linger very
long before an exhibit in the rear of one hall devoted to the
history of ballooning. This is a large Japanese balloon, constructed of laminated paper, along with the brief note that
balloons like this were once used in an attempt to bomb the
United States during World War II.

But that Japanese balloon is much more important than
the exhibit would suggest, for it is in fact a significant landmark in the history of espionage.

The exhibit is a tribute to the engineering ingenuity that
produced the balloon, and its Japanese inventors could have
had no idea that their interesting technology would someday
reside in an American museum. Nor could they have guessed
that they were producing the progenitor of a revolution in the
collection of intelligence—a technical system that has now
become so pervasive it rivals death and taxes among the certi-
tudes of life.

133

This revolution is worth examining, for it has become *the* single most important component in American intelligence. Thanks to the efforts of the Japanese balloon designers, along with a skeptical British flier, an Australian vagabond pilot, a cantankerous American aircraft designer, and an American college dropout, the United States has been able to construct an elaborate technical spy system undreamed of in the long history of espionage. It is an unrivaled system that has not only come to assume most of the functions of American intelligence but has caused the traditional human spy to all but disappear. He has been overshadowed by a huge web of electronic and other technical gadgets that promise fulfillment of the ancient dream of all espionage: specific, unequivocal, and detailed intelligence, safely beyond the reach of anyone trying to stop it.

So much for the dream. The reality seems to be quite something else, for American intelligence has discovered an unsettling fact: However wondrous and encompassing modern intelligence technology may be, it has proved unable to answer every intelligence question with complete certitude. And ironically enough, the more detailed, accurate, and sweeping these technical collection systems, the more arguments they seem to incite about just what they are seeing (and whether they have seen *everything* worth seeing).

This appears an odd development, and yet the implication was there, right at the very start, when Group Captain F. W. Winterbotham of the Royal Flying Corps had plenty of time to wonder why his country's military knew so little about what was happening on the Western Front in World War I.

Winterbotham had been shot down in 1917 while flying fighter escort for a slow-moving photo-reconnaissance plane, part of a failing effort to get above the battlefield and photograph German positions in France. While in a prisoner-of-war camp, Winterbotham reflected on what had gone wrong. Just about everything, he concluded. The British followed the same procedure each time, rendezvousing fighters with a two-man reconnaissance plane. The planes then dove to the low height at which the reconnaissance plane had to fly. Because of a problem with air temperatures—which at higher altitudes fogged over the camera lens—reconnaissance planes were forced to fly lower than 8,000 feet to take pictures, an altitude that made them vulnerable to ground fire and attacks by enemy fighters. The trick was to get much higher than that, but how?

After the war, Winterbotham began working for the British SIS, all the while trying to come up with a solution to the problem of cameras that fogged over at any height above 8,000 feet. His intelligence specialty was Germany, and with the advent of Hitler—and the gradual tightening up of internal security by the Gestapo—Winterbotham found it increasingly difficult to get information on the Nazi military buildup. He was especially concerned about German naval developments and reports that the Germans were constructing large-scale fortifications on their western border with France.

As Winterbotham discovered, the French were having similar intelligence problems. Georges Ronin of the Deuxième Bureau, like Winterbotham concerned about German military developments, also had the idea of taking air-reconnaissance photos. But his one attempt ended in failure. Ronin flew an old biplane along the Rhine River, searching for German fortifications while his passenger, a terrified Paris photographer hired for the occasion (complete with beret and beard), tried to take snapshots from the observation seat. But the resulting photographs were too blurry to be of any use.

Winterbotham then hit upon the idea of getting the SIS to buy the very latest in airplane technology, the American Lockheed 12A, a two-engine aircraft that could operate at a ceiling of 22,000 feet—higher than any current German fighter. However, the central problem remained—how to take pictures from that height.

The answer came quite by accident in the person of Sidney Cotton, a vagabond Australian pilot who had a reputation for daring and fearlessness. He also was reputed to be a little crazy, a trait that made him unwelcome in the Royal Flying Corps but suitable for the more open-minded atmosphere of SIS. Winterbotham hired Cotton in 1937 and explained the problem: It was vital to get overhead reconnaissance on the German military—human sources were drying up all over Europe—so somehow cameras must be made to work at the Lockheed's highest altitude. What could be done to get pictures from 20,000 feet, safely out of the reach of the German fighters?

Cotton's solution was subterfuge. Assuming he would have to fly at low altitudes, he cut three holes for Leica cameras in the fuselage of the Lockheed, an arrangement that would give maximum coverage of a "strip" passing underneath the plane as it flew. The holes were cleverly concealed by shutters operated from inside the plane. Then Cotton made an astounding discovery. Flying the newly equipped Lockheed in a test flight over England, he found that at high altitudes, warm air from the plane would be drawn out over the camera lens when the shutters were opened, thus preventing the lens from fogging.

Equipped with this important secret, Winterbotham and Cotton went into action. They set up a front—Aeronautical Research and Sales Company—and began flying all over Europe on the pretext of trying to drum up business for the firm. Included were at least two dozen flights to Germany, where no objection was raised to a British plane overflying anywhere it wanted to at maximum altitude. The Germans were certain that the British did not have the ability to take aerial-reconnaissance pictures from above 20,000 feet (although a secret reconnaissance squadron of the Luftwaffe at that point was already taking pictures from above 30,000 feet). Winterbotham and Cotton's secret went undetected, although there were some close calls. A particularly heart-stopping scare came one day in 1939 when General Albert Kesselring and other top Luftwaffe officers asked if they could fly the Lockheed. Cotton obliged, and as Kesselring himself took the controls, his curiosity was piqued by the flashing green light on the dashboard. Asked what it was, a thoroughly frightened Cotton responded that the flashing light (actually indicating continuity of the automatic cameras' exposures) was a special device showing "petrol flow to the engines."

The adventures of Winterbotham and Cotton contributed to one of British intelligence's greatest achievements during World War II, its large-scale aerial-reconnaissance and photo-interpretation operation. Because of a lack of resources and a lack of air superiority, especially toward the end of the war, the Germans were never able to match the British effort, although they were still far ahead of the Americans at the war's outbreak. At that point, U.S. intelligence technologically—with the exception of code-breaking operations—was somewhere in the Dark Ages. In 1941, air force officers were stunned to discover that the U.S. military had accurate maps for less than 10 percent of the earth's surface, and its aerial-reconnaissance facilities were of World War I vintage. Early American bomber crews were sent out without target folders or accurate navigation maps, and they also lacked reconnaissance photos of the targets they were supposed to bomb. Worse, there was no system for assessment of bomb damage, meaning the bomber crews had no idea of whether they had hit their targets.

A crash program put the United States, almost overnight, in the forefront of aerial reconnaissance, but the key to that achievement, aside from the collective efforts of American industry and the lessons learned from the British, lay in the American bases ringing Germany and German-occupied territory. From those bases, they could fly missions and return. That advantage disappeared with the advent of the Cold War; even the newest-model planes had no hope of carrying out unescorted strategic reconnaissance missions (several thousand miles) over Eastern Europe and the Soviet Union. The Red Air Force was large and alert; backed by ground-based radar, it was capable of checkmating any reconnaissance overflight. Yet the need for such reconnaissance was growing more acute. The answer, obviously, was some sort of airborne platform that could overfly the vast distances of the Soviet Union out of the range of fighter planes, take pictures, and return safely to base. The most advanced U.S. reconnaissance aircraft of the postwar period, the RB-47 (essentially a souped-up reconnaissance version of the B-47 jet bomber), was not the whole answer. The plane carried seven precision cameras that, operating automatically, could record without break the territory passing underneath. At 40,000 feet, the RB-47 could photograph 1 million square miles of territory during a three-hour flight, recording a strip 490 miles wide by 2,700 miles long.

But the Soviet Union's most important strategic facilities —its largest military airfields, nuclear testing sites, major industries—lay thousands of miles inland; however impressive the RB-47's capabilities, it could not possibly get pictures of those sites without overflying the Soviet interior. And that, given the formidable Soviet defenses, was not feasible. How, then, could it be done?

He didn't realize it at the time, but Reikichi Rada of Japan had provided the answer. Or what appeared to be the answer.

Rada in 1933 had been named head of the Japanese military's scientific laboratory, which among other assignments was trying to solve the problem of how to bomb enemy targets at intercontinental ranges. No foreseeable development in airplane technology seemed capable of producing such an aircraft, so Rada hit upon an innovative idea. Balloons would be armed with bombs, then sent to drift into enemy territory, where the bombs would be automatically released. The idea excited no interest in the Japanese military until 1942, when the surprise American air raid on Tokyo threw the entire Japanese high command into a paroxysm of rage and demands for "revenge."

Rada's idea, which promised immediate results, was resurrected. Rada soon demonstrated that his idea would work—with prevailing winds unique to Japan, he discovered, a balloon launched from Japan's east coast would drift 6,200 miles to the United States' west coast. Next, Rada developed an ingenious automatic system for the balloon, which dropped ballast to keep the balloon at a constant altitude during the flight, then loosed an incendiary or other type of bomb as the balloon settled to earth someplace in the United States. Made of laminated paper from the kozo bush (part of the mulberry family) and painstakingly assembled in strips by battalions of Japanese schoolgirls, the Rada-designed balloons were launched eastward in the fall of 1944. Operation Fu-Go, as the Japanese called it, was on.

As the world's first intercontinental military attack, Fu-Go was not a glittering success, although it did cause some panic in American intelligence. Clamping on a tight lid of secrecy in order to prevent the Japanese from learning whether their balloon attacks were successful, navy and army intelligence sought to figure out their purpose. The major fear—that the balloons were designed to dump biological weapons on the U.S. mainland—proved unfounded, but there was still cause for concern. The first balloons began floating over the United States in November 1944, and by April of the following year, when the Japanese gave up Fu-Go (they thought the operation a failure, since there were no press reports of bombs falling on the United States), a total of 285 balloons were spotted. Most were intercepted over the ocean or malfunctioned, although one woman and her five children were killed in Oregon when a Fu-Go bomb exploded.* The Japanese had launched nearly 4,000 of the balloons toward the U.S. mainland, and given the fact that only a small percentage of them ever reached their target, Fu-Go was a failure. It had been defeated by the vagaries of the atmosphere over the Pacific Ocean—much less predictable than Rada believed—and a secret but extensive American operation called

*The Japanese were unaware that one Fu-Go delayed the atomic bombing of Hiroshima, albeit briefly. The balloon's incendiary started a forest fire near Hanford, Washington, cutting off electrical power to the Hanford nuclear processing plant, which was producing U-235 for the Hiroshima bomb. The incident held up production of the bomb for three days.

139

Firefly. Using radar, fighters on instant alert, and a battalion of paratroopers standing by in loaded cargo planes ready to douse any fires, Firefly was able to defeat any large-scale balloon attack.

The failure, however, was only in military terms. From an intelligence standpoint, Fu-Go was a success, to the Americans at least, for it provided them with the germ of an idea on how to get intelligence on the Soviet Union.

The idea was born in the series of intelligence reports prepared by the army and navy on the Fu-Go flights. To those frantically searching in the years just after World War II for a quick, feasible way to get photographic intelligence on the Soviet Union, one glaring fact stood out in those reports: The Japanese had managed to fly by remote control a very stable airborne platform for distances over six thousand miles. Instead of bombs, what if such balloons were armed with cameras? Could similar types of balloons be launched into prevailing winds sweeping over the Soviet Union?

By coincidence, the air force at the time was running an extensive meteorological research program called Moby Dick. Operated in conjunction with the U.S. Navy's Office of Naval Research, Moby Dick aimed to uncover some of the mysteries of the upper atmosphere, where future aircraft (and missiles) were to operate. The program used the latest development in high-altitude weather-research balloons, a large gasbag called Skyhook. The first models were about 300 cubic feet in capacity, capable of rising to more than 120,000 feet. The high altitude was made possible by use of an innovative, partially transparent plastic material that showed a rainbow of colors when partly reflected and diffused by sunlight. More significant, in the context of the curious role Skyhook was to play later on, the balloon also changed shape as it rode into less dense air and its helium gas expanded. The balloon would change from an ice-cream-cone shape to a near circle, then, as it moved violently in the winds of the upper atmosphere, would become almost saucer shaped.

The tendency of Skyhook to change shape, especially

into the form of what appeared to be a saucer, caused a major and unanticipated headache in the Moby Dick program. The initial test flights of Skyhook in 1947 set off the first of what would eventually be many flying-saucer sightings. As the people running Moby Dick were aware, the sightings almost perfectly described what happened to the Skyhook balloon as it encountered the strong winds of the upper atmosphere. The balloon flattened out in the shape of a saucer and was yanked around violently, while reflecting diffused sunlight in shades of blue, red, and green. In other words, a classic flying-saucer (or, later, UFO) report.

The flying-saucer scare became serious; in 1948, an air-force pilot was killed while chasing a mysterious UFO (actually a Skyhook test flight), and there was no end to reported UFO sightings. The difficulty was that no one who knew anything about Moby Dick could discuss the program publicly, for by that time, it had become an intelligence operation. The idea was simple: Operating from secret launching sites in Europe (where they precipitated another UFO scare), Skyhook balloons were launched into the prevailing winds sweeping west to east over the Soviet Union. They were equipped with cameras and radio gear; when they reached Japan after a flight across the Soviet heartland, a radio signal sent from the ground would tell Skyhook to detach its instrument package. (Later, air-force pilots developed a special trapezelike hook attached to cargo planes that caught the balloon's shroud lines and recaptured the entire Skyhook, ready to be flown another day.)

Ultimately, Moby Dick was a failure. Many of the balloons crashed in the Soviet Union, and those few that made the entire flight produced spotty results. Subject to the vagaries of weather, some Skyhook cameras took pictures of clouds, and those that managed to snap pictures in clear weather had the disadvantage of not being subject to ground control, meaning that they were very much a hit-or-miss proposition. There were continuing refinements in the Skyhook balloons, but improvements in Soviet air-defense radars—balloons, because of their large surface area, make perfect radar targets

—eventually spelled the end of Moby Dick. The last balloon flight over the Soviet Union took place in 1958.*

Despite its overall failure, a number of valuable lessons were learned from Moby Dick. Most important, it was proved that overflights of the Soviet Union were possible, and that reconnaissance pictures could be taken from high altitudes. The central problem remained, however. A stable, safe platform was needed, something that not only would be impervious to the Soviet air-defense system but would not risk the lives of valuable pilots. In other words, it had to work and it had to be *safe.*

It is interesting that by that time, the growing sophistication of photo interpretation had convinced the interpreters that, given sufficiently detailed photo coverage, they could provide intelligence at least equal to (and possibly better than) that produced by any human agent on the ground. That may or may not have been true, but the assertion underscored a significant fact: The technology of photo interpretation had moved far beyond the relatively puny technology of obtaining those photos. In effect, the interpreters were waiting for surveillance technology to catch up with their skills.

The CIA's first photo-interpretation section had been set up in 1953, when Arthur Lundahl, a brilliant navy photo interpreter, joined the agency with a mandate to organize its first interpretation shop. Lundahl started with twenty interpreters (there are nearly fifteen hundred working there today), and they quickly proved that photo interpretation had come a long way from the days when Winterbotham and Cotton were taking pictures over Germany.

The interpreters still like to call their business a science, although it is more nearly an artful skill. The skill rests on the

---

*Moby Dick rose from the dead briefly in 1978, when U.S. Navy Intelligence and the National Security Agency collaborated on a large-scale eavesdropping effort against Cuba. Under an operation called Seek Skyhook, the navy took a large tethered balloon, jammed it with electronic eavesdropping and radar gear, then floated it 12,000 feet in the air above Cudjoe Key, Florida, 18 miles northeast of Key West. The balloon managed to snatch virtually every electronic transmission in Cuba, 150 miles away.

most important pieces of information with which the inter-preters work—the altitude from which a particular picture was taken and the focal length of the camera lenses. From those two details, the interpreters can measure with great accuracy the dimensions of what is shown on the ground, and well-trained interpreters can deduce an amazing amount of infor-mation. Shadows, measured for height and depth, will reveal the size of an object. The length of air-base runways can tip off what kind of planes fly there. Measurements of burn marks on runway tarmacs can reveal a plane's acceleration rate at takeoff and landing. Serial numbers on military vehicles, ships, and planes give important clues about the locations of military units.

In addition, interpreters trained in special skills can divine even more from a photograph. For example, an interpreter who is an expert in steel production can tell from a photo of a steel mill that plant's capacity, production rate, and other significant facts. An even more important aid has been the manifold increase in photographic technology since World War II, especially "false-color" photography. Among the more important developments for intelligence interpreters was Aerial Kodacolor, first developed by Eastman Kodak dur-ing the Korean War. The film is coated with an emulsion that is especially sensitive to the blue end of the spectrum, which means that pictures record all natural vegetation in red; at the same time they record all unnatural foliage and the spectral-enamel paints used for camouflage colors in green. The film makes it easy for interpreters to spot anything concealed under camouflage, and further reveals movement of tanks and vehicles, whose tracks show up as distinctive marks on a false-color photograph.

Still, no matter how ingenious the interpreters' skills, the intelligence they could produce during the first decade of the Cold War was limited. They simply did not have enough material to work with. The reconnaissance planes, equipped with the latest technology, skirted (and often strayed inside) the Iron Curtain borders and managed to photograph strips of land sometimes up to two hundred miles inside. That still left vast areas of Eastern Europe, China, and the Soviet Union total blanks. Worse, Soviet defenses were beginning to exact a high price for those flights. By 1948, forty American planes had been shot down while flying along or across the Iron Curtain, forcing reconnaissance missions to become more cautious. The trend was obvious: As Soviet radars and MiG fighters improved, the American spy planes would be increasingly endangered. Then too, it was only a matter of time before the Russians developed surface-to-air missiles capable of hitting American planes even at altitudes of up to 30,000 feet.

The possibility of a complete cutoff of American reconnaissance on the Soviet Union presented an especially dangerous situation. If there were no reconnaissance, how would it be known that Russian intercontinental bombers or missiles had been launched against the United States? (Since incoming Soviet bombers would not be detected until they were noticed by American air-defense radars on the American continent itself, that meant, as a practical matter, that no effective early warning existed against the possibility of a Soviet surprise strategic attack.)

It was the fear of Soviet surprise attack—and the realization that American intelligence had no real way of detecting it—that led President Eisenhower in 1954 to appoint a special panel of experts under Massachusetts Institute of Technology President James R. Killian, Jr., to come up with a solution to the problem. As both Eisenhower and Killian were aware, the chief deficiency of American intelligence at that point was its lack of sources inside the Soviet Union. That meant intelligence not only had no idea of Soviet military capabilities, it also had no idea of when and if the Russians might decide to use those capabilities.*

The Killian panel had a number of subcommittees exam-

*In 1949, air force officers requested the CIA to provide agents to monitor activity at military airfields in the Soviet Union, mainly to check when Soviet intercontinental bombers took off. Asked how many agents this job might entail, the air force replied that it required *two thousands agents,* since that was the number of military airfields in the Soviet Union. The CIA politely rejected the request.

ining the problem of detecting surprise attack, the most important of which was the group studying U.S. intelligence capabilities. The subcommittee included a remarkable character named Edwin H. Land, inventor, founder, and president of Polaroid. A notoriously reticent man (he has given only two press conferences in thirty-five years), Land was in the classic tradition of the great American tinkerer/inventor. He had dropped out of Harvard during 1937, then taught himself the intricacies of polarized light, mostly by holing up in a room at the New York Public Library and reading his way through anything about the subject he could get his hands on. When General Motors refused to buy his polarized material (used to cut headlight glare), Land went into business for himself in an old Massachusetts garage, ultimately developing 530 patents —including his most famous, the self-developing camera. Polaroid, the name he coined to describe the process, became an American household word.

Land was very much in the "can do" spirit of American inventiveness, and to him, the problem of getting intelligence on the Soviet Union was soluble provided the customary bureaucratic inertia was overcome, as well as the reluctance of experts who decreed that taking clear pictures from heights above 70,000 feet was impossible. Land's insistence was no small factor in the Killian panel's final conclusion that the solution to the problem of American intelligence was strategic reconnaissance, using a stable platform that could overly targets above 70,000 feet and take detailed photographs.

Land had vowed the photographic problem could be solved, but what about the platform? That seemed to be a more knotty problem, but the panel noted that a number of high-performance test aircraft possibly might be converted into such platforms—assuming that considerable technological problems could be solved.

At that point, the panel had the good fortune to encounter Kelly Johnson.

By the time the Killian panel began its deliberations in 1954, Clarence (Kelly) Johnson of Lockheed was already a legend in the airplane-design business. Considered a genius, he had made his mark with a number of aeronautical miracles, among them design of the first American jet fighter, the F-80 Shooting Star, in 1945, which took the unheard-of total of 141 days from design to production.

Johnson did not suffer fools gladly, and his independent style, hands-on philosophy, and disregard for bureaucratic convention were nervously tolerated by Lockheed executives, a number of whom Johnson did not hesitate to upbraid when he thought they were interfering in his projects. (Once asked the secret of his success, Johnson snapped, "I get a few good men and drown the rest.")

Lockheed had the sense to leave its brilliant, if somewhat irascible, designer alone. Johnson spent most of his time in what was officially known as Air Force Plant No. 42 on the edge of the desert at Lockheed's Palmdale, California, operation, working out designs that were literally made by hand to his specifications. Plant No. 42 was more familiarly known around Lockheed as the Skunk Works, after the mysterious still in the "L'il Abner" comic strip that produced the famous Kickapoo Joy Juice.

Among the designs Johnson was working on in 1954 was a test airplane known innocuously as Utility-2, used to test engines and other systems at high altitudes where the next generation of jet fighters were expected to operate. One of Johnson's more innovative designs, Utility-2 was difficult to describe: something of a glider-sailplane with turbojets, long, light wings, and needlelike shape. Although it had a phenomenal four-thousand-mile range, it looked unlike any other plane ever to take to the air, especially in its seamless appearance—Johnson had kept rivets and joints as smooth and flush as possible to keep friction down at the 90,000-foot level where Utility-2 operated.

But no matter how odd it looked, the Killian panel realized that Utility-2—which soon was most often referred to by its nickname, U-2—was that perfect reconnaissance platform they had been seeking. Johnson promised he could make the

U-2 into a spy plane. And hooked up with a new Land invention, special long-focus cameras that could scan continuously through seven apertures, the U-2 that Johnson produced was the most astounding technical development in the history of espionage up to that point. Here at last was the perfect spy. It could overfly at the then astonishing altitude of up to 90,000 feet and snap detailed reconnaissance pictures, safely out of the reach of any known jet fighter, missile, or other hazard.

However, espionage is espionage, and any U-2 flight over another nation, most particularly the Soviet Union, was technically a violation of that country's air space. It was a tricky question of international law, but the U-2's proponents hoped to persuade President Eisenhower to approve a program of U-2 spy overflights by using the argument of expediency—the need for the intelligence it could provide was so great that the risk was worthwhile. But to make sure Eisenhower understood just how revolutionary the U-2 was, CIA officials arranged that one of the U-2's reconnaissance photographs taken during test flights over the United States during 1955 was a shot from 55,000 feet of one of Eisenhower's favorite golf courses in Augusta, Georgia. As Eisenhower noted smilingly, the picture clearly showed golf balls lying on a putting green.* Eisenhower was convinced, but as he told CIA Director Allen Dulles and his deputies, "Well, boys, I believe this country needs this information and I'm going to approve it. But I'll tell you one thing. Someday one of these machines is going to get caught and we're going to have a storm."

---

*This incident was the first in what came to be a long string of instances in which senior government officials took special delight in reconnaissance pictures, often brandishing them for political reasons. During the Cuban missile crisis, French President Charles de Gaulle, shown U-2 pictures of Cuban airfields, muttered, *"C'est formidable,"* and spent a long time with a large magnifying glass, picking out the individual planes parked on the runway. American officials love to flourish the latest spy pictures. In 1970 Assistant Secretary of Defense William Clements confronted a French Defense Ministry official at a state dinner with the charge that France was supplying jet fighters to the Middle East. When that charge was denied, Clements threw a batch of U-2 pictures onto the startled Frenchman's plate; the pictures showed that the French were indeed shipping the planes.

WARRIORS OF THE NIGHT

Eisenhower was more of a prophet than he realized, for only a few people connected with the U-2 knew that for all its marvelous qualities, the plane had an Achilles' heel: a tendency to flame out at high altitudes. Flameout—the stalling of jet engines in thin air because of the lack of oxygen—was a special concern to the U-2 pilots, for it meant they had to glide down to a lower altitude, then restart the engine. But the U-2's fuel, specially refined kerosene oil, was difficult to ignite, and the pilots often would have to drop even lower, somewhere around 30,000 feet, to get sufficient oxygen for restarting the engines. And 30,000 feet was where jet fighters and surface-to-air missiles could operate.

That is precisely what happened to pilot Francis Gary Powers on the afternoon of May 5, 1960. When Puppy 68—Powers' special radio frequency to notify the CIA of trouble —suddenly reported a flameout that afternoon, CIA officials knew immediately that he was in serious difficulty. Powers at that point was overflying the Soviet industrial city of Sverdlovsk, ringed with the most advanced surface-to-air missiles; if he had to drop to a lower altitude to restart his engine, he would come into missile range. Powers dropped to that altitude, and that is when the U-2 was struck by a Russian surface-to-air missile.

The Powers incident did not completely end the U-2 program—the plane is still used to this day for flights over poorly defended areas—but it did shatter the American confidence that they had found the final answer to the problem of obtaining strategic intelligence on the Soviet Union. It was inevitable, of course, that the Russians would manage someday to shoot down a U-2. For one thing, they had known about the U-2 since 1955, and their source was none other than Eisenhower himself.

At the 1955 Geneva summit, Eisenhower had made his dramatic "Open Skies" proposal, under which the United States and the Soviet Union would allow reciprocal overflights of each other's territory to reduce the fear of surprise attack. As Eisenhower finished reading his proposal to the assembled delegates, there was an enormous clap of thunder outside, darkening the room. Despite this hint of divine approval, the Russians rejected Eisenhower's proposal out of hand, denigrating it as "a bold espionage plot." At the same time, however, the Russians realized that if Eisenhower was making so grandiloquent a proposal, the Americans already must have the means to carry out such overflights; ergo, there must be some sort of sophisticated American spy plane all ready to go. Sure enough, alerted Soviet radar tracking stations several months later picked up the blips of the first U-2s to overfly the Soviet Union.

Still, despite the worst American fears about the political fallout sure to occur the day a U-2 crashed or was shot down over somebody else's territory, there was surprisingly little international outrage expressed over this new development in espionage. Soviet Premier Nikita Khrushchev used the U-2 incident as an excuse to abort the 1960 summit meeting in Paris, but as he discovered to his shock, he seemed to be the only one really upset. "I have been overflown!" he yelled during one meeting with de Gaulle as he pointed at the ceiling. De Gaulle calmly replied that France had been overflown by Soviet spy satellites.* Startled by this assertion, Khrushchev replied, "We are innocent," whereupon de Gaulle asked him how the Soviets had managed to take pictures of the moon from their *Lunik* satellite.

"In that satellite, we had cameras," Khrushchev said.

"Ah," said de Gaulle, moving in for the kill, "in *that one* you had cameras. Pray continue."

As the dialogue between de Gaulle and Khrushchev indicated, the controversy over the U-2 had hardly died down

---

*Actually, de Gaulle was wrong. The Soviets right up to 1963 were consistent in their attitude that all overflights of another country's territory, either by plane or satellite, constituted espionage and that the violated country had the right to take any means to destroy them. But in 1963, the Russians developed their own spy-satellite capability and there was no further talk from Moscow about espionage being implicit in overflights.

when intelligence technology was already moving onto the next plateau. That was satellite reconnaissance, and unknown to Khrushchev, the United States only a month before his encounter with de Gaulle had secretly taken the first step toward replacing the U-2 with an even more awesome intelligence-collection capability.

Just before dawn on April 1, 1960, a Thor-Able rocket lifted off from Cape Canaveral, Florida, with a 290-pound satellite in its nose. Called *TIROS* (television and infrared observation satellite), the satellite was first designed to photograph cloud formations from above, fulfilling a long-standing dream of meteorologists who had urged for years that high-altitude observation was required to make accurate forecasts. In addition, the scientists hoped that observation of weather patterns on earth would afford early warning of major weather disasters, including hurricanes and typhoons.

But *TIROS* was also a bold experiment in espionage, designed to test whether a high-orbiting satellite—far from radar, missiles, and fighters—could carry out photographic reconnaissance. There was some question whether such reconnaissance, hundreds of miles up in space, could duplicate the U-2's capabilities; some experts argued that so much of the earth's surface was socked in by weather systems at heights of 100 miles and above, it was very doubtful that a satellite could ever see ground targets.

TIROS carried the latest marvels of American technology, especially two television cameras powered by nickel-cadmium batteries, recharged by nine thousand solar cells. Each camera—actually a Vidicon tube and focal-plane shutter—could store on a tube screen the pictures it snapped. An electron beam converted the stored image into electronic signals, which were then transmitted directly to ground receivers or recorded on magnetic tape. When the satellite came within range of a ground station, it could be ordered by radio signal to "play" its tape for the station to pick up.

Two hours after its maiden flight began, *TIROS*'s first pictures shocked the meteorologists and the more expectant

CIA and air-force experts who were awaiting the results. *Everything* could be seen clearly. To the surprise of all the experts, *TIROS* showed that in clear weather, satellite cameras saw in detail everything within sight of their lenses; the pictures from the first pass over the Soviet Union and China were so clear that the smallest details of air-base runways, planes, missile sites, and military bases could be picked out easily, even by the untrained eye.

The glittering success of *TIROS* revolutionized intelligence collection almost overnight. It proved that a satellite was not only capable of obtaining sharp reconnaissance pictures but also offered the added advantage of eliminating the need for a pilot. As an extra bonus, the satellite was invulnerable to any conceivable threat, since it operated high in space.

Reconnaissance-satellite technology proved to be hydra-headed; from the original patriarch *TIROS,* the American electronic wizardry has spun off many specialized and subspecialized variations. Among the more complex have been *Midas* (programmed to detect the flame exhausts of Russian missiles), *Vela Hotel* (parked in stationary orbit 22,000 miles over the equator to detect nuclear explosions), and newer satellites equipped with special telescopes to monitor any military objects in space. On a clear night, they can spot an object the size of a basketball 22,000 miles away.

The United States took a quantum jump in spy-satellite capability in 1971, when the first of the Big Bird satellites was launched. These are equipped with high-resolution television cameras, which can scan wide swaths of land on every pass, supplemented by highly sophisticated cameras that take detailed pictures. Even more amazing were the KH (for "keyhole") satellites launched three years later. KH has special heat-sensitive cameras that can measure images in the past (thus detecting even subtle changes), along with multispectral scanning devices that register wavelengths, picking up images that even the most sensitive photographic films can't detect. (The KH satellite pictures have provided the bulk of the CIA's intelligence on Soviet industry; KH has also been used to photograph Soviet satellites and spacecraft in flight.)

WARRIORS OF THE NIGHT

The key to the success of the American spy satellites has been U.S. technology's dramatic improvements in ground resolution—the size of the smallest object distinguishable in a satellite camera's picture. A good deal of that capability has been tipped off by the U.S. space program, which routinely publishes amazingly detailed pictures taken by its nonmilitary spacecraft and satellites. The *Apollo 17* flight in 1968, for example, took reconnaissance pictures of the moon from 160 miles above the surface, with a ground resolution of sixty feet. That's child's play for spy-satellite cameras, which can achieve ground resolution of about four inches from 100 miles away.

Technology has also made a number of dramatic improvements in how much data can be received from a spy satellite. In the beginning, the air force borrowed an old idea from the Moby Dick program and began retrieving photo capsules parachuted from satellites, using the trapeze-hook method that once snared Skyhook balloons. The method is still used for photos produced by "quick-look" spy satellites that sweep in relatively low (about 100 miles up) over a particular target to take pictures. Most satellite imagery, however, is returned by electronic signal, produced by a system aboard the satellite that takes the pictures, instantly develops them, then stores the images on a television scanner that transmits the data to earth, where they're fed into large computers for processing.

The technological revolution that created the spy satellites has also been packing ever more sophisticated capabilities into them. Breakthroughs in microcircuitry mean that future spy satellites will be miniature laboratories, reconnaissance vehicles, computer banks, and data-processing centers, all rolled into one. The reason is microcircuit chips, which can now be made five to seven microns wide (each micron is one millionth of a meter), much thinner than a human hair. American intelligence, however, is in the forefront of an effort to develop VHSIC (very high speed integrated chips), only one micron wide, that can store prodigious amounts of data.

How much data? A map of the United States printed on a sheet of paper only twenty inches wide, with lines of the map a half-micron wide, would show every single street in the entire country. In intelligence terms, that means a satellite would be able to cover huge areas with great accuracy, with the ability to store (and transmit) everything it saw, sensed, or read.

Combined with other advances in various sensing devices, that would give spy satellites a truly awesome capability. The newest-generation satellites now operating include such advances as imaging radar (which can "see" and map ground targets even through heavy clouds); infrared radiometer and thermal infrared scanners (which can detect underground construction); mosaic infrared detectors (which can spot heat sources at night, especially missile and aircraft exhausts); and multispectral scanners (which use separate lenses to take several pictures at the same time in different regions of the visible light spectrum and infrared bands). In addition, new computers allow analysts to manipulate this data to bring out subtle details.

Although specifics about the capabilities of American photographic satellites are officially classified top secret, a great deal can be deduced about them, for much of the technology is used in other areas. (The computer-enhanced pictures of Jupiter and Venus, for example, were sent by a satellite using the same technology as the spy satellites overflying the Soviet Union; more routinely, the satellite weather maps shown on local television newscasts each night use technology common to all spy satellites.)

Much less is known, however, about a second type of spy satellite—the ones that collect ELINT and COMMINT (electronics and communications intelligence). These remain the deepest intelligence secrets in the entire American government, and even the seven-page presidential order creating the National Security Agency—the organization responsible for COMMINT, ELINT, and American codes—is still classified, thirty-two years after President Truman signed it. The information produced by NSA and its predecessors is regarded as American intelligence's greatest achievement, yet it is an achievement that may not be as complete as sometimes heralded.

If espionage is the world's second oldest profession, then communications intelligence is of at least equal vintage. Ever since nation-states began warring with each other, a high premium has been put on the ability to read the secret communications (coded and uncoded) of the other side. It was not until World War I, however, when the new science of electronics began to put most military communications in radio or telegraph form, that the business of trying to intercept those transmissions became a major intelligence preoccupation. The most successful were the British, whose large-scale intercept and decoding operation managed to break the German codes used for transmitting orders to U-boats. (The British also broke a number of other codes all over Europe.)

But there was an even greater success in the United States. The man responsible for it was a twenty-four-year-old telegraph operator when he joined the State Department in 1913. Off duty, Herbert Yardley became fascinated with cryptography, a fascination that grew into a full-fledged obsession. And the more he studied the subject, the more he was struck by how hopelessly ancient U.S. codes were—which he proved one day by solving in less than two hours a highly sensitive message from President Wilson's personal representative in Berlin. He then went on to solve every other American diplomatic code then in existence. As Yardley shrewdly surmised, if he could break American codes so easily, then the more sophisticated British, who controlled the transatlantic cable over which all messages from Europe passed, certainly were doing the same thing.

Yardley analyzed the whole problem and wrote up a one-hundred-page report titled "Exposition on the Solution of American Diplomatic Codes," which he presented to his angry superior—who just happened to be the man who had devised the "unbreakable" codes in the first place. Yardley added insult to injury by opening the man's locked office safe, whose combination, Yardley noted with some amusement, was based on the telephone number of President Wilson's fiancée.

Upon the entry of the United States into World War I, Yardley was made a lieutenant, and with what must have been a large sigh of relief in the State Department, he was shipped off to the U.S. Army Signal Corps. There, Yardley's brilliance was quickly recognized; he was promoted to major, largely for his solving of most German espionage ciphers. With the end of the war, Yardley's code-breaking days seemed over, but General Marlborough Churchill, head of Army Intelligence, was determined to keep Yardley's operation—known as MI-8 —in existence. Churchill arranged for Yardley and a small crew of code breakers to be set up "unofficially" in a New York City brownstone. Using secret State Department funds, Yardley christened the operation "The Black Chamber" (after the French code-breaking operation known as *Chambre Noire*).

The American Black Chamber quickly scored some major coups. It solved the Soviet ciphers used to send instructions to Cheka agents in Europe and China, then turned to what was considered an impossible feat: breaking the incredibly complex Japanese diplomatic code. In July 1919, Yardley promised he would break the code by the end of the year, and on the night of December 12, according to his own account, the solution came to him in a deep sleep. Armed with that information, the United States was able to win a major diplomatic victory two years later, when the 1921 Washington Naval Conference opened. The conference, designed to set limitations on naval arms of the major powers, was deadlocked on the question of big-ship ratios. Under the formula then being debated, each nation would be permitted a certain amount of tonnage of large warships in proportion to the tonnage of other nations. The United States was particularly eager to get a tonnage ratio with Japan to curb the escalating

Japanese naval buildup. The Americans insisted firmly on a 10:6 ratio (1 million tons of American naval strength for each 600,000 tons of Japanese strength), but the Japanese just as adamantly insisted on a 10:7 ratio. Just when it appeared the Americans might have to compromise, Yardley's Black Chamber, which had been reading messages between the Japanese delegation and Tokyo, provided the game's fifth ace. Yardley's intercepts revealed that the Japanese had been given secret instructions to compromise at the American 10:6 figure "to avoid a clash." Armed with that priceless intelligence, the American attitude stiffened until the Japanese caved in.

The Black Chamber was closed in 1929, when the new Secretary of State, conservative Henry L. Stimson, learned the source of the intelligence reports that began "We learn from a source believed reliable that . . .", followed by the text of the intercepted message. "Gentlemen do not read each other's mail," Stimson pronounced, ordering the Black Chamber dissolved.*

That was not the end of America's COMMINT skill, for there was another cryptanalyst who may have been an even greater genius than Yardley at the arcane business of reading other people's secret communications. He was William F. Friedman, a brilliant mathematician who headed up the U.S. Army Signal Corps Code and Cipher Section, which ran a network of intercept stations, including one in the basement of a house owned by the head of the Signal Corps on the West Coast.

Friedman's teams concentrated their attention on Japan, considered America's most likely potential enemy, and between 1938 and 1940, pulled off what still ranks as the most amazing feat in the history of espionage. Based on inter-

---

*Out of a job, Yardley wrote the immensely popular book *American Black Chamber*. He then wrote the manuscript of a second, *Japanese Diplomatic Secrets*, but the government seized it during a landmark case upholding the government's right to prepublication review of the writings of its intelligence agents. Yardley subsequently worked for Chiang Kai-shek in China—to the fury of the Japanese, who began to regard him as a nemesis—and later for the Canadians during World War II. He wrote a classic treatise on poker and died, virtually forgotten, in 1958.

cepted electronic signals, they painstakingly reconstructed, in perfect detail, the most complex Japanese coding machine, known as Purple, which they then used to solve Japanese messages. As fast as the Japanese changed the settings on the machine, Friedman and his code breakers kept pace with the changes. It was a supreme triumph, the technical equivalent of creating the perfect human clone without ever seeing the original. This operation, known as Magic, led to such victories as Midway, where the U.S. Navy had advance word of the precise dispositions and plans of the Japanese fleet.

The war extended what was once a relatively simple code-breaking operation into the much broader area of communications intelligence. The reason, again, was technology. Radar, phone scramblers, radio-communication networks, and electronic-warning complexes had become an important part of a nation's arsenal—and therefore a prime target for intelligence.

In the case of the Soviet Union, getting at those electronic webs presented a problem, for most of them were deep in the Soviet heartland, out of the range of eavesdropping devices. The solution was to attack the web at its outer fringes.

Beginning in 1946, U.S. "ferrets," most of them cargo planes jammed with electronic listening gear, flew missions along the Iron Curtain borders. Inside the planes, military or NSA electronics experts moved the controls of their receivers slowly across the dial, hoping to pick up an interesting transmission from the other side of the border. The hunt was for anything that might be of use—a conversation between a control tower and the pilot of a jet fighter, a radioed order from a division command post to a battalion, a coded transmission from Moscow to a field command. Whatever sounded interesting was taped for later analysis.

Some of the ferrets, however, played a much more dangerous game. They would make a headlong dash across the Iron Curtain into the air space of an Eastern European country (or, in other areas, across the Soviet border itself), setting off air-defense alarms. That was the point: The ferrets were deliberately dashing across the border at top speed to ignite air-defense radars and orders to scramble fighters. Those transmissions, invaluable for showing the strength, response time, and pulse levels of radars, were recorded as the ferret suddenly turned tail and headed back at top speed for home. Some didn't make it. Almost half of the several dozen American spy planes shot down by the Russians while flying the "fringe route" from 1946 to 1960 were electronic ferrets. (One of the worst incidents occurred in 1958, when a ferret strayed too far into Soviet Armenia and was jumped by a flight of MiGs. U.S. monitors at ground stations in Turkey, listening in on Soviet Air Force communications, were horrified to hear MiG pilots reporting to base their shooting down of the American plane. Of the eighteen-man American crew, seven were killed and eleven were never heard of again.)

The ferret missions were supplemented with a wide range of sometimes ingenious operations to tap into Soviet communications nets, including the CIA's famed Berlin tunnel in 1955. The tunnel, dug under the main line for Soviet military communications in East Berlin, came about because the CIA had devised a way to recover conversations from telephone lines outfitted with scramblers. The Russians were angry when they discovered the wiretap operation and the tunnel a year later, although there were no serious international repercussions. But another, similar, operation that remains a closely guarded secret to this day almost brought the United States and the Soviet Union to the brink of war.

The episode involved one of the more bizarre operations designed to gather communications intelligence on the Soviet Union: monitoring stations set up on several small ice islands near the North Pole, where they were ideally suited to pick up Soviet military transmissions from Russian territory on the other side of the Pole (and provide warning of Soviet strategic attack). But a freak early spring thaw in 1954 suddenly caused one of the islands to begin floating into Soviet territory—while the resident air-force detachment wondered what would happen to them and all their monitoring equipment when they fell into Russian hands. The air force sent a plane to pick up the men and their equipment, but it crashed on landing and was unable to take off.

Meanwhile, Russian planes began buzzing the island, and the leader of the detachment, fearing imminent Soviet attack, ordered his men to dig in—and discovered that it was impossible to dig into the thick pack ice. To compound matters, the monitoring equipment detected what was thought to be a flight of Soviet bombers headed for the North American continent. An alarm was radioed, and the entire American air-defense system went on alert—only to find that they had been alerted for a flight of migrating Siberian fish ducks.

An emergency air-force helicopter finally got the men and their equipment off the ice island before the Russians grabbed them,* but the incident demonstrated again the dangers of operating communications intelligence even on the fringes of the Soviet Union.

With the advent of satellite technology, a considerable amount of ELINT and COMMINT was put aboard special ferret satellites that were piggybacked onto photo-reconnaissance satellites. The first ferret satellite was launched in 1962, and with advances in sensor technology, they are now able to record a vast amount of electronic transmissions while orbiting about 300 miles high. At that altitude, the satellites are invulnerable to attack—although there are recurring attempts to jam them electronically—but there has been much more danger associated with some of the supplements to the ferret satellites. One was an operation that converted old World War II Liberty merchant ships into floating electronics interception platforms; packed with radars and radio receivers, the ships slowly sailed in waters just off the borders of assorted

---

*This episode served as the basis for Alistair MacLean's novel *Ice Station Zebra*. A movie version of the novel was reputed to be a particular favorite of Howard Hughes, who for some odd reason watched it more than three hundred times.

hot spots, recording every electronic transmission they could reach. But the deliberate attack on the *Liberty* by Israeli planes in 1967 during the height of the Middle East war, and the capture by North Korea of the *Pueblo* a year later underscored the fact that the ships were too vulnerable. The program ended in 1972.

Equally problematical were several other highly provocative operations, among them Holystone, under which U.S. submarines infiltrated Russian harbors to take photographs through periscopes and collect electronic transmissions of the Soviet Navy. One American submarine managed to tap underwater telephone cables at Vladivostok, but recurring incidents of collisions between the submarines and Soviet naval craft finally made Holystone too dangerous to continue, and the program was ended in 1975 after thirteen years. Even more dangerous was the De Soto program, patrols of U.S. Navy destroyers packed with electronic interception gear that during the early 1960s deliberately provoked coastal defense radars in North Vietnam—a program that finally led to the fateful attack during 1964 on two De Soto destroyers in the Tonkin Gulf.

Why would these dangerous operations continue, even after COMMINT and ELINT functions were put aboard satellites? Because unlike photo reconnaissance, collecting electronics transmissions involves much more (and much heavier) equipment. The EC-121 American ELINT plane shot down by North Korea in 1969, for example, had a crew of thirty-one and *six tons* of eavesdropping equipment aboard; it will be quite some time before that amount of equipment can be miniaturized for use aboard satellites. Another reason is that ELINT must collect a prodigious amount of data before analysts can begin to draw conclusions about the significance of the transmissions they're reading. Moreover, much of the data is encrypted; miles and miles of digital tape recorded by ELINT have to be fed into huge computers called "numbers crunchers" as analysts try to break the encrypted enigmas, searching for the one tiny clue that will unlock the codes.

(Tapes of nonencrypted transmissions are often worked on by NSA's large number of blind employees, whose sensitive ears can detect sounds others cannot.)

Because so much of important communication moves around the world in code—only a small fraction of the Russian codes, the most difficult, have ever been broken—American intelligence, especially the NSA, has exerted great effort toward sweeping up as much as it possibly can of *all* potentially valuable transmissions. This vacuum-cleaner approach sometimes can pay dividends. In 1956, routine electronic eavesdropping by the CIA on the U.S. Communist party headquarters in New York City led to one of the agency's most successful operations, exposure of the Khrushchev "de-Stalinization" speech. On April 28 of that year, the political secretary to Eugene Dennis, the American Communist party's general secretary, stood before a meeting of the group's national committee and read the text of Khrushchev's speech that had been delivered in secret earlier to the Twentieth Party Congress in Moscow. The committee members sat shocked as Khrushchev's words piled vituperation on the memory of Joseph Stalin. The CIA later arranged to have the text of the speech released publicly, an event that created a schism in the world Communist movement, including the Sino-Soviet split. (The CIA has never admitted the wiretapping, for the simple reason that it was an illegal violation of the agency's charter banning domestic operations, to mention nothing about warrantless eavesdropping.)

Less successful was Gamma Gupy, an NSA operation in 1971 that managed to eavesdrop, from a listening post inside the U.S. Embassy in Moscow, on the two-way radio conversations exchanged between Soviet government officials riding in their limousines to work each morning. The eavesdropping, which produced a worthless pile of such trivia as the revelation that some of the Soviet leaders were much taken with the charms of Olga the masseuse, backfired when the Russians found out about it—they beamed strong microwaves to balk the eavesdropping, causing some of the Americans to become deathly ill.

By the beginning of this decade, American intelligence had surrounded its perceived enemies, notably the Soviet Union, with a vast electronic eavesdropping web whose size, complexity, and thoroughness remain unmatched in the history of espionage. Besides the satellites, there were two thousand posts all around the world to listen in on military communications, half a dozen huge radar complexes to monitor missile tests, and a sprawling communications interception operation in Cheltenham, England—run in conjunction with Canada and Great Britain—that picked up virtually all military communications in Eastern Europe.* Moreover, the Americans began to deploy the very latest in COMMINT, a robot electronic snoop that was planted at various sites inside the Soviet Union. About the size of a small handbag, the device is an unbelievably sophisticated electronic eavesdropping device, capable of automatically gathering transmissions from super-high frequencies being broadcast miles away, then encoding and transmitting them up to three hundred miles to a passing plane or satellite. (Although the robot is still highly secret in the United States, the Russians found out about it when one of the robots was carefully concealed inside an artificial tree stump, then sited in a forest near Moscow. But the CIA agents who did the job made a serious mistake. They put the robot inside a fake pine-tree stump, which they placed in a grove of aspen trees. A pine tree in an aspen grove is very rare in Russia, and the attention the stump got soon revealed the robot inside.)

There were supplements to the great electronic web:

*The eavesdroppers heard some poignant conversations. In 1967, they listened as a doomed Soviet cosmonaut, his spacecraft tumbling through the atmosphere out of control, screamed into his radio, "Somebody do something! I don't want to die!" At about the same time, a Soviet Air Force general, putting a MiG fighter through its paces over East Germany, angrily rejected ground control's orders for a flight correction. "Don't tell me how to fly this plane, you mother of a whore!" he shouted. He died as the MiG then crashed.

planes and unmanned reconnaissance drones. The planes were something really new, still another brilliant design perfected in 1959 by Kelly Johnson. Called the SR-71 (SR for strategic reconnaissance), it made the U-2 look like a Model T car. It could fly at three times the speed of sound—more than 2,000 miles an hour—at 100,000 feet, and packed with cameras and ELINT devices, the SR-71 in one hour could take pictures and record electronics transmissions covering an area up to 60,000 square miles.

Oddly enough, when President Lyndon Johnson announced existence of the plane in 1964, he called it the YF-12A and described it as a "fighter plane," part of an American deception plan to convince the Russians that the United States had not yet developed a high-altitude successor to the U-2. The Russians could hardly have been fooled; since there were no Soviet aircraft capable of operating at the SR-71's altitude or speed, what possible threat was the American plane supposed to counter? Obviously, it was a spy plane.

The Russians detected the SR-71 on their radars, but the fighters could not reach the American plane's altitude, and surface-to-air missiles exploded harmlessly many thousands of feet below. (More than nine hundred Russian missiles have been launched against SR-71s during the past decade, but none ever hit the plane.) Nevertheless, the fear of losing an SR-71 has induced caution; SR-71 missions over the Soviet Union are confined to relatively narrow areas just inside the border. The SR-71 is used much more boldly over less well-defended areas, primarily the Middle East and China.

Considerably less caution is used in conjunction with the drones, unpiloted jet aircraft that are miracles of miniaturization. Aboard are sensors, inertial-navigation systems, and a twenty-four-inch focal-length camera that can take strips of photographs forty-five inches long and about five inches wide. About a tenth the size of a conventional aircraft, the drones were first used over China in the early 1960s, later in larger numbers over North Vietnam. Now subdivided into various specialties, from ELINT to electronic interception to photo reconnaissance, the advantage of the drones is that they are cheap, do not risk a valuable pilot, and are remarkably stable. The chief disadvantage—aside from limited range—is political. The air force, which handles the operations end of all American intelligence reconnaissance, has never liked the drones, since they involve that most horrible of air-force nightmares, no pilots. Despite the air force's dislike, the drones have had some spectacular successes, among them detailed poststrike photographs following the B-52 bombing of North Vietnam in 1972. The pictures were so clear that individual pieces of blasted steel could be seen in areas where the bombs had struck.

At first glance, all the foregoing seems breathtaking, a huge clockwork so ingenious and so airtight that nothing can escape. And yet that is not what has happened; the supreme irony of modern American intelligence is the discovery by many of its practitioners that the more sophisticated the collection systems, the more ambiguity there seems to be.

The central problem is the sheer mass of information flowing in every day. Each new development in photo reconnaissance or electronic interception produces that much more data, and as the technological empire grows larger and larger, the interpreters and analysts are being overwhelmed by a mountain of paper. The problem has been growing especially acute over the past eight years, ever since an alarmed Pentagon warned Congress in 1976 that American intelligence was rapidly reaching the point when it "simply cannot screen all of the imagery that is available." And that statement covered only photo reconnaissance.

A good deal of this ocean of technical intelligence has turned out to be more ambiguous than originally supposed. Consider what happened in late 1970, when U.S. photoreconnaissance satellites detected the building of what appeared to be eighty new Soviet ICBM silos. That triggered an intelligence alarm, but three years passed while various components of the American intelligence community argued over its significance. Not until 1973 were the Russians asked formally about the silos—they responded they were command and control silos, not missile emplacements—and it took until 1977 for the debate finally to be cleared up. (The Russians were telling the truth.)

There was also the case of something called Shilka, American intelligence's code name for the Soviet ZSU-23-4, a radar-directed, computerized antiaircraft gun mounted on tank tracks. Spy-satellite pictures revealed a pretty formidable weapon—until one Shilka was captured intact by the Israelis during the 1973 Yom Kippur War. Subjected to rigorous testing by the U.S. Army, Shilka was revealed to be a turkey —its fire-control computers were inaccurate and slow, it had insufficient ammunition, it was hard to reload, and its radar was so bad it could barely hit maneuvering targets. (And at that point, the army had already spent $5 billion in an attempt to build Divad, the American answer to what was originally thought to be the formidable "threat" of Shilka.)

Another shortcoming in technical collection systems is their vulnerability to deception. The Soviets have been honing the art of concealment to a fine edge, and one entire factory in Czechoslovakia produces nothing but rubber MiGs, phony submarines, and a wide range of decoys, all designed to hoodwink American satellites and spy planes. The very precision of spy satellites—their tracks can be predicted exactly, allowing analysts to pinpoint what the sensors will detect—is also a major disadvantage; the Russians know when the satellites are overhead and when they're on the other side of the world, allowing a wide range of concealment activities when the satellites aren't around.

Even when the satellites are looking, there is some question whether they're detecting what they're supposed to detect. On September 22, 1979, for example, an American Vela satellite scanning the southern Atlantic for any sign of a nuclear explosion registered two intense bursts of light, the characteristic double pulse of an atomic detonation. The Vela sighting caused a sensation in the American intelligence community, but however conclusive intelligence analysts regarded the evidence—they were convinced that either Israel or South Africa had carried out a test of a nuclear-warhead missile—it was insufficient for the White House. As President Carter noted, with some justification, the United States was not about to make the sensational charge that Israel, a close American ally, or South Africa had set off an atomic weapon. Not, that is, without more conclusive evidence. Where was the fallout from the blast? Was there any confirmation from other intelligence sources? Could the intelligence agencies certify that no natural phenomenon—such as a meteor—was responsible for the flash the Vela detected?

The intelligence agencies could not, and in that admission lay the crux of the problem connected with technical collection systems. They are fundamentally ambiguous, particularly when too much reliance is placed on them. As the Vela and other incidents proved, technical collection systems, no matter how vast and complex, are at root dumb machines, able to record but not to think. To make them work effectively, the machines must operate in conjunction with human-intelligence sources.

But, as American intelligence discovered the hard way, talking about the necessity for human sources and actually developing them are two very different things. And it turned out to be an especially difficult problem in the face of an enemy that was past master of the art.

five

THE MOLE WARS (I)

> It is right to be taught, even by an
> enemy.
>
> —OVID

JOSEPH STALIN OFTEN WOULD HECTOR his intelligence chiefs to keep away from what he called "hypotheses and equations with many unknowns." The only intelligence he wanted to see, Stalin admonished, was the facts and figures his espionage minions could obtain "from the vaults of foreign governments."

Soviet intelligence has a word for it—*razvedka,* roughly translated as "true intelligence," which is defined in one Soviet intelligence manual as that "procured by undercover agents and secret informants in defiance of the laws of a foreign country in which they operate."

American intelligence calls it HUMINT (human intelligence), and the difference in how each nation approaches this most traditional of all espionage techniques is striking. The Russians, as events have proven, are highly adept at HUMINT; such intelligence argot as "moles," "double agent," "triple agent," and "disinformation" have been popularized by some of the more spectacular cases involving Soviet intelligence. The Russians have devoted a great deal of effort toward perfecting human-intelligence operations, and they remain unsurpassed in that field.

American intelligence, on the other hand, has been much less successful in the art of human-intelligence collection, especially on its central concern, the Soviet Union. Part of the reason has been the traditionally fragmented makeup of American intelligence; another is the historic American uneasiness with spies (although all American schoolchildren are taught the story of the revolutionary spy-hero Nathan Hale). The most important reason is that American intelligence has tended to focus on technical collection systems, which supposedly eliminate the two key problems connected with human-intelligence operations: time and ambiguity. Developing human-intelligence sources takes a vast amount of time; they require patient and detailed handling, a process that can take years. Moreover, all human intelligence carries a counterintelligence implication: Always subject to manipulation and penetration, HUMINT operations necessitate large-scale efforts to ensure their validity while at the same time identifying and neutralizing the HUMINT efforts of the other side. And in the final analysis, an element of ambiguity always remains—is it 100 percent certain that the intelligence being provided by a source is correct? Is it guaranteed that the source has not been turned and is not now feeding false information? Is it a certainty that the source has not applied his own biases to the information he is reporting?

The complexities of HUMINT operations can become dizzying, but no technical system can ever come close to that most perfect of all intelligence-collection machines, the human being. As noted earlier, the central weakness of technical systems is that they cannot think or interpret; they will collect only information that is either visible or recoverable, a process that involves its own ambiguities.

Reluctantly, American intelligence has been compelled by the press of world events to enter the difficult and complex business of human-intelligence operations. This requirement became especially acute as the Cold War began, because the United States suddenly found itself confronted with two large enemies, the Soviet Union and China, about whom next to nothing was known, either of their capabilities or of their intentions. But American HUMINT operations have been marked by bitter failures, a bleak record that continues to this day. Why?

Fundamentally, because American intelligence—and its allies—realized, belatedly, that their chief enemy had mastered the game very early and had been able to frustrate virtually every human-intelligence effort. Too late, it slowly dawned on those agencies that they had failed to pay attention to an important object lesson provided many years before by a genius at the art of intelligence.

His name was Feliks Edmundovich Dzerzhinsky, and as a spymaster, he clearly ranks as the century's greatest. Son of a Polish nobleman, Dzerzhinsky was, nevertheless, a fanatical Communist who had spent eleven years in the czar's prisons before the Russian Revolution, most of them under sentence of forced labor in Siberian mines. The experience had wrecked his health; thin and racked with tuberculosis, he spoke in a hoarse whisper, interrupted by bouts of coughing.

But above all else, Dzerzhinsky had the mind and heart of a secret policeman. It was that trait that moved Lenin to appoint him in December 1917 as head of the All-Russian Extraordinary Commission for Combating Counterrevolution and Sabotage—the Cheka, Soviet Russia's first secret police force. Lenin's move was shrewd: Dzerzhinsky was totally honest and without political ambition despite his pronounced fanaticism, which meant he would never threaten the regime. He sought only to be the "watchdog of the revolution," to destroy the vast array of enemies, within and without, that confronted the new Bolshevik regime.

The task seemed overwhelming. At the moment of his appointment, the Cheka had only two dozen agents in all of Russia, and no cars or any other vehicles. Yet they were supposed to defeat the machinations of the anti-Bolshevik forces (the Whites), checkmate a series of destabilization efforts by the United States, Great Britain, France, and other nations, and at the same time safeguard the secrets of a very vulnerable regime.

But the infant Cheka did have one very powerful weapon: the brain of Feliks Dzerzhinsky. Like an ascetic monk in his cell, he spent days and nights closed off in a small room at the Smolny Institute in Petrograd—and later in the Lubyanka Prison in Moscow—poring over records and files. He sat there for hours under the glare of a single, powerful electric light, absorbing details and slowly hatching his plans.

As we saw in Chapter One, Dzerzhinsky's Cheka scored its first success just after the end of World War I when it rolled up the Western intelligence networks in Russia and, at the same time, the large-scale sabotage operations they were running. But as Dzerzhinsky was aware, that was only the first battle in what was certain to be a long, underground war.

The immediate problem centered on the nearly one million anti-Bolshevik Russians who had fled the country in the wake of the Bolshevik revolution. Dzerzhinsky realized that these émigrés, many of whom were fanatically anti-Communist, would provide fertile ground for recruitment by intelligence agencies; as they moved back into Russia across still-porous borders, the Cheka soon would be overwhelmed, not to mention the beleaguered regime itself. The Cheka had unleashed "the terror," a widespread police roundup throughout Russia just after the war to crack down on domestic opposition to Lenin, but there was no guarantee that the regime's internal enemies had been silenced.

Dzerzhinsky discovered that there was at least one opposition group thriving during the terror, an organization called the Monarchist Union of Central Russia. Composed of former czarist officers and officials who had gone to work for the Bolshevik government, its members had become progressively disenchanted and were seeking ways of getting rid of the Bolsheviks, with the eventual goal of forming a constitutional monarchy. The group's members were what the Cheka called "radishes" (red on the outside, white on the inside), but given their positions in important government ministries, they represented to the Cheka an internal-security threat of the first order.

Dzerzhinsky, who had built up Cheka's strength a thousandfold since the end of the war, had also enlisted battalions of secret informers all over Russia, and it was not long before he knew the dimensions of the threat. By 1922, he had thoroughly infiltrated the group, but although he seemed ready to strike and arrest all the members for "counterrevolutionary activities," the Cheka chief stayed his hand. He had a much more involved plan in mind.

The plan was breathtaking: Dzerzhinsky's scheme was to take over the entire anti-Bolshevik organization, convert the group into a virtual Cheka branch office, then use it to snare some of the bigger fish he was trying to catch. Primarily, Dzerzhinsky wanted to eliminate the two biggest threats to Lenin's regime: (1) the extensive intelligence operations being run by the Western nations, especially Great Britain; and (2) the even more dangerous and widespread sabotage operations by Russian émigrés in cross-border forays, under the sponsorship of the same intelligence agencies.

Dzerzhinsky set his plan into motion like a grand master plotting intricate moves in a chess game. First, he secretly arrested Alexander Yakushev, one of the highest-ranking leaders of the monarchist group. It was a carefully thought out choice: Yakushev was opposed to the Bolsheviks, but he was not a fanatic and did not agree with some of the other leaders of the group, who advocated violence and sabotage operations. During lengthy interrogations, Dzerzhinsky shrewdly manipulated his prisoner, showing him evidence of atrocities committed by anti-Bolshevik forces, along with detailed information on the stupidity of the czar and his family. Dzerzhinsky convinced Yakushev that restoration of the monarchy, even a constitutional one, would be taken over by the more fanatic of the émigré groups, leading to horrendous bloodshed in Russia. The Cheka chief played his trump card: Did Yakushev and his organization want that on their consciences? Then

Dzerzhinsky took the extraordinary step of letting Yakushev go, over the strong protests of other Cheka officials.

But Dzerzhinsky had read his prisoner well. By now convinced that the Cheka chief himself was sympathetic to the group, Yakushev offered to help. Dzerzhinsky had just the right suggestion: The monarchist should contact the émigré groups in Europe, tell them of the opposition organization operating inside Russia, and convince them that further sabotage efforts would only jeopardize the chances of the "radish" group to take power.

Yakushev began visiting the various émigré groups in Europe, armed with a subtle but persuasive argument: His organization—now called The Trust—was poised to take power in Russia (within three or four months, Yakushev claimed), but continued sabotage operations by the émigrés threatened to upset a delicate political situation. It was important, Yakushev argued, that the Cheka, thus far unaware of the extent and power of The Trust, not be aroused into action that could destroy the organization just as it was about to achieve its great victory. Sabotage operations were dutifully suspended.

The operation then proceeded to succeed even beyond the Cheka's wildest hopes. The convincingly engaging Yakushev, as Dzerzhinsky had anticipated, soon began attracting intelligence-agency interest. Yakushev whetted that interest by recounting to émigré leaders and intelligence officers how The Trust had managed to infiltrate virtually every aspect of life in the Soviet Union, thus representing an unparalleled intelligence resource. Within a year, Western intelligence agencies, including the United States, began funneling money into The Trust, in return receiving reams of "intelligence" that was carefully prepared by Dzerzhinsky's Cheka. If that wasn't enough, Yakushev was able to convince the intelligence agencies that they should infiltrate agents into the Soviet Union only via special "windows" (clandestine entry points) operated by The Trust. The Cheka was soon able to spot every single intelligence agent entering Russia.

For those skeptical of Yakushev's claims, special tours inside the Soviet Union were arranged. All of them were elaborately staged by Dzerzhinsky: a large "underground religious service" held by Trust members inside the country (with Cheka agents playing the roles of priests), an entire trainload of Trust "supporters" (all of them Cheka agents), and assorted other shams, amounting to a gigantic sting operation that managed to fool just about everybody. The few disbelievers were gradually silenced by a long string of Trust "successes" inside Russia, including the remarkable feat of springing from jail the brother of a high-ranking British intelligence officer—a smart move by Dzerzhinsky that guaranteed blind faith in The Trust by the British Secret Intelligence Service (SIS).

Even at that supreme moment of triumph, Dzerzhinsky patiently bided his time, for he hoped to lure two even bigger fish into his widening net: Sidney Reilly, the leading British intelligence operative against Russia, and Reilly's chief émigré contact, Boris Savinkov, leader of a group of Russian émigrés responsible for most of the sabotage missions against the Bolshevik regime.

Reilly was a special obsession for Dzerzhinsky, who had just missed grabbing the British agent in 1918, when the Cheka broke up the Western intelligence operations that were aimed at destroying the new Bolshevik regime. (Reilly fled the country just one step ahead of the Cheka.) An incredibly daring and resourceful agent, Reilly—born Sigmund Georgievich Rosenblum in Odessa before emigrating to England and anglicizing his name—had been a thorn in the Cheka's side ever since. Not only was he running the most active émigré sabotage and intelligence operations against the Soviets, he was also responsible in 1924 for the forgery by British intelligence of the infamous "Zinoviev letter." (The letter, allegedly from Grigori Zinoviev, a close ally of Lenin, called on the British Communist party to "revolutionize" their country. Revealed in a London newspaper, it caused the downfall of the Labor government and balked developing trade and diplomatic relations between the two countries.)

In the summer of 1925, Dzerzhinsky moved his chess game into the final phase. First, Savinkov was lured across the border into the Soviet Union, followed by Reilly, both men taking this dangerous step on the firm conviction by the SIS that The Trust was genuine. Indeed, the SIS had urged Reilly to cross into Russia to handle an especially delicate operation The Trust was trying to arrange: selling the czar's crown jewels to raise money for further operations.

Reilly and Savinkov promptly disappeared, an event that raised the first real suspicion about The Trust. A year later, the Polish intelligence service decided to test The Trust by asking Yakushev to obtain a copy of the latest Soviet mobilization plan. Yakushev stalled while Dzerzhinsky, no military expert, worked with Red Army officers to forge a passable plan. The result, however, was a flawed forgery that the Poles easily exposed, and the resulting alarm moved all intelligence agencies to halt any further dealings with The Trust. Clearly, everything up to that point had been a Cheka ruse. In retrospect, of course, it seems unbelievable that the émigrés and the intelligence agencies should have been so completely taken in (their gullibility was an important reason for the ruse's success), but it is also true to say that Dzerzhinsky and the Cheka had played the game with consummate skill.*

Dzerzhinsky, his fragile health destroyed by the days and nights spent on the job, died at the moment of his supreme intelligence triumph. His value to the infant Soviet regime

---

*Almost all the Cheka officials involved in the operation were later executed during Stalin's Great Purge in the 1930s, including Yakushev and Dzerzhinsky's brilliant chief aide, Jacov Peters, head of the Moscow Cheka. Savinkov was executed before the purge began by being thrown out a window. As for the mysterious Reilly, there are conflicting accounts of his death, variously described in Soviet writings as occurring in 1925 or 1927. His friend and former case officer, Captain George A. Hill of MI6—who was directly involved in the anti-Bolshevik plots after World War I—ironically enough was posted to Moscow during World War II as a British intelligence liaison officer with the NKVD, successor agency to the Cheka. Hill heard a rumor there that Reilly was alive as late as 1944, but he was never able to obtain any confirmation.

was nearly incalculable, measured today in the Moscow square that is named after him and the large statue that stands before the headquarters of the organization that he fathered, the KGB. In plain terms, Dzerzhinsky saved the nation in which he believed so fervently and to which he literally gave his life.

In intelligence terms, The Trust was one of the most brilliant intelligence operations in modern history. Over a period of nearly five years, the Cheka completely neutralized its émigré enemy, blinded all Western intelligence agencies, captured the two leading operatives working against the Soviet regime—and for good measure got the intelligence agencies to finance their own destruction. When the Cheka closed down the Trust operation in 1927, following the disappearance of Reilly and Savinkov and the exposure by the Polish intelligence service, a huge dragnet pulled in several hundred Russians who had been working for émigré organizations or Western intelligence agencies—including the unfortunate members of the monarchist underground group, who died before Cheka firing squads without knowing of the role they had unwittingly played in the complex operation.

The practical effect of The Trust operation was that Western intelligence on the Soviet Union shut down almost completely; so thoroughly had the Cheka shattered the Western networks, those agencies never quite recovered. There was an important lesson in the entire episode: The West was up against a very formidable enemy, an enemy that had already demonstrated a remarkable ability—even with limited resources—for completely frustrating human-intelligence operations. Clearly, in order to gather intelligence on the increasingly closed society that was the Soviet Union, much more sophisticated and elaborate operations would have to be mounted, including the patient building of new networks and development of sources.

However, that did not happen. Preoccupied with other concerns, understaffed and underfunded, the intelligence agencies of the West did not comprehend the very clear lesson Dzerzhinsky had provided for them. They continued to repeat the old mistakes, chiefly the enlistment of émigré groups—all of them thoroughly penetrated by Soviet intelligence—for operations inside the Soviet Union. The lack of success of these operations seemed to have no impact, and there was even less impact when both the United States and Great Britain received unmistakable evidence that what meager operations they were running against the Soviet Union were being balked by an even more elaborate (and dangerous) chess game than the one run by Dzerzhinsky.

It was a clear warning that the unthinkable had happened: Western intelligence had been deeply penetrated by its Soviet counterpart.

The alarm was delivered by a slight, elderly man whose apparent frailty was belied by restless eyes that seemed to miss nothing. He was Walter Krivitsky, a general in the GRU (Soviet military intelligence) and head of all GRU operations in Western Europe. In 1937, after refusing an order from Moscow to murder a disillusioned agent, Krivitsky himself was marked for death, a circumstance that compelled him to defect to the United States. Krivitsky might as well have defected to Mars, for all the interest the Americans showed in him. He was initially refused entry, and after hiding out in the Russian émigré community for a short while, finally managed to catch the attention of Isaac Don Levine, a Russian émigré who had become a prominent anti-Communist journalist.

To Levine, Krivitsky poured out details of Soviet intelligence operations that seemed unbelievable—massive espionage rings everywhere, providing Moscow with detailed intelligence on virtually every military and political secret in the West, and a huge security apparatus inside the Soviet Union itself that had made the country impervious to penetration and unleashed a reign of terror surpassed only by the excesses of Ivan the Terrible. More ominously, Krivitsky began to talk about several spectacular penetrations Soviet intelligence had made at high levels of Western government and intelligence agencies, especially in Great Britain.

Levine made arrangements for Krivitsky to talk with skeptical officials at the British Embassy in Washington, and they became gradually more convinced as the Russian intelligence agent gave them specifics—including the unsettling news that a senior clerk in the government cipher department of the Foreign Office in London was a Soviet spy, handing over to the Russians every top-secret cable that came across his desk. (A hasty investigation by MI5, the British counterintelligence organization, revealed that Krivitsky was right: John Herbert King, a senior cipher clerk, was indeed a Soviet agent.)

The revelation about King thoroughly alarmed the British, who asked that Krivitsky go to London and extensively brief MI5 officials on what he knew about Soviet intelligence penetrations in the British government. Krivitsky at that point betrayed some evidence of paranoia—or so it seemed to the British—arguing that his life would be in constant danger while in Great Britain, since the Russians had high-level spies everywhere there. The British played along with this seemingly excessive fear, sending him to London aboard a Royal Navy submarine. Once at his destination, however, Krivitsky demonstrated to stunned British intelligence officers that he was not paranoid; there *were* Soviet agents everywhere. He revealed the existence of one hundred high-level Soviet agents scattered all over the British Empire, including thirty-five in Great Britain alone (all were British citizens working for Moscow). Six of them, he noted, were in the British civil service, and two more were prominent journalists. Krivitsky did not know their names—for security reasons, agents are usually known only by their cryptonyms within an intelligence agency—but he did provide several tantalizing clues that in the light of later events have particular irony. One of the key agents, Krivitsky said, was a Scotsman and a Communist with artistic tastes who worked at the Foreign Office; another was a journalist for a prominent London newspaper who had covered the Spanish Civil War; and still another was a recruiting agent for Soviet intelligence in academic circles at Cambridge University.*

Unfortunately, Krivitsky's disclosures came on the eve of World War II, and British intelligence, concerned with the threat of Nazi Germany, had neither the time nor the resources to follow up Krivitsky's leads, which pointed unmistakably to the Soviet intelligence moles Donald Maclean (the Scotsman in the Foreign Office), H.A.R. (Kim) Philby (the journalist who had covered the Spanish Civil War), and Anthony Blunt (the recruiter at Cambridge). But even if the British had had the time, it remains an open question whether they would have pursued those clues with the vigor that Krivitsky thought warranted. What the Soviet defector was proposing seemed beyond belief: that the British government (and every other Western government, for that matter) had been so thoroughly penetrated by Soviet intelligence that there was literally no important secret that Moscow did not know.

And the most important secrets, Krivitsky emphasized, were the ones connected with Western intelligence agencies. Any attempt at infiltration of the Soviet Union was being frustrated because of high-level penetrations of the agencies planning the operations. In simple terms, *the Russians knew when and how they were coming.*

The claims about moles met with even less interest in

---

*Krivitsky also revealed how Red Army Marshal Mikhail Tukhachevsky was murdered by Stalin in a cunningly conceived NKVD plot that managed to involve Adolf Hitler. An émigré leader (actually an NKVD agent) informed the Nazi S.D. in 1936 that Tukhachevsky was plotting against Stalin. The information was a deliberate lie, but as the NKVD and Stalin correctly guessed, S.D. chief Reinhard Heydrich, after consulting with Hitler, decided to use that information as a means of disrupting the Red Army. Assuming that Stalin would never believe such sensational intelligence directly from the Nazis, Heydrich had a number of documents forged, implicating Tukhachevsky in treason. The documents were then slipped to the NKVD via Czechoslovakian officials eager to curry favor with Stalin. The Soviet dictator used the forged documents to arrest Tukhachevsky, who was shot a year later, along with a good portion of the rest of the Soviet military leadership. Heydrich and the S.D. congratulated themselves on a successful operation—not realizing that it was Stalin himself who had pulled all the strings, right from the beginning.

the United States, where only the FBI seemed to attach any importance to what he was saying. But Krivitsky persevered, testifying before a U.S. congressional committee on how the American Communist party had been turned into an espionage adjunct for Soviet intelligence. By then, Krivitsky had become something of a public figure and indications began to accumulate that the NKVD had marked him for death. He encountered one notorious NKVD executioner on a New York street and afterward told friends, "If you hear that I've committed suicide, don't believe it." Some time later, on February 10, 1941, he was found dead in a Washington, D.C., hotel room with three suicide notes. Officially, the death was ruled a suicide, but nobody who knew Krivitsky doubted for a moment that he had been murdered by the NKVD to protect its deepest secrets. It is significant that Krivitsky's death came just before he was due to return to England for further discussions about Soviet moles in the British government.

If Krivitsky was murdered—as seems most likely—then it illustrated the lengths to which Soviet intelligence was willing to go to protect its moles. But Krivitsky's murder was soon forgotten, and by war's end, the GRU general had faded into obscurity.

By that time, however, there was a small, but growing, awareness that much closer attention should have been paid to Krivitsky's important clues about the range and depth of Soviet intelligence operations, particularly its extensive ability to checkmate the intelligence operations of the Soviet state's enemies. Some of the first clues were noted by Harry Rositzke, a young OSS officer who had decided to stay in intelligence work. After the war, Rositzke was posted to the Strategic Services Unit of the War Department, which had inherited the intelligence section of the fractured OSS organization. Assigned the job of discovering the breadth and depth of Soviet intelligence, Rositzke worked his way through stacks of captured German and Japanese intelligence files for clues about what the counterintelligence services of those defeated nations had learned concerning the Soviets.

A great deal, as it turned out, and the realization slowly dawned on Rositzke that what little the Americans had seen of the Soviet intelligence effort was only the tip of a huge iceberg. Rositzke was especially struck by how the Russians concentrated their efforts on human-intelligence operations, an effort that had paid off in a number of stunning successes. Among them was the *Rote Kapelle* (Red Orchestra), as the Gestapo called it, actually a number of centrally directed spy rings that blanketed Europe, with small branches in Canada and the United States. Eventually consisting of 118 agents, the Red Orchestra was first formed in 1936 and until the Germans finally managed to close it down in 1942, provided Moscow with detailed intelligence on German military plans and capabilities (including the precise date for the German invasion of the Soviet Union, intelligence Stalin refused to believe).

There was also *Rote Drei* (Red Three), a smaller ring based in Switzerland that produced intelligence of equal quality, until it too was closed down in 1944, this time by the Swiss. And in the Orient, Soviet intelligence had developed its greatest prize: Dr. Richard Sorge, a German journalist with high-level connections who was based in Japan. Sorge, a secret Communist and NKVD agent, formed a spy ring that penetrated the highest levels of the Japanese government, in the process discovering Japan's decision in 1941 to strike in the South Pacific and not north against the Soviet Union. This priceless intelligence, which Stalin accepted, enabled him to shift large reserves of troops westward and defeat German armies about to capture Moscow.

"The British worked with machines; the Russians worked with men," Rositzke recalled much later, in a perfect summation of what happened during the war. The few minor human-intelligence operations mounted by the United States and its allies seemed positively puny by comparison, and the gap became even more obvious as intelligence interest turned to the postwar Soviet Union. In the early years of the Cold War, nothing seemed to go right for American and other Western intelligence services when they attempted to develop human-intelligence sources. Attempts to turn Soviet diplomatic or intelligence officials were mostly failures, defectors were few and far between, and efforts to introduce agents into the Soviet Union in wholesale lots were defeated as soon as the agents set foot on Soviet soil. Indeed, the failures were unmitigated disasters: Operation Climber, a British MI6 operation to infiltrate agents into the Caucasus area of the Soviet Union, resulted in the capture of all twenty agents involved; a joint American-British effort to send agents into Albania aborted when all the agents sent in were shot upon arrival; and an extensive CIA operation to parachute agents into the Soviet heartland was easily rolled up by Soviet counterintelligence, which captured all the agents.

Even the most brilliantly conceived operations seemed to go wrong, somehow, the moment they became directed at the Soviet Union. One such failure involved Western intelligence's greatest World War II triumph, the Ultra code-breaking operation.

Ultra was the code name assigned to a huge (and very secret) British intelligence operation that succeeded in breaking Enigma, the main German code-making machine. Great Britain and the United States shared in the secret, and both nations took extraordinary efforts to make sure the Germans would never find out that their codes had been compromised. There were also efforts to ensure that the Russians didn't find out either, in part because the British were using Ultra in a Byzantine intelligence intrigue designed to hoodwink Moscow.

The intrigue centered on a central British objective: The Soviet Union, which was fighting the bulk of the German Wehrmacht, must be kept in the war, to avoid the possibility of a Russian defeat and the full unleashing of Hitler's military power against the British. The British stood no chance of ever defeating Germany unless Hitler was continually preoccupied with the life-and-death struggle on the Eastern Front. Ultra was solving all the German military operational orders dispatched in code, including those being sent to units fighting in Russia. There was no hope of the eternally suspicious Stalin accepting this priceless intelligence directly from the British. (One problem was that the Ultra material would have to be summarized to protect the secret.) MI6 thereupon worked out an elaborate plan.

To keep Stalin unaware that the Ultra secrets emanated from the British, they were laundered through Soviet intelligence networks operating in Switzerland, notably *Rote Drei*. With the connivance of Swiss intelligence, the British arranged for Ultra information, its source concealed, to be fed through Rudolph Roessler, a leftist German refugee who had fled to Switzerland after Hitler's accession to power and was later recruited into Swiss intelligence. Roessler, code-named Lucy, became part of the *Rote Drei* operation, and his intelligence soon caused a sensation in Moscow Center.

The intelligence was a godsend: Lucy, who worked for Soviet intelligence only on the condition he would never reveal his sources, provided amazingly detailed information on the latest movements and plans of German forces in Russia, down to the regimental level—often before the units themselves had received the orders. An initially skeptical Soviet intelligence soon became convinced of Lucy's value, since his reports were proven right, time and again. (The most sensational result of Lucy material came in 1943, when the Russians, warned of an impending effort by the Germans to take the city of Kursk, anticipated the offensive and completely smashed the Wehrmacht in history's greatest tank battle, which spelled the end of German offensive power in Russia.)

From the British standpoint, the Lucy operation was a brilliant success; the Russians had been thoroughly convinced of the genuineness of Lucy and his Ultra material, and the operation had played a major part in the defeat of German forces in Russia. Even more significant, the success raised the possibility that the source, representing a pipeline directly into Moscow Center, could be used later in intelligence operations involving the Soviet Union. The British began testing this idea by feeding cooked intelligence through Lucy, including alleged information about the Vatican's attitude toward Stalin and high-level data from the upper reaches of the British government reporting that the British never entertained the idea of a separate peace with Nazi Germany.

Moreover, MI6 was working an even more intricate twist to the Lucy operation. One of the *Rote Drei* radio operators, an English Communist named Alexander Foote who had been an NKVD agent since 1936, was a double, working for British intelligence. Foote represented an even greater opportunity for possible operations against the Soviets, since Moscow apparently trusted him completely. But Foote was to reveal to MI6 that the Russians had caught on to the Lucy game.

The revelation did not come until 1947, when Foote defected to the British in Germany. He recounted that he had returned after the war to Moscow, where he was to be trained for a new NKVD assignment. But Foote upon his arrival was subjected to hostile interrogation, during which the NKVD wanted to know about the "British material" Foote and the other *Rote Drei* radio operators had sent to Moscow. Foote realized that the Russians somehow had found out about the Ultra intelligence fed through Lucy, but he feigned ignorance about the source of the material he encoded and sent on to Moscow Center. The Russians believed him, and subsequently readied him for operations in Argentina. However, Foote defected at the first opportunity and, once in England, delivered the bad news to his MI6 debriefers. The questions he had been asked by the NKVD indicated clearly that the Russians knew about Ultra and knew also that the British had fed some of the Ultra material via the Lucy connection.

Foote's revelation was unsettling to both MI6 and U.S. intelligence, both of whom had to confront the unsettling fact that the war's most secret intelligence operation, one that promised unbounded opportunities later on, had been blown. The Russians had been carefully kept in the dark about Ultra; how was it possible for them not only to find out about it, but additionally to discover the Lucy connection?

Part of the answer was already being provided by what seemed, at first, to be a relatively low-level defection in Canada of a disgruntled Soviet Embassy cipher clerk. But the case of Igor Gouzenko was to have ramifications far beyond that event.

On September 2, 1945, Gouzenko, a twenty-six-year-old cipher clerk at the Soviet Embassy in Ottawa, fed up with the Soviet system, fled from the Soviet diplomatic compound with his wife and family and asked for political asylum. Following a tragicomic series of errors—at one point, Gouzenko tried to tell a newspaper his story, only to be turned away as a crank—he wound up, fortunately, in the care of Sir William Stephenson, a Canadian citizen and the famed Intrepid of World War II British intelligence. Stephenson recognized at once the importance of Gouzenko, for the Russian not only had access to Soviet intelligence flowing in and out of the Ottawa embassy—an important Russian espionage control center for operations in North America—he had also served at the main cipher section at GRU headquarters in Moscow.

In those capacities, Gouzenko had been exposed to a wide range of GRU secrets, the most important being the cryptonyms and general descriptions of many important agents. In what would later become the most publicized series of cases in Cold War espionage, Gouzenko revealed that the GRU had extensively penetrated the joint American-British-Canadian nuclear weapons program. Three scientists connected with the program were funneling information to Moscow, and other atomic secrets were being fed to the GRU by a large ring in Canada and a smaller industrial espionage ring in the United States, the latter including a GRU courier named Harry Gold and a man-and-wife team of spies, later identified as Julius and Ethel Rosenberg.

That much became public knowledge, but what was not

revealed outside the small circle of American, British, and Canadian counterintelligence officers who spent weeks with Gouzenko during his debriefing was some much more sensitive intelligence information. And it was information that went right to the heart of Western intelligence operations against the Soviet Union.

His debriefers never told him so, but almost all of what Gouzenko was revealing was already known to them, although in much more fragmented form. The source was the deepest secret of Western intelligence: the cracking of codes used by Soviet diplomatic missions abroad to forward intelligence to Moscow. At the end of World War II, British and American code breakers went to work on the Soviet codes, and discovered that they could read a considerable amount of the traffic dispatched from Soviet diplomatic posts during the war. Part of the reason was sheer volume. After the invasion of the Soviet Union, GRU and NKVD networks, especially in the United States, started cranking out a huge mass of intelligence. Dispatched via embassy ciphers, the volume overwhelmed cipher clerks, who began to make a number of serious mistakes. In some instances, the Russians repeatedly used the same normally unbreakable "one-time pads,"* and on other occasions sent highly sensitive intelligence in ordinary commercial codes. (The cracking of the Soviet commercial code was aided by an FBI break-in at the New York offices of Amtorg, the Soviet trading concern; the Russians were unaware that FBI agents during that break-in had photographed Soviet commercial code books.)

Reading a large backlog of Soviet intelligence transmis-

---

*Under this highly secure system, cipher clerks in Moscow were equipped with a set of small gummed pads, each page containing a long series of random five-digit number combinations arranged in columns. The pads were identical to the ones used by cipher clerks in outlying stations; after a message had been sent and decoded, the clerks discarded the cipher sheets from their respective pads and went on to the next page. The pads were never used twice, making the code unbreakable, since code breakers did not have enough traffic to analyze. But some Russian cipher clerks during the war, apparently short of pads, repeatedly used the same sheets for many messages, thus providing the code breakers with enough traffic to deduce the code.

sions provided disturbing evidence of the depth of Soviet intelligence operations in the West, although details were often maddeningly elusive. The American intercepts—called Bride—combined with the British versions (known as Black Jumbos), revealed three high-ranking Soviet agents operating in London, apparently at the highest levels of the British government. Known by their GRU cryptonyms—Stanley, Hicks, and Johnson—they were sending topflight intelligence, but there was insufficient detail to track them down.

More revealing were the intercepts referring to a spy code-named Homer; a slipup by a Russian cipher clerk, revealing too much personal information on that cryptonym, led analysts to suspect that Homer was a diplomat who had been stationed at one point in the British Embassy in Washington. A process of elimination led to the conclusion that Homer was Donald Maclean, former first secretary at the embassy. Other intercepts revealed clearly that one of the scientists involved in the Manhattan Project was a Soviet mole. Again, too much personal information revealed that he was Klaus Fuchs. Confronted with an MI5 bluff, he confessed, leading in turn to his GRU contact, Harry Gold, who in turn led the FBI to the Rosenbergs. (Actually, the FBI already had their suspicions. The Bride intercepts had pointed to the existence of an American man-and-wife espionage team with a relative who worked in a secret American weapons program —a near-perfect description of the Rosenbergs and Ethel Rosenberg's brother, David Greenglass, who worked on the Manhattan Project.)*

Gouzenko was able to fill in many gaps in the intercepts, and while his value was inestimable in helping in the roundup

---

*The intercepts also revealed a mole operating someplace in the highest level of the U.S. government. Called Agent 9, the mole was providing details of top-secret diplomatic and military discussions among President Roosevelt and his chief advisers. Agent 9 was never found, although mole hunters deduced that he was probably connected with the State Department. Initially, some suspicion was attached to Averell Harriman, but further analysis suggested that Agent 9 was probably Alger Hiss, although no proof was ever found.

of the assorted spy rings, there was a much more significant implication in part of his information. It was an implication that echoed the forgotten warning of General Krivitsky: The counterintelligence services in the West had been penetrated very deeply by the Soviet Union, and the Russians were in a position to frustrate nearly all intelligence operations directed against Moscow. Among other significant clues, Gouzenko revealed that while he was stationed in Moscow, a senior GRU officer bragged to him that the Russians routinely received reports directly from their mole in MI5. The reports, Gouzenko said, were high grade and could only have come from a very high-ranking MI5 official.

Gouzenko said the code name for this source was Elli, which caused some skepticism among his listeners. Elli was also the GRU cryptonym for a Canadian official who had already been arrested; was it possible that the GRU would commit so elementary a blunder as to assign the same code name to two different moles? The skepticism threw doubt on Gouzenko's entire thesis of moles deep inside Western intelligence agencies.

It would take more than twenty years before Gouzenko's thesis was revived by unmistakable evidence that the cipher clerk had been all too correct.

At the very moment that Gouzenko was encountering skepticism, evidence was already mounting that there was indeed extensive Soviet penetration of Western intelligence services. One especially disturbing development was the drying up of the Bride and Black Jumbos sources, which after the end of World War II represented the most important intelligence resource on the Soviet Union. Only a handful of intelligence officials on both sides of the Atlantic were in on the secret, yet by 1949, it was clear that the Russians were carrying out a massive and systematic overhaul of their cipher systems. Obviously, somebody had tipped them off, and what was worse, that somebody had to be very highly placed. As a result, there was a dramatic improvement in

Soviet signals security, and the Russian traffic became unreadable.

More publicized evidence came in 1951, when Maclean, an MI5 and FBI net closing around him, suddenly fled to Moscow in the company of an ex-British Foreign Office official, Guy Burgess. It was the flight of Burgess that caused the most consternation, for there was absolutely no suspicion attached to his name; who had warned him that the impending arrest of Maclean would lead counterintelligence agents inevitably to another Soviet mole named Guy Burgess?

FBI Director J. Edgar Hoover's suspicions focused on the man who must have seemed at that point the unlikeliest of suspects—H.A.R. "Kim" Philby, head of MI6's Section IX (Eastern Europe and the Soviet Union), then working in Washington, D.C., as liaison between British and American intelligence. An engaging man who seemed to know everybody in the intelligence trade, Philby was on a first-name basis with virtually all high-level CIA officials, whom he was supposed to be instructing in the arts of counterintelligence and infiltration of agents behind the Iron Curtain. The ever-tenacious Hoover, however, was more impressed by some interesting discoveries his agents had made while investigating the Burgess disappearance. For one thing, it turned out that Burgess and Philby had been close friends (in fact, one witness told FBI agents of seeing the men in bed together). Additionally, a review of Burgess's telephone records showed most of his long-distance calls from outside Washington had been made to Philby.

There were two other men who shared Hoover's suspicions, and they were to play significant (and controversial) roles in what was to become an almost unbelievably intricate controversy over the extent of Soviet penetration of Western intelligence.

One was James Jesus Angleton, head of counterintelligence for the CIA. A thin, gaunt man, Angleton had worked in the X-2 (counterespionage) branch of the OSS during the war, where he first showed his brilliance while running operations in Italy. An esthete devoted to the poetry of Ezra Pound, Angleton's hobbies showed the character traits that made him an uncommonly gifted intelligence officer—making jewelry and raising orchids, both of which require infinite patience, doggedness, subtlety, and devotion to detail. These were perfect traits for a counterintelligence officer, and they were shared by the second man, Arthur Martin of MI5. A former British Army NCO who had worked in communications-interception operations, Martin later joined MI6 but became more intrigued with spy-catcher work, and wound up in MI5. A short, plump man with narrow eyes, Martin seemed to have the perpetually suspicious squint of a policeman. He was no esthete like Angleton, but shared his American counterpart's ability for counterintelligence operations, notably a subtle mind capable of piecing together a series of seemingly disjointed clues. And as did Angleton, he finally came to be consumed by the intricate ambiguities that lie at the heart of such work.

Like the unraveling of a sweater from one loose thread, the defection of Guy Burgess exposed the extensive high-level Soviet network that had been so carefully put together by the Russians many years before. Simple police work put FBI and MI5 hounds on the trail. By questioning everybody who knew or ever had any dealings with Burgess, they were slowly able to piece together the dimensions of the network.

What was finally uncovered showed an intelligence disaster of the first magnitude. Not only had the network managed to cause a wholesale hemorrhage of top-level American and British secrets, but more important in the context of this study, had also managed to frustrate Western intelligence operations against the Soviet Union. Kim Philby was the star of the network, for his position in British intelligence afforded him an unparalleled overview of a wide range of operations, especially when he was posted to Washington, D.C., in 1949. He not only tipped off the Russians about the Bride and Black Jumbos decryptions but also blew a long list of American and

British penetration operations. Philby's position in British intelligence was so secure (he was widely regarded as a candidate for future MI6 director), that no suspicion was attached to any of his actions.

No one, for example, questioned why Philby remained strangely silent during one MI6-CIA meeting in Washington in 1950 when a CIA official wondered aloud whether a group of agents dropped into Lithuania were really sending back all those radio messages, chock-full of valuable intelligence. How was it possible, the CIA man asked, for the agents to operate so openly in the midst of a pervasive KGB and Soviet military presence in that area? Philby said nothing because he knew the answer: He had warned the Russians the agents were coming, allowing the KGB to round them up as they landed, then play back their radio under KGB control.*

The Burgess defection provided the answer to why so much had gone wrong, and the striking thing about the entire Soviet network was the obvious effort by its Soviet taskmasters to get the network's members into various components of intelligence agencies, particularly counterintelligence. As the KGB had demonstrated, it attached the highest priority to infiltration of enemy intelligence services, for such infiltration allowed a double benefit: protecting KGB moles working in other areas, and checkmating any intelligence agency attempts at penetration of the Soviet Union. And from there, the intelligence benefits of such infiltration extended even further. High-level intelligence-agency moles could protect other moles; they could recruit still others, forming a self-perpetuating system; they could plant false clues, leading

*CIA and MI6 realized only much later that Philby had also eliminated a potentially valuable source for Western intelligence. In 1945, Konstantin Volkov, a high-ranking KGB official in Istanbul, indicated to the MI6 station there that he wanted to defect and promised that among other things he would reveal the identity of a high-level KGB mole in British intelligence. The MI6 station dutifully informed London. Philby, the very mole to whom Volkov was referring, assigned himself the case. He tipped off the Russians, who disposed of Volkov while Philby deliberately took an inordinate amount of time getting to Istanbul. Volkov disappeared, an event Philby explained away by saying that the Russian had been too "indiscreet" in his contact with British intelligence.

counterintelligence astray, and they could carefully control or eliminate intelligence operations against the Soviet Union while ensuring that suspicion did not fall on themselves.

This multispectrum of deception, a hallmark of KGB operations from the days of Dzerzhinsky, was clearly revealed by the activities of the Philby network. Its members concentrated on getting into intelligence agencies, and they were able to score a number of notable successes. Besides Philby, there was Anthony Blunt, who had worked for MI5 during the World War II (he revealed MI5 operatives to the KGB and the existence of a MI6 spy working on the staff of Politburo member Anastas Mikoyan), and Leo Long, who revealed a number of British and American intelligence assets while working for MI5 in Germany.

But the Burgess defection and the resultant rolling up of Philby and the rest of the network did not brighten the bleak record of attempts at intelligence infiltration of the Soviet Union. In fact, things continued to get worse, and there grew within the FBI and the minds of Angleton and Martin a very disturbing possibility: What if the Philby network were only part of a much larger KGB infiltration operation? How many other KGB moles were still operating in Western intelligence, continuing to blow operation after operation?

Not too long after the end of the Philby network in 1951, evidence began to accumulate that there were other KGB moles at work.

The first significant clue came right about the time that Burgess and Maclean fled to Moscow. In Vienna, MI6 agents were congratulating themselves on one of the Cold War's most brilliant intelligence operations. Known as Classification/Lord, it had succeeded in tapping into the main communications cables connecting the Soviet military headquarters for Austria in the old Imperial Hotel with Moscow. MI6 agents had ingeniously run the tap by digging a tunnel under a busy thoroughfare from a shop across the street. The shop, run by MI6, was supposed to be a textile import outlet, although it was actually full of wiretapping gear that intercepted revealing conversations between Vienna and Moscow.

MI6 agents finally had to abandon the operation—a sudden rage in Austria for British tweed caused too many customers to enter the store, disrupting eavesdroppers—but by then, both MI6 and the CIA had already decided to replace the Classification/Lord operation with something more ambitious. The new operation, known as Prince, was a considerable expansion of the Vienna operation. This time, it was proposed that both agencies tap into the even more sensitive communications lines leading from Soviet military headquarters in East Berlin to Moscow.

From the start, the CIA dominated Prince, for it was not only underwriting the $25 million cost of the operation but also providing the significant technological breakthrough that made it all possible in the first place. The technology had solved a central problem of eavesdropping. It had seemed impossible to detect conversations carried over "scrambled" phones—devices that disarranged conversations at the transmitter end and rearranged them at the receiver end to frustrate eavesdroppers. But Carl Nelson, one of the CIA's leading scientific brains, had discovered that a "shadow" of the actual voice transmissions remained for a split second on the telephone line, and he developed special equipment that could recover these traces.

Thus, with great promise, MI6 and CIA agents began digging a fourteen-hundred-foot-long tunnel into East Berlin, using as cover construction of a new American radar base on the western side of the border. On April 25, 1955, the ingenious "Berlin tunnel"—equipped with air conditioning and a host of devices to ensure it would not be discovered—began tapping into Soviet landline communications. A vast ocean of information flowed forth, so much that MI6 had to hastily recruit a small army of 250 Soviet émigrés just to listen and transcribe the eavesdroppers' recordings.

Less than a year later, on April 21, 1956, the Russians

suddenly broke into the tunnel, following what was described as its inadvertent discovery by an East German unit on routine patrol. The Soviets sought to make a grand propaganda show out of the discovery, leading delegations of journalists through the tunnel to witness the American perfidy. The Russians, however, had miscalculated badly; instead of condemnation, the general reaction was admiration for the CIA's ingenuity, and the Russians wound up looking ridiculous.

But there was little rejoicing in the CIA and MI6 over the Russian discomfort, for the tunnel episode raised disturbing questions. The central one: How had the tunnel been discovered? No one believed the Russian version of inadvertent discovery, for a review of the operation proved that the most elaborate precautions had been taken to keep it concealed. Suspicion grew that Prince had been revealed by a KGB mole. Moreover, only two days before the tunnel operation was blown, another important intelligence operation had collapsed.

That one involved a hard-drinking, aging British frogman named Lester "Buster" Crabb, who had worked on a number of missions over the years for MI6. It was proposed that Crabb would carry out a secret underwater reconnaissance of the Soviet cruiser *Ordzlonikidze,* which was berthed in Portsmouth Harbor with two destroyer escorts. The ship, one of the most advanced in the Soviet Navy and the subject of much Western intelligence interest, had brought Soviet Premier Nikita Khrushchev and Red Army Marshal Nikolai Bulganin to their state visit in Great Britain.

The idea for this mission began in the Royal Navy's Department of Naval Intelligence, which tended to see such an operation as routine, since British warships on similar visits to the Soviet Union had noted harbor waters virtually alive with Soviet frogmen the moment they berthed. There was little concern, then, as Crabb dove into the waters of Portsmouth Harbor. But as the hours ticked by with no sign of Crabb, it became clear that something had gone very seriously wrong. MI5 agents, fearing the worst, rushed to the hotel where Crabb had been staying and tore pages out of the guest register as part of a desperate attempt to cover any trace of intelligence-agency involvement. (Perhaps, it was reasoned, Crabb had died in some sort of accident unrelated to the Soviet cruiser, so it was still possible that Crabb's real mission could remain concealed.)

But the Russians made it clear that they knew all about Crabb, and that they were responsible for the headless body of the British frogman that was found several weeks later. When the British Admiralty announced that Crabb was missing—and gave his last location far from the actual spot where he dove—the Russians sent a diplomatic message noting pointedly that perhaps the Admiralty might want to reconsider its "error" in giving the location of Crabb's last dive.

The evidence that both operations had been known to the Russians from the start was now irrefutable. An extensive postmortem of the Prince operation showed that while the eavesdroppers were recording a vast volume of Soviet traffic, it all amounted to a mountain of trivia, with almost nothing of intelligence value. Was it possible that high-ranking Soviet military officers discussed only trivial matters with headquarters in Moscow? No, and there was little doubt that they had been alerted beforehand not to discuss anything sensitive over the tapped lines.

But the question was: Who had revealed those operations to Moscow Central?

six

THE MOLE WARS (II)

The enemy I knew almost like my own
side. I risked myself among them a
hundred times, to *learn.*

—LAWRENCE OF ARABIA

"WE'VE GOT A MOLE, JIM," says the old spymaster in John le
Carré's *Tinker, Tailor, Soldier, Spy,* and there is no word that
strikes such dread in an intelligence service. Like a cancer, a
mole inside an intelligence agency causes a rot that is invisible
from the outside, while inside, the entire structure is gradually crumbling away. Agents are being killed or captured,
intelligence collected from the other side is a hopeless mess
of deceptive half-truths and lies, and the intelligence service
comes to be in effect a tool of the opposition.

The Philby case suggested clearly that the rot afflicting
Western intelligence agencies was in an advanced stage, but
had the problem been eradicated in 1951? Clearly not, for
only the presence of other moles seemed to explain the circumstances under which every single important intelligence
operation directed against the Soviet Union after 1951 had
failed. Elaborate postmortems over the failure of these operations revealed a disturbing pattern: On each occasion, either
the Russians knew beforehand or learned about them shortly
after they began.

Intelligence services tend to shy away from the implications of such conclusions, for damaging as moles may be, the process of tracking them down can be even worse. The problem is that a "mole hunt" is an exercise in triangulation; counterintelligence agents begin with the assumption that *anybody* can be the traitor. The hunt, featuring elaborate cross-checking of every possible aspect of the careers and personal backgrounds of all intelligence operatives, is conducive to paranoia and suspicion, an atmosphere that can paralyze an intelligence agency just as surely as moles. For that reason, almost any rationale or bit of evidence, however flimsy, is advanced to explain the consistent failure of so many operations. In the case of Prince, what about all those Soviet émigrés recruited suddenly to handle the Prince traffic? Might one of them have tipped off the KGB? And perhaps Crabb had been too obvious; maybe the Russians realized that MI6 would try such a stunt and were prepared for it?

Such explanations were tempting, for they offered reasons for the shambles that Western intelligence operations against the Soviet Union had become. Moreover, they were explanations that avoided the distasteful (and to some intelligence officers unthinkable) prospect of moles at work.

But in 1955 came convincing evidence that the unthinkable was fact.

It began with what seemed to be a very obvious KGB provocation: Lieutenant Colonel Petr Popov of the GRU volunteered his services to the CIA one spring day in 1953 by dropping a handwritten note into the car of an American diplomat in Berlin. The CIA moved cautiously, and assigned Popov to George Kisvalter, its leading handler of Soviet defectors (and the man who was to play an important role in the case of Oleg Penkovsky some years later). Kisvalter at that point, however, had only been in the CIA's SR (Soviet Russia) Division two years. But despite his junior status, Kisvalter, who had been born in Russia and spoke four languages, was a man of decisive opinions—and he decided quickly that Popov was genuine. Kisvalter aimed straight for Popov's most valuable asset. The Russian knew the cryptonyms of 370 Soviet "illegals" (KGB slang for agents operating under nondiplomatic cover), information that led to the uncovering of a number of GRU rings in the West.

As the only high-level source operating for the CIA and MI6 inside the Soviet intelligence apparatus, Popov was carefully protected. Only a small number of CIA and MI6 officials were aware of Popov's existence, and fewer still knew that Popov had agreed to work as a double agent for the CIA once he was routinely rotated back to Moscow, at which point he would become what was thought to be the West's first really important mole.

In 1955, Popov was ordered back to Moscow, news that he imparted by secretly handing a letter to a member of a British military mission touring East Germany, with a request that it be forwarded to the CIA. The British officer in turn gave it to the MI6 station in Berlin, which then forwarded it to the CIA, a presumably safe route.

In Moscow, Popov was assigned to one of the CIA's most experienced and capable case officers under diplomatic cover in Moscow, Russell Langelle, who worked out a complicated system of dead drops and contact meetings, during which Popov conveyed his information. Langelle ran this dangerous operation for nearly three years until 1959, when he and Popov were arrested by the KGB on a Moscow bus while allegedly "exchanging papers." Charged with espionage, Langelle was ordered to leave the country, but Popov suffered a more horrible fate. Sentenced to death, he was slowly fed live into a blazing furnace while his GRU colleagues were forced to watch.

The loss of Popov, a source treated with the care of a crown jewel, touched off an extensive postmortem: How did the KGB find out about this critically important source? There was the possibility of a KGB mole, of course, but there were also many other possible answers. A review of every step of the Popov case noted several points where something might have gone wrong. First, the letter in which Popov announced his posting back to Moscow had been given to the MI6 station in Berlin, where it was handled by one of MI6's best officers, George Blake. Had Blake been indiscreet somehow? Then there was the matter of Langelle; he was considered a very effective case officer, but given the KGB's thoroughness, it could be that the Russians simply had Langelle under intense surveillance and noticed a meeting between the CIA agent and Popov. More intriguing was the matter of the FBI. At one point, Popov had revealed that a man-and-wife team of GRU illegals was about to enter the United States. Once they arrived, a large-scale FBI surveillance operation trailed them at every moment. But the team suddenly went back to the Soviet Union, apparently having aborted an intelligence mission. Was it possible that they had noticed the FBI surveillance, despite the bureau's insistence that its watchers had not been spotted? Such surveillance, reported to Moscow, would have told the Russians that the dispatch of the agents had been betrayed to the Americans by one of the few intelligence officials connected with the operation.

All these possibilities existed, yet there was one nagging clue that did not seem to fit. Langelle reported that in one of his last meetings with Popov, in a Moscow restaurant, the Russian led him into the men's room, where he silently made whirling motions with his hands. Langelle understood immediately: Popov was wired with a tape recorder. Then Popov ripped off a large bandage from his hand; underneath were several strips of paper, which contained a message to the effect that the KGB had caught on to him, had subjected him to terrible torture to find out what he had told the CIA, and was now "playing" him out to hoodwink the agency. (Popov had deliberately slashed his hand so that he could conceal those strips underneath.)

This incident pointed to a more ominous explanation for Popov's uncovering, although there was no way of knowing how long the KGB had known about Popov. Still, they had *known,* which at least indicated that a mole had betrayed him.

Not everyone accepted this possibility, for its implications were severe. A mole someplace in Western intelligence, either in MI6 or the CIA, was in a position to betray even the most secret operations.

But about the same time as Popov's execution, undeniable proof arrived that the operation indeed had been betrayed by a mole. And it came in the form of one of the CIA's most unusual cases.

He called himself *Heckenschütze*, "Sniper," the name signed to an extraordinary letter that arrived at the U.S. Embassy in Berne, Switzerland. Addressed to J. Edgar Hoover, the letter was written in German and announced the author's willingness to give intelligence to the Americans. A series of thirteen typed letters followed over the next year, each one containing a few intelligence gems, mostly dealing with KGB operations in Western Europe. The CIA, quite naturally, was skeptical, since it had no idea of the identity of *Heckenschütze*, where he was from, and how he knew about such KGB secrets. CIA scientists carried out an exhaustive analysis of the letters, finally concluding that the writer was not Russian, that the typewriter was made in Europe, and that the paper had been manufactured in Eastern Europe. Apparently, he was an intelligence officer working in Eastern Europe.

But whoever he was, *Heckenschütze* obviously was in a position to know, because the information contained in his letters turned out to be accurate. Among other items, he revealed the presence of a KGB spy in the British Admiralty, a KGB illegal running a spy ring that collected Admiralty secrets, and, most intriguing to Hoover and the FBI, two other KGB illegals, operating in England, named Peter and Helen Kroger—which turned out to be new identities created by the KGB for two American citizens, Morris and Lona Cohen. The FBI had been searching for the Cohens for years, ever since they had fled the United States in 1951, when the FBI found out they were part of the Rosenberg spy ring.

But however impressive to the FBI and MI5 these cases

might be, to Angleton there was much less here than met the eye. As Angleton argued, *Heckenschütze* was revealing a number of small fish, low-level agents whose utility was limited anyway. Very possibly, Angleton pointed out, the mysterious correspondent was part of a larger KGB deception operation designed to build up his bona fides, to the point where he became completely trusted by the CIA—and then he would begin to feed the agency false intelligence (most often called "disinformation" in intelligence parlance).

Angleton got a chance to test his belief in December 1960 when *Heckenschütze* suddenly turned up unannounced in West Berlin, with his mistress, and offered to defect. He turned out to be Michal Goleniewski, a high-ranking Polish intelligence officer. The blustery Goleniewski cut quite a figure: A barrel-chested man with a large flourish of a mustache, he reminded his CIA handlers of a cavalry officer straight out of the nineteenth century.

Taken to Ashford, then the CIA's most important safe house, on a Maryland farm, Goleniewski began a series of debriefings that astonished his CIA listeners. What he had revealed in his letters turned out to be chicken feed; Sniper now began playing his high cards. For starters, he informed his debriefers that inside a tree in Warsaw he had hidden a cache of three hundred microfilms that contained "interesting information." In fact, the material, recovered by a CIA team in the Polish capital, turned out to be devastating, for it revealed that one of MI6's most important officers was a KGB mole.

His name was George Blake, the very same MI6 officer who had handled the Popov letter and thus revealed the CIA's mole to the KGB. Worse, it was further revealed that Blake had blown the Berlin tunnel operation to the Russians, as well as the Crabb mission, plus a long string of MI6 and CIA agents working in East Germany and Eastern Europe.

The news could not have been more devastating. Simply stated, it meant that CIA and MI6 intelligence operations originating in Berlin against the Soviet Union had been betrayed to the KGB as soon as they had started. Even more significant, the Blake case showed the extraordinarily patient efforts the KGB undertook to build up their moles inside Western intelligence. Blake, considered a talented intelligence officer, had been captured during the Korean War while under cover as a diplomat at the British Legation in Seoul. Later cited for his courage and leadership during a horrifying captivity in North Korea and Manchuria, Blake was a genuine hero marked for great things. Yet, despite his experience with Communist brutality, he had been recruited into Soviet intelligence—according to some speculation, he had been brainwashed into such a role during his Manchurian captivity. (Richard Condon's famous novel *The Manchurian Candidate* is partially based on this incident.)

However recruited, Blake was almost impossible to spot as a KGB operative, and it required a defector's irrefutable evidence to reveal his double role. An even more disturbing pattern emerged in another revelation by Goleniewski: Israel Beer, a close friend and aide of Israeli Premier David Ben-Gurion, involved with many aspects of Israel's defense and intelligence apparatus, was a KGB mole. Shocked Israeli counterintelligence agents followed up the lead and caught Beer red-handed as he tried to transfer a briefcase of top-secret documents to a KGB contact. But there was even more dismay when the counterintelligence agents made the unsettling discovery that they had caught a phantom; Israel Beer did not exist. An exhaustive check into Beer's background revealed that virtually every aspect of his life story was false, the result of a "legend" carefully constructed by the KGB. The real Israel Beer apparently died in Austria during the 1920s, and the phony Israel Beer assumed his identity. Then who was the man caught by counterintelligence agents? Only "Israel Beer" knew the answer, but he died in an Israeli prison in 1968 without ever saying who he really was.

Like Krivitsky, Gouzenko, and others before him, Goleniewski took pains to warn his newfound Western protectors that they had badly underestimated the extent of KGB penetration of their intelligence services. Moreover, they had underestimated its depth; as he noted, the major moles uncovered thus far showed a common pattern of lengthy and painstaking planning. The Beer case, for example, showed that the Soviets had spent nearly thirty years on the care and feeding of its mole, to the point where he could burrow deep inside Israel's secrets.*

Goleniewski was right, but it took another important Soviet defector to make the lesson sink in. And what he had to say was to rock Western intelligence to its foundations.

The CIA had known about Colonel Anatoli Golitsin of the KGB for quite some time, ever since 1954 when a KGB counterintelligence officer named Petr Deriabin defected in Vienna. During his CIA debriefings, Deriabin went through the standard exercise of identifying KGB officers in Vienna who he thought were potential defectors. Deriabin put Golitsin high on the list, pointing out that he was in a very difficult marriage and did not get along with his wife, Svetlana. Further, Deriabin noted, Golitsin was an obnoxious personality who was hated by his colleagues. Clearly, he was an unhappy man, the perfect candidate for defection.

The CIA set in motion a plan to induce such a defection, but before it could act, Golitsin was suddenly reassigned to KGB headquarters in Moscow. And there he remained for the next six years, until 1960 when, under the alias of Anatoli Klimov, he was assigned to the Soviet Embassy in Helsinki. CIA interest perked up, but before the agency could make a

---

*Goleniewski, however, began to lose credibility at this point. He informed his startled CIA case officers that he was in fact the only surviving member of the Romanov royal family, and as the czarevitch, asked CIA support for his plan to claim the throne of Russia. He also insisted, without proof, that Henry Kissinger was a Soviet mole. Gradually, Goleniewski drifted under the influence of the right wing of the U.S. intelligence community and the John Birch Society, which supported his claim to the Russian throne. In 1964, by then ignored by the CIA establishment, he was married in a Russian Orthodox Church ceremony under the name Aleksei Nikolaevich Romanov.

move, Golitsin acted. This time, he casually turned up one December night in 1961 on the doorstep of the CIA station chief's house, and announced his intention to defect. To prove his bona fides, Golitsin brought with him a list of all KGB operatives working in the Helsinki embassy, and promised to reveal the identities of KGB illegals around the world.

Golitsin wound up at Ashford, but if the CIA thought Goleniewski was a problem with his talk of being the czar's son, he was nothing compared to the trouble that Golitsin represented. Golitsin treated his debriefers like idiots, insisting they knew nothing about intelligence work. He claimed there were KGB moles everywhere, and refused to talk with any CIA man who spoke Russian on the grounds that the agency's entire SR Division was "tainted."

Code-named AE/Ladle, Golitsin was unlike any Russian with whom the CIA had ever dealt, and the agency was quite unprepared for such a character. The CIA put up with the abuse only because, when Golitsin began talking, he exploded a series of bombshells.

The first shock was that Golitsin had incredibly detailed knowledge about the inside workings of virtually every Western intelligence service. How could that be? Because, Golitsin said, every intelligence service had been completely penetrated by the KGB, which for years had been able to frustrate intelligence operations directed at the Soviet Union. And the rest of them had been manipulated by the KGB, Golitsin insisted. He ticked off the details:

- French intelligence was completely run by the KGB via a ring of moles code-named Sapphire, which had also penetrated the French government. The ring included high-level government and intelligence officials. When this astonishing assertion encountered some skepticism, Golitsin agreed to a test. He was presented with a large stack of NATO top-secret documents, some of which, he was told, included clever forgeries. He was to go through the stack and pick out the genuine ones. Golitsin slowly worked his way through the stack, unerringly picking out the genuine documents. Child's play, Golitsin told his shocked debriefers, for he had already seen the genuine documents in Moscow, where they had been sent by the Sapphire moles.*

- British intelligence was also completely penetrated. Philby was part of what the KGB called "the ring of five," controlled by KGB officer Yuri Moldin, a specialist in running homosexual agents. Further, British military and government operations were also extensively penetrated by the KGB.

- Canada's intelligence and government agencies were penetrated, and the Canadian ambassador to Moscow had become a KGB spy after being caught in a KGB-sponsored homosexual blackmail scheme.

- The West German intelligence service was penetrated by two KGB moles code-named Peter and Paul, who worked in high-level positions that enabled them to tip off Moscow about every operation directed eastward.

And on and on it went, a depressing recitation of KGB penetrations of Western intelligence, penetrations so pervasive and intricate, it appeared that Moscow had been manipulating those services for years. That was precisely Golitsin's point. Neither the United States nor its allies had the slightest grasp of the real depth of the KGB penetrations, and only an unprecedented major effort would root them out once and for all, followed by another even more extensive effort to "moleproof" Western intelligence.

To that end, Golitsin proposed the startling idea that a "special intelligence research department" be created by the CIA at a cost of $30 million, to be headed, he modestly suggested, by himself. Golitsin also insisted that he be granted a

*Leon Uris's novel *Topaz* (and the Alfred Hitchcock movie of the same name) is a fictional account of Golitsin, who is called "Boris Kuznetov" in the book.

personal audience with President Kennedy to explain the necessity for his proposal. However, the CIA began stalling its increasingly troublesome star defector, an attitude that made Golitsin sullen and uncooperative.

At this point, Golitsin passed exclusively into the hands of Angleton and his chief assistant, Raymond Rocca; only these two men, the Russian insisted, really grasped the dimensions of what he was saying. He also found another kindred soul in Arthur Martin of MI5, who had led a delegation of British intelligence officials to Washington to hear Golitsin's disclosures. If Angleton had been disturbed by Golitsin's revelations, Martin was positively horrified, for Golitsin told him in effect that both MI6 and MI5 had become jokes to the KGB, so thoroughly had they been penetrated. Great Britain had no intelligence service at all, Golitsin claimed; it was all run by the KGB.

Golitsin—code-named Kago by Martin and MI5—gave plenty of specifics, including the fact that a senior civil servant in the British Admiralty was passing secrets to the Russians, and that another senior civil servant had been inveigled into spying by his Yugoslavian mistress, actually a KGB agent. But this was small potatoes, Kago insisted; the real effort should be directed at analyzing why so many MI6 operations against the Soviet Union had been aborted, and why MI5 counterespionage operations against the KGB often went wrong.

Golitsin then proceeded to dazzle Martin and a small, selected circle of trusted MI5 and MI6 officials with some insights into the intricate subtleties of KGB penetration operations. Martin and his circle—collected into an *ad hoc* committee code-named Fluency—found that every one of their assumptions about their ability to combat the KGB was wrong. As they discovered, they had missed a lot of forests while looking at the trees. Consider, Golitsin lectured, why MI5 had not been able to recruit a single Soviet defector since the end of World War II, despite the fact that MI5 had run the brilliant "double-cross system" during the war, under which every German spy sent into England had been captured

WARRIORS OF THE NIGHT

and then doubled. The reason, Golitsin said, was that the Russians were aware of the success of the double-cross system, and took great pains to ensure that it would not be directed at themselves. They carefully debriefed Abwehr officers they had captured, isolating and thoroughly analyzing the elements that caused German intelligence to believe the false information being fed by turned German spies from England. And armed with that information, Golitsin pointed out, the KGB was able to frustrate all British attempts to induce defectors; the KGB used the attempts to develop pipelines into British intelligence, allowing their agents to become doubled, but then re-doubling them.

It was skull-cracking stuff in its complexity, but Golitsin had even more disturbing revelations. The most unsettling centered on the cases in which MI5 took great pride, the assorted Soviet spy rings and individual agents they had rolled up. Often, Golitsin said, such success was a deceptive illusion; agents were sometimes deliberately given away (called "discards" in the intelligence trade) to protect other, more important agents or to boost the stature of moles within the intelligence services. For example, Golitsin noted, MI5 had followed up his lead and managed to catch William Vassal, a senior official (and KGB spy) in the British Admiralty. But Vassal's case officer had fled England six days before Vassal's arrest; how could he possibly have known of the impending arrest unless a KGB mole someplace inside MI5 told him? Other espionage cases showed a similar dynamic. Some spies had been caught, but more important spies and case officers had always managed to flee before the arrests took place. Clearly, they were being tipped off ahead of time.

Subsequent events seemed to bear out Golitsin's contention, most notably in the long-simmering case of Kim Philby.

Philby had been forced to resign from MI6 in 1951, following the suspicion clouding his name in the wake of the Burgess-Maclean defections. Still, there was no solid proof against him, and Philby even held a press conference in 1955 to announce his "vindication" by British Prime Minister Harold Macmillan.* But by 1962, armed with the new revelations from Golitsin, MI5 sought to arrest Philby at last. The plan was to persuade Philby to accept a deal. In exchange for telling all he knew about KGB moles in England, he would be spared prosecution and a long prison sentence. (It was believed that the stiff forty-two-year prison sentence handed out to George Blake might serve as inducement for Philby's cooperation.)

High hopes were attached to this plan, for if it worked, then a Philby confession might clear up, once and for all, the question of KGB moles in British intelligence. Initially, at least, the plan seemed destined for success. Nicholas Elliott, an MI6 officer and longtime friend of Philby, was dispatched in late 1962 to Beirut, where Philby was then living and working. Elliott conveyed the offer of immunity, and to his surprise, Philby immediately agreed and gave him a limited confession. Philby further agreed to wind up his affairs in Beirut and then come to London for extensive debriefings.

But only a week later, Philby disappeared, subsequently turning up in Moscow. This turn of events seemed to confirm the darkest of Golitsin's warnings. Obviously, Philby and the KGB knew all about the arrival of Elliott. Philby gave a limited confession to lull MI5, and then slipped away, spirited out of Beirut by the Russians, who feared what a Philby under the control of MI5 interrogators might reveal. It seemed impossible. Since only a small group of five senior British intelligence officials knew about the plan concerning Philby, that meant at least one of them was a KGB mole. Further, Martin learned that CIA agents in Beirut had noted the sudden arrival (and equally sudden departure) in that city of Yuri Moldin, Philby's

---

*This "vindication" came about because of an abortive plan by J. Edgar Hoover to force the British to arrest Philby. Disgusted by what he perceived as an attempt by the British establishment to protect Philby, Hoover tried to force the issue by leaking a newspaper report that Philby was the "third man" in the Burgess-Maclean case. The newspaper story caused an outcry in England, and Macmillan, in response to a question in Parliament, was compelled to say Philby was *not* the third man, although at that point he knew that Philby was a KGB mole. But neither Macmillan nor MI5 had any proof at that point, certainly not enough to try him in court.

old case officer. It was clear that Moldin, alerted by the KGB mole in British intelligence, had gone to Beirut hurriedly to consult with Philby about the British plan, hatched a limited confession to keep the hounds temporarily at bay, then arranged for Philby to be spirited to Moscow. And that decision had been reached only after Philby's conversation with Elliott, which the KGB used to divine how much the British knew at that point about Philby and other moles. Elliott provided further confirmation, noting that Philby seemed to be prepared for him, and actually anticipated some questions.

And so the conviction hardened in Martin's mind that he was looking for a major KGB mole of very high rank, supported by a series of smaller moles, all very much in keeping with the scenario outlined by Golitsin. The Russian's stock had soared with Martin and the Fluency group, and while the CIA had no interest in Golitsin's plan for some sort of mole-hunt superagency, Martin agreed to set him up in England, where he would work with Fluency in uncovering KGB moles.

Events had enhanced Golitsin's reputation among the mole hunters to the point where he had become something of a demigod. In England, he moved from hotel to hotel under elaborate security, occasionally phoning Martin for secret meetings. At those meetings, there was what can only be called a religious atmosphere. Martin and his fellow hunters waited in respectful, hushed silence as the former KGB colonel settled himself in comfortably, then began reading through documents and files. Pudgy, with heavy jowls and a short military haircut, Golitsin exuded an air of omniscience, accentuated by his habit of long silences as he studied the files. "Deception," he would suddenly announce in his heavy Ukrainian accent after finishing one file, dismissing an elaborate MI5 or MI6 effort as merely a KGB manipulation. On other occasions, he would fire out questions and advice, much like a sergeant ordering privates around.

Golitsin had been in England only a few months when a London newspaper story revealed his presence, compelling him to return to the United States. There, Angleton and his deputies seemed to be the only CIA officials eager to see him back, for in truth, Golitsin was distinctly unwelcome throughout much of the agency. This was partly because Golitsin's tortuous accounts were regarded in many quarters as the hopelessly complicated musings of a paranoid. It was all well and good to scurry around in Great Britain, searching for what were clearly moles everywhere, but the much more stringent personnel-security systems for American intelligence meant that large-scale infiltration by the KGB was nearly impossible. Therefore, it was argued, the hunt for moles was a fruitless and disruptive exercise.

Against this line of argument Angleton could marshal two important facts. First, every other Western intelligence agency had been penetrated by the KGB; wasn't it reasonable to conclude that the KGB had attached the highest priority to infiltrating the CIA, its most powerful enemy? And second, American intelligence on the Soviet Union had been marked by a consistent record of failure; could all those failures be ascribed to inefficiency or bad luck? American intelligence was the victim of a fatal self-delusion, Angleton believed. Convinced of its ability to screen intelligence personnel (all CIA officers were required to take an annual lie-detector test) and thus keep out any KGB moles, it had become blind to the very clear indications from Golitsin that there was something seriously wrong. And the CIA, especially, seemed to suffer from a mole myopia, even when confronted with direct evidence that its most important operations were being blown. And one such unmistakable indication occurred in the case of Oleg Penkovsky.

Penkovsky had become a joint CIA-MI6 operation, which was run under the most stringent security precautions. Penkovsky's material was given a special CIA code, with access restricted to a small number of officials. Furthermore, even more elaborate precautions were used to obtain his material. Assigned to a post in Moscow in late 1961, Penkovsky communicated only via a series of innocuous postcards mailed anonymously to an MI6 cover address in London. To announce when a dead drop was ready, Penkovsky would call the American Embassy in Moscow with a previously arranged number of rings, then hang up. Dead drops were never used more than once, and to convey really important material, a very safe method of transfer was worked out. The key to the transfer was Janet Chisholm, wife of Roderick Chisholm, an MI6 case officer working under diplomatic cover in the Moscow embassy. She would regularly take her two small children for a walk. While out strolling through the park, they would be approached by a Russian man who would stop to remark on the loveliness of the children; sometimes he would give them some candy. And while this charming tableau was being enacted, the Russian man—actually Oleg Penkovsky—would slip batches of microfilm to Mrs. Chisholm.

Yet, despite these elaborate security precautions, as early as January, 1962, Penkovsky reported via one of his postcards that the KGB was onto him and had been monitoring his encounters with Mrs. Chisholm. He was not arrested until November, probably because the KGB had to move very carefully. Penkovsky was a senior government official, and incontrovertible proof was required before it dared move against him. Nevertheless, from the CIA standpoint, the Penkovsky case was a disaster. The most valuable human-intelligence source inside the Soviet Union had been nailed by the KGB only a short while after he had begun giving the CIA the best intelligence it had ever received from inside Russia. What had gone wrong? Postmortems could not find a single flaw in the way the Penkovsky operation had been handled, nor had any of the case officers involved made any mistakes. True, Penkovsky had been reckless—at one point, he had tried to pass microfilms during a July 4 party at the U.S. Embassy in Moscow—but by then the KGB knew about him, anyway.

The value of Penkovsky as an intelligence source would be difficult to overestimate. As Sir Dick White, head of MI6, said in a private discussion with his officers, "I would stress to all of you that if proof were needed, this operation has demonstrated beyond all doubt the prime importance of the human-intelligence source, handled with professional skill and expertise."

He was right, but the question remained: Had Penkovsky been uncovered through luck, or had the KGB been tipped off by a mole? The official verdict was luck—possibly the KGB's pervasive surveillance of Chisholm (they knew he was an MI6 agent) had revealed the connection between Mrs. Chisholm's walks and Penkovsky, or perhaps the KGB had been able to spot a particular dead drop.

But Golitsin had another explanation, and for the first time he mentioned a code word that ultimately was to tear the CIA apart. That word was Sasha.

According to Golitsin, Sasha was the KGB code name for its most important mole—a high-ranking official of the CIA who for years had been keeping Moscow informed about the agency's operations against the Soviet Union. In that position, Golitsin claimed, Sasha was directly responsible for the CIA's abysmal intelligence record. Golitsin had no proof that Sasha existed; the mole's presence was a postulate the Russian had elevated to fact. In a surprising move for a man who had always demonstrated cautious skepticism when dealing with revelations by Soviet defectors, Angleton came to accept Sasha's existence as gospel. In the process, Angleton descended into a Byzantine world of conspiracies and shadows, where nothing was as it seemed, where black was white and where suspicion was often considered sufficient proof of guilt.

How complicated the Sasha matter promised to become was underscored by another Golitsin assertion—that the KGB, alarmed over his revelations, would introduce a new twist into the game by producing false defectors whose chief assignment would be to deflect suspicion from Sasha and in the process cast as much doubt as possible on Golitsin himself.

Only Angleton took this assertion seriously, but just as

Golitsin predicted, several new Soviet defectors appeared, and what they had to say indicated that perhaps Golitsin had been right after all.

The first was a KGB officer named Yuri Nosenko, who in 1962 contacted the CIA in Geneva, Switzerland, while attached to the Soviet delegation for disarmament talks. Code-named AE/Foxtrot, he delivered a few items of intelligence, but among them was a claim that struck Angleton as pure disinformation—Nosenko claimed that Popov had not been betrayed by FBI surveillance of the two illegals in New York, or by a mole, but by routine KGB surveillance of known CIA agents attached to the U.S. Embassy in Moscow. That surveillance, Nosenko claimed, had spotted a CIA man emptying dead drops, so they had kept that agent under close watch until they could discover which Russian was filling those dead drops. As Angleton was aware, that story was nonsense; Popov had indicated at one meeting with his CIA contact, long before his arrest, that he was under KGB control, meaning that Nosenko's version was a lie. It was a version that the KGB obviously had concocted, but it did not include Popov's meeting with his CIA contact *because the KGB did not know about it.* However, the question was: Why would the KGB go through so much trouble to convince the CIA that its first important human-intelligence source in the Soviet Union had been blown by a routine surveillance? Because, Angleton reasoned, the KGB wanted to deflect attention away from Sasha.

That suspicion hardened when Nosenko, after formally defecting from the Soviet Union some months after his first contact with the CIA, told his debriefers that Viktor Kovshuk, one of the KGB's most senior operatives and a specialist on operations in the United States, had made a special trip to Washington, D.C., in 1957. The purpose of the trip, Nosenko claimed, was to meet with a KGB agent code-named Andrey, a U.S. Army sergeant who had been turned by the KGB while working at the American Embassy in Moscow. To Angleton, the story was a fairy tale; there was no way so senior an operative as Kovshuk would travel all the way to Washington simply to meet with a low-level agent. What was Kovshuk doing on that trip? Meeting with Sasha, Golitsin insisted; only a meeting with so high level a source justified such a journey.

Nosenko finally was to become the most publicized Soviet defector in American history, mostly because his assertion that the KGB had no involvement with Lee Harvey Oswald during the assassin's stay in the Soviet Union figured prominently in a new congressional probe of the Kennedy assassination. (Another KGB disinformation attempt, Angleton concluded, since the KGB obviously would have sought what Oswald knew about the U-2; he had served at one point during his Marine Corps hitch at a U-2 base in Japan.) Most important, the Nosenko case illustrated the great turmoil in which the CIA found itself as a result of the volatile combination of Angleton's suspicions, his obsessive hunt for Sasha, defectors telling contradictory accounts, and a continuing frustration over the failure of the CIA's human-intelligence operations.

The frustration was illustrated by the handling of the Nosenko case, which included a lengthy incarceration for the Russian, accompanied by what was apparently a program of psychological torture designed to make him confess what Angleton was already convinced was true: Yuri Nosenko was a KGB false defector, designed to sow as much confusion in the CIA as possible, while at the same time deflecting attention from the real high-level moles. Angleton was convinced, not only because of the growing list of inconsistencies in Nosenko's story, but also because the KGB made several moves to bolster his credentials. One such move involved two Soviet diplomats at the United Nations, code-named Fedora and Top Hat, who approached the FBI and began passing along a few intelligence tidbits. Their real purpose, however, was to underwrite Nosenko, leaking a number of details to convince their debriefers that Nosenko was the genuine article.

The greater the effort made by Top Hat and Fedora to

help Nosenko, the more Angleton was convinced that No-senko was part of an intricate KGB chess game to convince the Americans that Sasha did not exist. If such a chess game was under way, then that game raised a significant point: The KGB had already demonstrated its ability to frustrate human-intelligence operations, and was now apparently engaged in wrecking the one remaining human-intelligence source for Western intelligence, namely, defectors. That would be truly a major coup for the Russians, for defectors had been their weak point for some years. The weakness grew out of the very nature of Soviet intelligence, which was largely a closed world, cut off from the mainstream of Soviet society. And in this tight world, which skimmed off the elite of the Soviet leadership, there were surprisingly few office secrets, since its members lived, worked, played, and spoke only with each other. These *Kegebeshniki,* as the members of the privileged KGB elite liked to call themselves, formed a homogeneous cadre that had given the Soviet state a truly awesome intelligence capability.

As a result, if one member of that closed club became disillusioned and decided to defect, he would cause horrendous damage, given the wide range of operational intelligence to which he had been exposed. For that reason, even a low-ranking defector, such as the cipher clerk Igor Gouzenko, could reveal an astonishing amount of intelligence. The Nosenko and Top Hat/Fedora episodes indicated that the KGB had decided to close up this potential hemorrhage by introducing a new twist into the game: simply flooding Western intelligence with fake defectors as soon as a real defector showed up. That way, Western intelligence would become hopelessly confused, trying to sort out who was genuine and who was not.

If the KGB's central goal in this exercise was to confuse its opponents, the Russians succeeded admirably, for both the CIA and MI6 were thrown into turmoil over the whole question. The central dilemma was that Golitsin and Nosenko could not both be right; one of them was a false defector, creating the problem of trying to sort out the truth. That process was hindered by questions of evidence. Nosenko could claim, for example, that the KGB never had any interest in Lee Harvey Oswald, an assertion that was not provable, obviously, by double-checking with Moscow. Angleton and other counterintelligence officers were thus reduced to dealing with often-ambiguous circumstantial evidence.

In the case of Golitsin, Angleton came down foursquare on his side, convinced that a very clear pattern had been established. As soon as Golitsin began discussing Sasha, the KGB hurriedly dispatched several false defectors, an operation designed to preoccupy the CIA and cast doubt on the agency's star defector. However, in his eagerness to prove Golitsin right, Angleton made several serious errors of judgment. One was the mistreatment of Nosenko; another was his decimation of the CIA's SR Division, where, Golitsin said, the mole was almost certainly located. Angleton tore the division apart. With no concrete evidence to go on, only suspicion, the division's officers were subjected to elaborate checking that resulted in open accusations of treason against one of them, forced transfer of another, and broad hints that the division's chief himself was a KGB mole. CIA officers were shocked to find that Angleton had permitted Golitsin to pore over top-secret agency personnel and operational files in an attempt to find clues pointing to Sasha, an indiscretion that allowed Angleton's lengthening list of enemies in the agency to claim that his obsession over Sasha was beginning to unhinge his mind. Paranoia became rampant; not only was suspicion focused on several key officers in the SR Division but also on anyone who had ever had any contact with them. The division became paralyzed, a disaster worsened when Angleton contrived to have the division suspended from any role in the recruitment of human-intelligence sources on the Soviet Union.*

---

*A similar, although more low-keyed, concern over KGB moles suddenly erupted concurrently within the FBI's Intelligence Division. Assistant FBI Director

WARRIORS OF THE NIGHT

It all began to descend into farce: Golitsin betrayed increasing symptoms of paranoia, arguing at one point that any CIA officer with a Russian background or Russian language skills was suspect, while Angleton portrayed a gigantic KGB conspiracy that required considerable historical revision—"successful" intelligence and counterintelligence operations in the past might in fact have been KGB manipulations. The final depths were reached when one of Angleton's bureaucratic enemies produced an elaborate report that claimed, perhaps with tongue in cheek, that the KGB mole lurking within the CIA had been positively identified. The mole was James Jesus Angleton, aided and abetted by another mole named Anatoli Golitsin, who together had managed to nearly wreck the agency.

All this was bad enough, but it was positively benign compared with the disruption occurring at the same time inside British intelligence.

Like Angleton, Arthur Martin of MI5 had become convinced that high-level KGB moles existed, although unlike his American counterpart, he had more concrete evidence for their presence. The prime piece of evidence was the Philby case, which indicated almost certainly the presence of a top-level mole who had managed to alert the Russians and Philby.

Martin's suspicions focused, shockingly enough, on two men: his own boss, Roger Hollis, head of MI5, and Hollis's deputy, Graham Mitchell. In this connection, Martin's task was considerably easier than the mole hunt set off by Angleton; his American counterpart was looking for a needle in a haystack, while Martin knew that only five men—including himself and his secretary—knew of the top-secret plan to get Philby. And of the remaining three, one was Sir Dick White, head of MI6, a man Martin discovered was above suspicion.

William C. Sullivan, head of the division, became convinced that there was a KGB mole in the FBI. Sullivan imparted this suspicion privately to friends and some journalists, but never elaborated on the reasons for the suspicion before he was killed in a hunting accident in 1977.

That left Hollis and Mitchell, and Martin received White's approval to begin an investigation of both men.

The mere fact that the investigation took place at all was a tribute to the fears set off by accumulating evidence of KGB penetration of Western intelligence, for an investigation of the head of a nation's counterintelligence service—an American equivalent would be a probe to determine if J. Edgar Hoover had been a KGB agent—was unthinkable under ordinary circumstances. Yet White authorized it, for if the case of Philby and others had taught the British anything, it was that the unthinkable was often too sadly a fact.

Almost immediately, Martin and his sleuths turned up indications that perhaps they had not fallen victim to paranoia. They discovered that Mitchell some years before had approved a security clearance for an émigré atomic scientist, Bruno Pontecorvo, to work on the British nuclear-weapons program. Pontecorvo defected to the Soviet Union in 1950, and as Martin discovered, even the most cursory glance at the scientist's record would have convinced any intelligence officer that the scientist should not have received a security clearance under any circumstances: Virtually every member of his family in Great Britain and Italy was connected with the Communist party, and Pontecorvo himself was widely suspected of being a Communist. Yet Mitchell, an experienced intelligence officer, gave him a security clearance into the highly sensitive nuclear-weapons program, and how many secrets of that program Pontecorvo was able to take with him when he fled to the Soviet Union can only be imagined. Why did Mitchell do it?

There was even worse to come. MI5 agents, searching through Mitchell's garbage, found a discarded sketch map of paths in a park near his home. The map, marked RV (for "rendezvous"?), aroused MI5 suspicions, for it is standard KGB practice to give maps to their sources as guides to secret meetings. In addition, MI5 watchers noted other clues: Mitchell often drove his car aimlessly, a standard practice to avoid surveillance, and was seen often to sit in his office with his head in his hands, as though tormented by some overwhelming problem. There was also the matter of his elaborate evasive actions when leaving the office each night, another standard maneuver to throw off any agents who might be following him.

To Martin, these clues all amounted to unmistakable indications that Mitchell was hiding some sort of deep, dark secret, and the MI5 man thought he knew what it was: Mitchell was a KGB mole. But there was no proof, and Mitchell was allowed to retire quietly from MI5 in 1963 without being confronted by any accusations. Martin then turned to some other aspects of the Philby-network case, in the hope that some loose strands might clear up the mystery.

His first target was Sir John Cairncross, a prominent British Treasury official who had been friends with Guy Burgess during their days together at Cambridge University in the 1930s. In the process of checking up on Cairncross, Martin early in 1964 made an astounding discovery. Papers recovered from a trunk under a bed in Burgess's apartment, following his flight to the Soviet Union in 1951, included some sort of official, handwritten estimates prepared, possibly, by a government official. No one had ever bothered to track down their author, but on a hunch, Martin compared the handwriting on the documents with specimens of Cairncross's handwriting. They matched, and Martin made a quick trip to Cleveland, where Cairncross was lecturing at an American university. Confronted with the handwriting samples, Cairncross freely admitted spying for the Russians for sixteen years, until 1951, after being recruited by Burgess. He denied knowing any others recruited by Burgess, but Martin was convinced there had to be others, and perhaps one of them would lead him to the identity of the high-level mole he was sure existed in the person of either Roger Hollis or Graham Mitchell—or perhaps both.

On his way home from Cleveland, Martin stopped off in Washington, D.C., to pay a courtesy call on his American colleague, William C. Sullivan, head of intelligence for the

FBI. Martin found Sullivan in a morose mood; he was then locked in a bitter bureaucratic struggle with Hoover, and one of the chief sticking points between the two men, Sullivan related, was the question of how to approach counterintelligence operations. Hoover was too secretive and tried to amass too much power for the bureau, Sullivan complained, noting that the FBI director had cut off contact with MI5 because of his bitterness over what he perceived as British ineptitude in the Philby case. Martin then told Sullivan about his encounter with Cairncross, but to his surprise, he found the American strangely unimpressed. Martin was even more surprised when Sullivan told him why. The FBI knew all about Burgess and his friends, for the bureau had a full confession from one of Burgess's recruits, complete with details about other recruits. Hoover was keeping this information from the British out of spite, Sullivan revealed, and went on to explain that Michael Straight, former editor of the *New Republic,* had been nominated in the previous year for a federal arts post. The appointment, which required an FBI background check, compelled Straight to voluntarily reveal to the bureau his past as a spy for the Soviet Union after being recruited while attending Cambridge University in the 1930s.

Martin was now armed with a crucial piece of evidence, and an interview with Straight gave him another one. Straight revealed that the man who had recruited him at Cambridge was Anthony Blunt, by 1964 Sir Anthony Blunt, Surveyor of the Queen's Pictures and a renowned art expert. The revelation was not especially surprising to Martin, for Blunt had been high on a list of MI5 suspects ever since Burgess's defection in 1951. MI5 agents had long suspected that Blunt, as a close friend of Burgess and an avowed Communist in his university days, might have had some role in the Philby-Burgess-Maclean case, but could never prove any connection. However, Straight had provided MI5 with the link, and he agreed to testify if Blunt was put on trial. Blunt, who had been interrogated fruitlessly eleven times between 1951 and 1963, was confronted with Straight's confession and agreed on an arrangement: He would tell all in return for immunity from prosecution.

The debriefing of Blunt cleared up a number of mysteries connected with the Philby case, but Martin focused on any clues Blunt might provide about current high-level KGB moles in British intelligence. One fact to emerge during these debriefings struck Martin with particular force: Blunt during World War II had been an important official of MI5, yet by 1945, the KGB had showed no interest in his continuing in that organization (although they promised to spirit him to the Soviet Union if he should ever face prosecution in England). Martin was especially struck by this lack of interest, because as a counterintelligence officer with years of experience in duelling with the KGB, he found it inconceivable that the Russians would willingly give up a prime source right in the heart of British counterintelligence—*unless they already had an even more important mole inside MI5, thus obviating the use of men with known Communist connections who might later face close questioning on that score.*

Blunt's debriefing set Martin again on the trail of Hollis and Mitchell, for Blunt had revealed that Leo Long, another student recruited at Cambridge in the 1930s, had also become an MI5 official during the war, later rising to become deputy head of military intelligence in Germany and serving until 1951. Now Martin understood why so many cross-border operations had been foiled by the KGB, who always seemed to know when the agents were about to arrive. But it also solidified his suspicions about KGB penetration of MI5: Long had stopped spying for the Soviets in 1951 and, like Blunt, did not meet with any protestations from the KGB. Again, was it not logical to assume that the KGB no longer needed Long, because it already had an even better mole in place?

Martin went after Mitchell, who denied everything. As for the map, he said he had drawn it for his daughter's charity treasure hunt in a local park. He admitted taking evasive actions, but said that was standard procedure, a habit he had acquired over the years as an intelligence officer; the same reason applied to his seemingly aimless driving. And the scene of holding his head in his hands? He was discouraged about a deep rift between himself and his chief, Hollis. Pontecorvo? An honest mistake.

Mitchell would not budge from his explanation, and Hollis, subject subsequently of an extraordinary interview by MI5 agents on whether he was a mole, denied being one. So much for that, but at the same time Martin had been busy exhaustively checking MI5 and MI6 personnel files, looking for clues that would point him in the right direction. In the process, he made a disturbing discovery: Dick Ellis, a senior MI6 officer long involved with operations against the Soviet Union, had been the subject of suspicion during World War II. Questioned about this, Ellis astonished his MI5 interrogators by admitting that he had briefly worked for the Abwehr in 1939 when he was desperate for money—he betrayed a MI6 wiretap inside the German Embassy and revealed the names of MI6 operatives working in London against Abwehr agents. This was, to a certain extent, ancient history, but Martin grasped its implication: knowledge by the KGB of Ellis's dirty little secret would subject him to blackmail. Ellis denied he was ever a Soviet agent, but Martin was not so sure—a note on Ellis's file that former Abwehr officers after the war had revealed his treachery had been prepared by a senior officer of MI6 in 1945.

The man who wrote that note was Kim Philby.

Martin had become obsessed about the KGB mole lurking in British intelligence, whose identity, he was increasingly certain, was Roger Hollis. It was a suspicion accentuated when Hollis suddenly and unceremoniously fired his mole hunter in 1965, arguing that Martin had become a "disruptive influence." In that judgment, Hollis was correct—Martin and his Fluency hounds were sniffing in every back alley and corner of British intelligence in a relentless search for moles that most of their contemporaries believed did not exist. As in the

CIA, the predominant sentiment was that Martin, like Angleton, had become captivated by the arcane conspiracy theories of Golitsin, a master paranoid.

But Martin made the point that the evidence, although not yet conclusive, was compelling that a KGB mole—or perhaps a number of KGB moles—were still busily active in British intelligence, frustrating all operations against the Soviet Union. And however paranoid others might think Golitsin, Martin pointed to some important clues the defector had provided, among them the information that while working at KGB headquarters in Moscow, he had seen an index of important MI5 documents in the KGB's possession. Those documents, Golitsin related, were all dated *after* 1951, which would rule out Blunt or Long or any of the other known moles as suspects.

Unlike Angleton, who was later fired in 1974 from the CIA on the grounds that he, too, was "disruptive," Martin found another intelligence niche—high-level friends in MI6 who sympathized with his mole hunt gave him a job. And in that post, Martin set about to get Roger Hollis and end forever the KGB penetration.

His new line of attack was an echo from the dim past— Igor Gouzenko, by then nearly blind and barely eking out a living on his modest pension from the Canadian government. Martin was intrigued to learn that it was an MI5 operative named Roger Hollis who had been dispatched from London as representative of British intelligence at Gouzenko's debriefing in 1945. Martin contacted Gouzenko in 1972 and read to him Hollis's report on what he had said during that debriefing. Gouzenko listened carefully, then quietly announced that what Hollis had written was not what he had said.

Again, this was not an occurrence to inspire confidence in Hollis's abilities, but it did not amount to evidence of treason, or anything like it. For that, Martin and the Fluency group would need something much more concrete. They never did find it, and Hollis retired in late 1965 with a knighthood (he died in 1973), the case against him unproven. The problem, of course, was that the case was always mired in ambiguity—demonstrably, Hollis was not an especially effective intelligence chief, and it was not for nothing that he was known within his own organization as "Mr. Inertia," an uninspiring and unimaginative bureaucrat. Thus, when so many operations failed, was it because Hollis was incompetent, or because he was *deliberately* incompetent?

No one could answer that sort of question with certitude, and it was this ambiguity that finally ended Martin's mole search.* The same ambiguity confounded Angleton at the CIA. In counterintelligence terms, which amounted to a process of deductive reasoning, he might be convinced that so-and-so was a KGB mole, but how could it be proven? An intelligence officer might run a dozen operations, all of them spectacular failures; did it mean he had failed deliberately? Counterintelligence officers tend not to believe in coincidences, and they become especially suspicious when there are a number of coincidences—such as a succession of operations that appear to be appallingly executed. Was it *really* incompetence?

Not too long after Angleton had been fired, his chief aides reassigned in the CIA's outer reaches, and the counterintelligence division itself virtually atomized, several new attempts by the agency to run human-intelligence operations against the Soviet Union failed spectacularly. And the failures, amounting to a consistent record of disaster, raised some old questions about Angleton's suspicions.

In late 1974, only a short while after Angleton had left the CIA, the agency recruited a low-level, but nevertheless

---

*In the decade following the Great Mole Search, Angleton, Martin, and their former acolytes coalesced into several groups that kept alive the flame of controversy. They served as sources for a number of books and articles about actual or suspected moles in Western intelligence, in the process setting off still more arguments over who was or was not a KGB mole. The arguments are further confused by competing political factions among these groups, exemplified by the publication of an updated version of defector Anatoli Golitsin's two decades' old report, written for the CIA, on KGB deception operations. The publication of the report—arranged by Martin and other former intelligence officers—argues, quixotically, that the Sino-Soviet split and Yugoslavia's break with Moscow were Soviet deception operations.

interesting, source in Moscow. He was Sanaya L. Lipavsky, a Jewish neurosurgeon who claimed to have treated sailors suffering from radiation sickness aboard Soviet nuclear submarines. Additionally, Lipavsky was involved with the Jewish dissident movement, and shared a room with the movement's most noted spokesman, Anatoli Scharansky. Thus the Lipavsky recruitment promised a double benefit. He could reveal a great deal about operational details connected with crews of nuclear submarines, and at the same time provide a direct pipeline into an important dissident group.

For nearly three years, Lipavsky produced interesting intelligence from tidbits he had heard from Soviet nuclear-submarine sailors, and gave even more detailed intelligence on the Jewish dissidents, the latter representing a possibility for recruitment as CIA sources. But in 1977, the KGB struck, and revealed that Lipavsky had been a double agent all along, luring the CIA into a large trap. When it closed, the KGB disclosed that it had not only used its man to funnel false intelligence to the CIA, but also to round up the most important leaders of the dissident movement, notably Scharansky himself. Lipavsky testified at Scharansky's trial that the dissidents had provided him with intelligence for the CIA, an important lever the KGB used to discredit the Jewish dissidents and their movement within the Soviet Union as "spies," not genuine dissidents.

That was bad enough, but around the same time, the CIA suffered another defeat, and this one again revived some of the darker suspicions about a KGB mole operating someplace in American intelligence.

It was a fairly conventional operation, known in the intelligence trade as a "honey trap": A young Soviet cable clerk, far from home in Bogotá, Columbia, was set up with a woman working for the CIA. Their subsequent acrobatics in bed were secretly photographed by CIA agents, who then presented the pictures to the Russian with a standard offer—either agree to provide information to the agency, or the pictures would be shown to his superiors, with resulting disgrace, immediate reassignment to the Soviet Union, probable demotion, the end of a promising career, and who knows what other possible consequences. He agreed, for "nonauthorized" contact with foreigners was strictly forbidden in the Soviet diplomatic service and subject to severe punishment.

Aleksandr Dmitrevich Ogorodnik, the Soviet cable clerk, was a good choice for such an operation, for he was assigned to the Soviet Foreign Ministry's Global Affairs Department, which among other duties processed diplomatic reports from around the world. And among these reports was one particular type of strong interest to the CIA—required annual "assessment reports" by senior Soviet diplomats abroad, which were full of important clues to Soviet intelligence and diplomatic capabilities. Equipped with a CIA-provided "burst" transmitter (a radio that transmitted traffic in super-short electronic bursts, making tracking it very difficult), Ogorodnik was rotated back to Moscow some months later as part of a normal reassignment. Given the code name Trigon, he began to send details of messages that he handled.

But only a few weeks later, the CIA noticed that the quality of his messages began to slip, raising the suspicion that he had been caught by the KGB, which might be operating his transmitter under its control. The CIA kept the game going, however, until 1977, when Trigon sent a blockbuster: details of a secret cable Soviet Ambassador to the United States Anatoli Dobrynin had sent from the Russian Embassy in Washington back to Moscow. According to the cable, Henry Kissinger, in a meeting with Dobrynin in the embassy, told him not to take President Carter's SALT II negotiating position seriously, advising Moscow to wait for a better one.

Trigon's cable set off a furious dispute within the CIA over its genuineness, an argument that raged for nearly a year until further evidence made it clear that Trigon had been caught very early in his double-agent role, and that most of the material he had transmitted was cooked by the KGB. The Kissinger cable episode was designed to reestablish Trigon's bona fides, a not especially bright way of accomplishing that end, since, as Kissinger himself argued, he would hardly be so stupid as to make such a statement in the Soviet Embassy, of all places—known to be fairly alive with microphones.

But that did not end the controversy, for Trigon revived dormant fears of KGB moles, reminiscent of the Sasha episode, although there was a new twist. This time, a group of right-wingers within the U.S. intelligence community leaked stories to the effect that a National Security Council official named David Aaron had blown Trigon to the KGB by discussing the source with a Romanian official during a party; presumably, the Romanian had passed that intelligence on to the Russians. A further implication was that Aaron and similar-minded "liberals" were leaking CIA secrets, thereby exposing intelligence sources.

The claim was utterly without foundation (Aaron was completely cleared in an investigation), but it underscored some of the new tensions straining American intelligence. The strains were connected with the large-scale congressional investigations of the intelligence agencies in 1975 and 1976 that had exposed a long list of inept or illegal operations, leading to the first serious congressional oversight of intelligence-agency performance. But to the more conservative elements in the American intelligence community, the investigations were part of a broad conspiracy directed at U.S. intelligence efforts, a conspiracy that amounted to a KGB-inspired plot to emasculate those efforts through American "dupes" or "disinformation agents" of Moscow. This conspiracy, they argued, represented the real "KGB moles" who had been tearing American intelligence apart for years.

And in the descent to this sort of mindlessness, the great mole hunts, for all intents and purposes, came to an end. With Angleton fired and Martin retired from their respective services, the steam seemed to go out of them; even the continually dismal list of failures in human-intelligence operations brought forth no new mole hunters in the Angleton-Martin tradition. Nobody except the more conservative elements in Western intelligence services, especially the CIA, seemed to care much anymore.

Did Sasha ever exist? Was Roger Hollis—or perhaps another high-ranking official of British intelligence—really a KGB mole? No one outside KGB headquarters knows for sure, and it is possible, as some continue to argue, that the hunt for these alleged moles always amounted to a chase for phantoms, a mad pursuit of our own fears.

Perhaps, although there remains the small pile of evidence—however circumstantial most of it may be—that reasons other than incompetence and inexperience lay behind the nearly total failure of all human-intelligence operations by Western agencies in the past sixty-plus years.

There are those who continued to insist that the real failure in this regard was the inability to recognize the dimension and subtlety of the threat from Dzerzhinsky and his heirs. One of them was an ailing old man who could be seen occasionally on the streets of a small town outside Montreal. Almost totally blind and very sick, Igor Gouzenko every so often during his last few years would travel to Montreal, where he would look up a few old friends and debate the intelligence wars.

Embittered by what he saw as the deliberate failure to heed what he had been saying many years before, Gouzenko harped on his consistent theme: The West had never really learned how to run human-intelligence operations, they were always overmatched by the Soviets, they had never understood the extent of Soviet penetration, and so on.

Those who knew him tolerated these little lectures, for Gouzenko had been a hero those many years ago, when he had defected and opened the first real window into the intricacies of the intelligence war in which the West had suddenly been thrust. But he had long been forgotten; even the mole hunters from the CIA and MI5 didn't come around anymore. He died in March 1983, hardly remembered.

On a bitterly cold day there was a funeral for Igor Gouzenko. Just a few friends showed up for the man known to his neighbors only as an old immigrant with a heavy foreign accent. A clergyman who did not know Gouzenko was hastily recruited for the funeral service. Reading from a prepared text, he described the deceased as "Mr. Brown, who comes to us from Prague."

seven

EYELESS IN THE BIG MUDDY

> There are six or seven acceptable ways
> to win this war, two or three
> unacceptable ones, and only one way
> to lose it—and you've found it.
>
> —HERMAN KAHN, lecture to senior
> U.S. officers, Saigon, 1967

IT IS SAID THAT there are few secrets on the Mekong, the majestic river that fuels the heart of Indochina. And so it was in November 1982 that there was excited gossip up and down the riverbanks about what had happened at the tiny village of Ban Bonakah, Thailand.

A group of Americans, the story went, had slipped across the river in small boats from Ban Bonakah to Laos on the night of November 27, accompanied by fifteen anti-Communist Laotian guerrillas. The Americans, dressed in camouflage uniforms, were heavily armed and carrying some sort of equipment, as were the Laotians; what was going on? The local gossip accelerated a few nights later when some of this mysterious group filtered back to Thailand by swimming across the Mekong. The boats, weapons, and other equipment they had carried across the river were now missing, inciting talk about the fate of the men (there were rumors of shooting on the other side of the river).

It took some weeks for the authorities in Thailand to sort out most of the basic details, but even then, much remained a mystery. As best the Thais could determine, a group of half a dozen Americans led by a former U.S. Special Forces (Green Berets) lieutenant colonel had arrived in Bangkok several weeks before. They set themselves up in a house with a large amount of sophisticated radio equipment, began meeting with some of the assorted Laotian exile groups around the city, then traveled to the village of Ban Bonakah to make arrangements for the river crossing. Apparently, however, something had gone seriously wrong; once in Laos, according to fragmentary and sometimes contradictory accounts given by the former Green Beret in charge—one James B. "Bo" Gritz, pronounced "Grites"—the group was ambushed. One Laotian was killed, and the rest of the men scattered, their "mission" aborted.

And what mission was that? Things now began to get sticky, for the Thais—who had charged the Americans with assorted violations of Thai law—were told that it involved rescuing American prisoners of war still being held in Laos. Moreover, Gritz said, the attempted rescue was private but enjoyed unofficial support from the American government, and was financed by "private contributions," including some from companies with close ties to the American military. The Thais were puzzled, partially because they began to get subtle pressure from the American Embassy not to make too big a deal out of the case, and partially because they were confronted with an odd cast of characters. Besides Gritz, who seemed to talk nonstop, the group included an elderly Laotian man who claimed to be the main source for intelligence on Americans held prisoner in Laos, several American adventurer types, and a stunningly beautiful blond woman known in the group as "Angel East" (so called because she was detailed to handle communications with two women in California known as "Angels West").

Finally, the Thais gave up trying to make any sense out of all this, and ordered those involved to be deported forthwith. Their departure did not end the gossip, for there was much to speculate about in what seemed to be an *opéra bouffe* from start to finish. And it was a series of events that seemed

to encapsulate, for those with even short memories, the typically American approach to events in Indochina. Once again,
the Americans had come blundering in, loaded down with the
technical paraphernalia that was their trademark, intent on
solving a "problem" with the greatest dispatch. They had
worked assiduously to get themselves organized, then set
about collecting "intelligence" (from a somewhat unreliable
source) on their mission. That was followed by an alliance
with questionable allies, who proceeded to lead them to
disaster.

The Thais who, like most people in that part of the world,
delight in historical analogies, tended to see the Gritz fiasco
as a metaphor for what had happened to the United States
only a few years before in Indochina. Such metaphors can
often be overdrawn, but the parallels between what happened
in Thailand in 1982 and the American experience as a whole
in Indochina are quite striking: an overbearing presence, naïveté, highly suspect intelligence, and a thoughtless depen-
dence on allies of less than sterling reliability.

The entire episode awakened a disturbing echo of the not
too distant past, an echo of an experience that stands, still, as
the most tragic foreign adventure in American history. It is
known, in shorthand form, as the Vietnam experience—or,
more accurately, the Indochina experience. Even more accurately, it was the Indochina *disaster,* a series of errors, miscal-
culations, misperceptions, and downright stupidity that
teaches the costly lesson that even the most "advanced" nations, presumably with intelligent leadership, can fall victim
to the sins of blindness and self-delusion.

The disaster bears some examination, for it represents,
first and foremost, an intelligence failure of a magnitude unequaled in our history. And it was a failure of unequaled cost:
$352 billion and more than fifty thousand American lives, the
price exacted by history for failure to perceive events as they
really existed, to understand what was happening right under
our noses, if we had only taken the trouble to look.

When did that failure begin? Right at the first moment

that the United States decided to take an interest in Indochina. It was a time nearly forty years ago when, in an incident
few Americans know about, some American intelligence officers had their first encounter with an interesting group of men,
led by an even more interesting man they called "Uncle."

American intelligence literally dropped into Vietnam
during the spring of 1945, when a six-man team of OSS
agents parachuted into a wilderness area in the far north of
that country to make contact with Vietnamese guerrillas
fighting against the Japanese. Code-named Deer Mission, it
was supposed to arm and train the guerrillas for a series of
offensives that would drive the Japanese out of the northern
area of Vietnam. At the same time, the Americans were to
gather intelligence both on the Japanese presence and on the
guerrillas, called the Viet Minh.

The American presence represented an intelligence mission that had fallen through the cracks. The OSS, owing to
General Douglas MacArthur's open hostility, was unwelcome
in the Pacific theater, but Indochina—a French colonial empire occupied by the Japanese since 1940—was technically
part of the China-Burma-India theater, and therefore outside
MacArthur's jurisdiction. There, the OSS could organize
teams of guerrillas, the type of operation that was the agency's
hallmark. Vietnam was a backwater in assorted strategic calculations, for there was never any plan to invade that area outright; instead, the idea was to keep the Japanese preoccupied
battling guerrillas, so they would not move northward into
China itself.

The first American intelligence agents found that the
only effective guerrilla group in Vietnam was a tightly knit
organization of nationalists, under the leadership of a man
first introduced to them as Mr. C. M. Hoo, commonly called
Uncle. He was a small, thin man with a wisp of a beard, usually
dressed in an old shirt, shorts, and sandals. Mr. Hoo had
several thousand devoted followers, all of them dressed much
the same way. Their arms were equally nondescript, a mixture

of old rifles and more modern weapons captured from the Japanese, against whom they had been fighting for several years. The guerrillas had managed to take over vast areas of the countryside since the Japanese, without sufficient troops to patrol every square mile of Vietnam, pretty much kept to the cities and let the guerrillas have free run elsewhere.

It was not long before the OSS agents discovered that Mr. Hoo was in fact Ho Chi Minh, a longtime revolutionary who had run afoul of the French colonial authorities. (Ho before the war spent most of his time hiding out in southern China, from which he sallied forth regularly to organize opposition to French rule inside the Vietnamese section of Indochina.) The Americans were impressed with what Ho and his chief military aide, Vo Nguyen Giap, had been able to accomplish with few resources, and they were especially struck by Ho's ability at political organization. Indeed, Ho and his followers at that point completely dominated the nationalist movement.

The admiration of the OSS agents for Ho grew into a genuine friendship that moved the Vietnamese leader to confide his plans for the future. The plans included what seemed to the Americans an impossible feat: Ho planned to declare Vietnam's independence at war's end and expected that the French would recognize the new nation and incorporate it into the French Union. The Americans were openly sympathetic—at one point, Ho asked their help in writing a new Vietnamese constitution, modeled on the American one —but it was an enthusiasm that concealed some very pronounced political naïveté.

For one thing, the OSS agents did not understand that while Uncle Ho was a revered leader among his own people, he was regarded quite differently in London and Paris. There, Ho was known primarily as the most important leader of the Indochinese Communist party, a lifelong Communist functionary who was considered a tool of Moscow. The French, especially, saw Ho as a grave threat, for they fully intended to hold on to their Indochinese colonial empire after the war.

Certainly they had no intention of turning it over to the leader of the Indochinese Communist party.

For another thing, the OSS agents seemed to have no idea that political discussions with Ho thrust them into a very intricate and murky game of political intrigue that had geopolitical ramifications. The French and British considered the return of their Pacific colonies vital to their respective national security, and any attempt to hinder that would be regarded as betrayal by an ally. The OSS men did not realize that Indochina and other European colonies were in effect hostages in a larger political game; in return for support of American policy in Europe, the Europeans wanted American support for retrieval of their colonies.

Blissfully unaware of these larger political forces at work, Deer Mission trained Ho's guerrillas in the rudiments of such military arts as grenade throwing and rifle marksmanship, and spent the rest of their time listening sympathetically to Ho's plans for the future. Surely, Ho repeatedly asked, the United States would support the Vietnamese nationalists' bid for independence? Was it not precisely the same situation faced by American revolutionaries in 1776?

That remained Ho's fervent hope as the war ended and his forces prepared to take over Vietnam. Ho entered Hanoi and declared independence, an act that immediately put him at odds with the colony's French rulers. Conflict was inevitable, but the OSS did not have much understanding of the intricacies. To fill the intelligence gap, the agency dispatched one of its "city teams" (an intelligence-gathering group) to Hanoi with orders to find out what was going on.

The team sent to Hanoi in November 1945 was led by Frank White, a veteran OSS agent, along with a cryptographer and a radioman. White had no training or background for Indochina's complexities, but he was an intelligent and resourceful agent who immediately set about trying to gauge the strength of Ho's forces, French attitudes toward the nationalist leader, and what the probable outcome of the clash might be.

234

White and his fellow OSS agents were regarded with the gravest suspicion by the French, who pronounced the Americans hopelessly naïve amateurs under the spell of Ho. White found himself hindered at every turn by the openly hostile French, and only with the most stringent effort was he able to get some sense of what was happening. Essentially, White reported, events were heading toward a tragedy. Ho had proclaimed independence, and although the French said they were willing to negotiate, in fact they had no intention of doing so, certainly not to the extent of actually handing over the country to a Communist like Ho. For his part, Ho remained convinced that when all the chips were down, the United States would be compelled to support Vietnamese independence.

Like other OSS agents, White was sympathetic to Ho's aspirations, and as relations between the Americans and Ho grew warmer, the French became even more hostile and suspicious. To the French, the Americans, with their bumbling habit of unthinkingly embracing any anticolonial movement, were threatening vital French interests, a conviction that led to demands that OSS agents be removed from all of Indochina. Things began to get ugly: Colonel Peter Dewey, leader of an OSS team operating in the southern part of Vietnam, was especially despised by the French for his contacts with certain ethnic groups, who, the French suspected, were actually being organized politically by Dewey. That was not true, but on September 26, 1945, Dewey was shot and killed in an ambush. Officially, his death was blamed on trigger-happy guerrillas, but other OSS agents weren't so sure; they became convinced that the French had arranged to eliminate what they regarded as an especially dangerous enemy.

Dewey was the first American casualty in Vietnam. But in the year 1945, there was no hint of the blood and treasure that the United States would ultimately expend in Vietnam. What did exist was a sense of political cynicism. As the OSS agents soon became aware, the United States simply did not care whether Vietnam was independent. The country was of no consequence in the larger American strategic calculations, so it became a bargaining chip, given to the French in return for what was regarded as much more important—French support for American policy to rebuild Western Europe as a bulwark against the Soviet Union and Eastern Europe.

Part of the deal included removal of all OSS operatives from Indochina, and by early 1946 there were no American agents left there. The departure, accompanied by a French crackdown against Ho and the Viet Minh, was a source of some embarrassment to the OSS agents, who felt chagrined that their country was supporting a colonialist regime. It was an embarrassment clearly reflected in a farewell dinner that Archimedes Platti, chief OSS agent in Hanoi, held with Ho just before the Americans departed. Platti, whom the French openly accused of being a Ho sympathizer, tried unsuccessfully to explain to Ho why his government had decided to support the French. The United States did not support "French colonial ambitions," Platti told a puzzled Ho, but had not questioned "French sovereignty" over Vietnam.

The explanation made no sense, and Platti and his fellow American agents left Hanoi in an atmosphere of disappointment and embarrassment. Their departure was a milestone, for American intelligence was not to set foot in that area of Vietnam for another seventeen years. During all that time, American intelligence had no firsthand idea of what was happening in a part of the world that would later dominate so much of their concern.

It was the first step in a chain of events that was to result in a total disaster.

The French may have regarded the deal they cut with the United States about Vietnam as a great victory, but it was to turn to ashes. The French made the bad mistake of underestimating Ho, and his movement began to demonstrate a new form of warfare for which the general staff colleges of France (and America) had not prepared their soldiers. This was "people's war," a system of political and military action that sought to mobilize an entire people in an all-out struggle against an enemy. The doctrine, developed and put into practice by Mao Tse-tung, head of the Communist guerrilla forces in China, rested on the idea that the ultimate resource in war was people; if they could be totally mobilized politically so that an entire population in effect became a giant army-in-being, then no amount of military power could prevail against them.

The key was political mobilization, which Mao had described as the first stage in a three-stage process ending in full-scale military revolution against an enemy. Ho and Giap followed this precept exactly, and by the time the French decided to eradicate the Viet Minh, Ho had politically mobilized almost the entire Vietnamese population. And with the population so mobilized, the French were beaten before they started; no amount of conventional military power could defeat a revolutionary movement totally supported by the people.

The central French error was failure to understand the nature of people's war, for the French generals—in a mistake to be repeated some years later by the Americans—persisted in seeing Ho's forces in traditional military terms. In those terms, the guerrillas were mobile insurgents, so the solution was to bring sufficient conventional military force on those forces to destroy them. For generals trained in the traditional doctrines of military strategy, the solution made sense, but it ignored the real nature of the Viet Minh. Ho's forces, in Mao's classic phrase, lived among the people "as fish among the waters," avoiding set-piece battles with the French, and only standing to fight when the terms were completely favorable to themselves. The French encountered the central dilemma of all such wars: The guerrillas were very difficult to spot, and easily eluded the ponderous operations against them mounted by conventional forces laden down with equipment. The French might be able to clear out a village or patch of jungle, but when night fell, those areas belonged again to the guerrillas, whose subsistence depended not on conventional supply lines, but on the food and other essentials provided by the politically mobilized population.

The French–Viet Minh struggle ignited a new American interest in Indochina, which the United States began to perceive as the most important target in a series of advances across the map of Asia by monolithic Communism. The triumph of Mao's forces in China, followed by the invasion of South Korea and the war in Indochina, was accompanied by a Communist insurgency in the Philippines and another in British Malaya. The events focused attention on Vietnam, which the United States regarded as the last remaining bulwark against the Communist tide threatening to sweep all of Southeast Asia. Fall of Vietnam to Ho and the Communists, as Eisenhower claimed in his famous simile, would cause a row of dominoes to fall, isolating and threatening vital American interests in the Pacific.

In intelligence terms, the American domino theory betrayed some serious failures of perception. The assorted insurgencies, revolutions, and uprisings that had exploded all over Asia after World War II were not the result of a centrally directed conspiracy from Moscow, but an inevitable symptom of the tremendous political upheavals taking place on the continent, most of which had been touched off by the war. American intelligence had no real grasp of this mighty force for change sweeping the continent. It tended to judge those events in the narrow reference of the Cold War—Communists led most of the insurgencies, therefore there was some sort of master plan to subjugate Asia in the name of Communism. This narrow vision led the United States into a series of bad mistakes, one of which was to give full backing to the French in Indochina (including more than $300 million in aid), an act that convinced an entire generation of Asian revolutionaries that the United States, for all its professed commitment to self-determination of peoples, was a colonial power in disguise.

The errors were directly related to the very nature of American intelligence operating in Asia. The CIA in particular showed its OSS origins in that continent by concentrating its efforts in paramilitary operations designed to destabilize Communist regimes already in power or wreck Communist insurgencies in the making. The agency in Asia was action-oriented, dominated by a roster of cowboys who operated on the theory that the war in Asia was already almost lost and priority must be given to operations designed to roll back the Communist advance.

Intelligence collection was very much secondary in this atmosphere, and made more difficult by the suspicions French and British intelligence felt about Americans. The British, especially, caused problems, for they regarded the Americans as a threat to their own interests, which centered on retaining British colonial power in Asia. (MI6 officers complained that they had barely managed to retain the crown colony of Hong Kong in the face of American determination to turn the island over to the Chinese.)

The CIA, MI6, and the French Sûreté began to go their separate ways in Asia; divided by suspicions about one another's motives, they did not cooperate. In the process, the British missed the political undercurrents that were soon to sweep them entirely out of Asia, while the French, obsessed with proving that Ho was being directed by Mao and Stalin, failed to grasp the real nature of Viet Minh political strength.* American intelligence, meanwhile, missed just about everything of consequence, including Indochina itself.

The American belief that the problem in Indochina was essentially military caused intelligence reporting on events during the nine-year war between the French and the Viet Minh to be left in the hands of assorted military officers dis-

---

*The French also missed another significant fact: the quality of the Viet Minh intelligence service. Not only did Ho's agents completely penetrate the French command structure in Indochina, giving him advance word of French offensives, they also managed in 1950 to steal a copy of the top-secret Revers Report, a French master plan for forthcoming political and military operations in Indochina. Among other things, this master stroke tipped off Ho and Giap to French plans to build several huge fortified positions in the Tonkin area of Indochina—including one in an area called Dien Bien Phu.

patched there with a two-phase mission. First, they were to determine what American aid was necessary to help the French win, and second, to prepare intelligence on the nature of the Viet Minh and why the French seemed to be losing. The intelligence was most often framed in strictly military terms, the standard military equations of forces deployed, weapons systems, supply lines, and so forth. But these equations really said nothing about why the war was going so badly for the French. It did not occur to any American officer reporting on the Viet Minh phenomenon to wonder how an organization that began with a cell of nine people in 1925 had somehow grown to a force that was in the process of defeating one of the world's strongest military powers.*

The collapse of the French in Indochina created a vacuum that the Americans moved to fill as rapidly as possible, in the process setting themselves as the new bulwark against the Communist tide flowing south. The outer edge of this new bulwark was drawn at the 17th parallel, the demarcation line decided at the 1954 truce ending the Viet Minh–French war.

Under provisions of that truce, north of the 17th parallel lay Viet Minh territory, while south of the line was the new nation of Vietnam, a rickety entity composed geographically of Vietnam's richest agricultural areas and politically of supporters of the old French regime, people who had worked in various capacities for the former colonial power and assorted religious sects, all presided over by a French-installed ruler, the quixotic and weak Emperor Bao Dai.

---

*The depth of the American military's ignorance about events in Indochina was illustrated by the plan developed by Admiral Arthur Radford, Chairman of the Joint Chiefs of Staff, for a full-scale U.S. military intervention to save the French in 1954 at the time of the siege of Dien Bien Phu. Operation Vulture called for massive American air strikes against the Viet Minh, including the dropping of atomic bombs should the Chinese intervene in response. Eisenhower rejected the plan, mainly because Army Chief of Staff General Matthew Ridgway, a friend of Eisenhower's, pronounced it "militarily a mistake." As Ridgway pointed out, at least seven American divisions would be needed immediately in Indochina, simply to relieve Viet Minh pressure on the French, and much larger forces would be required eventually. Implicitly, Ridgway noted that Radford had no intelligence available justifying Operation Vulture.

The United States decided that the new nation would be the heart of its anti-Communist bulwark, and set about transforming it, almost overnight, into a viable political entity. Much of the task was assigned to the CIA, which reestablished a formal American intelligence presence in Vietnam in June 1954. It was disguised under the cover name of Saigon Military Mission; in fact it was not a military mission at all but a large-scale effort that was given a very broad range of tasks, from nation building to intelligence collection.

The first problem with this structure was its very scope, a mistake that the CIA had repeated over and over again. There was absolutely no way an intelligence organization could hope to mix the very different elements of intelligence and political action. The different processes are not compatible, and that central fact was to cause all sorts of difficulties with American intelligence in Vietnam. One of the problems was the man chosen to head Saigon Military Mission, Colonel Edward G. Lansdale, among the CIA's most famous cowboys. A mild-mannered former advertising executive, air-force officer, and OSS operative, Lansdale was a bundle of energy, brimming over with ideas for political intrigue and various dirty tricks to defeat the Communist enemy. He had been chosen for the Vietnam job because of his success in the Philippines in the early 1950s, when he led an American effort, spearheaded by the CIA, to defeat an insurgency of the Hukbalahaps, an ethnic group under Communist influence that had sought to overthrow the Philippine government.

Lansdale established a pattern in the Philippines that he sought to repeat in Vietnam. Essentially, it consisted of two tracks, one of which was a strong effort, using a whole catalog of dirty tricks, to undermine popular support for the insurgency. The second track was sponsorship of a carefully created "democratic alternative," which would emerge with powerful American support. The Huks, as the Americans called them, lacked a solid political base, even in their own territory, and they were ground down by relentless American and government pressure. Lansdale became famous within the CIA during this campaign for a number of tricks, among his most noted, the "vampire routine." Lansdale had discovered that many Filipinos in rural areas were deeply superstitious, especially about vampires. Using that fear, Lansdale arranged for some bodies of Huk guerrillas killed in a government ambush to be provided with two neat puncture holes in the necks. The bodies were then drained of blood, and left out in the open for the natives to see. As Lansdale surmised, word soon spread that vampires were killing Huks, convincing many of the more superstitious Filipinos that the Huks were "evil ones" marked for death.

The democratic alternative in the Philippines was another Lansdale creation—Ramón Magsaysay, whom an extensive American propaganda effort, along with considerable U.S. economic aid, transformed into a figure with only slightly less stature than Abraham Lincoln. It worked, in part because Magsaysay himself, despite his virtual creation by the CIA, was in fact a talented and dynamic leader.

Lansdale sought to repeat this scenario in Vietnam. His "Vietnamese Magsaysay," as some wits in the CIA called him, was Ngo Dinh Diem, an oddly mystic Vietnamese Catholic leader who was chosen for CIA support because of his visceral anti-Communism. At the same time, Lansdale moved to discredit Diem's Viet Minh opposition. The chosen method was a refinement of the vampire strategy used against the Huks: a lurid propaganda campaign designed to convince the Vietnamese that the Viet Minh were a bunch of sadistic savages, not "liberators" of oppressed Vietnamese peasants. Lansdale concentrated on Vietnam's Catholic population, about 1.5 million people, a large portion of whom lived in the Viet Minh territory above the 17th parallel. The 1954 Geneva Agreement ending the war called for a two-year period during which Vietnamese would be free to move to areas of their choice on either side of the 17th parallel. Lansdale wanted as many of the Catholics as possible in the south, to form a political base for Diem, so his central objective was to encourage as many Catholics as possible to move from the north.

The means of persuasion was a propaganda campaign

that pulled out all the stops. CIA-produced leaflets were circulated, with lurid stories of Viet Minh soldiers raping women, torturing men by crushing their testicles, and in a particularly gruesome touch, jamming chopsticks in the ears of children "to keep them from hearing the word of God." Unquestionably, there was some fear among the Catholics over Viet Minh retribution (most Catholics had supported the French), but Lansdale's propaganda bore little relation to reality. However, the campaign worked, and several hundred thousand Catholics, alarmed over stories that predicted their imminent torture and death, fled south via a U.S. Navy sealift.*

Lansdale had succeeded, but to what end? True, the bulk of the Catholic population had now moved south, but it did not seem to occur to Lansdale and the CIA that Catholics constitute only about 8 percent of Vietnam's twenty million people. Most of the Vietnamese were Buddhists or native offshoots of that faith, and despite the most ardent efforts over the preceding one hundred years, French missionaries had never been able to make much of a dent in the firm hold Buddhism has on the Indochinese peoples. The hope of building a viable political constituency in the south, based on the Catholic population under a Catholic president, was therefore doomed to failure. (Nine years later, the CIA mistake came home to roost: South Vietnam's Buddhists, angered over Catholic domination of all aspects of South Vietnamese life and Diem's repression, revolted. The revolt, which included highly publicized self-immolations by some monks, undercut American support for Diem, who was subsequently overthrown in an American-approved military coup during which the South Vietnamese leader was murdered.)

The CIA's intelligence errors, however, were even more

*The campaign received considerable help from an important CIA asset—Dr. Tom Dooley, a navy doctor who won worldwide fame for his moving stories of refugees and their suffering at the hands of the Communists. However, Dooley's humanitarian efforts were used to screen his real job, which involved reporting to the CIA on the political reliability of the refugees.

serious. They were connected with Lansdale's efforts to de-stabilize the infant Viet Minh regime in the north, after the Geneva ceasefire agreement, by leaving behind teams of anti-Communist Vietnamese operatives. The teams were supposed to be collecting intelligence, but the CIA had given them an additional assignment—carry out a widespread campaign of sabotage and disruption to cripple the Ho regime. These operations in the northern part of Vietnam—which became North Vietnam following the failure to hold elections in 1956 to unify the country—were under the direction of another CIA cowboy, Colonel Lucien Conein, who repeated almost precisely the mistakes made by the agency in Europe just after World War II.

The problem was that Conein had little interest in intelligence collection, so his teams spent most of their time in such activities as blowing up the largest printing plant in Hanoi, and sabotaging a fleet of government trucks. Conein also supervised another operation, very similar to the CIA's ill-fated "stay-behind" guerrilla operation in Europe: organizing arms caches for groups of stay-behind guerrillas who would spring into action the moment the Viet Minh tried to invade southward. However, the arms caches, many of them hidden in airtight coffins and buried in Hanoi graveyards, were never put to use, for there was no hope that any such anti-Communist guerrilla force could be organized in the north.

The overall American failure at this early point in the Vietnam debacle was compounded by the near panic that seemed to grip the American military establishment after the French defeat, and there was a great rush to formulate a "successful" counterinsurgency doctrine to forestall an anticipated wave of Viet Minh–type uprisings all over Asia.

American experts flocked to Malaya, where the British had managed to defeat a Communist-led insurgency, for the requisite lessons on how it was done. Malaya, however, was a poor example to emulate, for there was a world of difference between the British colony and Vietnam. For one thing, the political situation: The people of Malaya had already been promised future independence by the British on a specific timetable, so there was no "colonial oppressor" around which political dissidents could organize opposition. Vietnam, on the other hand, not only had a colonial regime detested by most of the population, the country itself remained divided even after that colonial power had been defeated. For another thing, the Malayan insurgents came mostly from ethnic-Chinese minorities, and Malays tended to regard the Chinese as interlopers. Even more important, some of the measures used in Malaya to defeat the insurgents—especially "resettlement" of entire villages into government-protected hamlets—were inapplicable to Vietnam, where many Vietnamese lived in ancestral villages, sacred soil from which it was unthinkable to move.

Yet, despite these important differences, the Americans sought to transplant the Malayan experience into a very different environment. The transplanting came complete with its own guru, Robert G. K. Thompson, a British counterinsurgency expert who had worked with British SOE operations in China and Burma during World War II. He had planned and developed the successful British counterinsurgency program in Malaya in 1948, and in 1961 was shifted to the British Advisory Mission in Saigon, which was supposed to advise Diem on how to deal with a growing insurgency movement in South Vietnam. Thompson discovered that Diem didn't have the vaguest idea what to do, except to increase the size and ferocity of his already repressive police apparatus and to undertake large-scale conventional military operations that blundered around the countryside to no good effect—save to antagonize the Vietnamese population further.

Thompson was appalled at what he saw in Vietnam—American military advisers who were creating a large conventional South Vietnamese army of little use against highly mobile guerrillas, and CIA advisers who were creating a large police and internal-security apparatus that had no understanding of how to find indigenous guerrillas living among

245

the people in the countryside. Thompson insisted that the correct approach in Vietnam was police action rather than military power, using some of the techniques he had developed in Malaya, including strict—but not repressive—control of the population to discover where the insurgents and their sympathizers were located. He was finally to clash with Diem's CIA advisers over his insistence on a different approach, and he left Vietnam in disgust when he discovered that Diem had adopted his advice selectively in order to set up a virtual police state.

Thompson predicted disaster if such policies continued, but the United States seemed unaware that the South Vietnam it had almost singlehandedly created was in danger of being subsumed by an indigenous guerrilla movement that called itself the National Liberation Front—although the South Vietnamese insisted on calling it the Viet Cong. Coincidental with the inauguration of John F. Kennedy, the Americans became increasingly convinced that such problems as the Viet Cong insurgency in South Vietnam were soluble, provided that the proper "system" was discovered and supported with sufficient funds. Less than a month after taking office, Kennedy told Secretary of Defense McNamara to put more emphasis on "counterguerrilla forces," and a month after that, he appointed former U.S. Army General Maxwell Taylor his chief adviser on "paramilitary activities." The appointment of Taylor signaled the Kennedy administration's interest in the realm of "limited war"—the theory that the international Communist movement would not directly challenge American strategic military superiority, but would seek to nibble the American giant to death by carrying out small conventional wars (mostly in the form of insurgencies) around the American periphery. Taylor had resigned his post as Army Chief of Staff during the Eisenhower administration because of strong disagreement with the "massive retaliation" theory, which, he felt, placed too many American military resources into strategic forces, while dangerously ignoring the necessity for strong conventional forces.

There was no small element of military politics here, for Taylor, a highly decorated paratroop commander during World War II, was a man dedicated to the service in which he had spent most of his life. Increasingly upset at what he felt was the steady erosion of the army's role in American military strategy, Taylor welcomed the limited-war ideas of the Kennedy administration, which promised a revitalization of the army, since that service, obviously, would be responsible for conducting those wars.

As so often happens in such circumstances, it turned out that the components for such limited-war strategy were already in place. One of them was the army's Special Forces, a unit created in 1952 but lying moribund since then because there was little money left for them during the Eisenhower era and the concentration on strategic nuclear forces. Now revived, the Special Forces—reorganized and given a distinctive green beret as part of their uniform—were seen as the perfect troops for the new limited-war strategy, considering their expertise in guerrilla operations. (Although this required a tricky shift in emphasis, since the original idea of the Special Forces was to conduct guerrilla operations behind enemy lines in the event of all-out war, not the other way around.)

Another component was more prosaic—the helicopter, a machine that had played only a minor role in the U.S. military for some years. But a number of army tactical experts, led by General Hamilton Howze of the 82nd Airborne Division, had developed new theories that called for a massive use of fleets of helicopters in future wars. The idea was to dramatically increase the army's mobility; troops would be moved quickly to the rear and flanks of an enemy, the soldiers and their artillery transported by helicopter and protected by helicopter gunships firing machine guns and rockets. It was a bold new concept, but had run into resistance from the air force, which objected to the army's taking over responsibility for close air support on the battlefield. In the summer of 1962, those objections were swept aside by McNamara himself, who watched a full-scale field demonstration of Howze's new concept and was instantly convinced. In a short while, the army began getting all the money it needed to develop the idea, and the 11th Air Assault Division was born—subsequently renamed the First Air Cavalry Division (Airmobile). It was later to use its unmatched mobility not against a conventional military enemy on the plains of Europe (the original idea), but to root out Viet Cong and North Vietnamese soldiers from the jungle.

But however impressive these tools of war, the Americans were to discover the hard way that the most essential weapon in a counterguerrilla war is good intelligence, for no success in such a war is possible unless, as the old U.S. Army phrase had it, the guerrillas can be "found and fixed." Where are the guerrillas? What is the extent of their political support among the populace? Where are their weapons caches? How do their food and ammunition supply systems work? And at least a hundred other questions.

The CIA, which would come to make Vietnam its largest operation—by 1973, there were about eight hundred CIA agents there, plus nearly thirty thousand non-American auxiliaries—had not been able to discover much about Vietnam since the OSS teams had been thrown out of the country. The central problem, as noted earlier, was the agency's habit of mixing paramilitary and intelligence-collection operations, and even the dramatically increased American involvement in Vietnam did not change that method.

The first major postwar intelligence operation was known as White Star. In late 1960, the CIA got the idea of obtaining critically needed intelligence through the back door—in Laos, where another Communist insurgent movement (the Pathet Lao) was festering. The plan was to enlist members of ethnic tribes in that country, arm and train them, then send them on intelligence-collection and harassment missions against Communist guerrillas. The hope was that the CIA-trained tribes would not only keep the Pathet Lao forces busy but would also divert Communist forces from South Vietnam. In addition, it was planned that the non-Communist forces would carry out intelligence operations, especially in North Vietnam, believed by the Americans to be the source of men and supplies for the Viet Cong forces in the south.

This rather tall order was assigned to the Green Berets, as the Special Forces had become popularly known, the first in what would be a series of operations carried out by that elite force under CIA control. But White Star revealed a basic flaw in this arrangement, for the Green Berets discovered that the intelligence on which the CIA based these highly dangerous forays into Laos (and later, North Vietnam and Cambodia) was often pretty thin. In the case of White Star, the 108 Green Berets who entered Laos discovered a mirage: The "non-Communist Laotian forces" they were supposed to organize and train did not exist. Under ordinary circumstances, the Green Berets would have turned around and returned home empty-handed, but White Star was led by one of the Special Forces' legendary officers, the ever-aggressive Colonel Arthur D. "Bull" Simons, who did not like missions to fail. Angered at the CIA's error in somehow believing that non-Communist Laotian forces existed, just waiting for orders to attack, Simons simply created such forces on the spot. His men literally kidnapped twelve battalions of Muong tribesmen, put them in compounds behind barbed wire, clothed, armed, trained, and paid them, then asked them how they liked the job. They liked it just fine, and the CIA was now in business in Laos.

White Star set the pattern for what would eventually become a large-scale operation under the general heading of Special Operations Group (SOG). The most secret intelligence operation of the entire Vietnam war, SOG eventually involved ten thousand Special Forces troops and CIA agents, along with more than thirty thousand native forces (all of them on the CIA payroll), running what amounted to their own secret war in South Vietnam, Laos, Cambodia, and North Vietnam. Technically, it was supposed to be an intelligence operation first and foremost, but the CIA's recurring habit of trying to combine intelligence gathering and boom and bang, using the same people, caused no end of problems.

A perfect illustration was Operation Fascination, a CIA plan to destroy the North Vietnamese fishing industry. Under this plan, seaborne SOG forces moved up and down the North Vietnamese coast, intercepting fishing boats. The frightened fishermen were told they would not be killed, but that the pressure of war forced the soldiers to interdict the North Vietnamese fishing industry; if the fishermen cooperated, then they would not be harmed. To show their good intentions and encourage an end to the fishing, SOG agents gave each fisherman a large basket full of food and other items. The fishermen promised to stop fishing, but just as the CIA assumed it had succeeded, SOG agents reported a manifold increase in the number of fishermen working off the North Vietnamese coast. What had happened? Human nature: The fishermen, eager to get more baskets of goodies, fished even more, hoping to be intercepted and rewarded again. The North Vietnamese fishing industry boomed.

Operation Fascination was one of the more interesting undertakings spawned by the CIA's SOG apparatus. In 1964, SOG put into effect a plan known as OPLAN 34-A, creating three large field offices called Command and Control Units. (The most important was Command and Control North, which operated SOG teams in North Vietnam and Laos.) The control units in turn operated a network of seven large bases stretching along the Laotian and Cambodian borders, each one containing 150 Special Forces soldiers and up to 600 indigenous troops from assorted ethnic minorities. From these bases—misleadingly called camps—the troops made forays into Laos, Cambodia, and North Vietnam, their chief assignment to collect intelligence on Communist troop movements, base camps, infiltration routes, and supply lines.

But the CIA could not resist throwing in some dirty tricks for these teams to carry out—such as having SOG teams scatter batches of ammunition for the Communists to find. The ammunition, at first glance of Soviet or Chinese manufacture but actually carefully forged by the CIA, was designed to explode the moment someone tried to use it. Of marginal military utility at best, such tricks had the serious disadvantage of calling attention to the SOG teams operating deep inside Communist-controlled areas. The same problem afflicted other SOG operations, such as Operation Timberwork, under which SOG teams carried out PT-boat raids in North Vietnamese harbors; about all that accomplished was to compel the North Vietnamese to increase their own sea patrols to stop the forays, thus denying another potentially excellent source of intelligence.

By 1967, SOG was failing badly, mainly because its assorted paramilitary actions touched off a strong effort by the North Vietnamese to stop them. SOG teams, which once found Laos surprisingly easy to infiltrate—in one instance, SOG troops spent the night sleeping right inside a North Vietnamese Army base camp—began to find such forays difficult and costly. The North Vietnamese, concerned about SOG operations along the Ho Chi Minh Trail in Laos (actually not a single trail, but a complicated network of supply routes), struck back with a vengeance. They stationed around their base camps and supply lines a large force of trail watchers who tapped sharply on the ground with bamboo sticks the moment they spotted any infiltrators. This "jungle telegraph," as the Green Berets called it, would alert North Vietnamese units for miles around.

The North Vietnamese counterattack began to close off any intelligence the SOG teams were collecting, and SOG missions became extremely hazardous, especially the operations into North Vietnam. Known as Kit-Cat, these operations by 1968 were a complete failure, in part because of the North Vietnamese crackdown, but more because a proper basis—development of on-ground intelligence sources and support facilities—had never been laid for them. Kit-Cat amounted to the classic CIA rush job to develop human-intelligence sources: SOG teams would run three- and six-man groups of hastily trained agents into North Vietnam. Equipped with radios and other spy paraphernalia, the agents were supposed to work their way near targets of interest, then begin reporting. But since safe houses, contacts, secure escape routes and other vital support systems had never been set up, the agents' task was hopeless. All were captured by the North Vietnamese, who either had them shot or turned them to feed back false information.

Similar disasters befell SOG missions into Cambodia and Laos, where SOG made the greatest use of indigenous troops. The problem here again was American impatience, trying to develop those forces as rapidly as possible into counterweights against the Communists. The indigenous forces, actually paid mercenaries, represented an attempt to fill an especially critical gap: Since the United States had no real hope of creating popular movements in South Vietnam, Laos, or Cambodia, it sought to buy them, building its own guerrilla armies that were supposed to preoccupy the Communist forces. But as mercenaries from ethnic minorities, there was no possibility that these groups could ever develop any widespread political support and present a viable political alternative. Furthermore, they often had their own special interests. The Hmongs of Laos, for example, were enrolled by the CIA in its largest indigenous army, a force of over twenty thousand men under General Vang Pao. But the Hmongs (or Meos, as the Americans preferred to call them) had been growing opium for many years, and it was a profitable business they were not about to close simply because they had become CIA-financed soldiers. In fact, business boomed as never before, in large part because CIA-provided transportation made moving opium that much easier. Needless to say, opium growing was not very conducive to either collecting intelligence or fighting the Communists, tasks for which Pao's CIA army demonstrated manifest incompetence. By 1968, what remained of his forces were decisively routed by Pathet Lao guerrillas.

While all these operations were failing, especially in intelligence terms, another major effort at gathering intelligence was also collapsing, and the failure in that case was even more disastrous.

The effort centered on the South Vietnamese police and security apparatus, a structure built entirely by the United States. From the first moment the Americans became seriously involved in Vietnam, high priority was placed on developing a large South Vietnamese intelligence capability. This was a laudable aim, but it ran into difficulty almost immediately. This was chiefly because the South Vietnamese did not share American goals and enthusiasm for this Asian CIA; in their view, it represented only a greater opportunity for more graft and squeezing of the population. The South Vietnamese internal security and intelligence apparatus existed during the Diem regime for the sole purpose of enriching its officers and repressing political opponents of the Diem family, which kept the apparatus under its strict control. Assorted regimes that came to power after the fall of Diem maintained that tradition and showed little interest in any intelligence unless it could be either turned to profit or used to forestall moves by potential and actual political opponents.

When the CIA began to reorganize this Asian Gestapo, the agency found itself confronted with a system of inbred corruption, administered by an interlocking network of cronies. The worst problem was the Military Security Service of South Vietnam, the organization directly responsible for gathering intelligence on the size and status of Communist forces in the countryside. Notoriously corrupt, it was headed up by General Nguyen Ngoc Loan, a close friend of Nguyen Cao Ky, the flamboyant South Vietnamese Air Force general. In 1965, when Ky became premier, he appointed Loan to the job, largely because Loan himself was notorious as an openly crooked police official who could be expected to protect a system of corruption (including opium trafficking) that extended from the presidential palace on down. The Military Security Service, amusingly enough, was responsible for "anti-corruption" investigations.

Despite this record, Loan became a popular figure with the CIA, which welcomed his first major operation, the cleaning out of Viet Cong political cells in the capital. (In 1964, following the political turmoil connected with Diem's assassination, Viet Cong political cadres in Saigon were operating openly, at one point holding political rallies in broad daylight.) Loan set up a brutally repressive police apparatus in the capital that soon put a stop to such things, but in the process betrayed evidence of the kind of corruption that marked all of South Vietnam's internal-security forces. Aside from brutal tortures, Loan's men operated on a sliding scale of bribes for various offenses, with release from confinement possible for the right amount of money.

The Military Security Service was not much of an intelligence organization, and neither was the Central Intelligence Office (CIO), South Vietnam's CIA. Wholly the creation of the Americans, the CIO began life as the Presidential Security Office in 1962, when it was brought into being by John Richardson, CIA station chief in Saigon and a fanatical anti-Communist. Richardson, a CIA cowboy who had operated in the Philippines with Lansdale, worked in Saigon with Colonel Le Quang Tung, head of the South Vietnamese Special Forces (another American invention, this one an attempted clone of the Green Berets). Tung was getting $3 million a year from Richardson, with orders to turn his two-thousand-man Special Forces into a crack unit that would root out and kill Viet Cong guerrillas, and at the same time collect intelligence on the Communists.

Tung, however, had no plans to do any such thing. A close ally of the infamous Ngo Dinh Nhu—Diem's brother, the head of South Vietnam's internal-security and intelligence apparatus—Tung turned his Vietnamese Green Berets into a political repression force. Among other things, he dispatched his men on a disastrous raid against Buddhist pagodas in an alleged hunt for "subversives" (but in fact to crush Diem's Buddhist political opposition).*

*The Buddhist incident infuriated U.S. Ambassador Henry Cabot Lodge, who demanded Richardson's recall. Later, CIA officials discovered that much of the money that Richardson had handed over to Tung was pocketed by the Diem family.

The CIO was to play a major role in another CIA scheme, an attempt to get at the so-called "Viet Cong infrastructure," by which was meant the political cadres, supporters, and other noncombat personnel who formed the political context in which the Viet Cong military forces operated. The theory was that in order to defeat the Viet Cong, that organization's large infrastructure would have to be defeated concurrently with defeat of its main military units.

How large was this infrastructure? Nobody seemed to know; CIA estimates ran from thirty thousand to ninety thousand, a range that illustrated the lack of intelligence on the entire Viet Cong organization. Despite this lack of information, the CIA set into motion what would become its most controversial operation in Vietnam, Operation Phoenix.

Phoenix technically was an intelligence-collection program. Dossiers on every Viet Cong from each village and hamlet in South Vietnam would be collected in order to prepare a detailed intelligence picture on the infrastructure. And once that material was collected, South Vietnamese forces would move in and eliminate those positively identified as Viet Cong. With the elimination of the infrastructure at the village and hamlet level, the Viet Cong itself would soon collapse.

The nearly eight hundred American CIA and military-intelligence officers attached to Phoenix obviously could not be expected to run a program of such vast scope by themselves, so direct participation by the South Vietnamese military and CIO was necessary. And that is where Phoenix failed, for the South Vietnamese security officials had no real idea of who was and who was not a member of the Viet Cong infrastructure. Moreover, the South Vietnamese did not seem to care; to them, Phoenix represented still another opportunity for graft. CIA officials were horrified to find that in some areas, government district chiefs applied red, white, and green markers to houses. Owners were informed that the different colors signified whether they were Viet Cong (red), pro-government (green), or neutral and therefore probably pro-Viet Cong (white). Those with white or red markers found that substantial bribes could get the colors changed.

Phoenix was to become notorious. Among other things, it was discovered that it took only two denunciations of someone to condemn that person for "Viet Cong activity." That was a sentence of death, for South Vietnamese security squads each night murdered those so accused and convicted, along with a large number of people only suspected of being part of the Viet Cong infrastructure. Ultimately, nearly twenty thousand people were executed under Phoenix, and the program was so badly administered that it is impossible to say how many of those victims were actually connected with the Viet Cong, and how many were simply the victims of spiteful denunciations.

Phoenix never did manage to collect even a rough outline of the Viet Cong. The program did not appear to affect the Viet Cong very much, and there was even less impact on other operations directed against the North Vietnamese, whose main military forces began to become seriously involved in the Vietnam war in the mid-1960s. In this case, the intelligence failure was of even greater magnitude.

The North Vietnamese represented a much more serious military threat to both the South Vietnamese and the Americans, but the CIA was handicapped in obtaining intelligence on North Vietnam and its forces in the south. One reason lay in some of the agency errors discussed earlier. Another was an ethnic fact of life: Native American agents could not operate undercover among the Vietnamese, since they obviously stood out among a sea of Oriental faces. That meant the South Vietnamese would have to shoulder most of the intelligence-gathering responsibility. The South Vietnamese, however, failed totally, and by 1967, it was clear to the CIA that there was no hope that their allies could gather even the most elementary intelligence on the North Vietnamese.

The magnitude of the failure led some CIA officials to conclude that the South Vietnamese CIO and other security operations might have been thoroughly penetrated by one of the Vietnam war's most mysterious organizations, Unit B-36 (the North Vietnamese intelligence service). Next to nothing was known about this organization, but early in 1967, CIA officials in Saigon discovered that a South Vietnamese CIO agent was actually a double for B-36. The agent had confessed his role for the North Vietnamese, and began to tell an incredible story about North Vietnamese penetration of the highest levels of South Vietnam's government and security agencies.

The agent's revelations were so alarming that a special CIA unit, code-named Operation Projectile, decided to take a close look at those revelations and discover just how deeply the South Vietnamese had been penetrated. Very deeply, as it turned out. The Communists had infiltrated the astounding total of nearly thirty thousand agents into the South Vietnamese security and government apparatus, including the two chief political advisers to South Vietnamese Premier Nguyen Van Thieu. The depth of the penetrations shocked the CIA (which also discovered that most of the indigenous Vietnamese on its payroll were B-36 agents), and the agency cut off virtually all contact with its South Vietnamese counterparts. From now on, the Americans decided, they would go it alone.

But there was no improvement in the intelligence picture, for very few Americans realized that the United States at that point had already lost the intelligence war in Vietnam. All the mistakes had come back to haunt American intelligence: the failure to develop sources in North Vietnam, the failure to understand the nature of people's war, the failure to perceive until too late the rot inside South Vietnamese intelligence, and the failure to understand the error of mixing paramilitary and intelligence-collection operations.

The failures were encapsulated by the Tet offensive in 1968, which was preceded by a squabble between the CIA and military intelligence over how many Viet Cong and North Vietnamese forces were operating in South Vietnam. The wide disparity between the two estimates—almost three hundred thousand men—illustrated the low state of American intelligence at that point, since it could not even decide so elementary a matter as how many enemy troops were in the field. The offensive itself was an even better illustration: a massive uprising by Communist forces all over South Vietnam, an offensive of such scope and violence that it belied official American statements about "light at the end of the tunnel"—and undercut political support for the war.

The intelligence blindness that led to the shock of the Tet offensive was part of a consistent pattern of myopia that seemed to afflict intelligence agencies and policymakers alike every time they tried to take some measure of progress in the Vietnam war. The myopia had been there in the critical year of 1963, when Maxwell Taylor and Robert McNamara, following a trip to South Vietnam to determine firsthand how well the South Vietnamese were holding up under the threat of a Communist-led insurgency, concluded that the South Vietnamese were holding up very well indeed. But in fact the South Vietnamese at that point were on the brink of collapse.

And the myopia was there in 1965 and 1966, when the reports of Rolling Thunder—code name for the American bombing campaign against North Vietnam—suggested that the campaign was successful, promising destruction of that country's supply lines and arsenals. Clearly, it was reasoned, the North Vietnamese could not stand up to such punishment long, and would soon end their support of the fighting in the south. But in fact the North Vietnamese were nowhere near capitulation, and had taken extensive measures—including diversification of industries and arms stockpiles—to frustrate the bombing, which never succeeded in even slowing down infiltration of men and arms southward.

And the myopia was there in 1970, when American forces were ordered into Cambodia, among their objectives the COSVN (Central Office for South Vietnam), supposedly the central headquarters directing Communist military operations in South Vietnam. But COSVN was a shadow; instead of the sprawling headquarters complex the troops expected to find, all they discovered were a few base camps and arms caches. Despite what the Americans believed, the great "nerve center" was merely a mobile headquarters aboard a few trucks, which promptly left the area as soon as the Americans invaded.

And the myopia was there in 1971 and 1972, when the much-heralded new plan for ending the war was put into full operation—"Vietnamization," the theory that the Americans could make the South Vietnamese capable of standing on their own two feet without American military support. But in 1972, only the intervention of American air power saved the South Vietnamese from collapse after another (and unexpected) Communist offensive was unleashed—an intervention that belied official pronouncements about the success of Vietnamization.

There were two final acts in this tragedy. The first came in March 1975 when South Vietnam's military headquarters, trying to get its forces organized to fight a massive North Vietnamese offensive, found itself unable to locate the Communist forces. The headquarters battle maps were all wrong; they showed incorrect locations for just about every major North Vietnamese unit, and as a result, South Vietnamese military intelligence could not tell unit commanders where the enemy was.

It was a development that caused a great deal of anger, mostly directed at Sergeant Le Er Tang, a young intelligence clerk who was responsible for preparing accurate battle maps. His infuriated superiors announced their intention to beat Sergeant Tang to a pulp, but he was nowhere to be found. He finally reappeared two months later, on the morning of May 2, when he walked into the headquarters—in a North Vietnamese uniform. Captain Le Er Tang of the North Vietnamese Army Intelligence Unit B-36 had arrived to claim the building in the name of his victorious army.

Nearby, the American Embassy already had been evacuated, including its CIA contingent. Its last action in South Vietnam had been to miss completely the impending North Vietnamese offensive. Having cut themselves off from their South Vietnamese CIO counterparts, they tried to wade through a mountain of communications intercepts, captured documents, and other raw intelligence, only to find that this often-contradictory mass provided them no answers. There were no human-intelligence assets anywhere to tell them of North Vietnamese plans, there were no assets anywhere in the jungles to tip them off about North Vietnamese troop movements, and none of their remaining South Vietnamese assets —mostly in the Phoenix program and internal-security forces —gave them a single clue about the impending disaster.

Meanwhile, the Viet Cong infrastructure, despite Phoenix, was as busy as ever. At Ban Me Thuot, a strategically important town in the Central Highlands, the people who constituted that infrastructure secretly half sawed through each tree in a grove where a large force of North Vietnamese tanks was hidden. Safe from any aerial observation by South Vietnamese planes, the tanks remained hidden until the moment of attack, when the trees were felled and the armor rolled into the town in a surprise attack that caught the defenders flatfooted. The successful attack unhinged the South Vietnamese strategic position in the entire Central Highlands, opening the door to later disaster.

History repeats itself first as tragedy, then as farce, as the aphorism has it, and nearly five years after this series of events, a farcical epilogue took place, the final act in the drama.

It began in Laos, when a group of Hmongs, part of a small CIA-funded "resistance" movement against the Communist government of the country, claimed to have seen a "prisoner-of-war camp" deep inside a Laotian jungle, at which several "Americans" had been spotted. The report caused a sensation within the American intelligence community, especially in the military intelligence agencies, since it concerned one of their central preoccupations: the fate of American prisoners during the Vietnam war.

Officially, there weren't supposed to be any prisoners; under the 1973 peace agreement, all had been released. But there were also 2,494 missing American servicemen, including 568 in Laos. Ever since 1973, the military intelligence agencies, particularly the Defense Intelligence Agency, had become convinced that the Communists were holding many of these missing men as prisoners, as possible bargaining chips in later negotiations. The more the North Vietnamese and Laotians denied it, the more U.S. intelligence officials were convinced that there were still American prisoners being held.

Among the more obsessed over this question was Lieutenant Colonel James B. "Bo" Gritz, a Special Forces officer who had won sixty decorations in Vietnam, where he worked on SOG operations into Cambodia. Part of the obsession was personal: Gritz's father had been shot down in a B-17 during World War II and been officially declared dead; in addition, like many Green Berets, Gritz felt a close bond with American soldiers who had been left behind.

Gritz's concern coincided with that of a number of DIA officers, who felt that the United States government had not done enough to hold the North Vietnamese, especially, accountable for the missing Americans. An idea began to take hold: If the United States could produce some of these missing, the resulting international outcry would compel the North Vietnamese to make that accounting.

The Hmongs' reported sighting moved the DIA to send an SR-71 flight over the area to confirm it. The resulting pictures became the subject of excruciatingly detailed analysis, although they did not prove the sighting one way or the other. The problem, clearly, was that a lot of DIA officials wanted to believe what the Hmongs had claimed was true, that there really were American prisoners held at the jungle site. So even the most slender clue was advanced as proof. The pictures showed vegetables being grown in fields around the camp, so this was adduced as evidence of an American presence, since Laotians usually grow only rice in such fields. And the pictures also showed what appeared to be men sitting cross-legged on the ground. Again, this was considered prime evidence, since Laotians usually squat on their haunches; most probably, it was argued, the cross-legged figures were Americans.

But the DIA was unable to obtain government approval for a rescue mission using American personnel to raid the campsite, mostly because the pictures were not in the least conclusive—certainly not conclusive enough to launch a highly provocative U.S. rescue mission that would violate sovereign borders.

Meanwhile, Gritz had retired from the army. Friends with a number of DIA personnel, he was aware of the Laotian sighting. When he learned that there would not be an official rescue mission, Gritz decided to mount his own—a private operation that would present positive proof of what both Gritz and many DIA officials already believed was fact.

Whether the DIA "unofficially" encouraged Gritz to carry out this private mission remains somewhat unclear, although, in fact, Gritz apparently received an extensive amount of official help in his quest. He mounted at least two operations into Laos, trying to find the camp. Both missions aborted before any sighting could be made, but by 1982, Gritz was convinced that the final proof lay just within his grasp.

Gritz began to talk about "special sources" reporting even more conclusive intelligence about Americans being held in Laos, sufficient for him to raise a stake of nearly $150,000 to mount what he called Operation Velvet Hammer into Laos. Some of the money was raised from actors William Shatner and Clint Eastwood, who provided the underwriting in return for the rights to what they assumed would be among the great adventure stories of our time.

It might have been, except that the prime source at that point for Gritz's conviction about American prisoners turned out to be an elderly Laotian mystery man who had been telling stories for some years about sightings of American prisoners in Laos. He had flunked three CIA lie-detector tests, and the agency long ago had pronounced him "unreliable" as a source.

But Gritz found the man reliable, possibly because he *wanted* to find him reliable. In any event, by November 1982 Gritz had quite an operation going in Bangkok, his chosen operational headquarters for Velvet Hammer. He had not only enlisted three other ex-American military men for the venture, he also had sophisticated communications equipment, weapons, and a full panoply of gear for the mission that all involved were certain would make them world famous.

But Velvet Hammer had all the security of an elephant entering a drugstore. It was not long before rumors swept all over Bangkok that something very big was up: There were several mysterious Americans about to run some sort of operation, and one of them was recruiting Hmongs. By this point, there was a total of nineteen people involved in Velvet Hammer, and security was made further porous when Gritz and the Americans traveled to villages along the Mekong seeking to buy boats. Since pleasure cruises are not a notable feature of the Mekong, only one possibility existed—the Americans and the Laotian guerrillas planned to invade Laos, although their purpose was unclear.

Thus, when Gritz and his team stepped off into the boats on the night of November 27, 1982, there were few people within miles of the village of Ban Bonakah who did not know about it. Possibly the Pathet Lao knew too, for only a few days later, while Gritz and the Laotians were walking through the jungle, they were caught in an ambush. One of the Hmong Laotians was killed, and the rest of the group scattered, never having gotten anywhere near the supposed prisoner camp.

As for Gritz, he made his way back to Bangkok by swimming across the Mekong, whereupon he was arrested by Thai authorities, who seemed more amused than angered by all the shenanigans. They wound up sending the Americans home, like chastened schoolboys, along with the blond woman who functioned as Angel East, the operation's communications specialist.

It had been a fiasco, but then people in that part of the world were used to seeing such fiascos. They had seen them for the years of the Vietnam war, when the helicopters, the big B-52 bombers, the tanks, the men in the Green Berets, and the troops with the best weapons and equipment had all stumbled around, trying to find and defeat the little men in black pajamas and rubber sandals.

Perhaps, some argue, it was all ordained, or, as American diplomat Charles W. Yost foresaw in 1968, "If indigenous dissidents, whether or not Communist . . . are able to mobilize and maintain more effective popular support than the government, they will eventually prevail."

eight

APPARATS AND SKYWRITERS

> I don't know what kind of intelligence
> I want, but I know it when I get it.
>
> —HENRY KISSINGER

UNLIKE MOST SUCH ENCOUNTERS, the rendezvous between Elihu Avraham* of the Israeli Mossad and the Eastern European intelligence agent was decidedly free of passwords and other such esoterica of espionage tradecraft. The Eastern European approached the Israeli in the Vienna restaurant crowded with luncheon diners, warmly shook his hand, and showed him to a table, while thanking him for punctually arriving at their prearranged meeting.

They sat at a table near the rear of the restaurant, carefully sizing each other up as they exchanged idle conversation about the oppressive heat of that summer of 1973. The preliminaries aside, and each man certain he had measured the other properly, talk got down to business.

The talk was direct and to the point, for each man already had many of the important facts about the man sitting opposite him. The Eastern European knew that the Israeli, ostensibly a trade expert involved in the import-export business, was in fact among a small group of Mossad agents handling that

*A pseudonym

265

service's most secret operation: assassinations of Palestinians all over Europe. And as much as the Eastern European disliked Israelis, he had to admit the assassinations had been carried off with great skill; a dozen of the Palestinian movement's top leaders had been shot or blown up (some with bombs that went off when they answered their telephones), crippling Palestinian operations in Europe.

As for Avraham, he knew that the Eastern European, supposedly a diplomat at his country's embassy in Vienna, was actually a senior operative of that country's intelligence service. Further, he knew that the Eastern European worked closely with the Soviet KGB and had important contacts with many of the Soviet military and intelligence elite. What Avraham did not know was why the Eastern European a week before this luncheon date had contacted him to set up a meeting. Possibly, the Israeli surmised, his opposite number was handling a KGB operation, perhaps preparing to give the Israeli a few names of Palestinian operatives the KGB wanted done away with because they had transgressed in some way. Or perhaps he had been detailed to pass along a warning that the KGB, aggravated over the slaughter of their Palestinian allies, would strike back at Mossad if it didn't stop.

But the Eastern European had something much less complicated in mind: money. Specifically, he wanted money in exchange for a secret that the Israeli agent found incredible: that the Russians had given approval to an Egyptian plan to cross the Suez Canal and invade Israeli-occupied Sinai, in conjunction with a Syrian attack from the east. Under this plan, at least three Egyptian armies would force a crossing of the canal, overwhelm Israeli troops guarding the canal's eastern banks, and subsequently dig in after capturing limited objectives. They would then hold off Israeli counterattacks and bring about a stalemate that would lead to peace talks, during which the strong Egyptian bargaining position would compel Israel to negotiate a settlement returning at least part of the Sinai to Egypt.

It was called Operation Badr, the Eastern European said,

adding that he had a copy of the entire operational plan, complete with maps and detailed orders for troop movements. D-day would be sometime during the first week in October, the Eastern European warned, so there was little time for delay; possession of the operational plan would allow the Israelis to checkmate this grave threat. And that plan was for sale. A mere $200,000—a small price to pay, the Eastern European noted—would give the Israelis the vital secret.

Avraham's immediate return to Tel Aviv with this offer set off an intense debate within Israeli intelligence. The agent heard nothing of this debate, for he was excluded from the inner councils that hashed and rehashed the Eastern European's offer. The debate, Avraham was told a few days later by his Mossad superiors, had been resolved. The offer was a plant, probably at the instigation of the KGB, to cause disruption in the Israeli armed forces. Nevertheless, Mossad decided, it would pay the $200,000 for a copy of the plan, "just to be sure." A quick return to Vienna, followed by a much more clandestine encounter, brought Avraham the plan for Operation Badr. And so the Israelis were in possession of a document that they were fairly certain was an elaborate deception, although they could not understand the point of the deception—unless it was simply to enrich the KGB (or the Eastern European) by $200,000. On the other hand, $200,000 is a relatively trivial sum in the marketplace of international espionage, especially for complete operational plans of major military offensives.

And while they pondered this turn of events, the shadow of war crept over Israel. For although the Israelis did not realize it, the document they were so certain was a fake was actually quite genuine. The Israelis, in fact, were at that point poised on the brink of disaster.

On October 6, 1973, Operation Badr unfolded just as the plan had foretold, and only the most extraordinary effort by the Israeli military—and a large-scale American airlift of critically needed advanced weapons—managed to stave off what initially appeared to be a defeat that threatened the very existence of Israel itself. The Yom Kippur War amounted to an intelligence failure of near-tragic proportions, but it is important to understand that it also involved some real deficiencies of American intelligence.

It seems surprising to include American intelligence in that indictment, yet the Americans share a major portion of the blame for what happened. There were two aspects of that American involvement: one, the relationship between American and Israeli intelligence; and two, the very nature of American intelligence itself in 1973.

The bond between American and Israeli intelligence had been close, much closer than similar bonds elsewhere in the world. It was a relationship that had paid great dividends for American intelligence, for the Americans never did manage to establish a firm foothold anywhere in the volatile Middle East; simply put, the Israelis had become America's eyes and ears in that area. The American-Israeli intelligence bond had been formed even before establishment of the Jewish state in 1948, when U.S. intelligence operatives in Italy worked covertly with the underground Zionist movement, ferrying people and supplies through the British blockade to Palestine. Those operations amounted to an intelligence prep school whose alumni later wound up in the highest levels of both the American and Israeli intelligence organizations.

To be sure, there were some problems in that relationship during subsequent years, for despite their close ties, the Americans and Israelis often had different ideas about the Middle East. In 1956, no one in Israeli intelligence bothered to tell their American friends of Israel's plan to invade the Sinai in concert with a British-French invasion of Egypt. Israeli intelligence carried out an elaborate deception plan to conceal the large-scale military deployments needed for the invasion, including several designed to hoodwink U.S. military attachés assigned the job of watching the Israeli armed forces.* Another deception plan was carried out by the Israelis in 1967 to conceal their preemptive strike against the Arabs. (That same year saw the most serious incident in the long Israeli-American intelligence alliance: The Israelis attacked the National Security Agency's spy ship *Liberty* off the coast of Sinai—mainly because the ship had detected Israel's greatest secret, a system of radio-traffic manipulation that not only concealed the true location of Israeli units but also fed false information over Arab communications networks.)

Despite these and other incidents, however, American and Israeli intelligence remained close, and by 1973 the Israeli Mossad amounted to the chief source for virtually all American intelligence on the Middle East. The arrangement was underscored by a number of formal agreements, which involved American financial support for many Mossad operations, in return for what the Americans considered a gold mine: Israeli intelligence on the Arabs, plus huge quantities of advanced Soviet equipment captured by the Israelis, allowing American intelligence to construct a detailed picture of Soviet weapon capabilities.

But such a close bond in intelligence terms eventually becomes too tight, resulting in a form of myopia, in which one side overlooks the first clues that its ally has begun to slip. It happened with the Americans and Israelis, for the brilliant Israeli victories of 1967, combined with the Mossad's soaring reputation for omniscience, blinded the Americans to some very real problems afflicting their most important intelligence ally. The blindness, very similar to the uncritical admiration by the Americans for British intelligence before World War II, caused them to miss some significant changes in Israeli intelligence prior to the Yom Kippur War. Among these was

*Chief among them was a deception designed to take advantage of what the Israelis knew was the American attachés' habit of monitoring Israeli radio broadcasts to hear mobilization orders for reserve units. The Israelis kept the orders out of radio channels monitored by the Americans, and as a result, American intelligence did not know of the Sinai invasion until after it had started. The intelligence failure annoyed Eisenhower, who was caught equally flatfooted by the CIA's failure to detect the British-French invasion before it began.

a pronounced deterioration in Mossad's intelligence-collection capabilities, mostly because Mossad had been saddled
with a new mission: a large-scale effort to destroy the Palestinian leadership by a program of assassinations. The effort,
born of the desire by the Israeli leadership for revenge following the massacre of Israeli athletes at the 1972 Olympics,
diverted too much of an already strained intelligence organization's resources; Mossad had to take away assets used for
regular intelligence collection and move them into the huge
effort required to track down and eliminate its Palestinian
enemies. Furthermore, the first generation of Israeli intelligence, a group of brilliant, dedicated men who had honed
their skills in a lifetime of clandestine work on behalf of the
oppressed Jews of Europe, were now passing on, into retirement or death. The succeeding generation, while perfectly
capable, lacked their depth of experience.

In simple terms, the Americans did not realize that by
1973, Israeli intelligence was not what it had been. The difference was summed up in the way the Israelis almost benignly
regarded a large-scale Egyptian and Syrian military buildup in
the summer of 1973, including extensive maneuvers near the
Suez Canal. Major General Eliyahu Zeira, director of Israeli
military intelligence, regarded the buildup as "defensive maneuvers," a judgment the Americans accepted. As Zeira and
other Israeli intelligence officers explained, their judgments
rested on something they called "the conception." This
amounted to a system of "intelligence indicators," specific
military moves that would tip off an impending Arab attack
against Israel. The system in turn stemmed from an especially
dangerous mindset of Israeli intelligence at that point: a fervent belief in overwhelming Israeli military superiority over
the Arabs. Thus, an Arab military attack against Israel was
considered "foolish," and the "indicators" were designed to
ring alarm bells only if the Arabs conducted any major, overt
military moves threatening Israel. (The Israelis believed, for
example, that the Arabs would attack with ground forces only
after paralyzing the Israeli Air Force by deep penetration

raids. Thus a simple equation was formulated: If the Arabs carried out such raids, then a major attack was imminent; if they did not, then an attack wasn't imminent.)

The Americans, especially the CIA, accepted all this un-critically, the chief reason they treated the Operation Badr documents with a great deal of suspicion when Avraham was dispatched to Washington in July 1973 to show them to U.S. intelligence. By that time, Avraham suspected that perhaps his superiors had been too hasty in dismissing Badr as a plant. The more he thought about it, the more it seemed to Av-raham that the documents had to be genuine; if the Egyptians were about to launch a surprise attack, they would concen-trate on lulling their Israeli enemy into a false sense of secu-rity. So how would leaking a false plan for an offensive help that deception? As the Russians and the Egyptians must have been aware, they stood the risk of alerting the very enemy they were trying to lull.

Avraham did not know it, but at the very time he was in Washington, listening as American military and intelligence experts debated whether the plan was genuine, another Isra-eli intelligence officer was drawing his own conclusion. Lieu-tenant Benjamin Siman-Tov (Hebrew for "good sign"), a young, bright Israeli military-intelligence officer assigned the job of watching Egyptian military moves, had sifted every clue and decided that the large-scale maneuvers on the other side of the Suez Canal were part of an elaborate deception. The Egyptians intended to attack, he concluded, probably some-time in October. Siman-Tov wrote up a lengthy report on his conclusion, but it went no farther than his superior, Lieuten-ant Colonel David Gedaliah, senior intelligence officer for the Israeli Army's Southern Command, who pronounced it wrong. The movements of Egyptian forces were for defensive deployment purposes only, Gedaliah insisted.

Even more positive that no threat existed was Zeira him-self, under increasing pressure to explain the huge military buildups both in the Golan Heights area in Syria and on the Egyptian side of the Suez Canal. In a showdown meeting on

October 5 in the office of Prime Minister Golda Meir, Zeira
sought to calm nervous Israeli Army generals about the buildups. The generals wanted an Israeli mobilization, a drastic
step in Israel, since large numbers of reservists suddenly
called away from their jobs would in effect bring the economy
to a standstill. Meir needed solid intelligence before deciding
on such a major action; could Zeira assure her that there was
no possibility of an Egyptian or Syrian attack? Zeira could;
there was a "low probability" of an attack, he told Meir, and
to clinch it, he went even further, insisting that the possibility
was "even lower than low." The Israelis did not mobilize, and
the Egyptians and Syrians less than twenty-four hours after
this meeting fell upon an unprepared Israel.

For a tiny nation where four thousand battle deaths represent a major calamity, the Yom Kippur intelligence disaster
exacted a terrible price from Israel. It featured every possible
mistake: underestimation of an opponent, preconceived no-
tions, refusal to listen to information contrary to those preconceptions, lack of solid intelligence, and blind faith in one's
own abilities. And the disaster was shared by Israeli intelligence's closest ally, the United States.

Aside from its uncritical acceptance of Israeli intelligence, American intelligence also failed in 1973 because of its
two worst shortcomings: one, an overreliance on technical
intelligence-collection systems; and two, lack of high-level
sources. The Yom Kippur War proved just how ambiguous
those technical systems can be. For months preceding the
outbreak of the war, American satellites and SR-71s constantly overflew the Suez Canal and Sinai areas. They produced a small mountain of very detailed pictures that showed
virtually every piece of equipment the Egyptians were deploying, down to individual machine guns. But the pictures could
not answer the vital questions: What were the Egyptian intentions? Were the Egyptians carrying out large-scale maneuvers, as the Israelis suspected, or did they actually intend to
attack across the canal? A considerable American SIGINT

operation had the same problem; the Americans intercepted virtually every electronic communication in that area for weeks on end, producing a large number of intercepts. But the signals were ambiguous; some suggested that the Egyptians might be planning to attack, while others suggested differently.

The ambiguity might have been cleared up by some high-level sources within the Egyptian military high command and government, or within the large Russian military-adviser contingent in Egypt that likely would have direct involvement in any major Egyptian military operation. However, the Americans lacked such sources, so they were compelled to make some sense out of the vast pile of conflicting information their technical wizardry had collected. What American intelligence did not know at that point was that the Egyptians and the Russians were perfectly aware that the Americans lacked good human sources, so they deliberately fed out vast amounts of ambiguity for American eyes and ears. The radio traffic the Americans so assiduously collected was part of an elaborate deception plan; radios were on the air constantly, broadcasting locations and reports for units that often did not exist. And what units did exist were shifted around aimlessly, all the while aware that every movement was being watched by American electronic eyes. As the Russians and Egyptians correctly guessed, analysts trying to make sense out of the rapidly shifting Egyptian deployments were frustrated by a bewildering series of rapid military shifts that appeared to make no sense.

The Egyptians and their Russian advisers were also aware that the Americans shared the prevailing Israeli assumption about the lack of Arab military capabilities, especially in Egypt. In fact, a major Russian advisory effort had managed to improve those abilities dramatically, but it was an improvement that the Russians wanted to keep as secret as possible, for underestimation was to play an important role in the plan to attack the Sinai. (Sadat had ordered the bulk of the Russian advisers home in 1972, but many remained.) To reinforce the underestimation, the Russians and Egyptians contrived a simple deception that was to fool both the Americans and their Israeli counterparts.

It took the unusual form of a large, public military parade and demonstration staged by the Egyptian government in July 1973. The parade was a high priority for every intelligence operative and military attaché anywhere near Egypt, for it promised a firsthand look at the Egyptian forces and all that new, advanced equipment with which the Russians had outfitted them since the debacle of 1967. What everybody saw was straight out of a Marx Brothers comedy, a parade and staged military maneuver that was fouled up so badly, the attachés in the audience had to stop themselves from laughing out loud. The Egyptians appeared positively inept, literally stumbling all over themselves. Intelligence reports of a half-dozen countries, including the United States, buzzed for weeks afterward with news of the Russian embarrassment; they had spent a fortune again outfitting a military force that would never learn how to fight.

However, it was all a deliberate sham, a carefully choreographed exhibition of ineptitude designed to lead whoever was watching to just that conclusion. It worked. Neither the CIA, nor the American military-intelligence agencies, nor the Mossad—nor anybody, for that matter—looked deeper, behind this elaborate charade, to discover what the Russians had been teaching the Egyptians for the past six years. Or why they had acceded to Egyptian requests for so much military equipment.

Thus, at the very moment the Egyptians stood poised for their strike into Sinai—an event that would cause a fundamental disruption in international politics, including the Arab oil boycott and a direct confrontation between Moscow and Washington—the United States had no idea that the dangerous Middle East cauldron was about to boil over.

To a large extent, the blindness stemmed from a curious circumstance under which American intelligence was operating at that point, for it had come under the dominance of one man. That man, Henry Kissinger, had managed to do what no other man ever had: take control over the disparate elements of the U.S. intelligence apparatus.

The circumstance explains much about the failure of that apparatus in the Yom Kippur War. How it came to be requires some explanation, for the events of 1973 climaxed years of a very trying relationship between the American intelligence community and the man it would come to regard as its greatest enemy.

In January 1969, a new President of the United States and his national security adviser, with remarkable unanimity of view, took office and set about immediately to transform the American decision-making process for foreign policy. Richard Nixon and Henry Kissinger shared the conviction that the foreign-policy apparatus was too clumsy and slow, riddled with competing voices that made American foreign policy essentially reactive and inconsistent.

An important part of their unhappiness with the foreign-policy machinery centered on American intelligence, which Nixon and Kissinger found nothing short of woeful. Privately, Kissinger complained that he found the intelligence product —particularly that of the CIA—very nearly a joke. It was produced by what Kissinger sneeringly called "theologians of intelligence," who most often seemed incapable of providing straight answers to simple questions. Kissinger perceived the intelligence community as bitterly divided, marked by squabbling among its various components; he complained that intelligence reports amounted to either shoddy attempts to cover up lack of knowledge or deliberate fudging to avoid controversy or elaborate efforts to protect the narrow interests of a particular intelligence agency.

The test of statesmanship, Kissinger had said often, was the ability to anticipate and evaluate threats before they occurred. But the record was clear that American intelligence wasn't giving much warning about anything—one of the reasons, Kissinger argued, that American foreign policy was such a mess. The memories of recent intelligence disasters was still fresh. Aside from Vietnam, the American performance in Europe obviously left a great deal to be desired, and Kissinger and Nixon were especially appalled over what had happened in Czechoslovakia several months before Nixon took office.

American intelligence was bewildered about events in Czechoslovakia, beginning with the coming to power of the liberal Dubček regime. By the summer of 1968, it was clear that the Soviets, increasingly jumpy about the threat the Dubček regime represented to their other satellite states in Eastern Europe, were about to take some sort of action. A large-scale buildup of Warsaw Pact forces on the Czech borders (described as "maneuvers" by Moscow) raised the possibility that the Soviets might intervene militarily, but intelligence reports reflected U.S. confusion over what the Russians intended to do. Some argued that the Russians would intervene, while others argued that the buildup was a pressure tactic, designed to bring the liberal Czechoslovakian regime back into line.

Again, the problem was lack of sources inside Eastern Europe; the CIA especially relied almost exclusively on reconnaissance and electronics interceptions to get some idea of what was happening. And that meant that when the Russians and their Warsaw Pact allies decided to move into Czechoslovakia under radio silence, the Americans had no idea that they had moved until it was too late. (The error was compounded when the CIA and the DIA somehow lost track of an entire Soviet division that later wound up in Prague. And the divisions the Americans did spot fed out a stream of deliberately misleading radio signals, leading to an intelligence judgment in July 1968 that there would be no invasion of Czechoslovakia. On August 20, the invasion took place.)

Matters did not improve in the following year, when the Americans were surprised by a military coup in Libya, an event that had severe repercussions, including Libya's close alliance with the Soviet Union and the first large Libyan-inspired increases in the price of crude oil. And a year after that, an infuriated Kissinger found the United States surprised by events in Cambodia,* followed in 1971 by disaster in Laos, when a U.S.-sponsored invasion of that country by the South Vietnamese was smashed by North Vietnamese forces the Americans had failed to spot.

Clearly, the acuity of American intelligence was declining, and part of the reason was the nature of the position of director of Central Intelligence. The job—its holder is usually described as "CIA Director," although technically no such post exists—was created by the National Security Act of 1947, and was intended to make the DCI the most powerful man in the entire American intelligence community. The DCI would work directly with the National Security Council, and in effect serve as the coordinator of all American intelligence, with direct access to the President via the NSC (no other American intelligence-agency head has such access). However, what looked so reasonable on paper was transformed into quite something else by practical experience.

The central problem was that the DCI had to possess sufficient political clout to maintain direct access to the President. Allen Dulles, the strongest DCI, had that access guaranteed because his brother was the Secretary of State and dominated American foreign policy. But the Bay of Pigs, which ruined Dulles, introduced a tendency by the White House to select more malleable men for the position. This was exemplified by President Kennedy's selection of an otherwise undistinguished John McCone as Dulles's successor—almost exclusively because McCone's impeccable conserva-

---

*Cambodia was the site of one of the more contentious arguments between the CIA and the DIA during the 1970s. The controversy concerned the port of Sihanoukville, which the DIA insisted was a major entry point for supplies for Communist forces in Cambodia and South Vietnam. The CIA rated the port's importance as insignificant, and there were protracted and bitter arguments about virtually every ounce of supplies moving through the port. In the end, the DIA was proved right, although it failed to persuade the White House to order an all-out bombing attack on the port. The argument was academic; by the time it was resolved, Cambodia's government was on the ropes.

tive Republican credentials would protect Kennedy's political right flank. That meant, however, that McCone did not enjoy Kennedy's full confidence, and everybody else in the American intelligence community knew it.

With the decline in influence of the DCI came a corresponding decline in the influence of the CIA, most apparent in the military-intelligence move to gain dominance over technical collection programs, the most important component of all American intelligence. McCone's already meager influence slipped further under Lyndon Johnson—who strongly disliked him—and he finally quit in 1965. Johnson's choice for a successor was a total disaster: Admiral William "Red" Raborn, former member of the Scientists and Engineers for Johnson-Humphrey organization and a fellow Texan who had won fame within the defense community for his successful management of the Polaris missile program.

Aside from his political connection, military management skills, and regional affinity with the President, Raborn had no real qualifications for the DCI job. He was in office only a short while before his CIA subordinates realized they were being led by a man of almost incomparable stupidity. A very slow learner, thickheaded, and in love with the navy—the only life he had ever known—Raborn could not pronounce the names of many capitals of the world (to say nothing of knowing what countries they were capitals of), and could not remember the names of heads of state. Appalled CIA deputies discovered that Raborn did not seem to have even the most elementary idea of world events, and at one meeting, they were stunned when Raborn expressed surprise that such a thing as the Sino-Soviet split existed. Faced with a demand by Raborn that he produce "evidence" of this development, Ray S. Cline, one of his deputies, blew up: "Well, what do you want me to use, Admiral, a *wheelbarrow*?"

A series of CIA-inspired press leaks about the admiral's more boneheaded activities began to undercut Raborn, and by the spring of 1966, he was finished. Johnson, in an impromptu conversation with reporters, claimed that Raborn had only been an "interim" choice for DCI. To underscore that political hint, Johnson told Raborn to bring one of his deputies along to White House meetings, a man who was to do most of the talking about intelligence—Richard Helms, a CIA deputy director. It so happened that Helms was the source for most of the leaks, a little covert action he had done at the behest of the CIA establishment, which felt that its already dwindling influence with the White House would be erased altogether if Raborn continued in office.

On one level, the plan worked, for Johnson, peppered with constant media reminders that his DCI was ineffective, decided that a change would have to be made, and further, that the new DCI should come from within the CIA itself. With all his other problems, Johnson did not want to begin the difficult task of finding another outsider; besides, there was Helms, a cool, confident, intelligent man, right there at hand. Helms became the new DCI in June 1966.

The appointment of Helms, an OSS veteran and charter member of the CIA, was cheering to the CIA establishment, but they failed to note that the new DCI had a major handicap: lack of a secure political base. This handicap was to prove critical in Helms's career, for as much as he enjoyed the respect and support of his own CIA, that counted for nothing in the Washington intelligence wars, where the name of the game was political muscle and degree of access to the President. Helms had the misfortune to take office at the point of deepening American involvement in Vietnam, when Johnson regarded intelligence's function as helping him win the war, not dispassionate analysis. And since the war was fundamentally unwinnable, that meant there was nothing Helms could ever have said or done that would have given Johnson the magic keys he so often sought for victory.*

---

*Not that Helms didn't try. During the great intelligence debate in late 1967 concerning the actual numbers of Communist forces in South Vietnam, he ordered the CIA to compromise the argument by accepting the military's lower estimates of Communist strength. Helms lacked the political clout to tell Johnson that there were more Communist forces than ever, a statistic that would have belied official optimism of "progress" in the war—and put the CIA squarely in the presidential doghouse.

The onset of the Nixon administration further exposed Helms's weakness, for as a Democrat with no strong political base, he was regarded suspiciously by Nixon, who had a marked distrust of what he saw as a CIA dominated by Ivy League liberals (although Helms himself was a Williams College man). Furthermore, Helms was an experienced intelligence bureaucrat, but he had no feel for the more rarefied world of high-level Washington politics, where the real action was. There, he had an important bureaucratic enemy: Nixon's Secretary of Defense, Melvin Laird, a former congressman with many years of experience in the jungle of White House and congressional politics. Laird sought to amass greater intelligence power at the Pentagon, and he was building on a strong base. At that point, the military actually had its hands on more than 80 percent of the total intelligence budget, since it had managed to gain operational control over the spy planes, satellites, and SIGINT collection systems that formed the heart of the increasingly technified American intelligence apparatus.

But Helms by his own admission was uninterested in technical intelligence. An "agents' man," as he was known within the agency, he had no interest in the increasingly arcane arguments surrounding such intelligence, and actually fell asleep during one meeting on Soviet missile strength—such discussions "frankly bore me," Helms was reported to have said. That attitude was ultimately to cost Helms his job, for by 1972, bloodied by many losing struggles with Laird, he was elbowed aside by Nixon and given the post of U.S. ambassador to Iran.

But by that time, the DCI had been reduced to very nearly a shadow anyway by the single-minded efforts of the man who was to become the de facto czar of American intelligence, Henry Kissinger.

The national security adviser made a dramatic first move upon taking office—ordering what amounted to a university-type final examination for every component of the American foreign-policy and intelligence machinery. All the agencies involved were ordered to provide independent answers to a series of searching questions Kissinger's National Security Council asked about the Vietnam War. The questions were so detailed that they served the double purpose of keeping those agencies occupied and at the same time providing Kissinger with a perfect method of evaluating just how good they were. The results, as Kissinger might have suspected, were uniformly revealing: Nobody, especially the intelligence agencies, seemed to have much of an idea of what was going on, and even less of an idea of what to do about it. At the same time, James Schlesinger, head of the Office of Management and Budget, carried out a Nixon-ordered analysis of American intelligence and concluded that it was plagued by overlapping jurisdictions, it spent too much money, and the intelligence it produced was not worth the cost. (Schlesinger himself became DCI in 1973 after Helms was forced out, and one of his first actions was to fire nearly one thousand CIA employees.)

Kissinger was dismayed at what he saw of the intelligence product, which he often called "skywriting," and was most unhappy with the national intelligence estimates and other analyses produced by the CIA, documents he found almost universally unfathomable. For one thing, Kissinger complained, the analyses and estimates did not reveal the sources of the intelligence judgments, so it was very difficult for anyone reading them to judge their worth. Moreover, Kissinger suspected, correctly, that the national intelligence estimates in particular were more monuments to the art of compromise than seasoned analysis. They were pockmarked with too many on-the-one-hand-this-and-the-other-hand-that statements, and dissents were buried in obscure footnotes. As a man seeking specific, unambiguous intelligence for the new, grand world design he and Nixon were trying to build, Kissinger was terribly frustrated by the fogginess he found in most intelligence judgments, many of which he scornfully called "Talmudic." (More bluntly, he once scrawled "piece of crap" across the first page of an intelligence estimate that he found especially vague.)

By deciding what questions he wanted answered in intelligence reports, Kissinger gradually began to control them, in an important sense becoming the final arbiter of American intelligence, all of which had to pass through his hands on its way to Nixon. Indeed, Kissinger's National Security Council, derisively known as *"der Apparat"* in the CIA, became for all intents and purposes the real American CIA, for it was the national security adviser, not the DCI, who had the precious access to the President.*

Kissinger by 1970 had achieved his goal as virtual czar of American intelligence, but that failed to guarantee any improvement in the quality of the intelligence. And the very first major intelligence controversy confronting Nixon and Kissinger showed some disturbing evidence that a one-man show was no solution to the problem.

On the morning of August 26, 1970, a routine U-2 flight crossing the southern part of Cuba passed over the Bay of Cienfuegos, a deepwater harbor of recurring interest to American intelligence because of its potential use as a naval base. A U-2 had overflown the area eleven days before, but the pictures developed from the August 26 flight showed some dramatic differences: A large wharf and military barracks were under construction—and most significant in the light of what happened later, there was also a recreational area behind those barracks.

The results of the August 26 flight spurred strong interest in what was going on at Cienfuegos, and daily U-2 flights were ordered. They revealed more construction in the har-

---

*Relations between Kissinger and the CIA grew very tense during this period, mostly because of Kissinger's habit of combining intelligence and policymaking roles. He and Nixon jointly decided on a Vietnamization strategy for ending the Vietnam war without bothering to consult either the State Department or the CIA on whether it had any hope of working. Both agencies concluded that it did not, and CIA-Kissinger relations further soured when the CIA prepared a lengthy analysis with the impolitic title "Why Vietnamization Won't Work."

bor, intelligence that dovetailed with another interesting development, this one picked up by the Office of Naval Intelligence: A Soviet naval flotilla appeared to be sailing toward Cienfuegos. Significantly, the seven-ship flotilla included a submarine tender and an amphibious landing ship with two barges, the type used for nuclear-submarine support operations.

Kissinger was shown the pictures, and he instantly decided that the Russians were constructing a nuclear-submarine base at Cienfuegos. This was a somewhat startling conclusion, for aside from the coincidence of construction of a wharf and the sailing of the Soviet naval flotilla, there was no hard evidence that the Russians intended any such thing. But Kissinger at this point fancied himself an intelligence analyst, and he pointed to one clue in the pictures that he said proved the Russians were busy at Cienfuegos: The recreational area behind the barracks included a soccer field. Cubans, Kissinger triumphantly announced, do not play soccer, but Russians do; therefore, there was no doubt that a "significant" Soviet military presence was stationed at Cienfuegos, undoubtedly to construct nuclear-submarine port facilities.

Kissinger, however, was wrong. Cubans *did* play soccer, and had for many years. That being the case, it was possible that the construction at Cienfuegos was *Cuban,* not Russian, and that the Cubans were building their own naval base of some sort, with berthing privileges to be extended to passing Soviet naval units. American intelligence was divided about developments at Cienfuegos, although majority opinion seemed to be that the facility was probably a relatively minor base that would also serve as a rest-and-recreation port for Soviet submarines. In fact, even the normally alarmist DIA concluded that the Cienfuegos construction did not amount to an important naval base.

But Kissinger persisted in his belief, and it was not long before a full-scale crisis began brewing, a distinct echo of the Cuban missile crisis eight years before. Kissinger argued that Cienfuegos amounted to a gross violation of the 1962 Soviet-

American understanding that prohibited the introduction of strategic weapons into Cuba. Basing nuclear submarines at Cienfuegos was not only a deliberate Russian challenge to the United States, Kissinger insisted, it also threatened to create a serious disruption in the American-Soviet strategic balance. The base, Kissinger charged, would dramatically improve the on-station time of Russian Yankee-class nuclear-missile submarines, normally on patrol along the east coast of the United States. Usually, those submarines were on station only about 20 percent of the time, given the lack of overseas bases and the long distances they had to traverse back and forth from their home base in Murmansk. (American missile submarines, which can use overseas bases, are on station at least 50 percent of the time.)

Kissinger wanted a showdown with the Russians over Cienfuegos, and the number of scare stories he leaked about the port soon brought him to a meeting with an ashen-faced Soviet Ambassador Anatoli Dobrynin, who sat shocked as Kissinger told him the "grave" threat the Americans perceived. Dobrynin angrily denied that any nuclear-submarine base was being constructed in Cuba, and insisted that there had been no violation of the 1962 understanding. Nevertheless, he grumbled, "in the interests of reducing tensions," the Soviet Union would formally agree not to base any nuclear submarines in Cuba, nor would any stop there temporarily. These guarantees were included in a series of "tightening-up" provisions negotiated by Kissinger and the Russians, and amounted to a revised understanding.

Both Kissinger and Nixon hailed the revisions as a diplomatic victory, but there is cause to wonder about the entire sequence of events. The basic question was whether in fact the Russians planned to do what Kissinger said they did. The question remains open, for there never was any conclusive intelligence that proved Cienfuegos was intended as a nuclear-submarine base. But the most disturbing aspect of the entire crisis was Kissinger's decision to precipitate it on the basis of his own intelligence judgment, itself based on an extremely flimsy piece of evidence. It was a judgment that caused some disquiet within the U.S. intelligence community —disquiet that grew into something much more serious when Kissinger began dabbling in another important area of intelligence, strategic weapons.

The question of strategic weapons—in intelligence terms, the quantitative and qualitative differences in the nuclear arsenals of the Soviet Union and the United States—attracted Kissinger's strongest interest, for in his view, those arsenals represented the real international political strength of each side. Since the onset of the Cold War, the issue of strategic weapons had been the most important question confronting American intelligence. It was also the most divisive, for intelligence judgments on Soviet strategic power not only had immense consequences for American military-budget questions, they also cut across a whole series of decisions on American military and foreign policy.

These judgments had been matters of intense dispute for years, and by the time Nixon took office, they were marked by great ambiguity and confusion. McNamara's original judgment that the Soviets would not seek a massive strategic buildup to match the overwhelming American advantage had been proved wrong by events—the Russians built more weapons at a much faster rate than intelligence predicted—but there was no consensus on exactly what the Russians were trying to achieve. Initially, the general view of American intelligence, sharply dissented to by the military, was that the Russians would seek "equality" in strategic weapons, but the continued strong pace of the Soviet buildup persuaded military intelligence, at least, to believe that the possibility existed for a Russian goal of "superiority" over the United States.

But there was no agreement within the intelligence community about what the Russians were doing, and a large part of the problem, aside from lack of real sources within the Soviet Union, was that the Americans tried to divine intentions from capabilities. This is always a tricky proposition, since it amounts to saying that a certain Soviet missile, for example, is designed strictly for a first-strike capability against the United States because its warhead is outfitted with MIRVs (multiple independently targeted reentry vehicles)—and thus for the sole purpose of blanketing American land-based missile sites with enough warheads to prevent their launching on a retaliatory strike. That assertion may or may not be true; there may be other possibilities to explain a MIRVed warhead. But intelligence that relies almost exclusively, as the Americans do, on technical collection systems, is reduced to extrapolating intentions from the nuts and bolts of the hardware it is observing.

This very ambiguous process of reaching intelligence conclusions about Soviet strategic weapons was largely responsible for the increasingly bitter disputes between the CIA and military-intelligence agencies. They were further sharpened by Laird's belief that the Russians intended to become vastly superior to the United States, at which point they would make a series of threatening moves; the United States, checkmated by Soviet strategic superiority, would be helpless to respond. One of the important effects of Laird's conviction was his tendency to accept the most alarmist intelligence about Soviet strategic weapons. These were mostly produced by the military-intelligence estimates, and by 1971, Laird was relying exclusively on them to buttress his contention that a very large American buildup was required to overcome the Russian lead. Laird openly distrusted the milder CIA estimates and agreed with military-intelligence officials who accused CIA counterparts of "arms-control bias," by which was meant the CIA's alleged domination by "liberals" of the Eastern establishment who sought to downplay the Soviet arms buildup because they wanted to reduce the levels of strategic weapons, especially in the United States. Thus, Laird and the military argued, the CIA "tailored" its intelligence estimates to deliberately underestimate Soviet arms levels.

These dark hints of conspiracy cast a shadow over American intelligence, and were shown to their most invidious effect when an old intelligence argument resurfaced—the ABM.

The ABM dispute appeared to have died a quiet death during Robert McNamara's reign, when it seemed clear that the original alarms over the Soviet ABM were mistaken, and that the United States did not face a grave threat. But the military had always waged a rearguard action against that judgment, arguing that the primitive Soviet facilities could be upgraded into the sophisticated ABM system they always feared might checkmate U.S. nuclear retaliatory capability. The military's argument persisted even in the face of what was supposed to be the ABM intelligence controversy's funeral, a flat statement by McNamara's successor, Clark M. Clifford, that the main Soviet ABM site in Estonia would never be upgraded into a real antimissile system.

But among Laird's first acts upon entering office was to ask for a supplementary budget request for a large-scale U.S. ABM system (known as Safeguard), which would counter what Laird insisted was a threatening, functional Soviet ABM system. With this action, Laird put his seal of approval on military-intelligence estimates, which at that point were almost diametrically opposite to CIA estimates. They also bore little relation to reality: Air force intelligence, for example, estimated in 1970 that there would be anywhere from seven thousand to nine thousand Soviet ABMs by 1972, meaning that the American nuclear arsenal would be completely checkmated by that year.

The intelligence supporting this alarmism was very thin, mainly a complicated series of deductions about the expected development and improvement of Soviet ABM rockets. It amounted to a number of assumptions about how the rockets would be built and deployed, based on what American technology would do in the same circumstances. It was pretty flimsy evidence on which to base a major military-procurement decision, but no more substantial than the intelligence that underlay another important decision, a new submarine nuclear-missile system called Trident. Costing nearly $2 billion each, Trident represented a substantial U.S. strategic investment that grew, primarily, out of a conviction by Laird that the Soviet Union had embarked on a breakneck campaign to build a nuclear-submarine force that would in a few years outstrip that of the United States. Again, this view stemmed mostly from the military-intelligence agencies, which took several facts—a professed new Soviet interest in submarine-launched missiles and the building of some new submarines—and extrapolated a whole series of assumptions about what the Russians planned to do. And since the military-intelligence estimates tended to put the most pessimistic interpretation possible on virtually every Soviet military development, the inevitable conclusion was that there was always a worst case at hand every time the Russians made a move.

Kissinger was not very much taken with these assorted intelligence alarms, for in his view the answer to the continued Soviet military buildup—all American intelligence agencies could agree on the fact of the buildup, if not on its dimensions—was not ever-larger American weapons programs, but an arms-control program that would cool the Soviet buildup and freeze it at current levels. In Kissinger's analysis, all the intelligence disputes were very much secondary to the main point, which was that the United States and the Soviet Union had achieved a form of rough parity in strategic weapons. Further buildups beyond these already high levels was pointless, not to mention the vast cost further increases implied.

The successful Strategic Arms Limitation Talks (SALT) eliminated several old intelligence disputes at once, notably the ABM. Both sides simply traded it away, an action that undercut the military's argument about Soviet ABM systems, since the Russians hardly would have traded away a system that worked as well as some components of American intelligence said it did. But SALT created a new intelligence dispute: compliance, known more technically as verification, the process of ensuring that the Soviet Union lived up to the terms of the agreement.

SALT provided for no on-site inspections, which had been a sticking point in U.S.-Soviet arms-control negotiations for years, mainly because the new art of technical intelligence collection and observation by satellite represented a way to monitor strategic-arms developments without people on the ground actually having to see them. Kissinger had great faith in technology as a method of ensuring compliance, but he did not reckon on the essential ambiguity of such systems, an ambiguity operating in the context of the suspicion with which the military services regarded the SALT agreement. The military had only reluctantly acceded to the agreement, partially because Nixon promised them some "qualitative" improvements in American strategic-arms programs, along with assurances that the machinery of American intelligence would be able to instantly detect any Soviet cheating. The military's suspicion augured a long, difficult road ahead, since there would be an endless number of complaints of Soviet cheating, particularly from military-intelligence agencies that had never been enthusiastic about SALT in the first place.

The complaints began almost immediately after the agreement was ratified in 1972, and they led to a major confrontation between the intelligence agencies and Kissinger. As intelligence officials discovered to their anger, Kissinger sought to forestall arguments about Soviet cheating by becoming, in effect, a one-man intelligence-arbitration process. In a series of moves designed to bolster his domination of intelligence, Kissinger first set up what he called the "verification panel" within the National Security Council, which, he ordered, would receive all intelligence relating to SALT verification, and then decide whether a violation had occurred; any such possible violations would be thrashed out secretly in a Soviet-American committee for final resolution.

At the same time, the U.S. Intelligence Board (USIB), a coordinating group for all U.S. intelligence agencies, had set up its own SALT Monitoring Group. It quickly discovered that Kissinger had no intention of letting it handle intelligence relating to SALT compliance; the group was told it could monitor but could not make any judgments on compliance or violations. That task, Kissinger decreed, would be handled by his own NSC subcommittee. There was worse to come: Kissinger began running a "hold" system, under which any raw intelligence (satellite photos and intercepted Soviet signals) could not be disseminated within the intelligence community; it had to be given only to the NSC staff.

The practical effect of these moves was to reduce the DCI, the CIA, and the other intelligence agencies to the role of clerks, merely collecting the intelligence and passing it directly to Kissinger, who further annoyed these agencies by referring to possible violations as "ambiguous situations." Many intelligence officers began to suspect that Kissinger's obsession with tightly controlling intelligence on SALT compliance was related directly to his continual amassing of greater power within the administration. This was exemplified by the NO DIS CHEROKEE stamped on some SALT compliance reports, meaning "No distribution to Cherokee," the government's communications code word for the Secretary of State, Kissinger's most hated bureaucratic rival, William P. Rogers.

The problem went deeper than bureaucratic politics, for the entire SALT verification episode illustrated Kissinger's worst fault, a tendency to try to control all aspects of a political or strategic problem. In the case of SALT, his move to have all raw intelligence come through his hands for his own analysis was a dangerous procedure, for it meant that a policymaker was the final arbiter of the success of his own policy. SALT was the crowning achievement in Kissinger's career at that point, and it is not likely that he would have concluded, on the basis of any intelligence available, that this considerable achievement was flawed or a failure.

By the same token, Kissinger was not about to admit that the assumptions he held about the area of his other great diplomatic achievement, the Middle East, were also wrong.

290

Therefore, when the question of possible Egyptian military action against Israel arose in 1973, Kissinger concluded that it wouldn't happen. He drew that conclusion not on the basis of anything American intelligence was providing but because his own diplomacy in that area had convinced him of certain "strategic realities." He believed that any Egyptian military action would not occur before new Middle East peace talks got under way in early 1974, that the Egyptians would not dare to challenge overwhelming Israeli military superiority, and that the various alarms in the summer of 1973 about an impending Egyptian military move were part of Sadat's effort to improve his bargaining position by a constant threat of war.

The SALT and Yom Kippur War episodes illustrate the danger of a policymaker's serving as his own intelligence agency. There is always a fundamental conflict of interest between policymakers and intelligence, for the people who formulate policy always have the biggest stake in its success or failure. For that reason, it is vital to separate the two processes. Kissinger violated that rule, and it was only a matter of time before that mistake would cause serious problems. One of those problems came in the Middle East.

The second came in Angola.

The Portuguese colony of Angola on the west coast of Africa had been the site of sporadic guerrilla action since 1961, when at least two separate movements sought to overthrow the colonial regime. One was a vaguely Marxist group called the MPLA, and the other was a non-Communist organization known as the FNLA. Neither had made much progress against the Portuguese, and in the context of more important developments in Africa, Angolan events remained on the back burner, simmering.

The CIA's goal was to keep all important bases covered, so while the United States was providing tacit support to the Portuguese regime—in return for which the Americans were given important military bases in Portugal—the agency was also establishing contact with the FNLA. The choice of the

FNLA was purely political for, as avowedly anti-Communist, it was considered the only anticolonial movement worthy of U.S. support. In this decision, however, lay the seeds of a future problem, for the FNLA was not only based entirely in neighboring Zaire—and therefore out of the Angolan political mainstream—it also had a well-deserved reputation for brutality (in March 1961 FNLA troops murdered 750 Portuguese settlers).

Holden Roberto, leader of the FNLA, had been recruited as a CIA agent in 1959, and since then had been providing intelligence on events inside Angola, along with information on what was happening with the anticolonial movements. However, Nixon and Kissinger discovered in 1969 that Roberto was hardly worth the $1,000 a month the CIA was paying him; the "intelligence" he had provided was mostly useless, and further, it had a number of curious omissions— such as the fact that the FNLA leader had established links with the Chinese in 1963. In addition, Roberto was almost entirely corrupt.

One of his lieutenants, Jonas Savimbi, became disgusted with Roberto's corruption and left to form his own organization, known as UNITA. But Savimbi attracted only nominal interest from the CIA, which was suspicious of his socialist background as well as of his tendency to play all sides against the middle. Savimbi had contacts with the PIDE (the Portuguese secret police), along with the Chinese and South Africans, a breathtaking pragmatism that eliminated him, in CIA eyes, from total U.S. support, although he was provided with some funds. Savimbi moved to the southwestern part of Angola and claimed most of it in the name of his organization.

By 1974, a very complicated situation existed in Angola. In the north were Roberto and his FNLA, making modest and infrequent forays against the colonial regime from its bases in Zaire (whose ruler was Roberto's brother-in-law). In the cities, the MPLA ran its operations while in the south, Savimbi's UNITA held sway. Collectively, they might have defeated the Portuguese, but individually, none could topple Portuguese rule, even with Chinese and Soviet aid to favored factions. In effect, a bizarre truce existed: Chunks of Angola were conceded to the various anticolonial movements, while important commercial and urban areas remained under Portuguese control. Big-power involvement, meanwhile, was kept at a low level, with Chinese and Soviets jockeying for influence, as the Americans kept a watch over events while supporting Roberto's FNLA.

But the CIA had badly misread what was happening in Angola. It had no real sense of the strong role tribal politics played in the intricacies of the various "liberation" movements, and its reliance for ten years on Roberto as an intelligence source guaranteed that information coming out of Angola during all that time was nearly worthless.

The shock, therefore, was all the greater when a revolution in Portugal in late 1974 suddenly ended colonial rule in Angola. All along, the CIA had operated on the assumption that the liberation movements would never defeat Portugal, yet that defeat had arrived and the United States found itself totally unprepared to deal with the consequences. Its main intelligence source, Roberto and his gang of thugs, had no idea of what was happening inside Angola itself, save in a fairly small area of northern Angola. There was no intelligence on what was happening inside Angola's urban areas, in the central part of the country, or in the large southwestern area that shared borders with the important nations of South Africa and Zambia. The American view became even more clouded during the several months of near anarchy that followed the precipitate collapse of colonial rule, for U.S. intelligence had no grasp of the political forces at work, among them the fact that the MPLA had become the dominant political force in the country.

This intelligence gap was exacerbated by Kissinger, who decided that the overt Soviet support for the MPLA faction represented a Soviet effort to establish a strong Communist beachhead on the continent. There was not the slightest shred of evidence for this belief, but in January 1975, Kissinger drew the line: The Communists would be kept out of Angola. To that end, the so-called 40 Committee—the White House-Pentagon-National Security Council group that decided covert operations—approved an outlay of $300,000 to be given to the political faction that the United States had designated to take power in Angola (several months later, another $14 million was approved). The chosen instrument for this American attempt to shape the political future of Angola was Holden Roberto.

It is difficult to imagine a worse choice to uphold the non-Communist cause, for there was almost nothing to recommend Roberto for his assigned task. His army was an untrained and inefficient rabble, he had no real popularity in the country, and aside from American support, he had no philosophy or ideal that might recommend him to the Angolan masses. The error of backing Roberto was fundamental, and the Americans proceeded to make a number of others that guaranteed Roberto's failure. Chief among them was Kissinger's decision that Angola represented some sort of front line in the Soviet-American competition; once the United States raised the stakes, it compelled the Russians to do likewise. And it was a dynamic that resulted in a considerable Soviet effort to arm and equip the MPLA for a civil war in which the MPLA already held a number of high cards, since it controlled Angola's urban population. Another, and in many ways more serious, error was the decision by Kissinger that the South Africans would be encouraged to invade northward against the MPLA. It may have made some military sense, but it guaranteed a political disaster since it tainted Roberto—and, to a lesser extent, Savimbi's organization—among black Africans with the unforgivable charge that they were allies of the hated South African regime.

Events moved to their fated conclusion. Roberto's forces fled in terror from the rockets and other weapons provided by the Soviets to the MPLA, the South Africans were checked by a large infusion of Cuban troops sent to Angola at the behest of Moscow, and when the dust settled a few months later, the MPLA had won what can only semiaccurately be called the Angolan civil war. And with that victory, every single American intelligence assumption about Angola was shattered. The U.S. Congress, disgusted with the whole episode, ordered all American covert aid cut off—over Kissinger's loud objections.

But there was still one last episode to come in this intelligence disaster, a tragicomic operation that is still one of American intelligence's deepest secrets.

His name was George Washington Bacon III, one of the all-American types who were drawn in those adventurous years of the early 1960s to the Green Berets. Sent to Vietnam, he worked on SOG operations in Laos. Bacon found his calling there, a holy crusade against Communism that became his driving obsession.

Five years later, Bacon was recruited into the CIA and, under the code name Kayak, went back into Laos to continue the fight, this time on behalf of the agency he often heard called "Christians In Action" by more cynical agents who knew the war was lost. It was a barb directed at some of the CIA personnel working operations in the hills and jungles of Laos, but Bacon ignored such talk, spending his days and nights working with the Hmong army of General Vang Pao. Technically, he was supposed to be an operations man, advising Vang Pao and his forces on how to attack the North Vietnamese and Pathet Lao, but Bacon, against orders, often would accompany the Hmong patrols.

Bacon's heroism and courage won him the CIA's second highest award, the Intelligence Star, but with the collapse of Vang Pao's army, he returned to the United States. Bacon was bored at home; there was no action to consume his restless energy, and nothing he took up seemed to satisfy his hunger to get back into the fight against Communism. He helped found an outfit called Veterans and Volunteers for Vietnam to enlist Vietnam veterans and get them back there to help the South Vietnamese fight off the last Communist assault, but that came to nothing.

However, in late 1975, opportunity came. The CIA,

Bacon learned, was organizing a secret operation that involved the hiring of mercenaries in the United States and Great Britain, who would then be moved into Angola to fight the MPLA and the Cubans. They were to be paid by CIA money laundered through Roberto, who would be in nominal charge of the operation from his base in Zaire.

Bacon had resigned from the CIA at that point, but the "resignation" was a formality. Known as "sheep-dipping" in the agency, this involved a formal resignation that could be produced in case the agent was ever caught; the CIA then could disavow any connection. Bacon had two missions: become part of the mercenary force in Angola, and at the same time function as a reporting agent to keep the CIA informed on what was happening within the mercenary operation.

The CIA needed to keep a watch, for it had recruited a motley group to handle the actual recruitments. In the United States, the chief recruiter was a California crop duster named David Bufkin, an ex-soldier who wore cowboy boots and a stetson and displayed a Hells Angels tattoo on one arm. Bufkin, who had a habit of telling everybody he knew that he was recruiting secretly for Angola (and that it was a CIA operation), managed to recruit six Americans, including Bacon. In Great Britain, meanwhile, a former British Army sergeant named Dennis Banks recruited ninety-six men, like the Americans a mix of former military men and adventurers looking for excitement.

They got more than they bargained for in Angola, where the mercenary operation turned out to be a fiasco. Ineptly organized, inadequately fed and armed, and atrociously led, the mercenaries stood no chance against the better-armed and organized Cubans. Within a month of their arrival in early 1976, thirty-six of the mercenaries recruited in England and two of the Americans recruited by Bufkin were killed; sixteen others were captured.

And among the dead was Bacon, killed on the morning of February 14, 1976, in a Cuban ambush. The death of this young American (the only CIA agent killed in Angola) was a tragedy, for the hope that this small, ragtag group of mercenaries for whom Bacon fought could ever have made a difference in Angola was an illusion. And it was the last tragic illusion that marked American intelligence's involvement in Angola.

The failure left a bitter taste, especially in the CIA, which for some years was to stay out of the covert-action business, mainly because of new congressionally imposed restrictions on such operations, a direct result of the Angola experience. The failure also marked the end of Henry Kissinger's career as American intelligence czar. A year after the Angolan disaster, Kissinger—by then a figure of considerable political controversy—was out of office.

No one could have foreseen it at the time, but the departure of Kissinger was to create a considerable vacuum that a new administration tried, unsuccessfully, to fill. And in the process, American intelligence was to undergo a disruption that it had never before experienced.

nine

THE CLUES OF SEMIPALATINSK

Oh, where hath our intelligence been
drunk?
Where hath it slept?

—SHAKESPEARE, *King John*

IT WAS SAID OF Major General George Keegan, assistant air force chief of staff for intelligence, that few men ever wound up winning an argument with him. Or even getting a word in, for Keegan's aggressive rhetorical style, something very much like a runaway locomotive, brooked no contradiction to a conviction he held to be immutable truth.

Reduced to its basics, Keegan's thesis—formulated during his tour of duty as head of air-force intelligence during the 1970s—was that the Soviet Union had surpassed the United States in terms of strategic military power and that the American intelligence establishment, led by the CIA, refused to recognize that fact. It was a conviction that Keegan pursued relentlessly in a series of skirmishes that marked the bitter wars fought at the rarefied upper levels of the American intelligence community during that decade.

Under ordinary circumstances, the battles would be of scant interest outside that little world, for internecine warfare between military intelligence and the CIA had been a prominent feature of American intelligence for years. But an unusual convergence of circumstances during the 1970s transformed the military-CIA war from just another argument into a deadly struggle for the very soul of American intelligence.

The chief catalyst was Keegan, and from the first moment he assumed his post as air-force intelligence chief in 1972, it was clear that there was going to be trouble. Part of it had to do with Keegan's personality. A former bomber pilot who had served a long apprenticeship in the military-intelligence field, he was a product of the Strategic Air Command, the air-force elite that tends to produce aggressive, tough-minded officers in the mold of SAC's progenitor, Curtis LeMay. Keegan gave the appearance of pugnaciousness; physically, he looked much like an ill-tempered bantamweight boxer, and this, combined with the chin-out style characteristic of many SAC officers, served to enhance his reputation as a bulldozer.

Like his predecessors, Keegan tended to take the darkest view of what the Russians were doing, a tradition that had made air-force intelligence notorious for what many CIA analysts felt were consistently alarmist (and consistently wrong) judgments on the scope and direction of Soviet strategic military programs. From the days of the bomber gap, the missile gap, and down through the great ABM controversies, air-force intelligence was everlastingly warning of a threatening Soviet specter. Its officers were the classic "hawks," always arguing that the United States was falling behind the Soviets, and that only bigger and better American strategic weapons would overcome assorted gaps.

Air-force intelligence played a considerable role in the debates over these gaps, because it was the most dynamic and best organized of all the military-intelligence services. Moreover, it was the most powerful. Under a series of arrangements with the CIA designed to end jurisdictional disputes, the air force had won operational control over technical collection systems, especially satellites and the U-2 and SR-71 planes. The air force also controlled American intelligence's most secrecy-shrouded component, the National Reconnaissance Office, which decided the priority of targets for aerial, satellite, and SIGINT collection resources.

Keegan ruled an empire of nearly fifty thousand people and a budget of over $3 billion, an apparatus that concentrated on the minutiae of Soviet military hardware—the types, capabilities, and threats represented by Russian weapons able to inflict strategic damage on the United States. And from that perspective, what Keegan saw was a growing danger of frightening dimensions, the largest and most powerful arsenal in human history, which was directed at a central objective: domination of the world.

Keegan became frustrated by what he regarded as a naïve tendency by American intelligence, notably the CIA, to deny the size and reality of that threat, and he became increasingly strident in his insistence that the United States was in grave danger. In 1972, he refused to sign memorandums that would give air-force intelligence's consent to the SALT I agreement, an act that infuriated Kissinger, but served to make Keegan something of an unofficial leader for a loosely organized group of similarly minded military officers, academics, and civilian strategists who felt, as Keegan did, that U.S. intelligence was badly underestimating the Soviet threat.

This development took place at a time of total confusion in American military policy. Clearly, the days of overwhelming American military superiority were over, but the much-heralded policy of détente seemed also a failure. Détente did not, as Kissinger and Nixon had hoped, brake the Soviet military buildup, nor did it end a series of dangerous Soviet-American confrontations around the world. In addition, the rapid pace of technology was threatening to unglue all the carefully constructed doctrines of mutual assured destruction and other strategic shibboleths that formed the basis for détente. One of the more important was the American presumption, first formulated by McNamara, that the only weapons that really mattered strategically were the weapons required to assure destruction in a second nuclear strike. In other words, it didn't make much difference how many nuclear weapons each side had, so long as both sides were always guaranteed "minimum deterrence"—enough weapons left over following a first strike to guarantee infliction of "unacceptable damage" on the enemy.

But the SALT negotiations proved that technology was rapidly undercutting these presumptions. As fast as issues were settled, new ones arose, all of them touched off by new technology. For example, both sides might agree to limit the numbers of individual missile silos, but they then faced the problem of MIRVed warheads, up to ten of which might be contained in a single missile. There were also neutron bombs, mobile ICBM missiles, and cruise missiles, new weapons systems that vastly increased the numbers of strategic nuclear weapons.

The intelligence implications were also serious, for the new weapons were very difficult to monitor, meaning that verification on their use and deployment represented a considerable challenge. In effect, intelligence began to run a race, trying to develop new technology to keep pace with the rapid improvements in strategic-weapons systems. The most serious concern was the so-called "CEP question," a bit of arcane technology that concerned the accuracy of ICBMs. It was an important technological question, for the more accurate missiles were, the more implications that had for the strategic balance between the United States and the Soviet Union. A missile arsenal of pinpoint accuracy raised the possibility that one side or the other would be tempted to carry out a first strike, since its accurate missiles would destroy the enemy's missiles in their silos, even before they were launched.

The accuracy was expressed as Circular Error Probable (CEP), defined as the radius of a circle centered on the target, within which at least 50 percent of the warheads would strike. By the early 1970s, ICBM warheads could achieve somewhere around a half-mile CEP, meaning that at least 50 percent of the warheads would hit within a half mile of the target. But rapid technological advances, mainly in satellite-directed guidance systems and laser beams on which warheads would "ride" with great accuracy to the target, began to dramatically improve the CEPs—to the point where the American-designed MX missile packed ten warheads aboard, each one capable of being individually guided to within one tenth of a mile of a target more than five thousand miles away.

The problem was that merely looking at a missile would not reveal anything about its real capabilities (for instance, how many warheads were inside the nose cone), so more and more ambiguity began to be introduced into intelligence judgments about the weapons. That led to even more ambiguous extrapolations. At one point, for example, Laird insisted flatly that one particular Soviet missile was designed strictly to achieve a first strike against the American land-based missile arsenal. Laird's data for this conclusion amounted to American monitoring of a single Soviet missile test, which featured the use of three separate warheads fired by the same rocket. The impact of the warheads—known as "footprints" in the technical intelligence field—showed, Laird claimed, that the warheads were for a first-strike weapon, since the approximate dimensions of the impacts roughly matched the pattern of American missile silos.

But this flimsy judgment was only the beginning of a long period of ambiguity in trying to divine the dimensions of strategic weapons in the Soviet Union. It featured a running series of arguments within the American intelligence community on whether the Soviets were trying to achieve a first-strike capability, whether their larger warheads offset the smaller but more efficient American warheads, whether megatonnage or accuracy was a more important standard to measure the power of strategic missiles, and on and on. The arguments became increasingly complex—so complex that very few people understood them, much less understanding just what constituted superiority or parity in strategic weapons in the first place. Kissinger was particularly annoyed by these arguments, insisting that given the increasing complexity of modern weapons, there was no real way to define such slippery terms as superiority. Besides, he argued, in a famous outburst, "What in the name of God is 'strategic superiority'? What do you do with it?"

George Keegan insisted, on the other hand, that the answer was quite simple: The United States must possess overwhelming superiority over the Soviet Union in all aspects of military power, especially in strategic weapons, for only such superiority would guarantee America's national security. In Keegan's view, there should be no confusion at all about Soviet intentions. The scale and volume of the Russian military buildup proved conclusively that the Soviets aimed for nothing less than military superiority over the United States.

However, the Keegan certitude at that point was very much a minority view; by the end of the Nixon-Kissinger era, American intelligence seemed more confused than ever over Soviet intentions, strategic and otherwise. The confusion was summarized in a lengthy CIA report completed in December 1975 in which the agency, drawing on all intelligence resources, tried to arrive at a central conclusion on what the Russians were doing—and what they seemed to be planning to do. The report, written by Fritz Ermath, one of the CIA's senior analysts, concluded that no one really seemed to know. American intelligence, Ermath noted, was hopelessly divided over the question, and had separated into three warring camps. The first camp, exemplified by Keegan and air-force intelligence (and other military intelligence agencies) believed that the Soviets aimed for complete dominance over the United States, which they would follow up by taking over the world. The second camp believed that the Russians were not aiming for such dominance, and instead were trying to hold off the United States, establishing conditions under which Soviet interests would not be threatened. This view, generally held by the CIA, was opposed by a third camp, which argued that the Russians were only trying to achieve a rough military equality with the United States. Essentially, this last view—held largely by State Department intelligence officers and analysts—argued that there were no long-range

Soviet goals; the Russians were opportunistic, taking advantage whenever they could to promote Soviet influence while at the same time trying to avoid direct confrontation with the United States, which they regarded as militarily superior.

Ermath's report, titled "Understanding Soviet Strategic Policy," demonstrated that there was little understanding of the question within the American intelligence community. Certainly, there was no consensus on whether this country had "fallen behind," as Keegan argued. But Keegan persisted, and his stubborn (and strident) arguments began to create a large number of bitter enemies, especially in the CIA, which resented his constant criticisms of that agency's intelligence conclusions.

CIA officials badly underestimated Keegan, a man they initially regarded as just another typical air-force man, like his predecessors a poorly trained intelligence officer who had been placed in an intelligence post first and foremost because of his unswerving loyalty to his own service. Traditionally, air-force intelligence leaders churned out a steady stream of alarmism that in large measure was related to the air force's push for larger and more expensive strategic-weapons programs. As the CIA and the rest of the American intelligence community understood, the air force always had a strategic investment to protect, and only the most alarming intelligence possible on various Soviet "threats" to American strategic assets would persuade the White House and Congress to pour mounting billions into measures to strengthen those assets—most of which were under air-force control.

Undoubtedly, some of this traditional air-force politics animated Keegan, but there were important differences. For one thing, Keegan was unquestionably the most talented officer ever to head up air-force intelligence. As CIA officials discovered to their surprise, Keegan was a man of formidable intellectual gifts; as a Harvard graduate (with other advanced degrees), he could slug it out toe to toe with many of the Ivy Leaguers who dominated the CIA's upper echelons. In addition, Keegan was a man who had done his homework; when he argued about Leninist theory and Communist dialetics, he spoke as a man who had not only read, but also carefully analyzed, all sixty volumes of Lenin's collected works—a feat very few CIA officials had ever bothered even to attempt. Furthermore, Keegan had spent many years in a thorough study of military technology and had become something of a walking encyclopedia on even the most obscure aspects of Soviet science and technology.

"I had no personal life for thirty-five years," Keegan was to say later, explaining how he had managed these awesome feats, but whatever the reason, he became the most striking figure in American intelligence during the 1970s. His draconian pronouncements about the Soviet threat articulated what had become a steadily growing uneasiness within some quarters of the American military and intelligence establishments over Russian intentions. Keegan attracted not only disagreement from his enemies, especially in the CIA, but strong personal dislike as well, for he had all the political finesse of a sledgehammer. Keegan didn't just argue his position; he pounded his debating opponent with an apocalyptic speaking style ("I have no hesitancy in saying . . ." was a favorite opening) that portrayed a dark future menaced by a dominant Soviet Union while "well-meaning, but foolish" American officials rued the day they had failed to heed the clear intelligence indicating that it would happen.

"George's transceiver isn't always on," even his most ardent air-force admirers admitted, but Keegan had come to the fore when no equivalent strong personality had emerged anywhere else in the American intelligence community. Weakened by public revelations of incompetence and illegal activities—plus weak DCIs—the CIA was on the defensive, and lacked the real strength to argue effectively against Keegan's charges of sloppy intelligence work. To a certain degree, Keegan was right; as he found out when CIA conclusions were challenged, much of what the agency was saying was not backed up by good intelligence. A great deal of the CIA's intelligence, as a matter of fact, amounted to suppositions and thumb-sucking, with nothing more solid to support it than the shared wisdom of analysts who elevated their assumptions into proven conclusions.

By 1974, only two years after he had assumed the job as head of air-force intelligence, Keegan had managed to create a full-blown intelligence controversy, which centered on the question of whether the United States had underestimated the Soviet strategic threat. The underestimation, Keegan argued, stemmed directly from what he described as a "coalition" of like-minded advocates sprinkled throughout the American intelligence community—especially in the CIA and State Department intelligence—who shared the goals of détente and deliberately overlooked evidence of Soviet perfidy.

Keegan's conviction that this cabal existed led to a private session in 1974 with the President's Foreign Intelligence Advisory Board (PFIAB), a blue-ribbon committee of private citizens that was supposed to monitor American intelligence activities and make recommendations to the President about the structure and functions of the intelligence agencies. The board had never played a role of any consequence in intelligence, since it was not equipped with a staff. (What staff members it did have came from the CIA, an arrangement that guaranteed the PFIAB would never dig too deeply into CIA activities.) But an alarming Keegan briefing before the board, which came at a time of great disquiet over the American-Soviet strategic balance, moved its members to rare decisiveness. They began to exert pressure on President Ford to establish some sort of independent, outside review over CIA analyses and estimates.

Ford and his CIA chief, George Bush, both Republican hard-liners on defense, shared much of Keegan's concern about the Soviet military buildup. They also subscribed, at least in part, to the idea that many CIA estimates about Soviet military power had been biased by "liberals" in the agency, a belief that moved Ford to approve the idea of an independent panel that would examine all the raw intelligence on which the CIA had based its conclusions, then see if it agreed.

The result, an unmitigated disaster for the CIA that completely disrupted the agency, became known as the "Team B episode."

Team B was a stacked deck right from the beginning. Ford made sure its ten members included the most notable defense hawks he could find, including the team's chairman, Richard Pipes, a Harvard Russian-history professor and government consultant who was a visceral Russophobe. All the team members were pronounced political conservatives, a fact that led CIA officials to conclude, correctly, that Ford and Bush were not so much interested in discovering the quality of CIA's intelligence product as they were determined to ensure their conservative backing for the upcoming presidential election.

For three months, the Team B members stood over the shoulders of CIA analysts, second-guessing virtually every conclusion. It was three months of bloody warfare, with near-violent arguments marking even the most innocuous judgments about Soviet capabilities. In the end, Team B members wound up concluding that the CIA had underestimated every single aspect of Soviet political and military power, including military spending, numbers of strategic weapons, and the scope of its civil-defense program. Further, Team B claimed that the CIA had failed to credit the Soviets with developing a first-strike capability and a strategy for limited nuclear war (which, said Team B, they were convinced would defeat the United States).

At first glance, these conclusions were shocking, for taken as a whole, they meant that the United States was hopelessly behind the Soviet Union, which was now in the position of being able to defeat the Americans in a war. They amounted to a position of unrelieved bleakness, and since they differed so markedly from the much less alarming CIA estimates, the question arises as to what information Team B saw that was not available to the CIA analysts. The answer is that they saw precisely the same information; the difference lay in the pronounced bias with which Team B regarded the same data. In fact, the Team B episode is a classic demonstration of how powerful a role such bias can play in intelligence interpretation.

The problem with the Team B members, aside from their deep political conservatism—which made the most alarming deductions from ambiguous evidence—was their universal opposition to the policy of détente. Their favorite villain was Kissinger, a man who had, they felt, traded away American superiority to appease the Russians. Kissinger was regarded as naïve, a foolish egotist who had been tricked by the Russians into pursuing a policy of détente that Moscow wanted to use as a screen to move against the United States. Thus, every piece of evidence Team B examined was regarded in the context of conspiracy; each Soviet development was framed in the context of a master Soviet plan they were convinced already existed.

Pipes was the worst offender. He believed fervently, for example, in his own unique theory that the Russians were devoted disciples of the Prussian nineteenth-century military philosopher Karl von Clausewitz, who, Pipes claimed (incorrectly), had proclaimed the doctrine of "total war." And under that doctrine, Pipes concluded, the Soviets therefore believed that they could destroy the United States in a massive nuclear strike after achieving superiority in nuclear weapons. And so when Pipes examined satellite pictures of sprawling Soviet ICBM complexes, including their hardened silos, he found that they amounted to incontrovertible evidence of a Soviet desire to wipe out the United States in a single nuclear blow.

As intelligence analysis, this sort of thing was on the comic-book level, a tribute to paranoia that saw danger lurking under every bush. The Russians were regarded by Pipes and his cohorts as modern Huns armed with thermonuclear weapons, each day hatching their plans for world conquest in the Kremlin while laughing at naïve Americans who failed to recognize the signs of impending doom. This Team B world view* was a dangerous form of myopia, but it is important to understand that it took place in the context of some very real intelligence ambiguity. The fact is that for all the talk about the "Soviet threat," American intelligence at that point could not provide conclusive evidence of just what the Russians were up to.

This indecisiveness stemmed largely from the weaknesses of American intelligence itself, which, despite its ever more sophisticated technical collection capabilities, found that it was unable to develop a comprehensive picture of a world that had become increasingly complex and dangerous. It was this central failure that allowed such critics as Keegan and Team B room to maneuver; the very ambiguity of the intelligence made it subject to just about any interpretation. In this atmosphere, a talented intelligence officer on the scale of George Keegan could exploit the ambiguity and demonstrate some significant failings in how intelligence judgments were formulated.

And the most damaging example he found was in Soviet Central Asia, an intelligence failure that would eventually have very wide ramifications.

Keegan had long believed that American intelligence was failing to anticipate new, large-scale Soviet weapons developments. Part of the reason for that error, he argued, was that Americans continually saw Soviet developments through the American prism; if American science and technology had not been able to develop a weapons system or make an important breakthrough, then there was no reason to suspect that the Russians had any hope of doing so. It was a form of American egoism, the conviction that the Russians were always behind

---

*Team B's final report was never publicly released, although much of it was leaked after Ford's election defeat, mainly in the fear that President Carter would ignore its conclusions. Ironically for Keegan and the air force, Carter used one part of the Team B report, alleging that the Russians had constructed a huge air-defense system capable of defeating American manned bombers, as justification for canceling the B-1 bomber, a cherished air-force project.

technologically, so there was no possibility of a Soviet technological surprise, especially in military terms.

Keegan found this judgment a dangerous example of wishful thinking, for his close monitoring of Soviet scientific developments convinced him that the Russians were not nearly the scientific Neanderthals the American technical-scientific establishment seemed to believe them to be. He was most struck by the rapid Soviet developments in directed energy, especially lasers and fusion, and he began to suspect that such research might have important military applications.

It was a logical deduction, but Keegan discovered that nobody in American intelligence was monitoring any of the Soviet weapons laboratories and test centers to determine what progress, if any, had been made on developing directed-energy systems for military use.

In 1962, directed-energy weapons were discovered by accident when an Air Force/Atomic Energy Commission nuclear test exploded a thermonuclear device at high altitude. Code-named Starfish, the test almost caused a major disaster, for it spewed out a vast stream of high-energy electrons into space, damaging several satellites. As the scientists then discovered, a stream of electrons of sufficient power, strewn in the orbital paths of satellites, would destroy them. And so was born the idea of directed-energy weapons, but a series of development projects to make them practical—Project Saint, Project Seesaw, and the more ominously named Project Squanto Terror—failed, mostly because the scientists could not develop the extremely large power requirements needed to make electron beams into viable weapons.

The American abandonment of the projects several years later resulted partly from an inability to develop the high-power requirements but more from a prevailing conviction that the Russians had not (and would not) develop such weapons, given the fact that the much superior American technology had failed. Therefore, there was no compelling reason for an American push to develop directed-energy weapons. That conclusion persisted, even when evidence began to accumulate that the Russians had made a number of important break-throughs in directed-energy technology. Keegan especially became exercised about the Russian developments, and he argued to no avail that a major American intelligence effort should be launched to determine just how far the Russians had advanced in military use of that technology.

Keegan needed proof, and he finally got it in early 1976 when several mysterious events were detected at a desolate site near Semipalatinsk, in Soviet Central Asia. An American DSS early warning satellite—programmed to detect Soviet thermonuclear explosions—flew over what seemed to be an underground facility there and registered high levels of thermal radiation. Several days later, another American satellite, this one used for weather reconnaissance, noted some nuclear debris in the atmosphere some distance from Semipalatinsk. Analysis of the elements detected by the satellite turned up some usually associated with detonations of thermonuclear weapons, so an intelligence deduction was formulated: The facility near Semipalatinsk was undoubtedly an underground testing facility for Soviet thermonuclear warheads. Intelligence reports dutifully listed it as a "possible nuclear test site"—or PNUTS, in American intelligence parlance.

But Keegan disputed that judgment. For one thing, he noted, there was no supporting evidence, seismic or otherwise, to indicate that a nuclear explosion had taken place anywhere near that site. Furthermore, pictures from photo-reconnaissance satellites showed a railhead near the Semipalatinsk site, on which four tank cars loaded with liquid hydrogen were spotted. Hydrogen in that amount, used for special cooling experiments, was not necessary for a thermonuclear test of any kind; thus, there was something else going on at Semipalatinsk that had little to do with thermonuclear warheads.

Despite this evidence, however, Keegan was unable to convince the rest of the American intelligence community, especially the CIA. Rebuffed, Keegan set out on a one-man intelligence mission to prove his growing suspicion that the

Russians were testing a large-scale directed-energy weapon system at Semipalatinsk.

This was regarded as ridiculous by the intelligence establishment, which had long ago decided that no such development could possibly be approaching the testing stage, given the state of Soviet technology. But Keegan proved that assumption wrong, and in the process carried out a *tour de force* piece of detective work that stands as one of the more impressive in the history of American intelligence.

Keegan turned over every scrap of evidence he could get his hands on. He carefully examined the results of the weather-reconnaissance flight and discovered that among the materials collected on the flight relating to the Semipalatinsk event were traces of hydrogen, xenon, krypton, and other material not normally associated with a thermonuclear explosion. Keegan also tapped into his chief intelligence resource: a vast collection of intelligence tidbits gleaned from Soviet scientific literature and the clues dropped inadvertently over the years by visiting Soviet scientists. These clues were patched together by Keegan in a mosaic that convinced him the Russians were embarked on an extensive development program for charged-particle beams (a stream of atomic or subatomic particles pushed out at tremendous speed, resulting in a "death ray"), and high-energy lasers ("light amplification by simulated emission of radiation," a form of accumulated energy that is concentrated in a very powerful beam of light).

Ultimately Keegan concluded that the Russians were attempting to perfect miniaturized explosive generators for the huge pulse-power requirements of particle-beam weapons. That was the significance of what was detected at Semipalatinsk, he argued. The elements detected by the satellites were produced during a pulse-power experiment when radioactive pellets were "crushed," a process that releases certain elements. The Russians vented these elements, Keegan said, by the use of a very large flame that burned some of the material and caused it to rise rapidly into the atmosphere.

313

The conclusion was openly ridiculed by the American experts on such technology, and Keegan at this point found himself in a direct confrontation with prevailing wisdom—since the United States had not been able to make any significant breakthroughs in directed-energy research, there was no reasonable expectation that the Russians had succeeded. That presumption failed to take into account the voluminous evidence that Keegan had so carefully collected and collated, and paid even less attention to his final proof: He had a small group of civilian scientists, all of them attached to the air force's division responsible for evaluating foreign military technology, actually put together a small, workable charged-particle-beam system. As Keegan argued, if they could build it, using only currently available technology, there was no reason to suppose that the equally qualified Russian scientists couldn't do the same.

But the real clincher for Keegan's argument came not from the evidence he produced but, oddly enough, from the Russians themselves.

In July 1976 Leonid Rudakov, head of the Kurchatov Institute in Moscow, the Soviet Union's leading research center on high-energy physics, stopped off at the Livermore Laboratory in California as part of a scientific exchange visit. Rudakov, who directed the Soviet Union's electron-beam-fusion program, was scheduled to deliver a lecture to assembled American scientists on the progress of his research. It was a speech that drew several dozen American scientists, for Rudakov, among the most brilliant of the Russian scientific elite, was a prime attraction.

The Americans anticipated the typical lecture in such circumstances, a general overview of Soviet research efforts, with a notable lack of specifics. In this case, Rudakov was expected to be even more restrained in his remarks, since the research effort he headed had important military implications. But to everyone's surprise, Rudakov launched into a highly detailed discussion of Soviet research, revealing a number of important breakthroughs in fusion-beam technology. The lecture, as a matter of fact, was stunning, and scientists sat shocked as Rudakov quietly revealed some of the more important secrets of Soviet research.

His revelations represented a curious development, for it remains a mystery to this day why Rudakov took the extraordinary step—especially for a Soviet scientist—of revealing so much information, a good deal of it having direct implications for weapons research. (Possibly, the revelations were intended as a Soviet warning that it was far ahead in such directed-energy research and would be prepared to match whatever effort the United States might exert in that area.) In any event, Rudakov's talk precipitated a scene straight out of the Three Stooges: Officials of the Energy Research and Development Administration (ERDA, later the Department of Energy), administrators of the laboratory, rushed there upon the conclusion of Rudakov's speech and pronounced all of it "classified," meaning that no one in the audience was permitted to discuss it. Furthermore, a blackboard on which Rudakov had written some equations was also ruled "classified information," an action that puzzled the Americans, since they were under the illusion that security classifications were designed to protect American secrets from the Russians, not the other way around.

But the cat was out of the bag. Clearly, the Russians had a viable directed-energy program under way, just as Keegan had concluded, and what was more, they were ahead of the United States in that field. It took some time to get the bureaucracy moving, but in 1978, more than two years after the controversy had first surfaced, the Pentagon appointed a thirty-six-member scientific committee to assess the problem, with orders to develop a five-year plan for an American directed-energy weapons program.

Ultimately, it was all to result in a full-scale American "beam wars" buildup, exemplified by President Reagan's famous *Star Wars* speech in March 1983, in which the United States was committed to build an electronic Maginot Line of directed-energy weapons against Soviet missiles. Whether the multibillion-dollar cost of this space-age defense will be worthwhile remains to be seen, but in intelligence terms, the entire episode from start to finish was instructive, for Keegan's one-man crusade against established wisdom illustrates much about the weaknesses of American intelligence.

The deficiencies centered, as we have seen so many times, on the intelligence community's real lack of good sources, and its tendency to extrapolate from ambiguous evidence. Worse, there was the problem of preconceptions, and Keegan's most arduous task was trying to change minds that had already decided what was "fact." The prevailing intelligence-community wisdom that the Russians were not developing directed-energy weapons was based on the *assumption* they were not, in turn part of a complex series of deductions about Soviet scientific developments seen through the American prism. But when Keegan said the Russians were working on a proton generator, he knew it to be a fact. He found two American scientists who, while visiting Moscow, had actually seen computer printouts on such a device. And when Keegan said that the technology for building charged-particle-beam weapons was viable, he knew that to be a fact also, because his men had actually built one that worked. (Yet, when Keegan managed to get the CIA to convene its Nuclear Intelligence Advisory Board to hear his evidence, he was appalled to discover that even this august group of presumably open-minded scientists refused to budge; they simply would not accept any intelligence suggesting that the Soviets had managed to make scientific breakthroughs where American science could not.)

Keegan's criticisms of how the intelligence community arrived at its conclusions extended, of course, beyond the issue of directed-energy weapons, but his role in other intelligence controversies demonstrated that he was susceptible to some familiar sins.

Like the members of Team B, Keegan believed that the United States had fallen far behind the Soviet Union militarily. That conclusion encompassed the entire range of the American-Soviet military balance but focused particularly on two issues, civil defense and military spending. These areas were cited as key pieces of intelligence evidence that there was Soviet superiority, so they are worth some examination.

Most of the Team B members, concerned about the election in 1976 of Jimmy Carter—a man who during the campaign had publicly pledged deep cuts in the military budget —had formed a new citizens' group called the Committee on the Present Danger. Three days after Carter's election, the committee announced its perception of a "Soviet drive for dominance based on an unparalleled military buildup." The committee amounted to a lobbying organization, a regrouping of virtually all the important conservative hard-liners on defense, and their action was intended as a warning to Carter not to attempt any reduction in the American arsenal. The chief animus for the committee was détente, which, the group argued, had been used by the Soviets as a cover for a huge military buildup. Richard Pipes, the former Team B leader, now a prominent member of the committee, went even further, claiming that things had gotten so bad that the Soviets were powerful enough to contemplate starting a war with the United States.

The committee's assertions ran counter to the general conclusions of American intelligence (especially the CIA), which, although somewhat confused, basically claimed that there was a rough parity between the countries, and that there was no evidence that the Russians sought total dominance over the United States. A terrible error, the committee replied, and its arguments attracted a good deal of public attention. Its doomsday claims of imminent Soviet dominance touched off a strident debate about just where the United States stood at that point. It was also a somewhat confused debate, for it was difficult for anyone in the general public to sort out the often-complex arguments cited by each side. A loose coalition of experts in Congress and elsewhere found no merit in the arguments of declining American power in the

317

face of a massive Soviet buildup. That created a two-sided debate with the lines clearly drawn, but it was less clear which side was right.

On the answer hinged some important decisions about American military policy, for if the United States had fallen as far behind as the committee said it had, then only a massive American buildup would redress the balance. But on the other hand, if strategic parity did in fact exist, then there was no cause for panic. What, then, was the intelligence that showed the United States was now militarily inferior?

The most important, according to the committee members and their supporters, was civil defense. The Soviet Union, they claimed, was constructing a huge civil-defense apparatus, a program with an important implication—the Soviets were developing a first-strike capability. The sweep of logic was a little tricky to follow, but it worked something like this: The Russians had decided that at some future date they would carry out a first strike against the United States. To do that, they needed to protect their industries and population against any American counterstrikes. Thus the Soviet civil-defense effort amounted to clear evidence of first-strike intentions because once the Russians had managed to protect their industries and population, they could move to destroy the United States without fear of retaliation. As Pipes, in one of his more Strangelovian analyses put it, the Soviets were constructing a civil-defense system that would keep their casualties, in the event of all-out nuclear war with the United States, down to an "acceptable" level of twenty million dead. (Pipes believed, apparently without checking with the Russians, that the Soviet Union would consider "acceptable" the level of loss of life it had suffered during World War II.)

The CIA had examined the Soviet civil-defense program in some depth, and concluded in 1978 that it was not especially impressive. As the agency noted, the bulk of the program consisted of relocation—in the event of war, people would be evacuated into the countryside, where they would dig holes, cover themselves with a rough shelter, then emerge later to carry on with what was left of Soviet society. Aside from the problem of weather—the effort of digging holes in the frozen earth during a typical Russian winter would represent a considerable challenge, should war break out in that season—the entire Soviet civil-defense effort seemed to CIA analysts of little use against an anticipated rain of thousands of powerful American thermonuclear warheads. The Soviet effort, in their view, amounted to putting a Band-Aid over a gaping wound, for a nuclear war would mean huge areas seared by heat, blast, and radiation, against which any form of hole and primitive shelter stood no chance, the equivalent of trying to hide out in a chicken coop during a hurricane.

The committee strongly disagreed, and cited what it called "proof" that the Soviet civil-defense program was much more extensive than the CIA believed, and that it clearly demonstrated Soviet intention to win a nuclear war. The proof, however, was very nearly vaporous. It consisted, in the main, of one lengthy study by a Soviet émigré professor, whose conclusions, in turn, were the result of an extensive study of Soviet civil-defense publications, drills, and instructions—a fairly impressive pile of documents that he said attested to the extensiveness of the Soviet program. But it all amounted to pretty shallow intelligence; the mere fact that the Soviet civil-defense bureaucracy produced piles of pamphlets on how to survive a nuclear war did not necessarily mean the Russian population at large took them very seriously. Indeed, they did not; as a conversation with any ordinary Russian would have revealed, most Russians regarded civil defense as little more than a joke. For all the talk about survival, most Muscovites had never been involved in a civil-defense drill in their lives, and had not the slightest idea whether there were any fallout shelters in the city.*

Perhaps not surprisingly, Keegan subscribed to the thesis

---

*They might have been amused to learn that the civil-defense advocates in the United States had cited a huge, hundred-yard-long buried mound in Moscow as a special underground bunker for Soviet leaders in event of nuclear war. Actually, the "bunker" was an emergency water-supply facility.

of a large-scale Soviet civil-defense program, but it had a much more unexpected advocate: Jimmy Carter. There is no rational explanation for the President's advocacy (which resulted in a tripling of spending on civil defense), for he was otherwise a man seemingly committed to the most liberal positions on military policy. Only a short while after taking office, for example, he had almost given the Joint Chiefs of Staff collective apoplexy by casually suggesting that perhaps the American and Soviet nuclear arsenals ought to be reduced to two hundred missiles each. He had also canceled the B-1 bomber, sharply cut back on military spending, and pronounced himself totally committed to obtaining a SALT II agreement with Moscow.

But Carter also possessed a number of quirks, among them a fascination with the assorted intricacies of nuclear war. A former nuclear-submarine officer (he often referred to himself, not quite accurately, as a "nuclear engineer"), Carter became taken with the question of how such a war would be conducted. "Survivability" was a favorite Carter buzzword, and he ordered up a series of drills among the White House staff designed to test how well procedures for "continuation of government" worked. (Not very well: Most of the tests were comic operas, and White House staffers noted with some cynicism that the drills were sometimes called off if the weather was rainy.)

Despite his devotion to this issue, Carter took no interest in the second of the Committee on the Present Danger's major theses, Soviet military spending—although it was to have a much more disruptive effect on the intelligence process.

The question of how much money the Soviet Union actually spent on defense had been a matter of some interest to American intelligence for many years, since economics is the chief influence on the size of military establishments. But no one had ever quite gotten a handle on Soviet spending; the distinction between military and civilian production was so blurred that it tended to distort the Soviet price system and made next to impossible the job of separating what was spent on weapons and what was spent on nonmilitary items. The estimates of Soviet military spending ranged all the way from 17 million rubles to 80 million rubles, the latter figure cited by the Chinese, hardly an objective source.

Given the difficulty of pinning down those figures (the officially released Soviet government numbers were widely regarded as hopelessly inaccurate), the CIA shied away from the job, partially on the grounds that since the Soviet civilian and military economies were so inextricably mixed, even the most painstaking analysis would probably be wrong. The task was summed up by one State Department intelligence official as "an exercise in meta-intelligence . . . the exegesis of obscure texts, guesses and unexplained residues, a hunt after analogues and indulgence in assumptions."

But the increasingly sharp debate about the Soviet threat gradually pressured the CIA—where the bulk of economic intelligence was located—into attempting that daunting task. To a great degree, the attempt reflected the American obsession with quick, shorthand methods of summing up complicated military and intelligence problems. In this case, the search was for a simple set of figures that would show instantly and conclusively how much the Soviet Union was actually spending on its military, and how that compared with American outlays. To accomplish that goal, CIA analysts in the early 1970s began to use what they called the "dollar-comparison method," which involved converting Soviet military spending into dollars, then comparing that with American spending.

The method evolved into an esoteric system of intricate formulas for arriving at the figures on Soviet spending. Basically, it consisted of converting dollar prices for Soviet equipment into 1955 rubles, using specialized studies on conversion rates for civilian machinery comparable to military hardware, then converting them back again to adjusted dollar figures. Nobody except the specialists who did the studies understood how it worked.

Before 1976, the CIA studies estimated that the Soviet

Union devoted somewhere between 6 and 9 percent of its gross national product to defense, and that there had been a relatively modest increase in Soviet military spending over the years. But to Keegan, the Committee on the Present Danger, and other doubters, the figures were arrant nonsense; how was it possible, they demanded, for the Soviets to be spending a "relatively modest" amount of money, given all that new military equipment the Russians were deploying everywhere? The spending analyses were prime targets when Team B spent its three months at the CIA, and the figures were argued and reargued.

The CIA analysts were feeling defensive; they rightly surmised that nothing short of the most alarmist figures would please Team B members. "The only people in Washington," as one CIA official noted in a memo to his boss, "not presently engaged in the study of costing of Soviet defense are the people in the GSA [General Services Administration] charforce. I expect to hear from them momentarily."

The difficulty was, however, that as solid as the CIA analysts considered their figures, they actually were very nearly worthless. The system for determining the numbers, a highly complicated series of extrapolations and assumptions, bore little relation to reality. For example, figures showing how much it cost the Soviet Union to keep nearly four million men in uniform were devised by a method that was laughable. In the words of one CIA report: "We obtain these manpower costs by applying U.S. factors for pay and allowances to our estimates of Soviet military manpower. Soviet military personnel performing duties similar to those of U.S. counterparts are assigned the same rate of pay as their counterparts."

Obviously, this was ridiculous. Since American military personnel are all volunteers, they have relatively high rates of pay and allowances. Soviet forces, on the other hand, are largely conscripted, with very low rates of pay and very small allowances. To assign them rates equivalent to their American counterparts was highly misleading, and the sort of voodoo economics on which Keegan and the other critics pounced.

What really discredited the CIA studies, however, was the agency itself. In May 1976, on the basis of what the agency called a "new system" of preparing such estimates, the CIA suddenly doubled its figures on Soviet military spending, now claiming that the Soviets devoted nearly *13 percent* of their gross national product to defense. The new estimate caused an uproar, and managed to please nobody. To Keegan and the critics, the estimate proved that they had been right all along in accusing the CIA of underestimating the Soviets. But liberals argued that the glass was half empty; in their view, the CIA had caved in to the political pressures of the hawks from the air force and the Committee on the Present Danger by somehow discovering, virtually overnight, that the Soviets were supposedly spending 100 percent more than previously believed. In either case, the CIA estimates lost all credibility.

The spending-estimates controversy was still another demonstration of how the volatile mixture of intelligence and politics increasingly confused American perceptions in the 1970s. All of Jimmy Carter's predecessors had been guilty of that sin, in one form or another, and while the new President hinted that he was above such tactics—he had, after all, run on a platform of disdain for the "Washington system"—the temptation apparently proved irresistible.

One striking example occurred early in Carter's presidency when he declared "the moral equivalent of war," a solution to the energy crisis. In a nationwide address in April 1977, Carter sought to impress upon his audience the urgency of his energy plan, an effort that included citation of a CIA report showing that the world energy situation was much worse than previously believed. In fact, Carter said, it was so bad that the CIA predicted that the Soviet Union would actually *import* 3.5 million barrels of oil a day by the mid-1980s—which raised potentially serious problems of international tension when the Soviets tried to compete for the same Middle East oil markets as their American rivals.

This shocking assertion surprised oil experts, who were aware that the Soviet Union was among the world's leading oil producers, and was discovering still more fields; where did the CIA get the idea that the Russians would become oil-poor? That remains a mystery, for no reasonable evidence existed at the time which would have pushed CIA analysts toward that conclusion. As things turned out, despite a CIA prediction that Soviet oil production would peak at no more than 12 million barrels a day by the early 1980s—and then fall off sharply to somewhere around 8 million barrels by 1981—the Russians actually produced 12.2 million barrels in 1981, even in the face of a worldwide oil-production decline.

The error originated in the political ties between the Carter White House and the CIA. The President's new DCI —Admiral Stansfield Turner—was close to Carter and participated in foreign-policy discussions almost as a presidential adviser. That made him vulnerable to political pressure from the White House, since Turner, an outsider with no intelligence experience or power base inside the intelligence community, was totally dependent on the political connection with his boss. And his boss, avid to underscore the seriousness of the worldwide energy problem, wanted intelligence to support that belief. That is what Turner provided him, intelligence that seemed to have been prepared more with an eye toward telling the President what he wanted to hear, rather than as dispassionate analysis of a critical foreign-policy concern.

There is also cause to wonder about the influence of politics on another intelligence controversy, this one of long standing—the question of Soviet violations of the SALT agreement. Carter was determined to get a SALT II agreement, but he faced strong opposition from conservatives who insisted that there had been consistent Soviet cheating on the SALT I accords and that American technical intelligence was not up to the job of detecting a wide range of Soviet deceptions. A chief focus of their concern was encryption, the practice of encoding telemetry signals from missile tests. The telemetry is a key intelligence resource, for a missile test, which requires more than a dozen test functions that are transmitted by sensors to ground-control stations, is an open book to technical intelligence-collection systems. They can read all the signals, from which analysts can deduce a great deal of information about the missile's capabilities.

Conservative opponents of the SALT accords had for some time argued that increased Soviet encryption of missile-test telemetry represented a great danger, for it cut off the chief source of intelligence about the status of Russian missiles. But the United States had caused the problem in the first place. During the negotiations for the first SALT agreement, the CIA had wanted a total ban in the treaty on all encryption. Military-intelligence agencies objected, since, they argued, there is also some encryption of American missile tests, without which the Soviets would learn too much about American missiles.

What emerged finally was a compromise, which permitted encryption to both sides, but not if it "impedes verification of compliance with the provisions of the treaty." The Russians happily accepted this provision, for its vagueness meant they were agreeing to a loophole big enough to drive a truck through. The Russians almost immediately began encrypting some of the data from their missile tests, and when faced with American protests, blandly replied that they had not violated the treaty provisions—since the encryption covered data "not relevant" to treaty compliance. It was a neat checkmate. Since the Americans could not read the encrypted data, they had no way of determining if in fact the Russians were telling the truth.

Carter was stuck with this provision, and it put him in something of a squeeze. On one hand, he was facing strong pressure from the conservatives to demand "tightening up" provisions in the SALT II accord—most of them concerned with various verification provisions—and they were demands Carter had to heed, for any SALT II accord would be subject to Senate approval, with all the politics that implied. Clearly, Carter would have to satisfy conservative opponents that he had been sufficiently tough with the Russians to win concessions on verification. On the other hand, there was only so much pressure the Soviets could withstand; as much as Carter needed the conservatives to pass the treaty, he also needed the Russians, for their consent, obviously, was crucial. And it was a consent the Russians would not give if Carter demanded too much.

Carter was walking a tightrope, and the balancing act included the always troubling question about how to handle charges of Soviet violations of the original SALT I treaty. These charges had grown sharper since Carter took office, since they were directly related to assertions that the treaty had been used by the Russians to increase the size of their already huge arsenal. Carter thus had a large stake in resolving those violations charges, a delicate operation that included such flareups as an American reconnaissance satellite blinded by a possible Russian laser weapon (natural gas fires, the Russians claimed), replacement of a "light" Soviet ICBM with a much larger one (not covered by the treaty), and the recurring controversy over encryption.

Carter did not get the SALT II treaty he sought so long and hard; he withdrew it from Senate consideration because of the Soviet invasion of Afghanistan. In fact, the treaty was in very serious trouble anyway because of growing doubt over whether it could be effectively monitored. The conservatives had argued that improved Soviet deception measures had outpaced American ability to detect them, and they were furious over what they believed was Carter's willingness to resolve the assorted violations charged to the Russians in the Soviets' favor, on the rationale that he did not want to jeopardize his chances of getting the SALT II accord. There was no firm evidence for the suspicion, but in that atmosphere, the conservatives could seize on a wide range of vulnerabilities connected with the treaty.

One of them was the treaty language itself, which often seemed so ambiguous as to be opaque. Article Two of the proposed SALT II treaty, for example, had eight clauses, seventeen "agreed statements" and sixteen "common understandings." Not even the diplomats who had negotiated them were quite certain what all those words meant, and certainly none seemed able to explain this treaty definition of cruise missiles: "Unmanned, self-propelled guided vehicles which sustain flight through the use of aerodynamic lift over most of their flight path and are not weapon-delivery vehicles, that is, unarmed pilotless guided vehicles, shall not be considered to be cruise missiles if such vehicles are distinguishable from cruise missiles on the basis of externally observable design features."

Apparently, this definition means that if it doesn't look like a cruise missile, then it isn't one, but the language might mean something else entirely. Whatever the meaning, it served to underscore the argument of treaty opponents that trying to enforce it was like trying to nail pudding to the wall; how, it was argued, with treaty language like that, would it be possible to even begin discussing enforcement?

Carter really didn't have an answer, except to claim that the American technical intelligence capabilities could effectively monitor any SALT agreement, with full confidence that Soviet cheating would be detected. But the 1979 revolution in Iran* exposed a weak spot. The most important part of the American technical ability was dependent on a chain of radar and electronic monitoring stations stretching from the southern Soviet border all the way to Alaska, and the removal of any component would badly degrade the rest of the system. The most important stations were in Iran, since they were closest to the main Soviet missile-firing locations just across the border in southern Russia. There was some debate over how

---

*The inability to predict that revolution became one of the CIA's more notorious failures, but the public controversy obscured an even greater failure: CIA agents at the American Embassy in Tehran, which was later seized by radical students, failed to burn classified documents. Students retrieved the documents from the shredder and painstakingly taped them back together, in the process discovering that three of the hostages they had seized were CIA agents. Several months later, military planners for Eagle Claw, the attempt to rescue the hostages, were appalled when the CIA told them it had no on-ground agents inside Iran; a retired CIA agent was enlisted to infiltrate Tehran.

327

serious a loss those Iranian monitoring stations represented, but in the delicate political context of the entire SALT debate, Carter could not overcome even the mildest questions about American ability to monitor.

The slow strangulation of SALT II marked a curious period during which Carter had fought a rearguard action against demands that he reorient American military and foreign policy. His opponents perceived a Soviet threat growing ever larger while American resolve and power gradually eroded. Carter had denied this was so, but his zigzag policies tended to lend support to the critics, who pointed to evidence of American decline. From the time of his inauguration, Carter was undecided on how to handle the Russians, waffling between moralistic preaching to the Kremlin, and extending an olive branch. His own administration was bitterly divided on the extent and meaning of the Russian threat, and what finally emerged was a document that reflected Carter's confusion. Called Presidential Review Memorandum (PRM) 10, it said that the United States and the Soviet Union had reached "essential equivalence" militarily, so there was no necessity to dramatically improve the American arsenal. But PRM 10 also advocated "competition" with the Russians in certain areas, especially the Middle East and Europe. In other words, both sides were equal, but the United States would confront the Soviets directly in peripheral areas as a way of rolling back Soviet influence.

There was little that made sense about PRM 10, and the deficiencies were made glaringly apparent the first time Carter tried to implement it. The chosen battlefield was an old American concern—Cuba.

As Carter's most hard-line adviser, National Security Council chief Zbigniew Brzezinski focused Carter's attention on the matter of what he called the "surrogate" question—the Cuban troops operating in the Third World, especially in Africa. Key to that dangerous military adventurism, Brzezinski argued, was the Soviet-Cuban connection; obviously, Cuba could not afford to send those nearly thirty thousand troops around the world unless the Russians not only provided the aid and support but also filled the gaps created in Cuban ranks back home. Thus the question came down to determining the exact dimensions of the Soviet military presence in Cuba, toward the eventual goal of pressuring Moscow to remove as many as possible. And that, in turn, would effectively sever the Cuban-Russian connection.

This goal imposed a strong requirement on intelligence to produce specific information, but the task immediately encountered some serious problems. The worst was the unsettling discovery that American intelligence had no real idea of how many Soviet military personnel were in Cuba. In 1962, it had counted seventeen thousand soldiers and technicians, all of whom had stayed behind after the Cuban missile crisis. They attracted little American concern, for the understanding that settled the crisis covered only "offensive strategic weapons," and even a division-sized Soviet military presence was not considered a direct threat to the United States. A year later, the Russians began withdrawing men from Cuba, until there were about ten thousand troops remaining. But nobody in the American intelligence community was quite sure of the actual number, for the simple fact was that it had lost track. Russians moved in and out of Cuba in civilian clothes, and the movements of so many men, all dressed in identical tropical shirts, soon confused the U.S. intelligence monitoring effort —a difficult operation to begin with, since there was a real lack of on-ground sources.

In subsequent years, the question of the Soviet troops was put on the back burner and nearly forgotten. The Russians aided this amnesia by keeping a very low profile; there was a bare minimum of radio traffic, and they remained out of sight, generally staying in the countryside and away from urban areas where they would be more noticeable. Moreover, without extensive on-ground sources to monitor them, it was impossible to tell how many of the Russians were advisers and how many were part of organized combat units. Part of the reason for the American confusion was a decision by Carter in the first month of his presidency to order cancellation of SR-71 flights over Cuba. Intended as a gesture to Castro (and, by implication, to Moscow) of a desire for friendly relations, the cancellation went unrecognized by Cuba and the Russians and had the more serious result of reducing what was already a very limited American intelligence capability on the island.*

To get some answers, Carter ordered a maximum intelligence effort focused on the island, and in the summer of 1979, it detected what was regarded as a significant clue: an NSA intercept heard radio-communication references to a Russian "brigade." On the surface, this reference made no sense, for training units—which were supposed to be the only types of Russian forces in Cuba—are never structured in brigade form, which is impractical for anything other than combat operations. Military intelligence regarded the reference with alarm, concluding that the Russians had organized a full-scale combat brigade in Cuba, with the probable intention of using it someday elsewhere in the Western Hemisphere—possibly the United States. Turner of the CIA took a more cautious view, arguing that the intelligence to that point showed only that there was an "entity" separate from the Russian advisory force, but the United States had no idea of its size, organization, or mission.

It would have remained an in-house intelligence argument except that politics intervened. Senator Richard Stone, a Florida Democrat facing a tough reelection battle against conservative opposition, was casting about for an issue that would establish his conservative credentials, particularly for the politically important Cuban exile community in Miami. In July 1979, while Stone was participating in the Senate Foreign

---

*One of the rare CIA field agents in Cuba managed in November 1978 to get a snapshot of a Soviet MiG-23 fighter that had been recently shipped into the island. The picture was a lucky break, for it showed that the MiG-23 had an intake valve not used on models of those planes configured for delivery of nuclear weapons—thus relieving an American fear that the Russians were trying to sneak in such planes.

Relations Committee's hearings on the Panama Canal treaty, one of his aides passed along an interesting piece of information: There was an argument within the administration on what to do about a Soviet "combat brigade" in Cuba. Stone pounced on it, asking embarrassed administration officials, during the public hearing, about the brigade reports.

Stone had brought the matter into the open, and it very quickly became a full-fledged political controversy, worsened when Senator Frank Church of Idaho, also facing a tough reelection fight against conservative opposition, not only decried the presence of the Soviet brigade in Cuba, but went on to demand its withdrawal as a precondition for Senate ratification of the SALT II treaty. (Only a month before, he had said publicly that there was "no change" in the numbers and status of Soviet forces in Cuba.)

In other words, a political circus, and combined with Carter's fumbling attempt to straighten out the controversy, it served to make the brigade matter a thoroughly confusing intelligence episode. Not one single shred of solid evidence existed for the assertion that a Soviet combat brigade was operating in Cuba. Besides which, even if it were, so what? As the CIA discovered, the Russians had no airlift or sealift capability stationed in Cuba; if they were going to invade anywhere, they would have to swim there. The judgment by military-intelligence agencies about the brigade turned out to have rested on a very thin piece of evidence: The layout of tents and other equipment was "very similar" to layouts used by Soviet combat brigades while they were on maneuvers in East Germany and the Soviet Union. Therefore, the unit in Cuba was also a combat brigade.

The Russians were puzzled and alarmed by the whole episode ("Are you saying, Mr. Secretary, that our soldiers may someday swim to Key West?" an exasperated Ambassador Dobrynin twitted Secretary of State Cyrus Vance), and they insisted that the troops had been in Cuba since 1962. Soviet diplomats began to hint that some sort of intricate American maneuver was in the works, since, they argued, how could American intelligence—known to have been micro-scopically interested in Cuba since the days of the missile crisis—have failed to spot the Soviet troops?

Finally, the matter was settled with some private diplo-macy. Vance, who thought the whole business about the combat brigade a silly bit of nonsense right from the begin-ning, got the Russians to affirm the "training status" of Soviet troops in Cuba, while Carter, to assuage his conservative critics, announced "increased surveillance" of Soviet activities, along with expanded American military man-euvers in the Caribbean under the new Joint Caribbean Military Task Force, which was supposed to forestall any in-vasion emanating out of Cuba—by the Russians or other-wise.

Part of the reason for the distinct lowering of the volume in this Cuban tempest was some rethinking in the intelligence agencies. More sober analysis of the data at hand suggested that perhaps the Russians had been there all along, and that they were organized largely for training Cuban units and filling the gaps left by regular Cuban army units sent overseas. Then too, there was the matter of the lack of sealift or airlift capability; obviously, without such transportation, a combat brigade stuck on an island in the middle of the Caribbean was useless for combat operations anywhere else.

Another reason was increasing congressional skepticism. Congressmen and senators had been ushered into the CIA's National Photographic Interpretation Center in Maryland to be shown satellite and SR-71 pictures of the Soviet military presence. Very interesting, many congressmen noted po-litely, but then asked how anybody in intelligence knew that there were Russians inside those tanks shown on the pictures. Because, they were told, the pictures also showed Russian infantrymen near the tanks; therefore, it could be deduced that there were also Russians inside the tanks. And how could that be proved? Well, it couldn't, CIA analysts replied with some irritation; they believed the Russians wouldn't have Cuban crewmen in the tanks and Russian infantrymen alongside, for they wouldn't be able to communicate with each other.

The latest Cuban imbroglio closed on that note of petty argument, but the effects were much broader, since the entire affair illustrated the fumbling, conflicting signals and ambiguous intelligence that seemed to mark the direction of American policy in the latter part of the 1970s.

Like most other conservative opponents of Carter's policies, George Keegan watched these antics with an increasing aversion. He had suddenly retired from his post early in 1977 following a series of nasty run-ins with Secretary of Defense Harold Brown about the scope of the Soviet threat. Ordered by Brown's office to tone down his statements—after one especially apocalyptic Keegan briefing, Brown privately pronounced him a "madman"—Keegan was infuriated when he found that a much milder CIA briefing had been substituted for his own remarks.

Brown's displeasure with Keegan was partially personal. A nuclear-weapons scientist, Brown belonged to the military-scientific establishment that had openly scorned Keegan's claims of Soviet advances in directed-energy weapons. At one point, before taking office, Brown had announced that the Russians could not possibly succeed in building such weapons, a possibly biased conclusion since he was one of the scientists involved in the American failures. Keegan called this "scientific smugness," a remark that made Brown one of his most bitter enemies.

But as a private citizen, Keegan caused Brown even more headaches, for now free of certain constraints connected with the uniform, Keegan galvanized the entire conservative opposition with a number of dramatic public appearances that set off an extensive debate about whether the Russians were ahead militarily. Upon his official retirement, he gave an interview to *The New York Times* in which he pronounced the Soviet Union possessed of military superiority over the United States, and followed that with a Washington news conference that claimed the American intelligence community had completely underestimated the Soviet military threat for ten years, the worst such intelligence failure in American history.

Over the next several years, Keegan was to hammer home this theme in a series of speeches and seminars across the country. (These appearances caused grave disquiet within the Carter administration, to the point where two of Brown's deputies openly threatened Keegan with some sort of unspecified retribution if he did not end his strident criticisms of Carter's defense policies. It is not known whether Brown knew of this approach, but in any event, the threat served only to increase Keegan's pugnacity, and he was not threatened again.)*

But by late 1979, no threat would have stopped Keegan anyway, for he had set forces into motion that were impossible to control. In large part because of his efforts, the prevailing wisdom within the American scientific-military-intelligence establishment was shifting toward the Keegan view of a massive and threatening Soviet specter.

And that shift, combined with an even more spectacular shift in the country's political outlook, was about to cause nothing less than a profound revolution in the way it perceived its greatest rival and the world at large.

In simple terms, Team B was about to become Team A.

*Even the air force learned that Keegan was not a man to be trifled with. Back in the late 1950s, he became openly skeptical that all those nuclear bombs and B-47 bombers, the heart of the American retaliatory capability, actually worked. SAC finally agreed to a test, and Keegan discovered not only that the B-47 was unflyable at high speed but that all the bombs got stuck inside the bomb bays. It turned out that a seventy-five-cent microswitch on the bomb-release mechanism became bent by the wind stream, and jammed, preventing a single bomb from being dropped.

ten

OMENS AND ORACLES

> "'Pon my word, Watson, you are coming along wonderfully. You have really done very well indeed. It is true that you have missed everything of importance, but you have hit upon the method. . . ."
>
> —SHERLOCK HOLMES, in "A Case of Identity" by Sir Arthur Conan Doyle

IN THE LATE FALL of 1980, while presidential candidate Ronald Reagan crisscrossed the United States, making speeches about the "Soviet empire of evil," Jim Smith* was in its very lair, trying to decide how to carry out à very puzzling intelligence mission.

Smith was an admirer of Reagan, and like the conservative Republican, believed fervently in the doctrine of the Soviet Union as the fount of the world's troubles. And also like Reagan, Smith believed that the United States had been in a dangerous torpor for years, benignly regarding a looming Soviet threat that was close to taking over the world. To some extent, Smith's convictions stemmed from his deep religious faith. A fundamentalist Baptist, he had heard for years about Soviet government oppression of fundamentalist Christian sects inside Russia. To Smith, the Russians were not only deadly political enemies, they were godless ones, too.

Smith had majored in Russian language and history studies at a midwestern university, and by the time of his gradua-

---

*A pseudonym.

tion in 1979, he had resolved to enlist as a soldier in a crusade against Soviet Communism. He tried the CIA and was rejected on unspecified grounds, but after getting a job with an oil-exploration company, Smith was recruited for intelligence service by one of the firm's executives who did some undercover work for the CIA.

Initially, the spying task was described somewhat vaguely; Smith would be one of a group of company executives who were scheduled to visit Moscow for an extended stay during negotiations over a possible business deal involving the Soviets. While there, Smith was told, he would be assigned the job of personally checking out a piece of technology the Russians might be using, illegally, for military purposes. In fact, the technology was American, a forty-ton "super magnet" that had been shipped to the Soviet Union in 1977 as part of a scientific exchange agreement. The magnet, given to the Russians because their own superconducting technology was far behind similar American technology, was supposed to be used strictly for nonmilitary experiments involving a new form of power generation called magnetohydrodynamics—the process of generating electricity by the interaction of superheated gases.

Smith was puzzled about this assignment. If the Americans were so worried about the magnet's use for some sort of military purpose, why had they given it to the Russians in the first place? Smith did not know it, but he had been assigned a role in still another of those endless American intelligence arguments. The argument centered on Soviet weapons programs, especially directed-energy weapons— the crux, as we have seen, of an especially acrimonious intelligence dispute during the past several years. The magnet issue was especially contentious, since military-intelligence agencies, especially the air force, claimed that the United States had been hoodwinked; the magnet, supposedly for peaceful scientific research, was actually being used to help develop small, superpowerful engines for space weapons and charged-particle-beam blasters. American scientists involved in the exchange program were highly skeptical of that claim.

The answer, obviously, was to get a firsthand look at the magnet in the Soviet Union, and that's where Smith came in. Although he eagerly accepted the espionage assignment, he was not very well equipped to do it. He had the advantage of fluent Russian, along with the fact that he was not known to the Soviets as an intelligence operative. But he had no idea of how he was supposed to track down this magnet. There was also the matter of that small camera—about the size of a matchbox—he had been given by the company executive; Smith had visions of twenty years in Siberia should the Russians ever discover it in his pocket.

It was thus a very nervous Jim Smith who embarked on his spying mission. Immediately, he had a run of good luck. A relative of a woman he had met in Moscow knew a man who worked at some sort of scientific laboratory north of Moscow. There were power-generation experiments going on there, the Russian confided after Smith had plied him with much vodka, and he finally agreed to provide Smith (whom the Russian believed to be a scientist interested in those experiments) with a special pass to get inside the building.

The run of luck continued. Smith took a train to the laboratory site and discovered that, unlike almost all scientific research facilities in the Soviet Union, it was virtually unguarded. Once inside, Smith managed to find the magnet—which he learned had been completely taken apart by the Russians, apparently in the process of analyzing how it worked. Fearful of being discovered, Smith snapped off several dozen pictures, then left.

But Smith's luck had run out. All the pictures were indistinct blurs, mainly because the camera had been jiggled by its very nervous holder. Smith was asked to go back and take better pictures. This time, Smith dressed in a set of plain overalls, the type worn by most Russian workmen, and simply wandered into the research site, pretending to be just another worker. However, no sooner had Smith shot just one picture than he was spotted by a watchman who turned him over to local police. When they took a look at the camera, the KGB was called in, and Smith very shortly found himself in an interrogation room at KGB headquarters in Moscow. Smith was frightened, but soon realized that the KGB men were more puzzled than angry. What, they wanted to know, was this American doing in a scientific research center trying to photograph a large magnet that had come from the United States? Smith had no answer to that question, save to insist, over and over again, that he merely wanted some pictures of the large magnet. Nearly ten hours of questioning went no-place, and finally the KGB gave up. Apparently convinced they were dealing with some sort of crazy American, they let Smith go, with firm warnings to stay away from "unauthorized areas."

And so the great magnet mystery remained unsolved, although the episode involving Smith provided at least some clues. For one thing, it was clear that the magnet was not being used in weapons-related research, since if it were, such research would have been carried out at a tightly guarded facility, with rigid security checks for anyone moving in and out. Moreover, when Smith found the magnet, it had been dismantled, indicating perhaps that the Russians had never intended it for any scientific experiments, but instead simply wanted to get their hands on a piece of advanced American technology for study and duplication.

In any case, the entire affair illustrated perfectly some of the very real tensions tearing apart the American intelligence community at that point. Here was still another of those divi-sive arguments over a relatively simple intelligence matter, the difference this time being an attempt to settle it by an intelligence rush job: an untrained "asset" sent into the So-viet Union, with vague instructions. But the majority of other disputes hadn't been settled, turning much of the intelligence community into a raucous debating society.

However, just as this amateur production was ending,

political events were bringing an end to all the squabbling. A revolution was about to take place, one that would subsume all of American intelligence.

During the fall of 1980, there was hardly a television screen in the entire state of South Dakota that was not filled at some point with the images of horror. Sixteen times a day for a month, viewers were treated to the pictures and sounds of Soviet troops, tanks, missiles, gas warfare, thermonuclear bombs, submarines, bombers, and fighters, an ominous tableau of brute military force—accompanied by a background of dolorous music that gave an impression that great hordes from the East were about to strike.

And that was precisely the point. The images were in a film called *The SALT Syndrome,* a thirty-minute compendium of alarmism on the Soviet military and political threat to the United States. Produced by the American Security Council, a conservative group that advocated increased U.S. military spending, it was often shown during the bitter campaign against incumbent Senator George McGovern. Conservative Republican opponents of McGovern bought huge swatches of television time and ran the film repeatedly, a tactic they felt would dramatically underscore their charges that McGovern had been "soft" on defense spending, and was among those seeking to "unilaterally disarm" the United States.

There is no way to judge the role of that film in McGovern's eventual defeat, but *The SALT Syndrome* as a political statement bears some examination, for it offers important clues to what happened later. The film was a slick production, designed to convey the impression of a massive, threatening Soviet military machine that had come to dominate a weakened United States. It encapsulated the doctrines and convictions of a group of people who for nearly a generation had argued that intelligence was consistently underestimating the dimensions of the Communist threat. In their view, the United States was undeniably losing the Cold War and on the defensive from a militarily resurgent Soviet Union, which was aided by a number of Moscow-dominated "clients" around the world (notably, Fidel Castro of Cuba). It was a view of the darkest foreboding: Only a fundamental revolution in the way the United States perceived its greatest enemy (accompanied by a large-scale military buildup) would redress the balance.

But how had its proponents arrived at this perception? What intelligence persuaded them that the generally prevailing view—the ragged consensus of the U.S. intelligence community that the United States and the Soviets were in rough parity—was so completely wrong? Many of the people who subscribed to the thesis of grave U.S. weakness had been privy to the same top-secret intelligence, especially the members of the old Team B and some of the members of the Committee on the Present Danger, yet everything they had seen persuaded them that American intelligence had badly underestimated the threats that came from every direction.

The conservative opposition stood the world on its head; there was danger everywhere, they argued, and the fact that intelligence did not see it proved only that the assorted intelligence agencies had fallen victim to their own preconceptions. Any belief in American security was an illusion, they insisted, and *The SALT Syndrome* documented their grim arithmetic: The Russians were spending three times the U.S. investment in defense, the United States was unilaterally disarming, the idea of arms control was a Soviet sham designed to lull the Americans, and the Russians had a six to one advantage in "missile firepower" (whatever that meant). A number of on-camera statements went even further: Defense policies of previous administrations were "immoral and self-defeating" (Alexander Haig), attempts at arms control were "pure appeasement" (Senator Henry M. Jackson), and the Soviets had spent "one hundred and four billion dollars more on defense" since 1970 than had the United States (former Deputy Secretary of Defense William Clements).

By 1980, the Committee on the Present Danger, where

these views flourished, included 191 members, all of them conservative critics of détente and advocates of a full-scale American military buildup. Of that total, Republican candidate Ronald Reagan—the most noted proponent of the America-is-far-behind thesis—selected 68 as "advisers" for two campaign panels to advise him on military and foreign policy. Significantly, the panels did not include Henry Kissinger, a favorite conservative whipping boy, or anyone who had ever been connected to Kissinger in any way. Or any liberals, for this was strictly the hardball team, made up of visceral anti-Communists who felt the time had come for America to exert forceful world leadership. "History," as one of them said, "is ours to define."

Reagan's campaign rhetoric was very much a reflection of this group, with an insistent theme of American military inferiority and drift. Reagan's victory transformed the Committee on the Present Danger from a government-in-exile into the actual government; fifty-one of its members were appointed to high-level Pentagon, State Department, and intelligence-agency posts in the new administration.

The conservatives' highest priority was the intelligence agencies, especially the CIA, for it was there, they believed, that most of the "bias" about Soviet intentions resided. A special target was the CIA's SR (Soviet Russia) Division, whose 250 employees were marked for immediate dismissal by some of the more rigid hard-liners in the Reagan transition team. However, cooler heads prevailed, and the SR employees were sentenced to exile instead of death— removed from CIA headquarters in Langley, Virginia, they were relocated in an office building in nearby Vienna, although their classified files had to remain permanently behind at Langley.

The eviction of the CIA's SR Division illustrated clearly the scorn in which the new regime held American intelligence's chief resource on the Soviet Union. It can be argued that this purge was a serious mistake, since its central motive was an ideological housecleaning, part of an effort to impose a rigid, doctrinaire outlook on an entire administration, its intelligence agencies included.* That is partially true, but it is also true to say that the SR Division, especially, had little to offer in its defense. The years of internecine argument, politicization, and assorted other bureaucratic wars had taken their toll; the CIA's performance on intelligence relating to the Soviet Union was simply not very good. By the time Reagan took office, there had been a steep decline in the quality of the analysts coming into the agency (nearly half of the people who worked in the SR Division didn't even speak Russian), and the agency's overall intelligence record was decidedly mixed.

The CIA's decline was accompanied by a rise in the influence of the military intelligence agencies, most especially the DIA. For some years after its founding by Robert McNamara, the DIA had been something of an open joke—its work was shoddy, there were poor career incentives for its officers, and its intelligence estimates were notoriously sloppy. The core of the problem was that the DIA did not want to antagonize the military services—from which its personnel and resources were drawn—so it tended to run with the pack. In 1970, Army General Daniel O. Graham took over the agency. A vigorous, very bright officer who was determined to establish DIA as a viable intelligence organization, Graham admitted that much DIA work was self-serving and budget-oriented. He completely reorganized and invigorated the agency, improving the quality of its officers and bringing in large numbers of civilian analysts. By 1976, the DIA had become a full-fledged rival to the CIA, and its growing independence was marked

*The housecleaning also included the President's Foreign Intelligence Advisory Board, but one of Reagan's choices for that board was unfortunate: Alfred Bloomingdale, a rich Reagan crony from California. Following Bloomingdale's death in 1983, CIA and FBI officials were alarmed to discover that he had not only carried on a semipublic liaison with his mistress, he had also videotaped "sex parties" involving his mistress and some of his politically prominent friends. CIA officials, concerned over the opportunity for KGB blackmail of Bloomingdale had it ever learned of his secret life, carefully suggested that in the future, more care be taken in the background checks of PFIAB appointees.

by regulations that created a new deputy secretary of defense, to whom the DIA reported directly.

Yet when Reagan set about in 1980 to build up American military power, intelligence played almost no role at all in his decisions. Reagan had long been committed to the theory that the United States was militarily inferior to the Soviet Union and that a large-scale military buildup was required to redress the balance. This conviction seems odd, for at the moment he took office, the American strategic arsenal was so vast and overpowering that its destructive effects in the event of war could not even be measured. The arsenal amounted to twenty-six thousand nuclear warheads, spread over twenty-five different types, ranging from the W54 nuclear land mine of four kilotons in explosive power (four thousand tons of TNT), to the nine-megaton W53 ICBM warhead (nine million tons of TNT).

But like the other conservatives, Reagan believed that the Russian arsenal was always bigger and better, and that however large and impressive its American equivalent, there was always the constant danger of a continuing Soviet military buildup checkmating the United States. In Reagan's phrase, "the window of vulnerability" always existed, for the Soviet Union would never rest until it had managed to build a military machine capable of defeating the United States at one blow.

Reagan's prime source of information was the *Reader's Digest,* whose pithy reportage on various political and military questions tended to be extremely conservative, and often alarmist. Thus, when Reagan read a *Digest* article by Edward Teller—the chief scientist behind development of the American hydrogen (thermonuclear) bomb—advocating an American *Star Wars* defense in space against incoming Soviet ICBM warheads, Reagan embraced it enthusiastically. Teller, the leading disciple within the American scientific community on the efficacy of nuclear weapons, believed that the Soviet ICBM threat could be balked by a plan to explode numbers

343

of small nuclear weapons in space; the X rays from these explosions, he claimed, would destroy Soviet warheads.

Reagan embraced this idea and went it one better during his noted Star Wars speech in March 1983, laying out a plan for an extended defense line of directed-energy weapons that would make America impervious to nuclear attack. But Reagan at that point had not the slightest shred of any intelligence indicating whether this defensive system would work, how new Russian weapons might overcome the defenses, and whether it was worth the multibillion-dollar cost. In fact, he had no intelligence to indicate whether the whole idea was necessary in the first place, and with the exception of his science adviser—a former protégé and acolyte of Teller—he had not consulted with any expert before making what amounted to a very serious statement on American military policy.

Reagan had a limited attention span, and was plainly bored by complex analyses or questions of any length. (At one point, CIA officials began videotaping the agency's daily intelligence bulletin for the President, using a CIA man professionally trained as an announcer—a desperate measure to ensure that Reagan would pay attention to at least some CIA intelligence.) Reagan tended to oversimplify complex problems, proceeding on a set of assumptions he held with the certitude of the true believer. He believed, for example, that the Soviet Union had built a massive civil-defense program, a program he was convinced would work in the United States. This conviction, as we saw earlier, was quite wrong, but Reagan underscored it by appointing a man named T. K. Jones to the post of under secretary of defense for research and engineering, strategic and theater nuclear forces, a mouthful of organizational chart that meant Jones was in charge of the American civil-defense program. Jones, a former Boeing Company official who had devised the theory that industrial machinery could be protected in the event of nuclear war, also believed that large segments of the American population could be protected. Like other civil-defense advocates, he insisted that there was a "civil-defense gap"—the Russians had a viable civil-defense program that would protect the bulk of their population in the event of war, while the United States had no program of similar size and scope.

This assertion, chillingly reminiscent of General Buck Turgidson's famous "mine-shaft gap" in the movie *Dr. Strangelove,* set the tone for the new American civil-defense buildup, beginning in 1981. It consisted, in the main, of plans for large-scale evacuation of urban populations. Once in rural areas, the people would dig crude shelters, survive, and then later emerge to carry on the business of civilization. As Jones summarized his theory in a widely noted interview, "You know, dirt is just great stuff. . . . If there are enough shovels to go around, everybody's going to make it."

If this sort of thing seems positively slapdash, it was no different from the general tenor of public remarks emanating from an administration that seemed to take a rather casual approach to such vital questions as nuclear war. (Administration officials had the distressing habit of openly discussing possible scenarios for "limited nuclear war.") A similar approach came in intelligence, exemplified by the appointment of William Casey as the new DCI.

Nicknamed "Cyclone," Casey was a blustery, self-made Republican multimillionaire businessman who had served in the OSS during World War II. A classic example of the typically combative New Yorker, Casey spoke in a Manhattan West Side mumble that made him all but unintelligible to people from other parts of the country. For those who understood what Casey was talking about, the new DCI seemed straight out of a time capsule. In line with the more aggressive stance of the Reagan administration, Casey sought to transform the CIA into a contemporary version of the old OSS. Called "the night parachute drop syndrome" by people inside the agency less impressed with the CIA's OSS heritage, it romanticized the OSS experience, arguing that since the United States faced a Soviet enemy that posed even greater danger than Hitler's Germany, it was time for the CIA to get back into covert action, to carry out a series of OSS-type offensive actions around the globe to confront the Soviet giant.

The renewal of covert political and paramilitary action, especially in the Far East and Latin America, was very much in keeping with Reagan's more activist stance against the Soviet Union, but the question is whether it contributed anything to the improvement of the product of American intelligence. And it did not, for fundamentally, intelligence was no longer the chief product of the CIA; the agency's intelligence was not especially welcome in an administration that already knew the answers. Richard Pipes, for example, had been named to the National Security Council as its Soviet expert, and as a man positive he knew all there was to know about Soviet intentions, he was in no mood to listen to any CIA intelligence. CIA officials, not surprisingly, also found that the White House preferred to see the raw intelligence that had been collected rather than a finished analysis, which they openly scorned as "biased" (meaning that it did not agree with their convictions).

This dangerous process was worsened by a number of measures taken by Casey to rebuild the CIA's tattered image in the eyes of the White House. For instance, he sprinkled a number of right-wing ideologues throughout the agency— partially as a means of paying off a few campaign debts to conservative supporters of Reagan, and also to demonstrate his own willingness to tailor intelligence to preconceptions.

One especially disturbing occurrence came shortly after Casey had taken over his post, when the CIA began preparing its annual intelligence report on world terrorism. Casey rejected the first draft, complaining that it did not have enough material on Soviet support for terrorist movements. A second draft included more material, but noted that no evidence existed that the Soviets were directly responsible for most terrorism. But Casey rejected the new draft, arguing that the evidence of Soviet control of terrorism must be there, someplace; besides, he noted, Reagan and Secretary of State Alexander Haig had already said that the Soviets were directly responsible, so it was now the duty of the CIA to find the evidence for that conclusion. (Casey also rejected drafts of CIA reports on political unrest in Latin America on the grounds that they failed to emphasize Soviet responsibility for the unrest.)

The events presaged that most dangerous of all influences on intelligence, politics. The CIA was attempting to produce intelligence for an administration that not only believed it already knew the answers, but saw world events through an extremely narrow prism—the Soviet-American conflict. A number of intelligence-community officials spotted the danger, notable among them Admiral Bobby R. Inman, former head of the National Security Agency.

Inman had been appointed Casey's deputy in the wake of the DCI's disastrous appointment of Max Hugel, a Reagan campaign official, as his deputy director. Totally loyal—he had once stood stiffly at attention during an outdoor Reagan campaign appearance while a stiff wind blew his toupee down the airport tarmac—Hugel otherwise had no qualification whatsoever for an intelligence post, and was hastily ushered out when he became involved in a business scandal. His replacement, Inman, was selected amid growing concern about the quality of people Casey was bringing into the agency.

No such question emerged about Inman, considered the most talented executive within the American intelligence community. A favorite of congressional committees for his no-nonsense briefing style, intelligence, and directness, Inman could be extremely enigmatic, sounding one day like a civil libertarian, and the next like a Reagan hard-liner, but he was, nevertheless, respected as an intelligence professional. He was clearly distressed by what he encountered when he joined the CIA in 1982—an agency whose intelligence product was being steadily downgraded while its resources were being increasingly diverted into a wide range of boom and bang operations. And these operations, Inman concluded, were not only a senseless waste of intelligence-agency assets, they also rested on the erroneous belief that such actions would make a dent in the Soviet threat.

Congressional committees gradually became aware of growing tension between Casey and Inman, and they learned to watch for an important clue during joint appearances by the men—when Inman's leg began to jiggle under the witness table, congressmen and senators knew that the restive admiral was finding whatever Casey was saying at that moment to be arrant nonsense. They also discovered that Inman often called his boss "the wanderer," for Casey's habit of constantly flying all over the world to various CIA stations, where he would attempt to encourage a widening range of covert-action operations.*

Inman, who quit nearly a year later, kept his complaints private, an act of loyalty that did not obscure the fact that he was quite right. The warping of intelligence and renewed obsession with covert action was bound to lead to trouble. It came in Latin America.

The Reagan administration judged events in Latin America strictly in a Cold War context, and it saw Fidel Castro's Cuba as the chief Soviet instrument for a plan to Communize the Latin American continent. There was no intelligence suggesting that this belief was in the least correct—in fact, social and political unrest in that continent were the result of much more complicated factors. The only intelligence the administration wanted to see was whatever would buttress its Castro-phobia—the fear that Fidel Castro was fomenting revolution all over the continent, as part of a master plan directed by

---

*Inman became distressed by Casey's rigid view of world events, especially regarding the Soviet Union. In one speech, for example, Casey showed a large map of the world, with "countries under significant degree of Soviet influence" painted a bright red. Those who looked closely at the map noticed that El Salvador was among those so painted; it had been written off by Casey on the grounds that it had an "active Communist insurgency." Inman was appalled when he realized that CIA analysts, who should have known better, had produced this map straight out of a 1950s-era civics lesson. The only thing missing was an octopus centered on Moscow.

Moscow. And that is the kind of "intelligence" the administration began to receive, passed along by Casey, who betrayed an incredible lack of knowledge of that area of the world. (In one rare interview, for example, he claimed that the 1962 American-Soviet agreement settling the Cuban missile crisis included a provision banning Cuba from "exporting revolution" throughout Latin America. Of course, the understanding said no such thing.)

The men who were supposed to be making decisions based on this intelligence also betrayed a distressing lack of knowledge. Among them was Thomas O. Enders, under secretary of state for inter-American affairs, who in 1981 pronounced Latin America in a "state of danger," and a year later proclaimed, "We believe the decisive battle for Central America is under way in El Salvador." Worse was Nestor Sanchez, another Reagan ideologue who had been appointed deputy assistant secretary of defense for international security affairs. A former CIA official in Latin America, Sanchez was notorious during a tour of duty in Guatemala, where he worked closely with right-wing death squads—so closely, in fact, that other CIA agents working in Guatemala demanded transfers elsewhere in protest. In his more important Pentagon post, Sanchez made a number of speeches around the country that took as their central theme the idea that Latin America was now officially a battleground between the Soviet Union and the United States, and that the side that won the struggle would determine the course of future history.

The first target of what the Reagan administration considered the new battleground in the East-West conflict was Nicaragua, where, it was argued, the previous Carter administration had made a terrible mistake. The error, the administration claimed, was in withdrawing military aid and political support from Nicaraguan dictator Anastasio "Tacho" Somoza Debayle in 1979 in the face of a revolutionary movement that eventually took over the country. Carter had claimed that while the revolutionary movement—known as the Sandinistas—had some Cuban help, and that some of its leaders were Marxists, it essentially represented a home-grown movement that had flourished in the face of a brutal and corrupt dictatorship.

Perhaps, but to the Reagan administration, Carter's action was heresy; Somoza was a strong anti-Communist and supporter of the United States, representing a bulwark against Castro that merited total U.S. support. There was also distress expressed about the loss of Somoza's less public advantage to the U.S.—as a CIA asset. He had not only allowed the use of Nicaraguan territory as training bases for the Bay of Pigs invasion, he had also permitted the CIA to use the country as a base of operations for missions against Cuba. At the same time, however, the CIA had repeated some of the mistakes it had made elsewhere in Latin America. In an operation that closely resembled the disastrous establishment of BRAC during the Batista regime in Cuba, the agency set up something called the Office of National Security (OSN) in Nicaragua. Like BRAC, the OSN was supposed to be an intelligence-collection agency, but Somoza was very much in the grand tradition of Latin American dictators—emulating Batista, he converted the OSN into an agency for internal repression, using CIA-trained agents and CIA money to hunt down dissidents.*

Nicaragua, with its avowed support for Castro, became the target of an extensive American intelligence effort, beginning shortly after the Reagan administration took office. Essentially, it was designed to prove that the country had become a beachhead for Communism in Central America, a new base from which Castro-inspired and -directed revolution would spread to all the surrounding countries. The shipment of Cuban and Soviet military supplies into the country

---

*Also like Batista, Somoza at the same time was very suspicious of the CIA. At one point, a handsome OSN agent was assigned the task of seducing a young woman who was working as a code clerk in the CIA station and who also was a heavy drug user. The combination of sex and drugs swept her off her feet, and she began providing copies of every cable she received or sent, one of them reporting that CIA agents had contacted a Somoza political opponent.

was regarded as the chief indicator of that master plan, so intelligence was directed toward uncovering the scope (and probable future use) of that material.

The effort, ranging from U-2 overflights to extensive ELINT monitoring from U.S. Navy destroyers off the Nicaraguan coast, concluded that Nicaragua was the focus of a massive military buildup, far out of proportion to the country's defense needs. Further, it was alleged, large numbers of Cuban and Soviet advisers were operating there, undoubtedly with the intention of directing an invasion by Nicaraguan troops elsewhere in the region.

At first glance, this wealth of technical intelligence seemed impressive, but a closer look suggests that perhaps it did not quite justify some of its alarmist conclusions. (Among the more interesting products of the intelligence effort was a reconnaissance picture of Nicaraguan Army training bases, showing, according to the CIA, "Cuban-style obstacle courses," presumably meaning that if Nicaraguan trainees were running such courses, this indicated clearly an intent by Cuba to have them performing in some uniquely Marxist style.)

In the spring of 1982, John H. Buchanan, a retired Marine Corps lieutenant colonel, spent several weeks in Nicaragua taking a firsthand look at this military buildup while serving as part of a delegation from the private Commission on U.S.–Central American Relations. Buchanan was struck by the wide disparity between what he saw on the ground and what American intelligence was claiming it saw from above. He noted, for example, that despite the intelligence alarm about Soviet-made T-55 tanks imported into Nicaragua, the country was marked by high mountains and narrow valleys cut by rushing streams, hardly suitable for armored operations. Further, even the Pan-American Highway has grades ranging from five hundred to five thousand feet, beyond the capabilities of the T-55, which can handle grades only up to 30 percent. In addition, Nicaragua had only one oil refinery and two large-capacity oil-storage tanks, a grossly inadequate logistical base for any military operations. As for the Sandinista army itself, Buchanan discovered it had about twenty thousand regular troops, somewhat fewer than Somoza's army, and was spread around forty-nine military garrisons in the country, most of them so small that they were hard to find. (And as for the "Cuban-style obstacle course," Buchanan found it precisely the same as the one he had sweated over during his marine recruit days.)

More serious was the significant gap between American claims about the number of Cuban and Soviet advisers in the country, and the actual numbers. Haig had claimed there were more than two thousand Cuban advisers there, but Buchanan discovered only a dozen, and while Haig had also claimed there were seventy Soviet advisers, the Nicaraguans were firm in insisting there weren't any. Buchanan reported later that he could find no evidence that there was a single Soviet adviser around.

There was no question, of course, that the Sandinista regime in Nicaragua was importing military supplies from Cuba to build up its armed forces—for strictly defensive purposes, Nicaragua claimed—but whether that buildup constituted quite the danger the United States said it did remains open to doubt. Yet, on the basis of its intelligence, the Reagan administration set in motion one of the largest covert operations in history, seeking to destabilize and ultimately destroy the Sandinista regime. It was also among the more public, for its very size soon made it the worst-kept secret in the world.

The covert action was related to another major intelligence concern in Latin America, a growing insurgency movement in El Salvador. Here again, there were important preconceptions at work, for that country began to be perceived as another important domino in a chain of Central American countries facing Soviet-directed revolution. The key preconception, most often enunciated by Haig, was that the guerrilla movement in El Salvador was not a genuine political movement at all, but a sham created and fostered by Castro and the Soviet Union, who were using it as a wedge to overthrow the government.

The American intelligence community mounted an operation in El Salvador that dwarfed the effort connected with Nicaragua—by 1983, there were more than two hundred U.S. intelligence agents (about two thirds of them from the CIA) operating inside the country, along with a $65 million effort to stabilize a Salvadoran government that lacked any real popular support. Essentially, this vast effort was designed to find out the source of the guerrilla arms—an effort that concluded, perhaps not too surprisingly, that Castro and the Soviets were the sole suppliers, mostly via Nicaragua. (Overlooked, somehow, in this intelligence judgment was the fact that many of the guerrillas' arms had either been bought on the thriving arms black market in El Salvador or been captured from the incompetent Salvadoran military. CIA reports spoke of "proof" of Soviet-directed arms supply, which amounted to some captured guerrilla arms that turned out to be American weapons left behind in Vietnam. Unfortunately, the CIA did not realize that most of these weapons had been sold by North Vietnam into the international arms market.)

This was not the only echo of Vietnam, for almost every problem the Americans had faced there was encountered anew in El Salvador. Chief among them was a badly trained, incompetently led government army that carried out large-scale (and low-risk) "sweep" operations that the guerrillas eluded with ease. A high-priority effort by American Army advisers to instill some sort of professionalism in that army met with fierce resistance—"You lost in Vietnam, didn't you?" Defense Minister Guillermo García snarled when American advisers tried to impress upon him the importance of improving the mobility of his clumsy army.

Equally eerie was the remarkable similarity of the intelligence problems in El Salvador and Vietnam. In this case, the CIA repeated all its Vietnam mistakes, mainly a foolish reliance on its assorted assets developed inside the Salvadoran secret police. These were useless assets, for among them was a collection of right-wing death-squad killers whose idea of intelligence was to identify all "leftists," then murder them. The second-in-command of El Salvador's intelligence apparatus, for example, was Roberto D'Aubuisson, who also happened to be head of the UGB (White Warriors Union), the country's most notorious death squad. D'Aubuisson himself was a notorious torturer, who took special delight in personally carving up victims with a knife. His reputation had deservedly earned the condemnation of former American Ambassador Robert White, who had called him a "psychopathic killer."

The inevitable result was an almost complete breakdown in even the most elemental intelligence about El Salvador, including the number of guerrilla fighters in the Farabundo Martí Liberation Front (FMLN), the main guerrilla movement. In a distinct echo of the pre-Tet numbers dispute in Vietnam nearly fifteen years before, the CIA and the military-intelligence agencies argued over exactly how many guerrillas were fighting in the Salvadoran countryside. Under White House pressure, the CIA concluded that there were about five thousand guerrillas, a statistic that reflected "progress" in the government's fight against the guerrilla movement. (In fact, the higher estimate by military intelligence, that there were seven thousand guerrillas, was correct, but such a conclusion, showing growing guerrilla strength, would probably have been rejected as unacceptable by the White House.)

It is no wonder that a House Intelligence Committee investigation into American intelligence's performance in El Salvador found that it was marked by "oversimplification" and "suggestion of greater certitude than warranted by the evidence," which was a polite way of saying that much of the intelligence was being cooked to please the Reagan hardliners eagerly seeking victory in Central America. And it was a failure that had two moments of high comedy—incidents that became known as "the grocery-store papers" and the "great confessor fiasco."

The grocery store papers episode began in November 1980 when Salvadoran police captured a pile of papers in an art gallery owned by the brother of Shafik Handal, leader of the Salvadoran Communist party. The papers, according to the Salvadoran government, described an arms-shopping trip to Eastern Europe by Handal, which had produced promises of arms aid from the Soviets and Eastern European nations. This incident aroused no particular alarm, but a year later, the new Reagan administration decided a closer look was warranted—the motive including a conviction by Haig at that point that arms for Salvadoran guerrillas were originating exclusively from Cuba and the Soviet Union. A State Department intelligence officer, dispatched to El Salvador, was told by the Salvadoran secret police that they had found still more papers—and produced a plastic bag filled with documents allegedly recovered from inside the wall of a grocery store suspected of helping to support guerrillas.

The documents, authenticated by the CIA, seemed to indicate a large-scale arms-shipment program by Cuba. Haig immediately ordered up a State Department report alleging that the documents proved that Cuba had decided on all-out support for Salvadoran guerrillas, who were actually spearheads of a Cuban effort to take over the country anyway. But to Haig's surprise, the evidence was not accepted with the same conviction with which he had unveiled it. For one thing, experts outside the intelligence community who took a close look at the papers noted a number of curious inconsistencies. Some words in the documents were clearly not in Salvadoran dialect, but appeared to be Chilean. Furthermore, periods and commas were used interchangeably, almost unheard of for anyone accustomed to writing Spanish. (One clue that something was amiss was the use in the documents of commas for figures over 1,000; Latin Americans invariably use periods for such figures, while Americans use commas.)

When some congressmen openly hinted that the papers might be CIA forgeries, the Senate Foreign Relations Committee convened a special closed session to hear intelligence-community testimony on how the papers had been obtained and verified. Casey's selection of a CIA representative to explain to the committee about the papers was an unfortunate choice—Constantine Menges, national intelligence officer for Latin America. Committee members were appalled to discover that Menges had been selected for this important intelligence post on the strength of his political credentials as a conservative ideologue and Reagan supporter. He possessed no real intelligence experience and had been appointed to the CIA post directly from his job as a policy analyst at the Hudson Institute, Herman Kahn's think tank. Before the committee, Menges launched into a shrill briefing that was almost unbelievable, featuring assertions that the Soviets and Cuba were directly responsible for all Central American unrest. It did not address the question of the grocery-store papers—much less their alleged authentication—and angry committee members sent an unprecedented letter to Casey complaining about Menges. In reply, Casey sought to soothe the committee by noting the "inexperience" of Menges, but pointedly did not contradict his simplistic view—presumably the same as the CIA's—of Central America as the front line in the Cold War between the Soviets and the United States.

Around the same time, the same Salvadoran secret police who had produced the grocery-store papers presented an even more interesting piece of intelligence—a nineteen-year-old Nicaraguan named Orlando José Tardencilla, a Sandinista allegedly captured inside El Salvador, where he later confessed to aiding Salvadoran guerrillas. American diplomats who spoke with the Nicaraguan in his jail cell were not impressed, for Tardencilla's account of Nicaraguan support of Salvadoran guerrillas lacked credibility—at one point, he claimed that Salvadoran guerrillas had trained in Ethiopia.

That appeared to be the end of it, but when the Reagan administration came under increasing pressure to produce solid intelligence to support its contention that the guerrillas were masterminded and outfitted by Nicaragua (acting as surrogate for Cuba and the Soviets), Tardencilla was resurrected. Haig dispatched one of his intelligence aides to El Salvador, and there Tardencilla was offered a deal: either come to the United States and repeat his story publicly, or be left to rot in jail. Not unreasonably, Tardencilla accepted the offer and was flown to Miami. Interrogated by relays of CIA Latin American experts, who also gave him psychological tests, he was pronounced "credible" and ready for public unveiling.

But a subsequent encounter with American reporters in Washington turned out to be a disaster. Tardencilla opened the proceedings by saying he had been terribly tortured by the Salvadorans to confess, and while embarrassed CIA and State Department officers looked on, he then recanted his entire confession. He was no Sandinista, he claimed, and had nothing to do with the guerrillas, but had been picked up by the secret police who saw an opportunity to "prove" Nicaraguan control of the guerrillas.

Both the grocery-store-papers and confessor episodes illustrate the very low state of American intelligence at that point, and further demonstrate how badly ideology was beginning to warp intelligence judgments. There were any number of other examples, but one of the more interesting was connected with the Sandinista government's decision to enlarge the country's main airport. According to Nicaragua, this project was part of an effort to increase tourism and trade, but an alarmed Reagan administration immediately branded it a key component of a military buildup, a clear attempt to base Soviet-built jet fighters and bombers there. One DIA briefing, in fact, stated flatly that the airport expansion was directly related to an ongoing Soviet plan to base long-range reconnaissance planes in Nicaragua, planes that would overfly American military installations in the entire Caribbean area.

However, there was cause to wonder about these intelligence judgments, for in fact the airport construction had been recommended not by the Cubans or the Russians but by the United States—specifically, a 1976 Agency for International Development study said that an improvement in Nicaragua's transportation system—especially its main airport—was vital to the country's economy.

Interestingly enough, the very same kind of intelligence judgment surfaced a year later, this time in Grenada. In a March 1983 speech, Reagan showed American aerial-reconnaissance pictures of the island, revealing an international airport being constructed on Point Salinas, in Grenada's southernmost section. The intelligence was of more than passing interest, for a revolution in Grenada in 1979 had brought the Marxist Maurice Bishop to power. Bishop, who had established strong links with Fidel Castro, was regarded by the Reagan administration as a dangerous enemy whose New Jewel Movement, it was feared, might set the tone for similar upheavals in other Caribbean island nations.

Among Bishop's more ambitious projects was an international airport, lack of which had hampered the development of Grenada's vital tourist industry. Construction of a new international airport had been recommended by the World Bank, and a British firm carried out a feasibility study for the project in 1969, but it was held up for some years by lack of funding. Bishop finally got developmental funding from European nations, plus promises of construction help from Castro.

It was the Cuban connection that ignited most of the subsequent controversy, for no one in the Reagan administration believed that Castro would help build an airport solely to aid Grenada's tourist industry. Other, more sinister, purposes were suspected, and a number of overflights of Grenada led to what can only be described as a full-scale intelligence panic over the airport project. U.S. Navy intelligence, for example, deduced that the airport would be used for Russian long-range surveillance planes, while the CIA claimed that it would be an important transshipment point for Cuban planes ferrying men and supplies to Cuban troop garrisons in Africa and elsewhere. This latter deduction was most curious, for the CIA should have been aware that those Cuban flights had been moving out of nearby Barbados, whose government was nothing if not evenhanded: It also permitted American RC-135 and other reconnaissance planes to land there.

More to the point, the cost of those overflights of Grenada was unnecessary; on the island itself, the airport construction site was completely unguarded, and tourists and Grenadians alike walked freely about the area taking snapshots.* Moreover, a British company handling the actual construction contract had seventeen employees working at the site, and as they firmly noted to anyone who asked them, they were not building a military airport. Among other things, they pointed out, the new airport had no navigation or surveillance radars (the weather there was good enough for the visual flight rules of civilian jetliners), no underground storage facilities, no aircraft-arrester gear, and no perimeter security, all vital to the operation of a military air facility. Then too, the airport's fuel-storage tanks were out in the open, hardly suitable for military operations, which require such fuel to be stored in underground tanks as a defense against a possible air strike that would destroy fuel reserves left aboveground.

The airport question played a major role in the subsequent American invasion of the island, and while it is difficult to define its role exactly, there is no question that the alarming intelligence about the airport, combined with the political direction of the island's government, made some form of direct American intervention inevitable. There was also the factor of Cuba, whose every move was subjected to the most minute American analysis, a microanalysis that tended to frame its judgments in the context of Castro as surrogate for Moscow. Thus, a Cuban offer to help airport construction on Grenada was interpreted as part of some sort of larger plan, undoubtedly hatched by the Russians. It was a process that made even the slightest tremors in the Caribbean and Latin America loom large. The problem, of course, was that Ameri-

---

*The CIA had no on-ground sources in Grenada after 1981, when its plan for the overthrow of Bishop was rejected by a scornful Senate Intelligence Committee, one of whose members, Lloyd Bentsen of Texas, said, "You've got to be kidding." The CIA thereupon pulled its agents out of the island and was caught flatfooted when its chief target, Bishop, was suddenly overthrown and murdered in a violent coup in 1983.

can intelligence had absolutely no insight into Cuba, so it lacked any real understanding of Cuban motives for such decisions as airport construction. And what little information there was eventually wound up filtered through the preconceptions of a strongly Castrophobic administration.*

Latin America and the Caribbean, of course, were not the only places where this sort of process took place. It also happened on the other side of the world, in Asia. There it played an important role in another intelligence controversy, which can be loosely called "The Case of the Yellow Rain."

On April 14, 1981, Soua Lee Vang, a twenty-nine-year-old Hmong villager from Laos, walked across the Thai border and into the Ban Vani Refugee Center, proclaiming his intention never to return to his homeland. Vang told an incredible story to refugee workers. Early one day the previous month, he was working in his village of Ban Paa Ngum in the Laotian Central Highlands when he saw an old propeller-driven biplane slowly circle the village. Suddenly, Vang related, the plane swooped low and flew directly overhead, releasing a trail of yellow smoke from its wings. People directly under the cloud collapsed in convulsions, bleeding from their eyes and ears. Vang fled, leaving behind, he said, twenty-one dead and more than five hundred hurt in his village.

Vang's account was the most dramatic of several such stories that the refugee workers had been hearing during the first several months of that year, including one from a defecting Laotian Air Force pilot who claimed to have fired "special rockets" filled with gas against Laotian villages suspected of fighting the government. The refugee workers were skeptical,

*There were continuing American attempts to develop intelligence sources inside Cuba, but almost all of them failed, sometimes ignominiously. One of the silliest concerned an American college student and antiwar activist who was enlisted by the CIA to infiltrate the Cuban community in Canada. He succeeded, and was invited later to settle in Cuba and pursue his studies in rocket technology. CIA officials gave him a burst transmitter to radio back information, but on his very first night in Cuba, he used the radio while sitting on the veranda of his house in Havana. Needless to say, this attracted local attention, and the American soon found himself faced with stern questions about what he was doing. Subsequently, he was used to feed cooked intelligence back to the CIA.

for almost all the reports came from Hmongs, mostly illiterate tribesmen who, it was felt, probably confused tear-gas attacks —relatively common in the continuing but small-scale guerrilla struggles involving Laotians, anti-Vietnamese Cambodians, and other assorted forces—with poison gas. In addition, other refugee workers inside Laos reported no evidence of a great number of deaths from any kind of gas, especially in the Hmong areas.

But that is not the way American intelligence saw it. Spurred by Haig, State Department officers were ordered to collect the refugee accounts, and at the same time obtain a "smoking gun"—an actual sample of the residues of the poison gas. That effort ultimately led to several samples of a yellowish substance that was subjected to extensive laboratory analysis. Dubbed "yellow rain," the substance was found to contain mycotoxins, a deadly form of fungus that, it was deduced, had been artificially manufactured and then dropped over villages in the form of a misty cloud. The resulting conclusion was obvious: Unquestionably, the Russians had manufactured this material and had given it to their Laotian allies as part of an effort to stamp out anti-Communist resistance in the countryside. (Later, it was further alleged that similar substances had been used against the Afghan resistance movement.)

However, this conclusion lacked several important pieces of supporting evidence. First, where was any intelligence suggesting that the Russians had managed the considerable scientific feat of manufacturing mycotoxins and then converting them into actual weapons? Was there any conclusive intelligence showing that the Laotians and the Russians had made any arrangement for use of this weapon? (And more significant, why would the Russians risk discovery of a truly important weapons development in the relatively unimportant struggle in Laos?)*

*Several years before, the CIA erred badly in suggesting that an anthrax outbreak in the Soviet city of Sverdlovsk was related to a Russian biological-weapons experiment that had misfired and contaminated city residents with deadly germs. Actually, it turned out that the outbreak was caused by the illegal sale of tainted meat

No such intelligence existed, and that lack began to cast grave doubts over the entire yellow-rain story. In addition, the scientific data Haig had presented as irrefutable evidence of yellow rain began to be given less dramatic interpretations. There was considerable debate within the American scientific community about the samples, but biologists discovered that the mycotoxins found in the samples are in fact relatively common in many areas of the world, Laos included, and that the yellowish substance was almost certainly bee excrement. And Australia's chief national-research laboratory ruled that the samples produced as evidence of yellow rain were definitely not man-made.

The Australian conclusion pointed up an invidious intelligence process on the part of the United States—offering very tenuous evidence in the context of preconceptions. Plainly, the Reagan administration *wanted* to find evidence of Soviet germ warfare, so it seized upon the most slender threads to weave its judgment. Nor should it be forgotten that at the very time the administration was making strong public charges about Soviet germ warfare, it was attempting to persuade a reluctant Congress to spend several billion dollars for a buildup in American gas-warfare weapons, largely on the rationale that the Russians had opened a wide lead in this area.

Aside from political preconceptions, the real problem of American intelligence at this point was its continued overreliance on technical collection, an obsession that led to a series of intelligence blunders. Over and over again, although the lesson never seemed to sink in, American intelligence found itself confused, led astray, or plain wrong each time it tried to draw deductions from that very ambiguous process. It found itself once again trying to keep up with the escalating pace of weapons technology, in the end confess-

---

in the city; most of the germs were spread by an anthrax-tainted cow that had been thrown down a well, contaminating the water supply.

ing that it had no real means of detecting SALT II violations by the Russians. An example of this problem was expressed by a new Pentagon buzzword—"breakout," the process by which the Russians would secretly violate the agreement by developing new systems that would be "broken out" in a surprise deployment. American intelligence had no answer to this possibility or to the Pentagon's worries over another buzzword, "dual-mode," this one meaning that the Russians might use advanced surface-to-air missiles for both antibomber and antimissile defense. How would intelligence know when the Russians intended a particular missile for one role or the other?

American intelligence couldn't, any more than it could accurately estimate exactly what the Russians were spending on defense or answer any number of other such questions. In fact, it could not shed much light on even so relatively simple a matter as a natural gas pipeline.

The Reagan administration expressed particular unease with a Russian plan to lay a 3,600-mile pipeline from vast fields of natural gas in Siberia all the way back to Europe, where the gas would be sold to energy-starved Western European nations. The fields had been discovered in 1973, the largest such find in the world, but Reagan became convinced that if the United States withheld vital technology from the Soviets—particularly special large turbines to relay the gas along the pipeline—the project would have to be abandoned. To that end, Reagan embargoed American technical equipment to the Soviets and pressured Western European allies to do the same.

To a certain extent, Reagan based his plan on an intelligence deduction that the Russians could not complete the pipeline without American technical know-how, a judgment that, again, was based on the narrow American intelligence capability for estimating Soviet science and technology. The judgment turned out to be wrong, for the Russians, in a maximum effort, developed their own technology to complete the pipeline—and what they didn't develop, they bought from the Western Europeans, who considered the whole Reagan idea silly.

The Europeans were equally unimpressed with a Reagan administration claim that one hundred thousand "slave laborers" (including ten thousand political prisoners) were being forced to work on the pipeline. This assertion, based on the reports of a Soviet émigré group in Germany, was openly scoffed at by Europeans, whose own media had extensively covered the pipeline construction, noting among other things that pipeline jobs—involving high pay—were much prized in the Soviet Union. Faced with this skepticism, the administration ordered the CIA to find some data to prove the slave-labor charge. The agency could not, and after several months of work, it produced a cautious report that said there was "no proof" of forced labor being used on the pipeline—but added that there were four million forced laborers in the Soviet Union, the latter intelligence designed to mollify Reagan administration officials angry over not being provided with evidence for their slave-labor accusation.

Satellites and other technical systems had no way of determining whether the men laboring on the pipeline had paybooks in their pockets. Another example of that kind of limitation came in Poland, where American intelligence badly misread the sudden crackdown on the Solidarity political movement in late 1981. The Americans were surprised by that development, since they had concentrated their considerable resources on the Soviet military presence around the Polish borders, alert for any sign of an imminent Russian move westward into Poland. And without good on-ground sources in the country, intelligence missed the fact that it was the Polish government itself that would carry out the crackdown. The Pentagon later described this as a "collective intelligence failure," but it actually knew only half the truth: Even the American monitoring of the Soviets was badly flawed, for heavy cloud cover over Eastern Europe during the month of

December 1981 virtually blinded intelligence—if the Russians had decided to move at that point, American intelligence would not have spotted them until they were inside Poland.

The same problem of ambiguity can be seen in the events leading up to the Falkland Islands War between Great Britain and Argentina a year later. American intelligence detected the Argentine naval movements and buildup of air units a considerable time before the actual invasion took place, but while that information answered the question of Argentine *capabilities* for an invasion, it did not answer the more pressing question of Argentine *intentions:* Did Argentina actually intend to invade the islands, in line with a threat to do so, or was it merely a bluff to induce greater British willingness to negotiate the islands' political future?

The British took the American intelligence at face value, but decided (on the basis of an assumption, not intelligence) that the Argentines would not attack before January 1983, the one hundred fiftieth anniversary of what the Argentines regard as the "illegal" British seizure of those islands. The United States accepted that conclusion, but just two days before the actual invasion took place, the Americans realized that the British were wrong—Argentine military movements made it clear that an invasion was imminent.

In the end, the British paid a price for its myopia, for the failure to send a force to the Falklands as a deterrent to an Argentine invasion as soon as American intelligence had picked up the first clues meant that they had to retake the islands by force.

And while the fight was raging, a small group of congressional staffers assembled in Washington to hear a classified briefing from the CIA on the Falklands situation. The congressional aides, connected with military and intelligence committees, were especially concerned about the airport captured at the capital of Stanley in the islands: Were the runways long enough for use by Argentine Mirage fighter-bombers?

And if they were, would the Mirages be able to destroy the British invasion fleet steaming toward the islands?

These were important questions, for there was the ever-present danger that the war between Great Britain and Argentina could widen into a much broader conflict that might involve the United States. But there was something less than confidence exuded by the CIA briefers; they seemed uncertain about events in the Falklands, and what was more, betrayed evidence of some serious gaps in their knowledge: They solemnly asserted that the runways at Stanley were long enough for Mirages. That raised the possibility of a very serious military confrontation.

However, the CIA data seemed not quite right, and the staffers set about to double-check what they had heard. It turned out that the information was dead wrong; conversations with Mirage pilots, especially some ex-Israeli Air Force officers, revealed that the planes could not operate from Stanley's runways. The judgment was confirmed when the staffers looked at maps in the Library of Congress; the runways were indeed too short for Mirage operating requirements.

The CIA officers, apprised of the congressional findings, immediately went to the Library of Congress and made Xerox copies of the maps—for the purpose, presumably, of telling headquarters that the agency's intelligence about the airport at Port Stanley (obtained at the cost of God knows how much taxpayer money) was incorrect.

One can imagine the possible difficulties that might have arisen if the congressional staffers had not been alert. A major international crisis might even have resulted had the United States warned Argentina not to base its Mirages at Port Stanley and thereby threaten the British fleet, and so on—all on the basis of a CIA judgment.

Still, it was a moment of some import in this saga, for there is much to heed in the sight of CIA officers in a library copying public maps of an area that has been the subject of satellites and high-flying reconnaissance planes. It reminds us, again, of the frailty of what we have come to understand as the very checkered process of American intelligence. And that process remains frail and subject to the gravest error, for it is first and foremost a process involving human beings.

As Ronald Reagan was to discover, no matter how much money is lavished on American intelligence, certain truths remain.

EPILOGUE: THE WORLD AND "MOTHER K"

The great thing is to get the true
picture, whatever it is.

—WINSTON CHURCHILL

ON A WARM SPRING day last year, President Ronald Reagan
was chauffeured across the Potomac River to Langley, Virginia, for one of those minor public ceremonies that nevertheless tell much about the direction of the American
government.

The occasion was the official ground-breaking for a new
wing of the headquarters building of the Central Intelligence
Agency. The cost of this new wing—around $20 million—was
a mere pittance by Washington standards, but Reagan's presence was meant to underscore his commitment to what has
been an unprecedented expansion of American intelligence,
the CIA included.

The commitment has indeed been impressive, judged by
the simple standards of fiscal arithmetic. Since coming to
office in early 1981, Reagan has asked for (and received)
enough money from Congress to increase the budgets for
American intelligence between 20 and 25 percent each year
for the past four years. There have also been sharp increases
in personnel (in 1982 alone, the CIA hired fifteen hundred
new employees). And perhaps more important has been a

distinct change in attitude. Following years of cutbacks and the infamy of assorted scandals, the American intelligence community under Reagan has enjoyed unparalleled official support.

As he stood beside CIA Director William Casey that spring day, contemplating the most recent concrete example of his largess for that community, Reagan could reflect on a record as czar of American intelligence—for that, fundamentally, is what all U.S. Presidents are—that may never be equaled. Certainly, no President had ever drawn up a seven-year plan, as he had, for the massive buildup of U.S. intelligence and then managed to get Congress to approve it—all in secret. And certainly no President had managed, as he had, to apportion all that money (the precise amount is secret) among the various components of the American intelligence community without any of them running to the press, complaining they weren't getting enough. And finally, Reagan had managed to persuade both Congress and the members of the intelligence community that all the money—by some estimates, around $50 billion—was worth it because, at last, the United States would be able to construct an intelligence apparatus of a quality and dimension unrivaled in history.

And yet, had he bothered to make the effort, Reagan might have wondered whether it was all worth it. Perhaps he did not know that despite all that money and lavish official support, nothing much has changed, really.

He might have begun with that new wing on the CIA building, its neo-Mussolini architectural style blending perfectly with the faceless, grim look of the rest of the sprawling headquarters. It might be expected that the new wing would house some of the people the CIA has been hiring straight off the college campuses these days. But in fact the new wing will house not people but computers. Very good computers, certainly, but computers nevertheless, still another reflection of American intelligence's historic fascination with technology.

Nobody is saying precisely what the computers will be

used for, but it does not require much imagination to deduce that they will represent still another effort to handle the mounting volume of raw intelligence being collected by the other technical systems. (One idea is to have the computers aboard satellites, and other such technical collection systems, send their data directly into computer banks at CIA headquarters, thus creating the first intelligence method untouched by human hands.)

And while those computers are performing their several hundred thousands of calculations per second, the question arises: Does the vast pile of data they're spewing out reflect any improvement in American intelligence?

No. For while Reagan, Casey, and other intelligence officials are congratulating themselves on the newly enhanced intelligence empire all that money has bought them, consider a few events occurring elsewhere at about the same time:

- In Costa Rica, the leader of a group of Nicaraguan exiles, organized and supported by the CIA in a "guerrilla army" to carry out armed forays against Nicaragua, is having an argument with his CIA controllers. He cannot understand why still another arms shipment, delivered in unmarked DC-3s, has somehow gone awry. Again, the delivery consists of large numbers of uniforms and boots instead of arms, the result of CIA headquarters' conviction that no guerrilla army can possibly succeed unless properly uniformed.
- Just down the road from Langley, the military-intelligence agencies at the Pentagon are preparing the annual edition of a slick booklet outlining the extent of Soviet military power. It is an alarming document, all the more because it claims that there is a dangerous "warhead gap"—the Russians have more nuclear warheads than the United States. This latest gap turns out to be the result not of detailed intelligence but of an odd extrapolation: Military-intelligence officials have counted all the Soviet missiles in deployment, then

multiplied by ten. The assumption is that each Soviet rocket carries a full complement of ten multiple independently targeted reentry vehicles (MIRVs)—thus the total number of warheads. But, those same officers admit, they have no idea how many Soviet warheads really exist, or whether each rocket in fact is fully MIRVed. At the same time, however, the Pentagon is seeking money to build more warheads, along with an advanced MX missile system to battle all those Soviet warheads.

- The CIA station chief in Rome is unceremoniously replaced by Casey after he tells his boss that there is insufficient evidence to support the Reagan administration's conviction that the KGB arranged with the Bulgarians for the attempted assassination of the Pope. Casey is reputed later to complain about "liberals" in the agency who are "sabotaging" assorted investigations ordered by the White House, all of them involving matters on which the White House has already passed judgment—such as its conviction that the KGB, via the Bulgarians, indeed tried to murder the Pope.

- A panoply of technical intelligence is brought to bear on Iran, whose armies appear poised for still another thrust into Iraq, with possibly fateful consequences for the Persian Gulf oil-supply lifeline. Satellites, spy planes, and electronic eavesdropping devices search all over Iran, trying to pick up the radioed orders that will reveal the dispositions and plans of the forces gathering on Iraq's border. Puzzlingly, however, the large electronics network detects very little—until French intelligence passes along a little tip: The Americans aren't getting anything because the Iranians, aware of the U.S. eavesdropping and unable to counter it with their own technology, have gone back to basics. Instead of radioing orders, they are dispatching them by relays of couriers, who carry sensitive messages throughout the Iranian military command. A little slow, perhaps, but it works—as the Americans discover the hard way, when they suddenly find they have no idea of what the Iranian forces are doing. Squads of young, barefoot runners render billions of dollars in intelligence technology useless.

- In Washington, D.C., the denizens of the CIA and their bitterest rivals, their counterparts at the Defense Intelligence Agency, are fighting again. This time, the argument is over how much the Russians have spent on weapons systems in 1983. According to the DIA, the Russians spent more that year on armaments than in the previous six years, an increase of about 10 percent because of new and costly weapons systems. The CIA, however, claims that Russian defense spending has actually gone down in the past several years. Despite efforts to reach a consensus position on the controversy, neither agency will budge, and a resulting intelligence estimate says that (a) Soviet spending on defense has gone down, and (b) Soviet spending on defense has gone up. In either case, nobody has the slightest idea of what the Russians actually spend on military arms.

- In Beirut, the marine commander is fairly besieged with a large stack of intelligence reports from every part of the American apparatus warning him of various dangers from the myriad factions in the political minefield that surrounds the marine positions. Try as he may, the commander cannot make any sense of the reports. They tell him everything except what he wants to know: Are there any specific military or terrorist threats against his men? Confused by the mass of contradictory intelligence, the commander decides to do nothing. Shortly thereafter, a terrorist attack kills more than two hundred of his men.

- In a Central American country, the CIA gets the bright idea of providing more effective "cover" for its agents operating there. The plan is to provide "families"—

local women and children—who will be paid to pretend they are the families of the agents. The local people find the plan hysterically funny, since the Americans in some cases do not speak the language and most do not look even remotely Hispanic.

● Planners from the Joint Chiefs of Staff planning the invasion of Grenada discover that nobody in the American intelligence community can tell them anything about that country, especially how many Cubans are on the island, and whether any of them are military personnel. The planners are told that collecting intelligence on the island is difficult—an explanation that strikes them as odd, since Grenada is only 133 square miles in size and is open to tourists. One military planner asks the CIA why it cannot simply send a man and wife team to the island, dressed as tourists and with an ordinary camera, to take pictures of everything they see and at the same time count the number of Cubans in sight. He receives no answer; instead, an urgent, CIA-requested effort begins, featuring U-2 planes crisscrossing the island just before the invasion, taking extensive pictures of virtually every man-made structure. But the pictures do not show an armed Cuban army construction battalion, which ambushes U.S. troops as they land.

If these incidents—and there are many more—seem somewhat familiar, it is because they are; they reflect the sins that have marked American intelligence from its very beginning. And they are sins no amount of money will solve, for they involve some serious weaknesses in the very structure of American intelligence itself. Consistently, American intelligence has failed to provide policymakers with effective, unbiased intelligence, has failed to gain control over what amounts to unrestrained intelligence collection, has failed to separate covert-action and intelligence-collection functions, has failed to unite in any way its disparate elements, and has failed to be adequately accountable either to Congress or to the American people.

What must be done?

Clearly, the United States, so long as it remains a major world power, will require an effective intelligence apparatus. Why it does not have one has been the subject of discussion within the intelligence community for many years, and what emerges is this general consensus on necessary reforms:

1. *Develop human-intelligence sources:* This is probably the single most-cited recommendation, for it remains American intelligence's most serious deficiency. The problem, as noted earlier, is primarily cultural; there is no tradition of human-intelligence operations on the scale necessary for effective intelligence, especially in the foreign-intelligence area. The answer is a long-term program to develop such a capability, and almost certainly the congressional intelligence-oversight committees will have to impose such a program (via funding imperatives).

2. *Overhaul the congressional oversight function:* It is clear that the present oversight system is not working. Talent and ability vary widely on the respective House and Senate commit-tees, and while some members are conscientious, there are also a fair number who are not up to the job. One problem is the number of members of Congress involved in intelli-gence committees. There should be one permanent joint committee of Congress for intelligence, with members appointed not on the basis of the conventional committee-assignment rotation system but on the recommendation of the joint leadership. The appointments should be made on a blue-ribbon basis. Committee members should be there because of a consensus judgment that they are best qualified for that thorny assignment, not because it's their turn.

3. *Charter intelligence agencies:* So long as the CIA and other American intelligence agencies operate without a charter, there will be recurring problems—such as the furor that erupted when Congress discovered the CIA hadn't bothered to inform them about the mining of Nicaraguan harbors. One

especially troublesome problem created by the lack of a charter is the way intelligence agencies, operating by White House fiat and executive order, tend to become subject to White House control. Every President since the end of World War II has found use of intelligence agencies for purposes other than intelligence-gathering irresistible, and they get away with it because there is still no overall charter spelling out the functions, limits, and controls of American intelligence agencies. Moreover, intelligence agencies, like every other component of this democratic government, sooner or later must be held accountable for their actions. Only a charter, combined with effective congressional oversight, will protect the democracy from the abuses that inevitably accompany intelligence agencies operating under control of an executive power that is impatient with the usual constraints of this system of government.

4. *Restore the "central" to American intelligence:* Technically, the man who heads up the Central Intelligence Agency—misleadingly called CIA Director, although no such post exists—is supposed to be Director of Central Intelligence (DCI). As a practical matter, however, there has never been a real DCI since the job was first created by the National Security Act of 1947. There are a number of complicated reasons for that development—outlined earlier in this book—and the result has been the fragmentation of American intelligence into a number of fiefdoms. The charter for intelligence noted earlier should include specific provisions for a true DCI function, including detailed requirements on what the DCI should be coordinating in terms of intelligence. At the same time, the DCI ought to be divorced from the CIA, which should be run by a director who would produce foreign intelligence only. The DCI should serve for a fixed term, similar to that of the FBI director, with an independent staff of analysts and coordinators, and should report directly to the National Security Council. His job would be to produce finished, analyzed intelligence, drawing from all sources in the American intelligence community. He would also determine intelligence-collection priorities.

5. *End the intelligence clutter:* The American intelligence community at the moment is composed, primarily, of a number of overlapping jurisdictions, and new fiefdoms seem to be springing up every day. (Only recently it was discovered that army intelligence had quietly formed a new agency unto itself whose functions seemed suspiciously similar to those of the CIA.) Again, a solid charter is required here, including a reorganization plan that would eliminate, merge, or reshape the various intelligence components and end the building of little empires. There is no reason, for example, for the Defense Intelligence Agency to have its own staff of civilian intelligence analysts, who are performing the same function as their counterparts in the CIA. Their presence may satisfy the dictates of bureaucratic politics, but it represents a terrible waste of resources, to say nothing of confusing an already very confused organization chart.

Whether any of these reforms will eventually be enacted remains an open question, for one of the more interesting aspects of American intelligence is how often it repeats the same mistakes—and how often it will draw the wrong lessons as a result of those mistakes. The evidence is everywhere: covert-action operations, run straight out of the OSS textbook from World War II, failing time and time again. The mixture of covert and intelligence-collection operations using the same assets, a dreadful error that was first committed in 1919 and is still repeated to this very day. Overreliance on a single, technological source for intelligence, ignoring the well-established truth that there is no such thing as an intelligence paragon. Continually fragmented intelligence organizations, overlooking the inevitable problems that fragmentation guarantees.

It all represents, of course, a flawed continuum, an attempt by the world's leading democracy to construct an intelligence service capable of lighting its way along the dark passages of an ever-threatening world of uncertainty and change. And it has been a continuum, as we have seen, that represents a tradition of flawed vision. From the progenitors of 1919, who were confronted in Russia with a revolutionary movement they did not even begin to understand, to the men who in 1942 tried to plan the invasion of North Africa (and found the only source intelligence had on the port of Oran was a 1923 French tourist guidebook), to the operatives of 1984, who tried, unsuccessfully, to understand the political convulsions of Central America, it has been a long, checkered history that has fashioned what is at once the most extensive and most flawed intelligence apparatus in the history of the world.

The central lesson, perhaps, is that it is still people who run American intelligence, and their frailties—their biases, their fears, their errors—constitute the real fabric of that institution. Despite the ongoing attempts to mechanize the process, people remain the real story of American intelligence—people like the "night warriors" who have drawn night duty this very evening at CIA headquarters.

During those hours, they will collect, collate, and digest all the intelligence that has arrived at "Mother K" (from the CIA cryptonym for headquarters, Kubark) during the past twenty-four hours. Just before dawn, this information will be prepared in the form of a daily intelligence brief for the President of the United States, the sum of what American intelligence believes is the salient intelligence on the world situation.

Carried to the White House by special courier, this brief will be on the President's desk at 7 A.M. He may or may not bother reading it. He may ignore its contents. He may be angry at reading something that does not suit his preconceptions, political and otherwise. The brief itself may be pocked with errors or may be missing a vital piece of intelligence. It may portray a relatively quiescent world, free of the crises that burden presidents—and several hours later, a major threat, not even hinted at in the brief, may suddenly erupt.

In the end, this is what the entire intelligence process has come to: a document that may or may not be true given to a chief of government who may or may not believe it. A flawed process, to be sure, but then, given the nature of the democracy served by the men on the night shift—and by the thousands of others working elsewhere and the people they are supposed to keep informed—perhaps it is inevitable that this should be so; democracy, after all, is a very flawed process.

NOTES AND SOURCES

Introduction: God and Ice Water—The American Intelligence Process

Page

13   "We can't tell you . . .": quoted in *National Defense,* March–April, 1976.

13   Intelligence failure: Willmore Kendall, "The Function of Intelligence," *World Politics,* July 1949; Richard K. Betts, "Analysis, War and Decision: Why Intelligence Failures Are Inevitable," *World Politics,* January 1979.

14   Size of U.S. intelligence apparatus: Definitive figures on the size and cost of the American intelligence community are difficult to arrive at, since almost all data bearing on them is classified. The estimate here is based on a number of interviews, plus the most definitive contemporary estimate, found in "Changing Intelligence Priorities," *Electronic Warfare/Defense Electronics,* May 1978. Data in that article have been updated to account for funding and personnel increases during the Reagan administration.

14   Intelligence process: Klaus Knorr, "Strategic Intelligence: Problems and Remedies," in Laurence Martin, ed., *Strategic Thought in the Nuclear Age,* Johns Hopkins University Press, 1981.

16   American intelligence development: Robert L. Pfaltzgraff, Uri Ra'anan, and Warren Milberg, *Intelligence Policy and National Security*, Archon, 1981.

17   OPEC: Staff Report, Senate Select Committee on Intelligence, *U.S. Intelligence and the Oil Issue, 1973–1974*, USGPO, 1977.

17   Obsession with technology: Thomas G. Belden, "Indications, Warnings and Crisis Operations," *International Studies Quarterly*, March 1977.

18   Intelligence collection, Lady Astor: Ernest Volkman, "The Problem with American Intelligence," *Military Science and Technology*, January 1981.

19   "The pleasure . . .": Roberta Wohlsetter, "The Pleasures of Self-Deception," *Washington Quarterly*, Autumn 1979.

19   Nine major attacks: Richard K. Betts, "Hedging Against Surprise Attacks," *Survival*, July–August, 1981; Lieutenant Colonel A. L. Elliott, "The Calculus of Surprise Attack," *Air University Review*, March–April 1979. The nine attacks were: German invasion of the Low Countries and France (1940), German invasion of Russia (1941), Pearl Harbor (1941), North Korean invasion of South Korea (1950), Chinese intervention in Korea (1951), Israeli attack on Egypt (1956), Israeli attack on Jordan and Syria (1967), Communist Tet offensive in Vietnam (1968), and the Egyptian attack on Israel (1973).

19   "British provocation": Department of the Army, DA Pamphlet No. 20-261A, *Historical Study: The German Campaign in Russia—Planning and Operations (1940–1942)*, March 1955; Barton Whaley, *Codeword Barbarossa*, MIT Press, 1973.

19   Rusk: Elliott, loc. cit.

19   Czechoslovakia: Betts, loc. cit.

Chapter One: Our Man in Moscow

23   Kalamatiano: R. H. Bruce Lockhart, *Memoirs of a British Agent*, Putnam (London), 1932; G. A. Hill, *Go Spy the Land*, Cassell (London), 1932. Lockhart and Hill, both British SIS agents, worked with Kalamatiano in the anti-Bolshevik plot.

24   Capture of Kalamatiano: Jacov K. Peters, "Reminiscences of Work in the Vecheka in the First Year of the Revolution,"

Proletarian Revolution (Moscow), No. 10 (33), 1924. Peters, a Latvian, later headed up the Kremlin Guard, the praetorian guard force that handled security for the innermost Kremlin sanctum. Apparently he ran afoul of Stalin during the purge era, for he disappeared in 1937.

25   Russian revolution: George F. Kennan, *Russia Leaves the War*, Princeton University Press, 1956.

25   U1: Rhodri Jeffreys-Jones, *American Espionage*, Free Press, 1977.

26   Somerset Maugham: Ted Morgan, *Maugham: A Biography*, Simon & Schuster, 1980.

26   Wiseman: W. B. Fowler, *British-American Relations, 1917–1918: The Role of Sir William Wiseman*, Princeton University Press, 1969.

27   American errors: Kennan, op. cit.

27   Kalamatiano's role: Peters, loc. cit.

28   Kalamatiano freed: Ibid. See also *New York Times*, August 11, 1921. Kalamatiano returned to the United States and took up his teaching again, but was later killed in a hunting accident.

28   Post–World War I American intelligence: U.S. Army Intelligence Center and School, *The Evolution of American Military Intelligence*, Fort Huachua, Arizona, 1973 (unclassified).

29   British intelligence: Richard Deacon, *History of the British Secret Service*, Taplinger, 1969.

29   Cumming: Compton McKenzie, *Greek Memories*, Chatto and Windus (London), 1932.

29   Tai Li: Robert Roman, "The Dwarf Who Roused a Giant," *Soldier of Fortune*, November 1979.

30   1928 war plan: U.S. War Department, War Plans Division, *Joint Army and Navy Basic War Plan Red*, 1928 (declassified 1974).

30   Rapallo: CIA, Office of Research and Development (ORD) *Covert Rearmament in Germany, 1919–1939: Deception and Misperception*, March 1979 (unclassified); F. L. Carsten, "The Reichswehr and the Red Army, 1920–1933," *Survey*, October 1962.

30   AAF bomber mafia, B-17: Ross G. Hoyt, "Metamorphosis of the Fighter," *Air Force*, October 1975.

31   Chennault: Mal Holcombe, "Flying Behind the Twelve-Pointed Star," *Wings*, October 1983.

32   Herr, Army cavalry: Herr's testimony is reprinted in full in *Journal of the U.S. Cavalry Association*, May-June, 1940. The

U.S. Army's horse cavalry was not officially disbanded until 1951.

32   Pearl Harbor: A number of navy officers before Pearl Harbor tried to warn a slumbering navy establishment that the Pacific Fleet anchored together closely in the Hawaiian base was a serious error. See especially Lieutenant Commander Logan C. Ramsey, "Aerial Attacks on Fleets at Anchor," *U.S. Naval Institute Proceedings,* May 1937.

33   Creation of OSS: CIA, Center for the Study of Intelligence, *Donovan and the CIA: A History of the Establishment of the Central Intelligence Agency,* 1975 (declassified, with some deletions, 1981, and later published in a commercial version by its author, Thomas Troy).

33   "You will have to . . .": Ibid.

33   FDR admiration for SIS: This admiration stemmed in large part from what Roosevelt observed of the multifaceted activities of British Security Coordination, the main SIS operation in the United States. Based in New York and headed by William Stephenson (known by his famous code name Intrepid), BSC had a virtual carte blanche from Roosevelt for intelligence, counterintelligence, and propaganda operations against the Germans. See H. Montgomery Hyde, *Secret Intelligence Agent: British Espionage in America and the Creation of the OSS,* St. Martin's Press, 1983.

33   FBI–military-intelligence hostility: Recollections, Ernest Cuneo, *Foreign Intelligence and Literary Scene,* October 1982.

34   Transformation of OSS: David Kahn, review essay, "Wild Bill Donovan and His Company," *Washington Post Book World,* December 19, 1982.

34   OSS record: Ibid.

34   German atomic bomb: David Irving, *The German Atomic Bomb,* Simon & Schuster, 1967; Rudolf Perels, "Atomic Germans," *New York Review of Books,* July 1, 1971.

35   Lack of intelligence: U.S. Atomic Energy Commission, *Manhattan Engineering District History,* 1946–1947 (35 vols.). See especially vol. XIX, *History of the Intelligence Division* (declassified, with extensive deletions, 1976). See also U.S. Army, Military Intelligence Division, *A History of the Military Intelligence Division, 7 December 1941–2 September 1945,* 1946 (declassified 1976).

35   Special intelligence teams: Ibid. The operation was code-named Alsos, a rather thin cover. *Alsos* means "grove" in Greek; the head of the Manhattan Project was General Leslie Groves. A spinoff operation, code-named Paperclip,

swept up the elite of the German scientists and technicians, especially the developers of the V-1 and V-2 rockets. (See Joint Chiefs of Staff report, *General Allocation Policy on Secret Weapons—Exploitation of German Scientists,* May 1, 1945 (declassified 1979); and C. G. Lasby, *Operation Paperclip,* Atheneum, 1971.)

36 Hiroshima, Nagasaki: Committee for the Compilation of Materials on Damage Caused by the Atomic Bombs at Hiroshima and Nagasaki (Tokyo), *Hiroshima and Nagasaki,* 1980.

37 Rescue in Romania: Office of the Assistant Secretary of War, Strategic Services Unit, History Project, *War Report of the OSS,* 1946 (declassified, with extensive deletions, 1975).

37 Wisner, Operation Bughouse: Ibid.

38 Von Bolschwing: Biographical material is contained in the government's court case against him, *USA* v. *Otto Albrecht von Bolschwing,* CIVS 81-308, USDC, Eastern District California, May 27, 1981; see also U.S. Air Force, Office of Special Investigations, *Statement of Civilian Suspect Otto Albrecht von Bolschwing,* December 22, 1970.

39 Reorientation of American intelligence: Joint Chiefs of Staff Directive 1496/2, *Basis for the Formulation of a Military Policy,* September 18, 1945 (declassified 1977).

39 U.S.-Soviet tensions: Interview, Averell Harriman, *Washington Post,* November 20, 1981; also, author's interview with Harriman, March 1977.

39 OSS report: OSS Research and Analysis Report 2669, *Capabilities and Intentions of the USSR in the Postwar Period,* January 5, 1945 (declassified 1980).

40 Crowcrass: Adalbert Ruckerl, *The Investigation of Nazi War Crimes, 1945–1978,* C. F. Muller (Berlin), 1978.

40 Recruitment of Nazis: Thomas M. Bower, *Blind Eye to Murder,* Andre Deutsch (London), 1981; Thomas O'Toole, "Nazi Cold Warriors Went Unpunished," *Washington Post,* November 4, 1982.

41 Von Bolschwing record: Report of Manfred von Killinger [German Foreign Office chief in Romania] to Foreign Minister Joachim von Ribbentrop, "Subject: Report to the Foreign Minister Regarding the Participation by Reich Germans in the Attempted Revolution by the Legionnaires," February 26, 1941 (in U.S. State Department, *Documents on German Foreign Policy, 1918–1945,* Series D (1933–1945), vol. XII, *The War Years, February 1–June 22, 1941,* USGPO, 1961.

41 Unearthing Iron Guard leaders: Charles F. Allen, Jr., "Fas-

cist Killers in Our Midst," *Jewish Currents,* February 1963. I
am indebted to Dr. Cornelius Savin for much information
on Romanian Nazis and their later whereabouts.

42   Nazis hoodwink Americans: Confidential interview.

42   Centralized intelligence: Harold Wilensky, *Organizational Intelligence,* Basic Books, 1967; Hans Moses, *The Clandestine Service of the Central Intelligence Agency,* Association of Former Intelligence Officers (McLean, Va.), 1982.

43   Central Intelligence Group: Robert L. Benson, "Early Efforts (and Failures) in Joint Intelligence: A Shaky Beginning," *Joint Perspectives,* Fall 1980.

43   Military hostility: U.S. Air Force, *AAF Headquarters Intelligence Policy and Programs,* 1946 (declassified 1976).

43   Congressional disquiet: House Committee on Expenditures in the Executive Departments, *Executive Hearing on HR 2319, the National Security Act of 1947,* June 27, 1947 (declassified 1982); House Military Affairs Committee, *A Report on the System Currently Employed in the Collection, Evaluation and Dissemination of Intelligence,* December 17, 1946 (declassified 1982).

43   Hoover intelligence: Confidential interview.

43   National Security Act: John L. Gaddis, *The United States and the Origins of the Cold War, 1941–1947,* Columbia University Press, 1972.

44   CIA covert operation in Europe: National Security Council Memorandum 10/2, June 18, 1948 (declassified 1981). This historic document directed the CIA to set up the Office of Special Projects to plan and conduct covert operations. Unfortunately, this final draft of the order eliminated the idea, first formulated in the early stages of deliberation by the NSC, of an advisory committee that would oversee covert operations. Elimination of this oversight proved to be a mistake later, when largely unsupervised covert operations began to backfire.

45   Wisner's operation: Trevor Barnes, "The Secret Cold War: The CIA and American Foreign Policy in Europe," *Historical Journal,* Part One, June 1981, and Part Two, September 1982.

45   Wisner's assets: Werner Rings, *Leben mit dem Feind,* Kindler Verlag (Munich), 1979; confidential interviews.

45   Wisner's errors: William Corson, *The Armies of Ignorance,* Dial Press, 1977.

46   Covert action budget: Ibid.

46   Red Sox/Red Cap: Ibid.

47   Wisner death: Thomas Powers, *The Man Who Kept the Secrets,*
        Knopf, 1979.
47   Von Bolschwing death: *New York Times,* March 9, 1982.
47   The Org: Louis Hagen, *The Secret War for Europe,* Stein &
        Day, 1968. The Org later was transformed into the BND,
        West Germany's intelligence service.
47, 48 Reinhard Gehlen: Heinz Hohne and Hermann Zolling, *Pul-
        lach Intern,* Hoffman und Campe Verlag (Munich), 1971.
49   American pressure: E. H. Cookridge, *Gehlen,* Random
        House, 1972.
49   MiG-15: Remarks, Charles (Chuck) Yeager, Smithsonian
        Air and Space Museum, October 9, 1981. Author's notes.
49   Soviet knowledge of parachute operations: *Caught in the Act,*
        Foreign Languages Publishing House (Moscow), 1962. An
        obvious KGB production, the book lists twenty-three cases
        of parachuted agents caught between 1951 and 1961. It
        reveals that the KGB knew beforehand of every drop. The
        Russians enhanced very effective counterespionage work
        with a shrewd political maneuver: In 1960, the Soviet Union
        amended its criminal code, waiving any penalties for para-
        chuted agents if they turned themselves in upon arriving on
        Russian soil. Most agents did just that.
49   Moles in The Org: Hohne and Zolling, op. cit. The chief
        KGB mole was Gehlen's right-hand man, Heinz Felfe. He
        was exposed by KGB defector Anatoli Golitsin.
50   "Worst case scenario": National Security Council Report
        20/1, *United States Objectives with Respect to Russia,* August 18,
        1948 (declassified 1978).
50   Soviet atomic bomb: Joint Chiefs of Staff Intelligence Re-
        port, *The Capabilities of the USSR in Regard to Atomic Weapons,*
        July 8, 1947 (declassified 1979).
51   CIG–air force dispute: Central Intelligence Group ORE
        3/1, *Soviet Bomber Production,* October 3, 1946 (declassified
        1979).
51   Russian defector: Asher Lee, *The Soviet Air Forces,* Harper &
        Row, 1956.
51   May Day shock: Leslie C. Stevens, *Russian Assignment,* Little,
        Brown, 1953. Stevens, a navy vice-admiral, was U.S. naval
        attaché in Moscow, 1947 to 1949.
51   Air-force fear: Testimony of General Curtis LeMay before
        Senate Armed Services Committee in *Study of Air Power,*
        USGPO, 1956; see also Charles A. Cannon, "Interest and
        Ideology: The Senate Air Power Hearings of 1956," *Armed
        Forces and Society,* August 1977.

NOTES AND SOURCES

52   Growth of "bomber gap": CIA NIE [National Intelligence Estimate] 11-3-55, *Soviet Capabilities and Probable Courses of Action Through 1960,* May 17, 1955 (declassified 1978).

52, 53 Taylor's mistake: Cannon, loc. cit.

54   CIA demolishes air force estimate: CIA NIE 11-3-55.

54   90 . . . 150 planes: CIA NIE 11-4-57, *Main Trends in Soviet Capabilities and Policies, 1957–1962,* November 12, 1957 (declassified 1978).

54   *Sputnik:* Albert L. Weeks, "When the Russians Discovered Cosmos," *Military Science and Technology,* 6 (1982).

54   SS-6: Colin S. Gray, "Gap Prediction and America's Defense: Arms Race Behavior in the Eisenhower Years," *Political Science Quarterly,* Spring 1972.

55   *Sputnik* alarm: Weeks, loc. cit.

56   Eisenhower unconcern: Gregg Herken, *The Winning Weapon,* Knopf, 1980.

56   Eisenhower panel: Known familiarly as the Gaither panel, its official title was Security Resources Panel of the Science Advisory Committee. The group's final report was titled *Deterrence and Survival in the Nuclear Age,* November 7, 1957 (declassified 1973).

57   CIA–air force squabbling: John Prados, *The Soviet Estimate,* Dial Press, 1982.

58   Alarming intelligence estimates: CIA NIE 11-4-57.

58   Missile gap: Daniel Yergin, *Shattered Peace,* Houghton-Mifflin, 1977.

58   1960 estimate: Prados, op. cit.

58   Eisenhower decision: Lawrence Freedman, *The Evolution of Nuclear Strategy,* Macmillan, 1982.

59   Ten thousand missiles: Alain Enthoven and Wayne K. Smith, *How Much Is Enough?,* Harper & Row, 1971.

59   McNamara's doubts: James M. Roherty, *Decisions of Robert S. McNamara,* University of Miami Press, 1970.

59   Disappearance of missile gap: Edgar Bottome, *The Missile Gap: A Study of the Formation of Military and Political Policy,* Fairleigh Dickinson University Press, 1971.

Chapter Three: Homage to Dumb Luck

61   Carter: Carter interview.

62   *Barbudos:* Ibid.

62   CIA support for Castro: Fidel Castro was among a number of anti-Batista political leaders in Cuba who received support in one form or another from the CIA in the 1950s, part of a plan to keep pipelines into all components of the Cuban resistance movement. Castro's major funding came from wealthy Cuban exiles living in the United States, who were persuaded by Fidel's oratory that he could overthrow Batista and form a popular government. The CIA was aware of the funding, and permitted the covert movement of money and supplies out of the United States. The tacit approval took place despite Castro's well-documented record as a Communist activist throughout Latin America during the 1950s. Castro had managed to persuade Americans and Cuban exiles alike that he was not a Communist.

63   American obsession: Jorge I. Domínguez, "It Won't Go Away: Cuba on the U.S. Foreign Policy Agenda," *International Security,* Summer 1983.

64   Kirkpatrick: Lyman B. Kirkpatrick, Jr., *The Real CIA,* Macmillan, 1968.

64   BRAC: Ibid.

55   Kirkpatrick cable: Ibid.

65   Batista's flight: David Atlee Phillips, *Night Watch,* Atheneum, 1977.

66   Split in CIA station: Confidential interview. See also hearings, Senate Internal Security Subcommittee, *Communist Threat to the United States Through the Caribbean* (Part II), August 13, 1959.

66   Ambassador Smith: Nathaniel Weyl, *Red Star over Cuba,* Devin-Adair, 1962.

66   U.S. Latin American policy: Hugh Thomas, *Cuba: The Pursuit of Freedom,* Harper & Row, 1971. For pre–World War II policy, see Samuel Flagg Bemis, *The Latin American Policy of the United States,* Harcourt, Brace, 1943.

67   Trujillo: Bernard Diederich, *Trujillo: The Death of the Goat,* Little, Brown, 1978.

67   Batista: Phillip W. Bonsal, *Cuba, Castro and the United States,* University of Pittsburgh Press, 1971.

68   CIA station in Havana: Testimony, U.S. Navy Captain Charles R. Clark, Jr., Senate Armed Services Committee, April 12, 1962.

68   Seizure of BRAC: Confidential interview.

68   Castaño: Confidential interview.

69   Che Guevara: The appeal was delivered by journalist An-

drew St. George, who later recounted the story widely to many, including the author.

69 Colonel Paget: Confidential interview.

69 "No Communist leanings": Allen W. Dulles, testimony, Senate Foreign Relations Committee executive hearings, *The Situation in Cuba,* January 20, 1959 (declassified 1982).

69 Nixon: Castro's version of this incident is in transcript, *Interview of Fidel Castro Ruz,* House Select Committee on Assassinations, April 3, 1978. (Author's files.)

70 Guatemala example: Stephen Schlesinger and Stephen Kinzler, *Bitter Fruit,* Anchor Books, 1983.

71 First CIA operation against Castro: NSAM [National Security Council Action Memorandum], *A Program of Covert Action Against the Castro Regime,* March 17, 1960 (declassified 1981).

71 Lack of intelligence on Cuba: Confidential interview.

71 Operation Zapata: Cuban Study Group, final report, *The Anti-Castro Cuban Operation Zapata,* June 13, 1961 (declassified 1981).

72 American assumptions: Ibid; see also Lyman B. Kirkpatrick, Jr., "Paramilitary Case Study—The Bay of Pigs," *Naval War College Review,* November–December 1972. This article is actually a revised version of a devastating report Kirkpatrick prepared while he was Inspector General of the CIA.

73 Cuban exiles: Peter Wyden, *Bay of Pigs,* Simon & Schuster, 1979.

74 Military review: JCSM-57-61, *Military Evaluation of the CIA Paramilitary Plan—Cuba,* February 3, 1961 (declassified 1981).

74 Artillery shipment missed: Confidential interview.

75 "Splinter into a thousand pieces": Arthur M. Schlesinger, *A Thousand Days,* Houghton-Mifflin, 1965.

75 Kennedy's revenge: Confidential interview.

75 Postmortem: Cuban Study Group, op. cit.

75 Operation Mongoose: Bonsal, op. cit.

76 Kennedy obsession: Arthur M. Schlesinger, op. cit.

77 Atmosphere of conformity: Confidential interview.

77 Shackley conclusions: Ibid.

78 Size of Mongoose: Ibid.

78 Exile raids: Details of these raids emerged in a number of trials of exiles later accused of various crimes connected with gun-running activities. See especially *United States* v. *Pedro Gil, Armando López Estrada, Juan Raimundo Arce and Isidoro Pinciro Castineira,* 77-481-Cr-Je, USDC Southern District Florida, January 6, 1978.

78   Martínez: Tad Szulc, *Compulsive Spy: The Strange Career of E. Howard Hunt,* Viking, 1974. Hunt was a CIA case officer to many of the leading Cuban exile operatives during Operation Mongoose, and he later recruited the same people for the Nixon campaign's program of dirty tricks.

79   Warping of intelligence: Confidential interview.

80   Harvey: David Martin, *Wilderness of Mirrors,* Harper & Row, 1980.

80   Rip Robertson: Confidential interviews.

80   Poor screening of exiles: Manuel Hevia Coscullena, *Pasaporte 11333: Eight Years with the CIA,* Cuba Ministry of Foreign Affairs, 1976. This is a Cuban intelligence production and laced with propaganda, but it is quite accurate on the ease with which the Cuban DGI—the Castro intelligence service—managed to infiltrate Cuban exile organizations in the United States.

81   Rivero: "Rivero Collado Interview," *Latin America and Empire Report* (Havana), December 1974. Another DGI production, but essentially accurate.

81   Sirgado: Remarks by Fidel Castro at XI Festival of Youth and Students, Havana, August 18, 1978; see also Sirgado interview, "Ten Years a Cuban Double Agent in the CIA," *Prensa Latina,* same date.

81   Suspected DGI penetration: Confidential interview.

82   First clues: Interview, John Erickson, *Manchester Guardian,* November 21, 1983.

82   IL-28 bombers: CIA, SNIE [Special National Intelligence Estimate] 85-3-62, *The Military Buildup in Cuba,* March 1962 (declassified 1977).

83   Confusing intelligence clues: CIA, OCI [Office of Current Intelligence] 3047/62, *Recent Military Aid to Cuba,* August 1962 (declassified 1977).

83   Caribbean Admission Center: Confidential interview.

83   Refugee stories, Russian missiles: Senate Armed Services Committee, Preparedness Investigating Subcommittee, *Interim Report on Cuban Military Buildup,* May 9, 1963.

84   CIA preconception: Klaus Knorr, "Failure in National Estimates: The Case of the Cuban Missiles," *World Politics,* April 1964.

84   Keating charge: Kenneth Keating, "My Advance View of the Cuban Missile Crisis," *Look,* November 3, 1964. Keating never did reveal his sources, but a number of them were actually U.S. Navy officers stationed at Guantánamo who had heard reliable reports of missile installation, but could

not get the navy's Office of Naval Intelligence to believe them. Keating became alarmed when he asked intelligence officials in Washington about the Guantánamo reports and was told that there was nothing to them. Keating argued that officers working in Cuba obviously knew what was happening on the island; why didn't Washington?

85 DIA disagreement: Confidential interview.

85 McCone: Thomas Powers, *The Man Who Kept the Secrets*, Knopf, 1979.

86 McCone disagrees with CIA analysts: Ibid.

86 "The accountant": Confidential interview.

87 Analysts refuse to budge: RAND RM 4328-ISA, *Cuba and Pearl Harbor: Hindsight and Foresight*, RAND Corporation, April 1965.

87 "Honeymoon cables": Confidential interview.

88 Cuban women afraid: *Interview of Fidel Castro Ruz.*

88 Problems of U-2 pilots: Don Moser, "The U-2, Cuba and the CIA," *American Heritage*, October 1977.

88 "Craterology": Victor Marchetti, "The Missile Crisis at CIA," chapter in Linda Obst, ed., *In the Sixties*, Random House, 1977. Marchetti resigned from the agency some time after the end of the Cuban crisis and became a bitter critic of the CIA.

88 First hard indication: Confidential interview.

89 DIA guess: Ibid.

89 U-2 pictures of San Cristóbal: Moser, loc. cit.

89 "No present likelihood": Remarks, National Security Adviser McGeorge Bundy, *Meet the Press*, NBC, October 14, 1962.

90 "Homage to dumb luck": Dean Acheson, "Dean Acheson's View of Robert Kennedy's View of the Cuban Missile Crisis," *Esquire*, February 1969.

90 Russian errors: Confidential interview; see also Arnold Horelick, "The Cuban Missile Crisis: An Analysis of Soviet Calculations and Behavior," *World Politics*, April 1964.

91 1962 "understanding": Bonsal, op. cit.

91 Pressure on Kennedy: Albert and Roberta Wohlsetter, *Controlling the Risks in Cuba*, Adelphi Paper No. 17, International Institute of Strategic Studies (London), 1965.

91 Pentagon briefing: Department of Defense, transcript, "Special Cuba Briefing by Robert S. McNamara," February 6, 1963.

92 Operation Red Cross: Confidential interview.

92 Eduardo Pérez: Ibid.

93   Proposal to CIA headquarters: Ibid

93   Pérez disappears: Ibid.

94   Passing of the exiles: Hearings, Senate Internal Security Subcommittee, *Terroristic Activity: Terrorism in the Miami Area,* May 6, 1976.

95   "We shall live up to this . . .": Quoted in Alan Brinkley, "Minister Without Portfolio," *Esquire,* February 1983.

Chapter Three: A Fly in Space

97   Mount Royal Hotel: Author's notes.

97   Soviet delegation: Ibid.

98   Oleg Penkovsky: Frank Gibney, Introduction to *The Penkovsky Papers,* Doubleday, 1965. The book was actually a CIA production, which patched together some oral statements and written documentation made by Penkovsky, along with some of the CIA's own words. However, the CIA made a number of sloppy linguistic and other errors, quickly establishing the book's genesis.

99   Greville Wynne: Greville Wynne, *Contact on Gorky Street,* Atheneum, 1968.

99   Turning of Penkovsky: Confidential interview.

99   Wynne's espionage operations: Confidential interview.

100   Penkovsky operation: Nigel West, *The Circus,* Stein & Day, 1983.

100   CIA skeptical: Confidential interview.

101   Alex operation: West, op. cit.

101   Kisvalter: David Martin, *Wilderness of Mirrors,* Harper & Row, 1980.

102   Penkovsky's revelations: *Penkovsky Papers.*

103   New CIA estimate: CIA, NIE 11-4-61, *Current Status of Soviet and Satellite Military Forces and Indications of Military Intentions,* September 9, 1961 (declassified 1976).

103   Air Force, camouflaged sites: John Prados, *The Soviet Estimate,* Dial Press, 1982.

104   Deficiencies of Soviet missiles: Edmund Beard, *Developing the ICBM: A Study in Bureaucratic Politics,* Columbia University Press, 1976.

105   Soviet warning, "now or never": Jerome B. Wiesner and Abram Chayes, eds., *ABM,* Harper & Row, 1969; Freeman Dyson, *Disturbing the Universe,* Harper & Row, 1979.

105   "A fly in space": Frederic S. Feer, *The Impact of Soviet Misin-*

formation on Military Operations: 1920–1979, Analytical Assessments Corporation (Marina del Rey, California), 1979.

105   Whalen case: Victor Marchetti and John Marks, *The CIA and the Cult of Intelligence*, Knopf, 1974.

106   American arsenal: David Alan Rosenberg, "The Origins of Overkill," paper prepared for Conference on the Theory and Practice of American National Security, 1945–1960, U.S. Military Academy, West Point, N.Y., April 21, 1983.

106   Polaris: William F. Whitmore, "The Origin of Polaris," *USNIP*, March 1980.

106   SIOP: Fred Kaplan, *The Wizards of Armageddon*, Simon & Schuster, 1983.

107   "Pure bull": George B. Kistiakowsky, *A Scientist at the White House*, Harvard University Press, 1976.

107   Inadequate maps: Confidential interview.

107   Huge American nuclear stockpile: Senate Armed Services Committee, hearings, *Military Procurement Authorization, Fiscal Year 1966* (Part I), USGPO, 1965.

108   "We find out . . .": Kaplan, op. cit.

108   Albania: Ibid.

108   Elusive nuclear forces: U.S. Air Force, Office of Air History, *The Air Force and Strategic Deterrence, 1951–1960*, 1967 (declassified, with extensive deletions, 1980).

109   McNamara: Desmond Ball, *Politics and Force Levels: The Strategic Missile Program and the Kennedy Administration*, University of California Press, 1980.

109   "How much is enough?": William Arkin, Thomas B. Cochran, and Milton M. Hoenig, "The U.S. Nuclear Stockpile," *Arms Control Today* (Arms Control Association, Washington, D.C.), April 1982.

109   McNamara's "New Look": Alain Enthoven and Wayne K. Smith, *How Much Is Enough?*, Harper & Row, 1971.

110   Civilian strategists: Lawrence Freedman, "The Strategist's Vocation," *Survival*, July–August 1983.

111   Bernard Brodie: Colin S. Gray, "What RAND Hath Wrought," *Foreign Policy*, Spring 1981.

111   Brodie insights: Gregg Herken, review essay, "The Built-in Obsolescence of Deterrence," *Manchester Guardian*, June 12, 1983.

112   McNamara's intelligence theory: Ball, op. cit.

113   "Action-reaction" phenomenon: Speech, Robert S. McNamara, "The Dynamics of Nuclear Strategy," Septem-

ber 19, 1967 (in *Department of State Bulletin,* October 9, 1967).

113   Birth of DIA: William R. Corson, *The Armies of Ignorance,* Dial Press, 1977.

114   ABM controversy: Ball, op. cit.

115   ABM systems, "hit one bullet . . .": Joint Committee on Atomic Energy, hearings, *Scope, Magnitude and Implications of the United States Anti-Ballistic Missile Program,* USGPO, 1967.

115   Hen House: Dr. John S. Foster, Jr., speech, April 23, 1970. Foster was then head of the Defense Department's Directorate of Research and Engineering.

115   Nixon observation: Confidential interview.

116   Soviet blast: Alan Platt, *The U.S. Senate and Strategic Arms Policy, 1969–1977,* Westview Press, 1978.

116   High-altitude test: Lawrence Freedman, *U.S. Intelligence and the Soviet Strategic Threat,* Westview Press, 1978.

116   Growing evidence: Robert S. McNamara, *FY 1964 Posture Statement,* February 3, 1963.

116   McNamara's displeasure: Ralph E. Lapp, *Arms Beyond Doubt,* Cowles Book Co., 1970.

117   McCone's role: Confidential interview.

118   Argument over Leningrad: Confidential interview.

118   McNamara testimony: Remarks, Robert S. McNamara, hearings, Senate Appropriations Committee, January 28, 1963.

118   CIA-military argument: Prados, op. cit.

119   Estonia construction: Freedman, *U.S. Intelligence.*

119   Griffon: Ibid.

119   ABM alarm: "Soviet ABM Deployment Expected in Year," *Technology Week,* November 21, 1966.

120   Mechanically operated scanners: Prados, op. cit.

120   "Technically feasible": Gen. Nikolai Talensky, "Anti-Missile Systems and Disarmament," in William R. Kintner, ed., *Safeguard: Why the ABM Makes Sense,* Hawthorn Books, 1969.

120   CIA-DIA argument: Prados, op. cit.

121   McNamara impoundment: Henry Trewhitt, *McNamara: His Ordeal at the Pentagon,* Harper & Row, 1971.

121   McNamara, CIA proven right: Freedman, *U.S. Intelligence.*

122   Intelligence predictions of Soviet missiles: CIA, DCID 3/4, *Production of Guided Missiles and Astronautics Intelligence,* April 23, 1965 (declassified 1976).

122   McNamara's assumptions: Summed up in his statement before the House Armed Services Committee, *Hearings on*

Military Posture and an Act (3293), April 30, 1968. McNamara became so captivated by this theory that he could ignore anything that failed to match his assumption. In a 1965 interview, for example, he said, "There is no indication that the Soviets are seeking to develop a strategic nuclear force as large as ours"—although the Russians at that point were seeking to do exactly that. (Interview, Robert S. McNamara, *U.S. News and World Report,* April 12, 1965.)

123   Analysts' assumptions: A prime critique of this "mirror imaging" problem is RAND R-2154-AF, *The Soviet Strategic Culture: Implications for Limited Nuclear Operations,* 1976.

123   Growth in American arsenal: Beard, op. cit.

124   Russian buildup: David Holloway, "Military Technology," chapter in R. W. Davies, et al., eds., *The Technological Level of Soviet Industry,* Yale University Press, 1971.

124   Fifty-one . . . forty-two analyses: Albert Wohlsetter, *Legends of the Strategic Arms Race,* United States Strategic Institute, USSI Report 75-1, 1975; see also his "Optimal Ways to Confuse Ourselves," *Foreign Policy,* Fall 1975.

125   Creation of Office of National Estimates: Freedman, *U.S. Intelligence.*

125   Langer: William L. Langer, *In and Out of the Ivory Tower,* Neal Watson Academic Publications, 1977.

125   Kent: Roy Goodson, ed., *Intelligence Requirements for the 1980's: Analysis and Estimates,* National Strategy Information Center (Washington, D.C.), 1980.

126   Factory smoke: Confidential interview.

126   Biakonur: "Soviet Cosmodrome," *Aviation Week and Space Technology,* October 11, 1982.

126   Microanalysis of writings: A classic example is Arthur J. Alexander, "Modeling Soviet Decisionmaking," paper prepared for Conference on Soviet National Security Decisionmaking, U.S. Navy Postgraduate School, UCLA Center for International and Strategic Affairs, Monterey, California, March 1971.

127   Kyshtym incident: Zhores Medvedev, "Nuclear Disaster in the Urals," *New Scientists,* June 30, 1977; Bryan Silcock, "Nuclear Accident Alters the Map of Russia," London *Times,* January 9, 1980.

128   Intelligence on China: Harry Temple, "Deaf Captains: Intelligence, Policy, and the Origins of the Korean War," *International Studies Notes,* Fall–Winter 1981–1982.

128   Purge of experts: Barbara W. Tuchman, "Why Policymak-

ers Do Not Listen," address before the Foreign Service Association, January 12, 1973.

129   Shock of North Korean invasion: House Foreign Relations Committee, *Selected Executive Hearings of the Committee, 1943–1950,* vol. VII: *U.S. Policy in the Far East,* part 2, USGPO, 1976. Only two days before the invasion, Assistant Secretary of State for Far Eastern Affairs Dean Rusk told the committee, "We see no present indication the people across the border have any intention of fighting a war."

129   Twelve-hundred-man army: U.S. Air Force, HQ Net Assessment Task Force, *The Critical Properties of Sudden Attack: A Study Proposal,* November 1976.

129   Chinese army in Burma: Anthony Cave Brown, *Last Hero: Wild Bill Donovan,* Times Books, 1982. One of Donovan's last government acts was to arrange transfer of this force out of Burma.

129   Tofte: Joseph C. Goulden, "CIA's Korean Caper: Hans Tofte Leads the Agency to Its First Major Coup," *Soldier of Fortune,* May 1983.

130   Operation Bluebell: Confidential interview.

130   Parachute operations into China: Confidential interview.

130   Shock of Chinese intervention: U.S. Army, OCMH, *South to the Naktong, North to the Yalu,* 1961. MacArthur's intelligence organization had confidently predicted no Chinese intervention, and indeed, its aerial-reconnaissance flights detected no large Chinese presence in North Korea. But they had made a fatal mistake: Assuming that Chinese soldiers had the same habits as their American counterparts, the reconnaissance pilots looked for the fires of troops trying to keep warm in the subzero Korean winter. But the Chinese troops, under strict discipline, built no fires, and nearly 300,000 of them crossed the Yalu River totally undetected. (Confidential interview.)

131   Death of Penkovsky: Gibney, loc. cit.

Chapter Four: "National Technical Means"

133   Balloon exhibit: Author's notes.

134   Winterbotham: F. W. Winterbotham, *The Nazi Connection,* Harper & Row, 1978.

135   Winterbotham's problems: Ibid.

135   Ronin: Ibid.
136   Sidney Cotton: Ralph Barker, *Aviator Extraordinary: The Sidney Cotton Story*, Chatto & Windus (London), 1969.
136   Operation over Germany: Andrew J. Brookes, *Photo Reconnaissance*, Ian Allan Ltd. (London), 1975.
136   Kesselring incident: Winterbotham, op. cit.
137   British photo-interpretation operation: Brookes, op. cit.; Constance Babington Smith, *Air Spy*, Ballantine Books, 1957.
137   American deficiency: Brookes, op. cit.
138   RB-47: Glenn Infield, *Unarmed and Unafraid*, Macmillan, 1970.
138   Reikichi Rada: Robert C. Mikesh, *Japan's World War II Balloon Bomb Attacks on North America*, Smithsonian Annals of Flight, No. 9, 1973.
138   Rada's balloons: George E. Weidner, *Japanese Bombing Balloons*, U.S. Army Technical and Technological Survey, PB Report 28880, January 2, 1946.
139   Fu-Go Operation: Yasushi Hidagi, "Attack Against the U.S. Heartland," *Aerospace Historian*, Summer 1981.
139   Fu-Go failure: Weidner, op. cit.
139   Delay of Hiroshima bomb: Mikesh, op. cit.
140   Balloon spawns an idea: Confidential interview.
140   Moby Dick: Ibid.
141   UFO scare: Ibid; see also Martin Gardner, "Flying Saucers," chapter in his *Fads and Fallacies in the Name of Science*, Dover, 1957.
141   Flights over Russia: "Russia Charges Balloon Forays by U.S. and Turks," *New York Times*, February 6, 1956; "Russians Display Balloons of U.S.," *New York Times*, February 10, 1956; "Soviet Again Says U.S. Is Spying: Shows Balloon, Accuses Attachés," *New York Times*, October 12, 1958.
142   Lessons of Moby Dick: Confidential interview.
142   Seek Skyhook: Ibid.
142   CIA's first photo "shop": John Prados, *The Soviet Estimate*, Dial Press, 1982.
143   Art of photo interpretation: General Electric Laboratory Report No. 62G-L78, July 27, 1962; R. V. Jones, *The Wizard War*, Coward-McCann, 1978.
143   Technical advances: CIA, DCID 3/4, *Production of Scientific and Technical Intelligence*, August 14, 1952 (declassified 1976).
144   Limitations of reconnaissance planes: U.S. Air Force, Air

University Research Institute, *Development of Intelligence Functions in the United States Air Force, 1917–1957* (declassified 1976).

144 Danger of reconnaissance flights: Testimony, Allen W. Dulles, executive session, Senate Foreign Relations Committee, May 31, 1960 (declassified 1982).

144 Killian panel: Report, Technological Capabilities Panel of the Science Advisory Committee, *Meeting the Threat of Surprise Attack*, February 12, 1955 (vol. 1) (declassified 1981).

144 Air Force seeks two thousand agents: Harry A. Rositzke, *The CIA's Secret Operations*, Reader's Digest Press, 1977.

145 Edwin H. Land, library: Information provided by New York Public Library staff.

146 Kelly Johnson: Duane Yorke interview.

146 "I get a few . . .": Ibid.

146 Skunk Works, Utility-2: Information provided by Lockheed Aircraft Corp.

147 Eisenhower, golf balls: Stephen Ambrose and Richard H. Immerman, *Ike's Spies*, Doubleday, 1981.

147 "Well, boys . . .": Ibid.

147 *"C'est formidable":* Vernon A. Walters, *Silent Missions*, Doubleday, 1978.

147 Clements: Confidential interview.

148 Achilles' heel of U-2: Confidential interview.

148 Francis Gary Powers: James A. Nahan, "A Fragile Détente: The U-2 Incident Reexamined," *Military Affairs*, October 1975. Powers's own version is in his *Operation Overflight*, Holt, Rinehart and Winston, 1970, a book heavily censored by the CIA.

148 Eisenhower tips off Russians: Herbert S. Parmet, *Eisenhower and the American Crusades*, Macmillan, 1972; Walt W. Rostow, *Open Skies: Eisenhower's Proposal of July 21, 1955*, University of Texas Press, 1982.

149 "In that satellite . . .": Walters, op. cit.

149 Soviet capability: Herbert F. York and Allen Greb, "Strategic Reconnaissance," *Bulletin of the Atomic Scientists*, April 1977.

150 *TIROS:* RAND P-1707, *Observation Satellites: Problems and Prospects*, RAND Corporation, May 1959.

151 Surprise of *TIROS:* Ambrose, op. cit.

151 Satellite intelligence: Ted Greenwood, *Reconnaissance, Surveillance and Arms Control*, Adelphi Papers No. 88, International Institute of Strategic Studies (London), June 1972.

NOTES AND SOURCES

151   *Midas, Vela Hotel:* Confidential remarks made at intelligence symposium, "Software Tools and Productivity," Armed Forces Communications and Electronics Association, November 16, 1982, San Diego, Calif. Author's notes.

151   Big Bird, KH: "The Military Applications of Remote Sensing by Infrared," *Proceedings of the Institute of Electrical and Electronics Engineers,* January 1975.

152   Ground resolution: Report, Hoover Institution, Stanford University, *Open Space and Peace: A Symposium of Effects of Observation,* 1964.

152   Satellite film recovery: Cecil B. Jones, Jr., "Photographic Satellite Reconnaissance," *USNIP,* June 1980.

153   Microcircuits: Report, *Scientific Communication and National Security,* National Academy of Sciences, Committee on Science, Engineering and Public Policy, September 1982.

153   ELINT, COMMINT: John M. Carroll, *Secrets of Electronic Espionage,* Dutton, 1966.

154   Code breaking: The MITRE Corporation, *Selected Examples of Possible Approaches to Electronic Communication Interception Operations,* January 1977; David Kahn, *The Code-breakers,* Macmillan, 1967.

154   Yardley: Ibid; James Bamford, *The Puzzle Palace,* Houghton Mifflin, 1982.

155   Black Chamber: Herbert O. Yardley, *The American Black Chamber,* Bobbs-Merrill, 1931.

156   "We learn from a source . . .": Bamford, op. cit.

156   Yardley's end: Ibid.

156   Friedman: Kahn, op. cit.; Ronald Clark, *The Man Who Broke Purple,* Little, Brown, 1977.

157   Purple: Kahn, op. cit.

157   "Ferrets": U.S. Air Force, Historical Division, Research Studies Institute, *History of the 3rd Reconnaissance Group,* 1957; confidential interview.

158   Violations of Soviet borders: R. P. Berman, *Soviet Air Power in Transition,* Brookings Institution, 1978.

158   Berlin tunnel: Nicholas Daniloff, "How We Spy on the Russians," *Washington Post Magazine,* December 9, 1979.

158,
159   Ice-station incident: Confidential interview.

159   Ferret satellites: *Hearings, 1978 NASA Authorization* (part 3) Senate Committee on Commerce, Science and Transportation, USGPO, 1978; *Hearings, Department of Defense Authoriza-*

tion for Appropriations for FY 1976 and 1976T (part 5), Senate Armed Services Committee, USGPO, 1975.

160   *Liberty, Pueblo:* Final Report, House Armed Services Committee, Special Subcommittee on the USS *Pueblo, Inquiry Into the USS* Pueblo *and EC-121 Plane Incidents,* USGPO, 1969.

160   Holystone: Seymour M. Hersh, "Submarines of U.S. Stage Spy Missions Inside Soviet Waters," *New York Times,* May 25, 1977; "U.S., Soviet Subs Treading Dangerous Waters," *Chicago Tribune,* December 4, 1977. A related program was the attempt in 1975 to raise a sunken Soviet Golf-class submarine from the Pacific Ocean floor after a U.S. Navy underwater listening station in Hawaii heard the sounds of the submarine breaking up. The operation, utilizing the *Glomar Explorer,* an ocean-mining ship, was only partially successful. It did not obtain the chief targets of the operation, the codebooks and other secret documents aboard the boat.

160   Size of ELINT requirements: Confidential interview.

161   Khrushchev speech: Confidential interview. Success, as they say, has a thousand fathers, and different CIA officials have taken credit for this dramatic incident (even the Israelis have claimed some credit). The fact is that there were many different copies of the speech available; the problem was that the CIA had decided on public release—thus, the copy had to be unquestionably genuine. The version read to the American Communist party meeting was considered irrefutably genuine, since it had been brought back directly from Moscow. That was the version publicly released, although the source was carefully concealed. Soviet émigré Lev Navrozov, in an interview with author, notes that there were thousands of copies available in the Soviet Union, and the speech was read aloud at many meetings. Somehow, the CIA was unable to obtain one of these many copies, and resorted to an attempt to buy a copy from Eastern European Communist officials.

161   Gamma Gupy: Paul Brodeur, "Microwaves," *New Yorker,* December 13, 1976, and December 20, 1976.

162   Cheltenham: Nick Davies and Richard Norton-Taylor, "Vast Exercise in Global Eavesdropping," *Manchester Guardian,* November 21, 1982.

162   Robot eavesdropper in Moscow: Confidential interview. Sources say that the Russians have developed similar, but much less sophisticated, devices and have planted some in the United States. These are believed to be involved,

mainly, with interception of long-line microwave relay transmissions of computer and telephone data.

162 "Somebody do something!": Confidential interview.

162 "Don't tell me . . .": Ibid.

163 SR-71: Lt. Col. G. Abe Kardong, USAF, "High, Hot and Headin' Out," *Air Force,* December 1971; Johnson's own version of the plane's development is recounted in "Development of the Lockheed SR-71 Blackbird," *Lockheed Horizons,* Winter 1981/1982.

163 Russians fail to down SR-71: Confidential interview.

163 Drones: William Wagner, *Lightning Bugs and Other Reconnaissance Drones,* Armed Forces Journal/Aero Publishers Inc., 1982.

164 Pentagon warning: *Hearings, FY 1977 Authorization for Military Procurement* (part 11), Senate Armed Services Committee, USGPO, 1976.

164 1970 incident: Report, *Principal Findings by the Senate Select Committee on Intelligence on the Capabilities of the United States to Monitor the SALT II Treaty,* Senate Select Committee on Intelligence, USGPO, October 5, 1979. This is a highly sanitized version of a much longer report. Its central conclusion, that the United States had the capability to effectively verify a SALT II treaty, was sharply dissented to by several senators, and the report was voted by a 9–6 margin.

165 Shilka: Gregg Easterbrook, "Divad," *Atlantic Monthly,* October 1982.

165 Vulnerability to deception: Michael Mihalka, "Soviet Strategic Deception, 1955–1981," *Journal of Strategic Studies,* March 1982; Bruce G. Blair, "Arms Control Implications of Strategic Monitoring Programs," paper prepared for Subcommittee on International Security and Scientific Affairs, House Foreign Affairs Committee, 1978; Amrom H. Katz, *Verification and SALT: The State of the Art and the Art of the State,* Heritage Foundation, 1979. Katz was head of the Verification and Analysis Bureau in the U.S. Arms Control and Disarmament Agency, 1973–1976.

166 Vela incident: Philip J. Klass, "Clandestine Nuclear Test Doubted," *Aviation Week and Space Technology,* August 11, 1980; Arnold Kramish, "Nuclear Flashes in the Night," *Washington Quarterly,* Summer 1980. Kramish argues that the incident may have been related to an Indian nuclear-weapons test.

Chapter Five: The Mole Wars (I)

167   "Hypotheses and equations": Alexander Orlov, *Handbook of Intelligence and Guerrilla Warfare*, University of Michigan Press, 1963. Orlov, a high-ranking NKVD officer, defected to the United States in 1938. This book is a compilation of lectures Orlov gave to NKVD recruits when he was chief of Soviet intelligence operations in Spain during the civil war.

167   *Razvedka:* Ibid.

168   Problems of HUMINT operations: Remarks, Dr. R. V. Jones at Colloquium on Intelligence and Deception, Los Alamos National Laboratory (Los Alamos, N.M.), August 19, 1982 (reported in laboratory's *NEWSbulletin*, September 3, 1982). Jones headed scientific intelligence for the British during World War II.

169   Feliks Dzerzhinsky: Viktor Brunovsky, *The Methods of the OGPU*, Harper (London), 1931; Clare Sheridan, *The Naked Truth*, Harper Bros., 1928. Brunovsky was one of the first defectors from Soviet intelligence. Sheridan, the beautiful daughter of an American financier, was a sculptress who went to Russia shortly after the revolution. There she became friends with many of the Bolshevik leaders, including Dzerzhinsky, of whom she did sculptured busts. This entrée caused British intelligence to recruit her as an agent, but she later became a rabid Bolshevik, aborting the operation.

170   Foiling of anti-Bolshevik plot: Robin Bruce Lockhart, *Ace of Spies*, Stein & Day, 1967; details of the plot were outlined in *Pravda*, September 9, 1918.

170   Cheka's beginnings: Ibid.; see also G. L. Leggett, *The Cheka: Lenin's Political Police*, Oxford University Press, 1981.

170   Threat of émigrés: Yona Liron, "J'etais un expert soviétique de contreinsurrection," *L'Est européen*, October 1964. Liron, a veteran NKVD officer, defected to France shortly before World War II to escape a Stalin-ordered purge of Jews in Soviet intelligence. He was a counterintelligence expert.

170   Monarchist Union of Central Russia: Roland Gaucher, *Opposition dans l'U.R.S.S., 1917–1967*, Editions Albin Michel (Paris), 1967.

171   Yakushev's arrest: Richard Deacon, *History of the British Secret Service*, Taplinger, 1969.

171   Dzerzhinsky's plan goes into motion: Geoffrey Bailey, *The Conspirators*, Victor Gollancz (London), 1961.

172   Cheka sham operation: Lev V. Nikulin, *Groundswell,* Foreign Languages Publishing House (Moscow), 1965. Nikulin, a prolific Soviet author on intelligence matters, was the KGB's "public relations man," churning out a long list of works on the triumphs of Soviet intelligence. See also *Subversive Activity of Foreign Espionage Services in the USSR* (Part 1), Foreign Languages Publishing House (Moscow), 1940. This was the first volume in what was apparently intended to be a multivolume history of Soviet intelligence. Although the book was anonymous, its contents suggest official authorship at a high level of the KGB. For reasons that remain unclear, the history was never completed.

173   Sidney Reilly: Sidney G. Reilly, *Britain's Master Spy, or The Adventures of Sidney Reilly,* Elkin, Matthews and Marriot (London), 1931. In fact, the book was not written by Reilly, but by his wife, Pepita Reilly, to raise money after her husband disappeared. She received some cooperation from former SIS colleagues of Reilly, although the SIS itself was distressed by the book.

173   Zinoviev letter: N. S. Grant, "The Zinoviev Letter Case," *Soviet Studies* XIX (1967–1968); Christopher Andrew, "The British Secret Service and Anglo-Soviet Relations, Part One: From the Trade Negotiations to the Zinoviev Letter," *The Historical Journal,* 20, 3 (1977).

173   Boris Savinkov: Winston Churchill, *Great Contemporaries,* Putnam, 1937; W. Somerset Maugham, "The Terrorist," *Redbook,* October 1943.

174   Polish intelligence test: Edward van der Rhoer, *Master Spy,* Scribner's, 1981.

174   Death of Savinkov: Bailey, op. cit.

174   Peters and other purge victims: Paul W. Blackstock, *The Secret Road to World War II,* Quadrangle, 1969.

174   Reilly mystery: Van der Rhoer, op. cit. Van der Rhoer is convinced that Reilly himself was part of an elaborate Dzerzhinsky deception and that he had been an OGPU agent all along. Furthermore, that he was not executed in the USSR, but became an important agent of Soviet intelligence, helping to arrange its spectacular penetrations of the British intelligence and government services some years later. However, no evidence exists to support this deduction.

176   Walter Krivitsky: Gordon Brook-Shepherd, *The Storm Petrels,* Harcourt Brace Jovanovich, 1977. Krivitsky wrote his own

account of his career: *In Stalin's Service,* Harper Bros., 1939.
176   Krivitsky and Levine: Brook-Shepherd, op. cit. Unfortunately, Levine's deep-seated anti-Communism caused him to give Krivitsky bad advice; an attempt was made to turn the Russian into a crusader against the American Communist party. In addition, some questions have arisen about whether Krivitsky really held general's rank, and whether, as was claimed, he headed up GRU operations in Western Europe. Perhaps not, but Krivitsky's knowledge of Soviet intelligence operations in Europe was obviously extensive.

177   John Herbert King: *Report of the Conference of Privy Councillors,* HMSO, 1956. This report was the result of an official British government investigation into security procedures following the Philby-Burgess-Maclean cases. The investigation revealed an incredible laxity, including use of former British Communist party officials such as King in sensitive government posts and a total lack of effective background investigations for government employees, failures that made Soviet penetration operations that much easier.

177   Krivitsky's clues: Blackstock, op. cit.

178   Tukhachevsky operation: Victor Alexander, *L'Affaire Tukachevsky,* Opéra Mundi (Paris), 1962.

179   American lack of interest: Brook-Shepherd, op. cit.

179   Krivitsky death: Ibid.

179   Rositzke: Harry A. Rositzke, *The CIA's Secret Operations,* Reader's Digest Press, 1977.

180   *Rote Kappelle:* CIA, Center for the Study of Intelligence, *The Rote Kappelle,* 1964 (declassified, with deletions, 1979).

180   *Rote Drei:* Ibid.

180   Sorge: F. W. Deakin and R. Storry, *The Case of Richard Sorge,* Chatto and Windus (London), 1966.

180   "The British . . .": Rositzke, op. cit.

181   Operation Climber: Confidential interview.

181   Ultra: Jozef Garlinski, *The Enigma War,* Scribner's, 1979.

182   British plan: Confidential interview. The arrangement worked like this: Ultra messages were handed over to top officials of Czechoslovakian intelligence, then part of the Czech government-in-exile and working closely with MI6. The operational details of the messages were in turn given to Roessler (Lucy), who sent them to Moscow. The Czech end of the operation in Switzerland was handled by Buro Ha, an "unofficial" branch of Swiss Military Intelligence that was working covertly on behalf of the Allies. Roessler

thus had no overt connection with British intelligence—a connection that might have given the game away to the Russians. Nevertheless, the Russians found out anyway, through Philby.

182   Lucy: CIA, *Rote Kappelle.* However, the CIA report is strangely vague on the very important question of Lucy's sources for his spectacular intelligence. Roessler's story that he had several "high-level sources" in the German high command is untrue. For one thing, German counterespionage units, aware of the hemorrhage of their country's top military secrets eastward via radios operating in Switzerland, looked for radio messages coming *into* Switzerland from Germany. There were none, and there was no way Roessler could have received such intelligence—hot from the press, so to speak—by any other (much slower) method. Obviously, Roessler's "sources" were *outside* Germany, but the Germans never drew the logical deduction that his intelligence stemmed from reading German codes, which were considered unbreakable.

182   British connection with Lucy: Confidential interview. To this day, both the British and American intelligence services have concealed this connection. Roessler himself never said.

183   Foote: Confidential interview. Foote's memoirs, *Handbook for Spies,* (Museum Press, London, 1949) were ghostwritten by M15 agents. Foote himself, like most double agents, was never fully trusted, and he was shuffled off to a boring job in the British Ministry of Agriculture and Fisheries. Later, he told friends of his connection to British intelligence, but few believed him.

183   Foote's revelation: Confidential interview.

184   Igor Gouzenko: The most complete account of Gouzenko's defection is his own, *The Iron Curtain,* Dutton, 1948.

184   Gouzenko's revelations: Report, Royal Commission to Investigate the Facts Relating to and the Circumstances Surrounding the Communication by Public Officials and Other Persons in Positions of Trust of Secret and Confidential Information to Agents of a Foreign Power, July 15, 1946. Extensive sections of this report remain classified; see also Robert Bothwell and J. L. Granatstein, eds., *The Gouzenko Transcripts,* Deveau (Ottawa), 1982. This work includes only 350 of the more than 6,000 pages of the Gouzenko debriefing transcript. The rest are still classified.

184   Gold, Rosenbergs: William Stevenson, *Intrepid's Last Case,* Villard Books, 1984.

185   Cracking of Soviet codes: Confidential interview.

185   "One-time pads": David Kahn, *The Code-breakers,* Macmillan, 1967.

186   Bride, Black Jumbos: Confidential interview.

186   Identification of Homer: Ibid.

186   Bride points to Rosenbergs: Ibid.

186   Agent 9: Ibid.

187   GRU officer's boast: Ibid.

187   Russians overhaul ciphers: Kim Philby hinted that he was responsible for this operation in an interview in *Izvestia,* December 19, 1967.

188   Maclean, Burgess flight: Memorandum, Col. Robert Totten, Joint Chiefs of Staff, to Hoover, FBI, "National Security Implications Resulting from the Defection of British Diplomats Donald Duart Maclean and Guy Fran deMoncy Burgess," October 18, 1955 (declassified 1975). Totten was director for intelligence in the JCS Secretariat.

188   Suspicions of Philby: Philby, in his *My Silent War,* Panther Books (London), 1980, describes the FBI web that slowly drew around him. Although Philby doesn't mention it, at one point in 1951, FBI agents tailed him to the Virginia countryside and observed him servicing what seemed to be a dead drop. Possibly aware that he was under observation, Philby hesitated, then began urinating into the bushes. The FBI agents found nothing incriminating at the site. (Confidential interview.)

188   Angleton: There is no overall account of Angleton's life and career, but he is the thinly veiled main character in the Aaron Latham novel, *Orchids for Mother,* Little, Brown, 1977. (Mother was Angleton's communications cryptonym at the CIA.)

189   Martin: Nigel West, *The Circus,* Stein & Day, 1983.

189   Unraveling of Philby ring: Douglas Sutherland, *The Great Betrayal,* Penguin Books, 1980.

189   Philby damage: Bruce Page et al., *The Philby Conspiracy,* Doubleday, 1968; Hugh Trevor-Roper, *The Philby Affair,* William Kimber (London), 1968.

190   Meeting on Lithuania: Confidential interview. Philby also admitted later betraying a CIA-MI6 operation in Albania. (Philby *Izvestia* interview.)

190   Volkov case: In an interview with the London *Daily Express*

on November 15, 1967, Philby was to describe this episode as "the happiest day of my life." He also noted that at the same time Volkov made his move, Gouzenko defected in Canada, confronting Philby with a difficult choice of which case to handle. He opted for Volkov, mainly on the theory that the defector in Turkey could probably harm him a lot more than a lowly cipher clerk in Canada.

190   Philby ring's priority: Confidential interview. Philby and other Soviet moles extensively damaged Western intelligence, although the full extent of that damage remains classified. Occasional tantalizing details slip out, such as the revelation several years ago that at one point Philby was assigned the job of weeding out Communist sympathizers from British intelligence services: Phillip Knightley, "Big Churchill Spy Purge Revealed," London Sunday *Times,* December 9, 1979.

191   Blunt, Long: H. R. Trevor-Roper, "Acts of the Apostles," *New York Review of Books,* March 31, 1983. Blunt's most extensive public discussion of his spying (and that of other "Apostles") came during an extraordinary interview with the London *Times,* November 21, 1979. The interview, however, was laced with evasions and untruths.

191   Classification/Lord: Confidential interview.

192   Operation Prince: David Martin, *Wilderness of Mirrors,* Harper & Row, 1980.

192   Carl Nelson's invention: Ibid.

192   Flood of transcripts, 250 émigrés: West, op. cit.

193   Berlin tunnel operation blown: Heinz Hohne and Hermann Zolling, *Pullach Intern,* Hoffman und Campe Verlag (Munich), 1971.

194   Crabb operation fails: West, op. cit.

Chapter Six: The Mole Wars (II)

195   "Mole hunts": Arthur A. Zuehlke, Jr., "What Is Counterintelligence?" paper prepared for Colloquium on Counterintelligence, Consortium for the Study of Intelligence, Washington, D.C., April 24, 1980. (Zuehlke is a Soviet analyst at the DIA.)

196   Popov: William Hood, *Mole,* Norton, 1982.

197   Langelle case officer: Ibid; see also the Soviet version of this

case, "Duel in the Dark," *Izvestia,* March 12 and 13, 1963.

197 Execution of Popov: Confidential interview.

198 FBI surveillance: Hood, op. cit.

198 Suspicion of mole in Popov case: Confidential interview.

198 Langelle information: Ibid.

199 *Heckenschütze:* David Martin, *Wilderness of Mirrors,* Harper & Row, 1980.

199 First Sniper revelations: John Bulloch, *Spy Ring,* Secker and Warburg (London), 1962.

200 Goleniewski appears: Martin, op. cit.

200 Blake revealed as mole: E. H. Cookridge, *The Many Sides of George Blake, Esq.,* Vertex, 1970.

201 KGB development of Blake: Ibid.

201 Israel Beer case: Dennis Eisenberg et al., *The Mossad,* Paddington Press, 1978.

202 Goleniewski's warning: Confidential interview.

202 Goleniewski's royalty claim: Martin, op. cit. For a right-wing view of Goleniewski's claim to the Russian throne, see Guy Richards, *Imperial Agent,* Devin-Adair, 1966. Richards first revealed Goleniewski's existence in this country in the now-defunct *New York Journal-American* on March 6, 1964. That precipitated what has become a strange obsession by the American right wing in the case of the Romanov "rescue" —allegations that members of the Romanov family were not killed by Bolsheviks, but were permitted to secretly emigrate to Western countries where they lived out the rest of their lives under assumed names and in straitened circumstances. Richards summed up this thesis in *The Rescue of the Romanovs,* Devin-Adair, 1975. Unfortunately for his theory, the Grand Duke Aleksei—whom Goleniewski claimed to be —was twelve years old at the time of his alleged escape. Goleniewski's birth certificate shows him to have been born in Nieswiez, Poland, on August 16, 1922, fully four years after he claimed to have escaped from Russia.

202 Deriabin lists Golitsin: Confidential interview. Deriabin told his story in *The Secret World,* Ballantine Books, 1982, co-authored with Frank Gibney. Deriabin, who worked for the CIA until his retirement in 1981, analyzing KGB counterintelligence capabilities, also worked with Gibney on producing *The Penkovsky Papers.*

203 Golitsin appears: Martin, op. cit.

203 AE/Ladle a problem: Ibid.

203 Sapphire: P. L. Thyraud de Vosjoli, *Lamia,* Little, Brown,

1970. De Vosjoli was SDECE (French intelligence) liaison officer in Washington during the 1960s. He remained in the United States after Golitsin confirmed his long-felt fears of extensive KGB penetration of French intelligence.

204   NATO documents: Martin, op. cit.

204   "Ring of five": Nigel West, *The Circus*, Stein & Day, 1983. See also *Report of the Tribunal Appointed to Inquire into the Vassall Case and Related Matters*, HMSO, April 1963.

204   Penetration of Canada: Confidential interview. This assertion was to lead, finally, to grave suspicions being attached to the head of the Royal Canadian Mounted Police's Security Service counterespionage section, Leslie James Bennett, who was later forced to retire following an extensive investigation of charges that he was a KGB mole. No proof was found on this charge, but the RCMP felt that since his effectiveness had been so badly debilitated, his retirement was necessary. I am grateful to John Sawatasky for sharing his insights on the Bennett case and related matters.

204   Peter and Paul: These were the KGB code names for Heinz Felfe and his friend Hans Clemens, both BND officials, whose role was discussed in Chapter One.

205   Martin horrified: West, op. cit.

205   Fluency revelations: Ibid.

206   Suspicions of a high-level mole: Ibid.

207   Hoover's plan: Confidential interview.

207   Philby "vindication": "Parliamentary Report," London *Times*, October 26, 1955.

207   Plan for Philby confession: West, op. cit.

207   Elliott: Ibid.

208   Respect for Golitsin, Golitsin's appearance: Confidential interview.

209   Angleton's support for Golitsin: Martin, op. cit.

210   Penkovsky: Deriabin and Gibney, op. cit. See also Greville Wynne, *The Man from Moscow*, Hutchinson (London), 1967. Wynne was irked that he had not been involved in the *Penkovsky Papers* book project, and despite MI6 opposition, produced his own book.

210   Mrs. Chisholm: West, op. cit.

210   KGB traps Penkovsky: Confidential interview.

210   "I would stress . . .": Remarks, Sir Dick White, head of MI6, to a meeting of MI6 senior officers, London, November 18, 1962. Quoted in Anthony Verrier, *Through the Looking Glass*, Norton, 1983.

211   Sasha: Martin, op. cit.
212   Nosenko: Edward Jay Epstein, *Legend,* Reader's Digest Press, 1978.
213   Angleton's suspicions: Ibid.
213   Kovshuk: Ibid.
213   Lee Harvey Oswald: Ibid.
213   Mistreatment of Nosenko: *Hearings, House Select Committee on Assassinations* (vol. II), USGPO, 1979.
213   Top Hat, Fedora: Martin, op. cit.
214   *Kegebeshniki:* Vladimir Sakharov interview.
215   Atmosphere of suspicion: Edward Jay Epstein, "The War Within the CIA," *Commentary,* August 1978; Thomas Powers, *The Man Who Kept the Secrets,* Knopf, 1979.
215   Wrecking of SR Division: Epstein, "The War Within the CIA."
215   Sullivan's suspicion: Interview with author, 1976.
216   Accusation against Angleton: Martin, op. cit.
216   Martin suspects Hollis: West, op. cit.
217   Mitchell case: Ibid.
217   Mitchell's garbage: Ibid.
218   Cairncross: Ibid.
219   Sullivan's shock: Confidential interview.
219   Michael Straight: Michael Straight, *After a Long Silence,* Norton, 1983.
219   Blunt caught: George Steiner, "The Cleric of Treason," *New Yorker,* December 8, 1980.
220   Leo Long: Ibid.
221   Dick Ellis confession: West, op. cit.
221   Martin fired, hired: Phillip Knightley, "What Was Really Tearing M15 Apart," London Sunday *Times,* March 20, 1981.
222   Gouzenko review: Confidential interview.
222   Hollis: Chapman Pincher, *Their Trade Is Treachery,* Sidgwick and Jackson (London), 1981. Pincher all but says Hollis was a KGB mole, but in all fairness to Hollis—who died in 1973—there is no conclusive evidence whatsoever to prove that he was a traitor.
223   Ambiguity of counterintelligence: Hans Moses, *The Clandestine Service of the Central Intelligence Agency,* Association of Foreign Intelligence Officers (McLean, Va.), 1982.
224   Lipavsky: Confidential interview.
224   Lipavsky double agent: Ibid.
225   Trigon: "The Rumor Mill in Washington: A Case History

Involves Death of a Valued Spy," *New York Times,* September 23, 1980; Daniel Schorr, "The Trigon Caper," *First Principles* (Center for National Security Studies, Washington, D.C.), December 1980.

225   Kissinger cable: Schorr, op. cit.

226   Aaron accusation: Ibid.

227,
228   End of Gouzenko: Confidential interviews.

Chapter Seven: Eyeless in the Big Muddy

229   Ban Bonakah: Confidential interview.

230   Gritz and the Americans: Ibid; see also "Daring Mission, Dashed Hopes," *Time,* June 1, 1981.

230   Gritz's Vietnam War mission: Gritz led a Green Beret team in a dangerous mission to recover the "black box" (highly secret electronic intelligence circuitry) from a U-2 plane that had crashed in a Vietnamese jungle while returning from a mission over North Vietnam. When Gritz discovered that Viet Cong guerrillas had removed the box from the plane wreckage, he led a foray into a Viet Cong base camp and literally stole the box from its captors. Among the more noted of Gritz's Vietnam War exploits, it is described in Gen. William Westmoreland's *A Soldier Reports,* Doubleday, 1972.

230   Thais order deportation: "Daring Mission, Dashed Hopes," loc. cit.

231   Cost of Vietnam War: U.S. Commerce Department, *Statistical Abstract of the United States,* USGPO, 1974.

232   Deer Mission: OSS, *Deer Report #1,* July 17, 1945 (declassified 1972), HQ OSS China Theater, *Report on Deer Mission,* September 17, 1945 (declassified 1972).

232   Mr. Hoo: Report, Maj. Allison K. Thomas, OSS Deer Mission, *The Vietminh Party or League* (annex to *Report on Deer Mission,* September 17, 1945); HQ OSS, Detachment 404 report, *Political Aims and Philosophy of the Viet Minh Government of French Indo-China, and Their Attitude Toward America and Americans,* September 30, 1945 (declassified 1972).

233   Ho and the Americans: Ibid.

233   OSS naïveté: Ibid.

234   Frank White: HQ OSS China Theater, *Report on Deer Mission.*

235   White's report: HQ OSS, Detachment 404 report.

235   Dewey's death: HQ OSS, Detachment 404, *Affidavit Cpt. Herbert J. Bluechel OSS, MLB-2739-B,* October 13, 1945 (declassified 1972).

236   Indochina deal: U.S. Army, OCMH, *Special Studies: Rearming the French,* USGPO, 1957; for an early expression of the Vietnam-as-domino idea, see NSCM 64, *The Position of the United States with Respect to Indochina,* February 25, 1950 (declassified 1971).

236   Platti: Archimedes L. A. Platti, *Why Viet Nam? Prelude to America's Albatross,* University of California Press, 1980.

236   Platti's explanation to Ho: Ibid.

237   Ho's plan: Huynh Kim Khanh, *Vietnamese Communism, 1925–1945,* Cornell University Press, 1982.

237   French failure in people's war: Bernard Fall, *Street Without Joy,* Stackpole Books, 1961. For the American failure to heed the lessons of such wars, see Ronald Schaffer, "The 1940 Small Wars Manual and the 'Lessons of History,'" *Military Affairs,* April 1972.

238   American perceptions: Robert M. Blum, *Drawing the Line: The Origin of the American Containment Policy in East Asia,* Norton, 1982; Frances Fitzgerald, *Fire in the Lake,* Little, Brown, 1972.

238   American perception of Vietnamese Communists: State Department, Office of Intelligence Research, Division of Research for Far East, Report No. 3708, *Political Alignments of Vietnamese Nationalists,* 1949 (declassified 1972).

238   Commitment to French: NSC 124/2, *United States Objectives and Courses of Action with Respect to Southeast Asia,* June 25, 1952 (declassified 1972).

239   Hong Kong: Joseph Smith, *Portrait of a Cold Warrior,* Random House, 1976. Smith was deputy chief of station for the CIA in Singapore in 1954.

239   Viet Minh intelligence theft: Confidential interview.

240   Operation Vulture: John Prados, *The Sky Would Fall: Operation Vulture, the U.S. Bombing Mission in Indochina, 1954,* Dial Press, 1983. Army planners told Eisenhower that it would take a U.S. military force of nearly 150,000 men to extricate the French from Dien Bien Phu (see Department of the Army, *Memorandum re: NSCAM 1074-A,* April 14, 1954, declassified 1973). Meanwhile, the CIA predicted—correctly, as it turned out—that the Chinese and Russians would not intervene directly if the United States were to give full back-

ing, short of troops and air support, to the French. (CIA Special Estimate SE-53, *Probable Communist Reactions to Certain Possible U.S. Courses of Action in Indochina Through 1954*, December 18, 1953, declassified 1973.)

241   Saigon Military Mission: Saigon Military Mission, *Lansdale Team's Report on Covert Saigon Mission in 1954 and 1955*, August 12, 1955 (declassified 1972).

241   Lansdale: David Halberstam, *The Best and the Brightest*, Random House, 1972. Lansdale's own version: *In the Midst of Wars*, Harper & Row, 1972.

242   "Vampire routine": Kenneth M. Hammer, "Huks in the Philippines," chapter in Franklin M. Osanka, ed., *Modern Guerrilla Warfare*, Free Press, 1962.

242   "Vietnamese Magsaysay": Confidential interview.

243   CIA propaganda campaign: Memorandum, Brig. Gen. Edward G. Lansdale, Jr., to Gen. Maxwell Taylor, *Resources for Unconventional Warfare*, n.d., but believe circa 1961 (declassified 1972).

243   Dr. Tom Dooley: Jim Winters, "Tom Dooley, the Forgotten Hero," *Notre Dame Magazine*, May 1979. Dooley had been proposed for sainthood, but the rigorous investigation required by the Catholic Church for such status uncovered Dooley's CIA connections, and the sainthood idea was quietly dropped.

243   Diem mistake: Fitzgerald, op. cit.

244   Colonel Conein: Confidential interview.

244   Airtight coffins: Ibid.

244   Malayan example: Douglas Blaufarb, *The Counterinsurgency Era*, Free Press, 1977.

245   Thompson: Ibid.

245   Thompson appalled: Ibid.

246   "Counterguerrilla forces": Charles M. Simpson III, *Inside the Green Berets*, Presidio Press, 1983.

246   "Limited war" theory: Stephen Peter Rosen, "Vietnam and the American Theory of Limited War," *International Security*, Fall 1982; Harry G. Summers, Jr., "Lessons: A Soldier's View," *Wilson Quarterly*, Summer 1983.

246   Maxwell Taylor: Blaufarb, op. cit.

247   Special Forces: Department of the Army, *Vietnam Studies: U.S. Army Special Forces, 1961–1971*, USGPO, 1972.

247   Helicopters: Gen. Hamilton Howze, "The Howze Board," *Army*, February 1974; "Airmobility Becomes More Than a Theory," *Army*, March 1974; "Winding Up a Great Show," *Army*, April 1974.

247 General Howze: Ibid.

248 Eight hundred agents, thirty thousand auxiliaries: Confidential interview.

248 White Star: Ibid.

249 Simons's Laos mission: Donald Duncan, "The Whole Thing Was a Lie!" *Ramparts,* February 1966. Duncan was a Special Forces NCO who quit the army in protest over American policy in Vietnam.

249 SOG: Confidential interview.

250 OPLAN 34-A: Ibid.

250 Forged ammunition: Ibid.

251 Failure of SOG: Simpson, op. cit. Meanwhile, military intelligence was having its own problems in Vietnam. It consistently failed to spot Viet Cong and North Vietnamese units and had great difficulty detecting supply lines and caches for the Communist forces. See Department of the Army, *Vietnam Reports: The Role of Military Intelligence, 1965–1967,* USGPO, 1974. The report was written by Gen. Joseph A. McChristian, head of military intelligence for MACV (Military Assistance Command, Vietnam). It reflected the bitter feelings that existed between military intelligence and the CIA in Vietnam. The agency is hardly mentioned.

251 Kit-Cat missions: Confidential interview.

252 Cambodia, Laos: Confidential interview. Cross-border missions into Cambodia were run under the code name Daniel Boone.

252 Hmongs, Vang Pao: Confidential interviews. The Hmong operation became the CIA's most notorious such paramilitary action because of the Hmongs' deep involvement in opium growing and smuggling. CIA officials had a bad habit of looking the other way when the Hmong opium business boomed. (See Alfred W. McCoy, *The Politics of Heroin in Southeast Asia,* Harper & Row, 1972.) Vang Pao and a number of his men were evacuated by the CIA from Laos following that country's collapse. The agency bought Vang Pao a large ranch in Montana, where he lives today. (Confidential interview.)

253 South Vietnamese intelligence apparatus: Fred Branfman, remarks, Conference on the CIA and World Peace, Yale University, April 5, 1975. (Author's notes.)

253 Loan: Confidential interview. Loan became immortalized after a fashion in 1968 when he was photographed in the act of shooting a Viet Cong suspect in the head with a pistol,

a picture that made the front page of virtually every American newspaper.

254 CIO: Ibid.

254 Richardson: Ibid.

254 Tung: Ibid.

255 Size of Viet Cong infrastructure: Michael Charles Conly, *The Communist Insurgent Infrastructure in South Vietnam: A Study of Organization and Strategy,* American University Center for Research in Social Studies, 1966.

255 Operation Phoenix: Joseph B. Treaster, "The Phoenix Murders," *Penthouse,* December 1975.

256 Phoenix corruption: *Pacification: The 100-Year Flight of the Phoenix,* Indochina Resources Center (Washington, D.C.), May 1973.

257 B-36: Confidential interview.

257 Operation Projectile: Ibid.

258 Numbers argument: Gains B. Hawkins, "Vietnam Anguish: Being Ordered to Lie: A Mississippi Colonel Explains How It Feels to Cover Up [Viet Cong] Strength Figures and How to Tell the Truth," *Washington Post,* November 14, 1982. Hawkins was the MACV representative during the CIA-military negotiations on Communist military-strength figures. For the CIA role in the controversy, see Final Report, House Select Committee on Intelligence (section II, part 1), *Tet: Failure to Adapt to a New Kind of War,* February 1976; and CIA, Interim Report, *Intelligence Warning of the Tet Offensive in South Vietnam,* April 11, 1968 (declassified 1975). The CIA concluded that American intelligence correctly assumed that a Communist offensive was imminent, but badly underestimated its size and intensity.

258 Tet disaster: Ibid. Several months before the offensive opened, a CIA report admitted that the agency had no real idea of the actual strength and size of Communist forces in South Vietnam (CIA, SNIE 14-3-67, *Capabilities of the Vietnamese Communists for Fighting in South Vietnam,* November 13, 1967 (declassified 1972).

258 1963 Taylor-McNamara visit: Office of the Secretary of Defense, Memorandum for the President, *Subject: Report of McNamara-Taylor Mission to South Vietnam,* October 2, 1963 (declassified 1973). However, at the very time McNamara and Taylor were reporting progress, a State Department intelligence report was noting that the war was in fact going badly for the South Vietnamese. The State Department

based its conclusions on a statistic that seemed to have escaped everyone's notice: The South Vietnamese were losing weapons (captured by the Communists) at a much higher rate than they were recovering weapons from the Viet Cong. At that rate, the report noted, the South Vietnamese would soon equip the entire Viet Cong military with weapons. (State Department, Bureau of Intelligence and Research, Research Memorandum RFE-90, *Statistics on the War Effort in South Vietnam Show Unfavorable Trends,* October 22, 1963, declassified 1973.) This report was ignored.

258   Rolling Thunder failure: John M. Van Dyke, *North Vietnam's Strategy for Survival,* Pacific Books, 1972; Hearings, Preparedness Investigating Subcommittee, Senate Armed Services Committee, *Air War Against North Vietnam,* USGPO, 1967; Air War Study Group, Cornell University Program on Peace Studies, *The Air War in Indochina,* 1972.

258   COSVN mobile trucks: Confidential interview.

259   Vietnamization: The concept was born in a report written by Guy J. Pauker of the RAND Corporation in March 1971 ("An Essay on Vietnamization," RAND R-604-ARPA). Kissinger seized on this idea and Pauker soon became the new guru of Vietnam War strategy. His suggestions were put into effect—they amounted to the so-called "secret plan" Nixon had announced for ending U.S. involvement in the war—but all of them failed ignominiously. For a devastating critique of the reasons for that failure, see Bernard Brodie, "Vietnam: Why We Failed," chapter in his *War and Politics,* Macmillan, 1973.

259   Sergeant Tang: Confidential interview.

260   CIA blindness: Frank Snepp, *Decent Interval,* Random House, 1978. Snepp, a disaffected former CIA agent, was supported in his account of the final weeks in Vietnam by another disaffected CIA agent, John Stockwell. (See Seymour Hersh, "Another Ex-CIA Official Alleges Agency Failed Some Saigon Allies," *New York Times,* November 23, 1977.)

260   Communist deceptions, Ban Me Thuot: Wilfred Burchett, *Grasshoppers and Elephants: Why Viet Nam Fell—The Viet Cong Account of the Last 55 Days of the War,* Urizen Books, 1977. Burchett, a pro-Communist Australian journalist, recounts a long list of deception measures designed to fool American intelligence. See also his review essay, "Dubious Hindsight," *Harper's,* March 1978.

260   Hmong "prisoners" report: Jay Peterzell, "Reagan's Covert
       Action Policy (II)," *First Principles,* Center for National Secu-
       rity Studies (Washington, D.C.), February 1982. A small
       force of Hmongs is now being covertly supported and
       funded by the CIA to carry out a small-scale guerrilla resist-
       ance against the Laotian Communist regime.
261   U.S. prisoners of war: Department of Defense figures, 1982.
261   Gritz obsession: Confidential interview. See also summary
       narrative, *Bo Gritz and Operations Velvet Hammer, Eagle and
       Lazarus,* April 1983, prepared by members of Gritz's teams,
       and *Intelligence Summary and Situation Report, Operation Laza-
       rus,* January 1983.
261   SR-71 pictures: Confidential interviews.
262   Operation Velvet Hammer: *Bo Gritz and Operations . . .*
262   Dubious Laotian source: Ibid.
263   Gritz mission common knowledge in Bangkok: Jim Graves
       et al., "Bo Gritz: Hero or Huckster?" *Soldier of Fortune,*
       Spring 1983.
263   Gritz fiasco: Ibid.

Chapter Eight: Apparats and Skywriters

265   Elihu Avraham: Avraham interview.
266   Operation Badr: Ibid.
267    $200,000: Ibid.
268   American-Israeli intelligence bond: Avraham interview; see
       also Final Report, House Select Committee on Intelligence
       (section II, part 3), *The Mideast War: The System Breaks Down,*
       1976.
268   1956 Israeli deception: Confidential interview.
269   *Liberty:* Ibid.
269   Radio deception: Ibid.
270   Mossad deterioration: Ibid.
270   Hit teams: George Jonas, *Vengeance,* Simon & Schuster,
       1984.
270   Zeira, "defensive maneuvers": Michael I. Handel, "Percep-
       tion, Deception and Surprise: The Case of the Yom Kippur
       War," Jerusalem Paper #19, Leonard Davis Institute for
       International Relations, Hebrew University of Jerusalem,
       1976.
270   "Intelligence indicators" system: Arganat Commission (Is-

rael), *Third and Final Report to the Government and the Defense and Foreign Affairs Committee of the Knesset,* January 30, 1975.

270   Deep penetration equation: Ibid.

271   Washington meeting, Avraham: Avraham interview.

271   Lieutenant Siman-Tov: Arganat Commission, op. cit.

272   Golda Meir meeting: Avigdor Haselkorn, *Israeli Intelligence Performance in the Yom Kippur War,* Discussion Paper 2033, Hudson Institute, July 1974.

272   "Low probability . . . lower than low": Ibid.

272   American intelligence technology over Sinai: Confidential interview.

273   Ambiguity of evidence: Ibid.

273   Lack of good sources: Ibid.

273   Soviet-Egyptian deception plan: Hassan el Badri, Taha el Magdub, and Mohamed Dia el Din Zohdy, *The Ramadan War, 1973,* T. N. Dupuy and Associates (Dunn Loring, Va.), 1978. The authors were senior Egyptian Army officers.

274   Military parade sham: Confidential interview.

275   Kissinger, Nixon: Memorandum, Henry Kissinger to Subcommittee on National Security and International Operations, Senate Government Operations Committee, *Subject: The National Security Council,* March 3, 1970.

276   Kissinger criticism of intelligence: Stephen Leacos, "Kissinger's Apparat," *Foreign Policy,* Winter 1971. Kissinger's critical view was shared by the House and Senate select committees who carried out an unprecedented investigation of American intelligence agencies, particularly the CIA, 1974–1976. Although the committees focused on assorted intelligence agency abuses, too-brief attention was paid to the question of the quality of intelligence the agencies were producing. See, especially, Hearings, House Select Committee on Intelligence, *The Performance of the Intelligence Community* (part 2), USGPO, 1975.

276   Czechoslovakia failure: Final Report, House Select Committee on Intelligence (part II, section 3), *Czechoslovakia: Failure of Tactical Warning,* 1976.

276   Lost Soviet division: David N. Schwarz, *The Soviet Invasion of Czechoslovakia: 1968: A Case Study of NATO Crisis Warning,* MIT Center for International Studies, July 1977.

276   Libya failure: Robert F. Ellsworth and Kenneth L. Adelman, "Foolish Intelligence," *Foreign Policy,* Fall 1979.

277   Cambodia argument and failure: House Select Committee on Intelligence, *Performance . . .*

277   The DCI problem: This difficulty was only recently addressed with a step that has been advocated for years: giving the DCI cabinet rank, as Reagan has done with William Casey.

278   Raborn: Thomas Powers, *The Man Who Kept the Secrets,* Knopf, 1979.

278   "Well, what do you . . .": Ibid.

279   Helms, chief leaker: Confidential interview.

279   Helms as DCI: Powers, op. cit.

279   CIA ordered to compromise: Confidential interview.

280   Laird's move: Paul Blackstock, "The Intelligence Community Under the Nixon Administration," *Armed Forces and Society,* Winter 1975.

280   ". . . frankly bore me": Powers, op. cit.

280   Helms elbowed aside: Ibid.

281   Kissinger's exam: Henry Kissinger, *White House Years,* Little, Brown, 1979.

281   Schlesinger's recommendations: Blackstock, op. cit.

281   Kissinger's criticisms, "skywriting": Confidential interview.

281   "Talmudic . . . piece of crap": Ibid.

282   *"Der Apparat":* Confidential interview.

282   Vietnamization: Guy J. Pauker, "An Essay on Vietnamization," RAND R-604-ARPA, March 1971.

282   CIA report: Confidential interview.

282   U-2 flight over Cienfuegos: Hearings, Subcommittee on Inter-American Affairs, House Foreign Affairs Committee, *Soviet Naval Activities in Cuba,* October 13, November 19, and November 24, 1970, USGPO, 1971.

283   U-2 pictures: Raymond L. Garthoff, "Handling the Cienfuegos Crisis," *International Security,* Summer 1983.

283   Kissinger's deduction: Kissinger, op. cit.

283   The soccer clue: Ibid.

283   DIA conclusion: Hearings, *Soviet Naval Activities.*

283   Kissinger's argument: Garthoff, loc. cit.

284   Showdown with Dobrynin: Kissinger, op. cit.

284   "In the interests . . .": Ibid.

285   Strategic weapons intelligence: Albert Wohlsetter, "Is There a Strategic Arms Race?" *Foreign Policy,* Summer 1974; see also his "Optimal Ways to Confuse Ourselves," *Foreign Policy,* Fall 1975.

285   No consensus on Soviet missiles: Ray S. Cline, "Policy Without Intelligence," *Foreign Policy,* Winter 1974–1975.

286   Overreliance on technology: Wohlsetter, "Optimal Ways."

286   Laird's belief: Hearings, Joint Economic Committee, Subcommittee on Priorities and Economy in Government, *Allocation of Resources in the Soviet Union and China, 1979,* June 26, 1979 (especially testimony of DIA Director General Eugene Tighe).

286   "Arms-control bias": A longstanding charge of the military-intelligence agencies. See, especially, testimony of DIA Director General Daniel Graham before Subcommittee on Priorities and Economy in Government, July 21, 1975.

287   ABM debate revived: Graham testimony.

287   Safeguard: Alan Platt, *The U.S. Senate and Strategic Arms Policy, 1969–1977,* Westview Press, 1978.

287   Seven thousand to nine thousand Soviet ABMs: Freedman, *U.S. Intelligence and the Soviet Strategic Threat.*

287   Trident: Members of Congress for Peace Through Law, *Report on ULMS: A Research Paper for Consideration by the Military Spending Committees,* April 1972.

288   Kissinger's arms-control theory: Kissinger, op. cit.

288   Compliance dispute: Gerard C. Smith, *Doubletalk: The Story of the First SALT Talks,* Doubleday, 1980.

289   Verification panel: Elmo Zumwalt, Jr., and Worth Bagley, "Soviets Cheat and We Turn Our Backs," *Washington Star,* August 10, 1975.

289   USIB restricted: Ibid.

290   "Ambiguous situations": Testimony, Ray S. Cline, Senate Select Committee on Intelligence, *U.S. Intelligence Agencies and Activities: Risks and Control of Foreign Intelligence* (part 5), USGPO, 1975.

290   NO DIS CHEROKEE: Seymour Hersh, *The Price of Power,* Summit Books, 1982.

290   Kissinger's assumptions: Cline, "Policy Without Intelligence."

291   "Strategic realities": Remarks, Henry Kissinger, press conference, Washington, D.C., December 9, 1975.

291   Angola turmoil: John A. Marcum, "Southern Africa After the End of Portuguese Rule," chapter in Helen Kitchen, ed., *Africa: From Mystery to Maze* (vol. XI in *Critical Choices for Americans*), Lexington Books, 1976.

292   Roberto, FNLA: Gerald J. Bender, "Kissinger in Africa: Anatomy of a Failure," chapter in Rene Lemarchand, ed., *American Policy in Southern Africa: The Stakes and the Stance,* University Press of America, 1978.

NOTES AND SOURCES

292 Roberto, CIA asset: Confidential interview.
292 $1,000 a month: Ibid; see also "Accusations of Savimbi Against Holden Roberto in 1964," *O Jornal* (Lisbon), January 24, 1975.
292 Savimbi breaks away: John Stockwell, *In Search of Enemies*, Norton, 1978. Stockwell, who was chief CIA officer on the agency's Angola Task Force, quit the CIA in 1975 to protest its actions in Angola.
292 CIA unease with Savimbi: Ibid.
292 1974 situation: Bender, loc. cit.
293 CIA misreads the situation: Gerald J. Bender, review essay, "Angola: A Story of Stupidity," *New York Review of Books*, December 21, 1978.
293 Faulty sources: Confidential interview.
293 Kissinger widens the intelligence gap: Bender, "Angola."
294 40 Committee: Stockwell, op. cit.
294 Decision to involve South Africa: Bender, "Angola."
294 Collapse of Kissinger plan: Colin Legum, "The Soviet Union, China and the West in Southern Africa," *Foreign Affairs*, July 1976; John A. Marcum, *The Angolan Revolution*, vol. II: *Exile Politics and Guerrilla Warfare, 1962–1976*, MIT Press, 1978.
295 George Bacon (Kayak): Confidential interviews.
295 Bacon's restlessness: Ibid.
296 CIA mercenary operation: Ibid.
296 "Sheep-dipping": Ibid.
296 Bufkin: Ibid; see also Robin Wright, "The Mercenary," *Washington Post News Service*, May 7, 1977; R. K. Brown, "David Bufkin: American Merc Destroys Cuban Spy Ring," *Soldier of Fortune*, March 1977.
296 Dennis Banks: Stewart Tendler and Hugh Noyes, "Somber Fate of British Mercenaries," London *Times*, March 12, 1976.
296 Fiasco: In 1983, three Americans being held in Angola, including two mercenaries and a pilot suspected of being a CIA agent, were exchanged for Soviet advisers being held prisoner by Savimbi's forces.
296 Bacon's death: Confidential interviews.

Chapter Nine: The Clues of Semipalatinsk

299   Keegan: Confidential interviews.

300   Air-force intelligence: Lee Lescaze, "Pentagon vs. CIA: Control of Intelligence Community Sparks Major Battle," *Washington Post,* June 10, 1977.

301   National Reconnaissance Office: Confidential interview.

301   Fifty thousand people, $3 billion: Ibid.

301   Keegan refuses to sign: Ibid.

301   American disquiet: Representative Les Aspin, "Debate over U.S. Strategic Forecasts: A Mixed Record," *Strategic Review,* Summer 1980; William T. Lee, "Debate Over U.S. Strategic Forecasts: A Poor Record," Ibid.

302   Intelligence tries to keep up: Ray S. Cline, "The Future of U.S. Foreign Intelligence Operations," chapter in Peter Duignan and Alvin Rabushka, eds., *The U.S. in the 1980s,* Hoover Institution Publication No. 228, 1980.

302   CEP: Lawrence Freedman, *Evolution of Nuclear Strategy,* Macmillan, 1982.

303   MX: Mary Kaldor, *The Baroque Arsenal,* Hill and Wang, 1981.

303   Laird belief in Soviet first strike: Raymond L. Garthoff, "On Estimating and Imputing Intentions," *International Security,* Winter 1977.

303   Running argument: Michael McGwire, "Soviet Strategic Weapons Policy, 1955–1970," chapter in Michael McGwire and Ken Booth, eds., *Soviet Naval Policy: Objectives and Constraints,* Praeger, 1975.

304   "What in the name . . .": Often attributed to Kissinger by many different sources, but no one seems quite able to place precisely when and where he said it.

304   CIA report: Confidential interview.

305   CIA underestimates Keegan: Ibid.

306   "I had no . . .": Keegan interview.

306   "George's transceiver": Confidential interview.

307   1974 PFIAB meeting: Ibid.

307   Team B episode: Arthur Macy Cox, "The CIA's Tragic Error," *New York Review of Books,* November 6, 1980.

308   Pipes, Team B hawks: Ibid.

308   Team B's conclusions: Ibid.

309   Team B's mindset: Ibid.

310   Carter uses Team B to cancel B-1: Confidential interview.

310   Weakness of U.S. intelligence: Daniel Graham, "The Intelli-

gence Myth of Washington," *Strategic Review,* Summer 1976.

311 Soviet directed-energy-weapons developments: Keegan interview.

311 Starfish: Ernest Volkman, "The Magic Bullet," *Defense Science and Electronics,* April–May 1982.

311 Project Saint, Seesaw, Squanto Terror: Ibid.

312 Semipalatinsk: Confidential interview.

312 Keegan disputes conclusion: Ibid.

313 Keegan's crusade: Ibid.

313 First important clues: Ibid. Keegan was aware of an earlier clue that he found significant: A RAND study of Soviet laser research noted that an important laser research group at Moscow University had suddenly stopped publishing scientific papers, a certain indication that they had been switched to classified military research. (RAND R-921/1-ARPA, *Soviet Chemical Laser Research,* 1971.)

313 Keegan's conclusion: Interview, Dr. Lowell Wood, director, Lawrence Livermore National Laboratory, *Defense Science and Electronics,* August–September 1982.

314 Rudakov: Confidential interview.

315 Rudakov's shocking lecture: Ibid.

315 Pentagon finally believes: "Beam Weapons Survey Team Formed," *Aviation Week and Space Technology,* October 2, 1978.

316 Nuclear Intelligence Advisory Board: Confidential interview.

317 Committee on the Present Danger: The committee was officially formed on July 4, 1976, and announced on that date at a Washington, D.C., press conference. Author's notes.

318 Battle lines drawn: William T. Lee, "Understanding the Soviet Military Threat—How CIA Estimates Went Astray," *National Strategy Information Center Agenda Paper No. 6,* 1977.

318 Civil defense: Paul H. Nitze, "Deterring Our Deterrent," *Foreign Policy,* Winter 1976. Nitze and other members of the Committee on the Present Danger became especially infuriated by CIA reports that generally took a benign view of Soviet civil defense and concluded that it was not very effective against a full-scale American nuclear attack. (See especially CIA, DCI NI 78-10003, *Soviet Civil Defense,* July 1978, unclassified.)

318 Twenty million Russians dead: Richard Pipes, "Why the USSR Thinks It Could Fight and Win a Nuclear War," *Commentary,* July 1977.

319   Committee's "proof": Leon Goure, *War Survival in Soviet
        Strategy: USSR Civil Defense,* Center for Advanced Interna-
        tional Studies, University of Miami, 1976.
319   Moscow "bunker": Confidential interview.
320   Carter and civil defense: William H. Kincade, "U.S. Civil
        Defense Decision Making in the Ford and Carter Adminis-
        trations," Ph.D. thesis, American University, June 1981.
320   Carter nearly causes apoplexy: Thomas Powers, "Choosing
        a Strategy for World War III," *Atlantic,* November 1982.
320   White House drills: Confidential interview.
320   Military spending argument: RAND N-1000-AF, *The Signifi-
        cance of Divergent U.S.-USSR Military Expenditures,* RAND
        Corporation, February 1979.
321   "Meta-intelligence . . .": Quoted in Michael R. Gordon,
        "Estimating Soviet Military Spending: An Arcane Art with
        Political Overtones," *National Journal,* June 26, 1983.
321   "Dollar comparison method": CIA SR78-10002, *A Dollar
        Cost Comparison of Soviet and U.S. Defense Activities, 1967–1977,*
        January 1978 (unclassified).
322   "The only people . . .": Confidential interview.
322   Military manpower costs method: Roger Boyes, "Hidden
        Figures Baffle Western Experts," *Financial Times* (London),
        October 5, 1978.
323   1976 switch: CIA SR 76-10053, *A Dollar Comparison of Soviet
        and U.S. Defense Activities, 1965–1975,* February 1976 (un-
        classified).
323   Carter uses CIA oil estimate: CIA OER ER 77-10270, *Pros-
        pects for Soviet Oil Production,* 1977 (unclassified).
324   CIA estimates proven wrong: "Energy Czar," *Scientific
        American,* November 1981.
324   SALT violations: Graham, loc. cit.
325   Telemetry: Ibid.
325   Encryption: Ibid.
325   Americans cause their own problem: Strobe Talbot, *End-
        game: The Inside Story of SALT II,* Harper & Row, 1979.
325   U.S.-Soviet compromise: Ibid.
325   Carter in a squeeze: Committee on the Present Danger,
        statement, *Where We Stand on SALT,* July 6, 1977.
326   Problem of treaty language: Talbot, op. cit.
327   CIA failure in Iran: Staff Report, House Intelligence Com-
        mittee, *Iran: Evaluation of U.S. Intelligence Performance Prior to
        November, 1978,* January 1979.
327   CIA documents glued back together: Confidential inter-
        view.

NOTES AND SOURCES

327   Eagle Claw: Harry G. Summers, Jr., review essay, "Delta Force," *Military Review*, November 1983.

328   Carter's divided policy: Robert Komer, "Soviet Strength and U.S. Purpose," *Foreign Policy*, Summer 1976.

328   Brzezinski: Gloria Duffy, "Crisis-Mangling and the Cuban Brigade," *International Security*, Summer 1983.

329   Intelligence loses count: Confidential interview. The last definitive estimate was in 1963 (see "Russians in Cuba Now Put at 12,500," *New York Times*, June 20, 1963).

330   Carter cancels SR-71 flights: Confidential interview.

330   MiG-23 snapshot: Confidential interview. On the recurring intelligence controversy over MiG-23s in Cuba, see Raymond L. Garthoff, "American Reaction to Soviet Aircraft in Cuba, 1962 and 1978," *Political Science Quarterly*, Fall 1980.

330   Maximum intelligence effort: Confidential interview.

330   "Brigade": Duffy, loc. cit.

330   Turner caution: Confidential interview.

330   Senator Stone: Remarks, Senator Richard Stone, Hearings, Senate Foreign Relations Committee, *Hearings and Markup on the Panama Canal Treaties* (vol. VI), USGPO, 1978.

331   Senator Church: Duffy, loc. cit.

331   "No change": Ibid.

331   Military intelligence: Confidential interview.

331   "Are you saying . . .": Ibid.

332   Vance works out a settlement: Duffy, loc. cit.

332   Intelligence rethinking: Ernest Volkman and Robert Shrum, "The Cuba Syndrome," *Politics Today*, November–December 1979.

332   National Photographic Interpretation Center: Confidential interview.

333   Brown-Keegan dispute: Ibid.

333   "Madman": Ibid.

333   Brown's skepticism: Remarks, Secretary of Defense Harold Brown, National Press Club, Washington, D.C., March 18, 1977. Author's notes.

333   "Scientific smugness": Confidential interview.

334   Keegan threatened: Ibid.

334   B-47 failure: Keegan interview.

Chapter Ten: Omens and Oracles

335   Jim Smith: Smith interview.

336   Smith recruitment: Ibid.

336   American supermagnet: Ernest Volkman, "The Energy Technology Nobody Knows," *Omni,* April 1982.

336,
337   Smith's mission: Smith interview.

338   Caught by the KGB: Ibid.

339   South Dakota: Lou Cannon, *Reagan,* G. P. Putnam's Sons, 1982.

339   *SALT Syndrome:* Author's notes.

340   Committee on the Present Danger: Barry R. Posen, "Defense Policy and the Reagan Administration: Departure From Containment," *International Security,* Summer 1983.

341   Sixty-eight advisers appointed: Ibid.

341   "History is ours . . ." Confidential interview.

341   Reagan appointments, defense and intelligence: Justin Gallen, "Intelligence: The Reagan Challenge," *Armed Forces Journal,* January 1981.

341   SR Division targeted: Confidential interview.

341   Eviction of SR Division: Ibid.

342   Bloomingdale: Ibid.

342   Decline in CIA performance: Gallen, loc. cit. Part of the decline is attributable to the continuing (and bloody) battles with the military-intelligence agencies and the DIA. See Richard Ned Lebon, "Misperceptions in American Strategic Assessment: CIA and DOD," *Political Science Quarterly,* Summer 1982.

342   DIA revitalization, Graham: Les Aspin, "Misreading Intelligence," *Foreign Policy,* Summer 1981.

343   American arsenal: William M. Arkin et al., *Nuclear Weapons Data Book,* National Resources Defense Council, 1982.

343   "Window of vulnerability": R. Jeffrey Smith, "An Upheaval in U.S. Strategic Thought," *Science,* April 1982. This phrase, often repeated by Reagan and the conservatives, summed up what they perceived to be an immutable strategic formula: The increasing superiority of the Soviet strategic arsenal would very soon put all American strategic weapons at risk, making the United States vulnerable to a Soviet first strike. The important implication was that a huge (and very expensive) overhaul of the American strategic arsenal was

necessary in order to make those weapons invulnerable.

343 Reagan, *Reader's Digest:* Cannon, op. cit.

343 Teller's scheme: Peter Pringle, "Sci-fi Guru Behind Reagan," *Observer* (London), March 27, 1983.

344 CIA videotapes: Confidential interview.

345 T. K. Jones, "dirt is just great": Robert Scheer, *With Enough Shovels,* Random House, 1982.

345 William Casey, "Cyclone": Confidential interviews. For an account of Casey's OSS career, see Joseph Persico, *Piercing the Reich,* Viking, 1979.

346 CIA and Pipes: Confidential interview.

346 Casey and terrorism report: Ibid.

347 Max Hugel: Confidential interview.

347 Bobby Inman: Admiral Bobby R. Inman, speech, "The State of U.S. Intelligence," annual American Defense Preparedness Association meeting, Arlington, Va., November 17, 1981; see also interview with Inman in *Military Electronics and Countermeasures,* January 1983.

348 Inman's foot-jiggling: Confidential interview.

348 "The wanderer": Ibid.

348 Casey's red map: Ibid.

349 Casey misunderstands Cuban understanding: Interview, William Casey, *U.S. News and World Report,* March 8, 1982.

349 Enders: "The Voice with Echoes of Cambodia," *Manchester Guardian,* December 21, 1982. The reference is to Enders's previous service in Cambodia in 1970, when he helped direct secret American bombing strikes in that country.

349 "Danger . . . decisive battle": Ibid. Alas, even these draconian pronouncements were not enough for the Reagan administration; Enders was replaced in early 1983, and his Latin American post was turned over to an even harder hard-liner.

349 Nestor Sanchez: Confidential interview.

349 Guatemala death squads: Ibid.

349 Nicaragua: During the 1980 presidential campaign, conservatives signaled that they were appalled by Carter's action, and would seek a reversal of American policy if Reagan was elected. Most of the hard-liners on Latin American policy were clustered in a group called the Council for Inter-American Security, in Washington, D.C., which in September of that year produced a report advocating a renewed American strategic presence in the Latin American continent *(A New Inter-American Policy for the Eighties).*

350 Somoza: Bernard Diederich, *Somoza,* E. P. Dutton, 1981.

350 Somoza as CIA asset: Confidential interview.
350 OSN: Ibid.
350 Seduction of CIA code clerk: Ibid.
350 Intelligence offensive against Nicaragua: Ibid.
351 "Cuban-style obstacle courses": State Department briefing, "The Military Buildup in Nicaragua," March 9, 1982. (Author's notes.)
351 Buchanan's findings: Testimony, John H. Buchanan, hearings, Subcommittee on Inter-American Affairs, House Foreign Affairs Committee, *U.S. Aid to Honduras,* September 21, 1982.
352 Number of Cuban, Soviet advisers: Ibid.
352 Large-scale covert operation: Because of extensive leaks, the covert operation soon became overt. The major leaks were in *New York Times* (March 17, 1981), *Washington Post* (March 10, 1982), and *Newsweek* (November 18, 1982).
353 Two hundred agents in El Salvador, $65 million: Confidential interview. See also Phillip Taubman, "U.S. Establishes Extensive Central American Intelligence Network," *New York Times,* March 20, 1983.
353 Source of Salvadoran rebel arms: Confidential interview.
353 "You lost . . .": "El Salvador's War," NACLA *Report,* North American Congress on Latin America, September–October 1982.
354 D'Aubuisson: "Death Squads: the Real Government of El Salvador," *Covert Action Information Bulletin,* April 1981.
354 "Psychopathic killer": Katharine Koch, "Salvadoran Contender Linked to Death Squads," *Boston Globe,* March 29, 1982.
354 Numbers dispute: Confidential interview.
354 Handal papers: Karen de Young, "Sleuth of the Salvador Papers," *Washington Post,* March 14, 1981.
355 "Grocery-store papers": Ibid.
355 Haig claim: State Department Intelligence and Research Report, *Arming of the Guerrillas in El Salvador,* February 19, 1981.
355 Flaws in papers: Detailed critiques of the papers' authenticity were contained in *New York Times* (June 10, 1981), *Washington Post* (June 13, 1981) and the Pacific News Service (March 1981).
356 Constantine Menges: Confidential interview. Menges left the CIA but later was appointed as Latin American expert on the National Security Council.

356   Orlando Tardencilla: NACLA *Report,* September–October, 1982.
356   Tardencilla offered deal: Ibid.
357   Tardencilla recants: Author's notes.
357   Nicaraguan airport: CIA/DIA briefing, "Evidence of Military Buildup in Nicaragua," Washington, D.C., March 9, 1982. (Author's notes.)
357   American recommendation: Don Oberdorfer, "Nicaraguan Says U.S. Urged Airfield Work," *Washington Post,* March 11, 1982.
358   Grenada airport: Alan George, "President Reagan's Fantasy Island," *Defense* (Great Britain), July 1983.
358   Intelligence deductions: Confidential interview. For two opposing views of events on the island, see "Reagan's Big Lie," *Covert Action Information Bulletin,* Spring–Summer 1983, and "The Castroization of Grenada," *National Review,* September 17, 1982.
359   Airport construction nonmilitary: "Grenada Airport Project Halted by Invasion," *Aviation Week and Space Technology,* November 7, 1983.
359   "You've got to be . . .": Patrick E. Tyler, "CIA Planned Grenada Operation," *Washington Post,* May 6, 1983.
359   American suspicions: Staff report, Subcommittee on Oversight and Evaluation, House Intelligence Committee, *U.S. Intelligence Performance on Central America: Achievements and Selected Instances of Concern,* September 22, 1982.
360   Failed CIA Cuban operation: Confidential interview.
360   Soua Lee Vang: Ibid.
360   Refugee workers skeptical: Ibid.
361   Haig convinced: State Department Special Report No. 98, *Chemical Warfare in Southeast Asia and Afghanistan,* March 22, 1982. This report claimed, without any confirmation whatsoever, that ten thousand people had been killed by Soviet poison gas in those areas.
361   Lack of confirming intelligence: Gene Lyons, "Mainly on the Brain," *Inquiry,* March 15, 1982.
362   Scientific skepticism: Jamie Kalven, "Yellow Rain: the Public Evidence," *Bulletin of the Atomic Scientists,* May 1982.
362   Sverdlovsk incident: Zhores Medvedev, "The Great Russian Germ Warfare Fiasco," *New Scientist,* July 31, 1980.
362   Australian verdict: Australian Department of Defense, Defense Science and Technology Organization, Materials Research Laboratories (Organic Chemistry Division), *Technical*

Report: the Examination of "Yellow Rain" Specimens Received at MRL in April, 1982, October 1982.

363   SALT violations, "breakout": Jack Anderson, "Soviet Subterfuge a SALT Concern," *Washington Post,* May 23, 1980.

363   Gas pipeline: "Soviet Pipeline Goes Full Speed Ahead," *New Scientist,* January 27, 1983.

364   Europeans unimpressed: "Au coeur de la Siberie secrète," *Paris Match,* March 4, 1983.

364   CIA report: CIA, Directorate of Intelligence, *The Soviet Forced Labor System,* November 1982 (unclassified).

364   Poland failure: Confidential interview.

365   Falkland Islands: "A Failure of Intelligence," *The Economist,* April 10, 1982.

365,
366   CIA briefing, maps: Confidential interview.

Epilogue: The World and "Mother K"

369   Reagan in Langley: Author's notes.

369   Intelligence budget increases: William Ellsworth-Jones and Mark Hosenball, "CIA: Back to Dirty Tricks," London (Sunday) *Times,* April 15, 1984.

370   Reagan buildup of intelligence: Confidential interview.

370   CIA computers: Ibid.

371   Costa Rica: Ernest Volkman and John Cummings, "Our Man in Los Chiles," draft Mss.

371   "Warhead gap": Department of Defense, *Soviet Military Power '84,* May 1984.

371   Warhead-counting method: Confidential interview. See also William M. Arkin and Jeffrey I. Sands, "The Soviet Nuclear Stockpile," *Arms Control Today,* June 1984.

372   CIA station chief in Rome: Confidential interview.

372   Iran: Ibid.

373   CIA-DIA argument: Ibid.

373   Beirut: Ibid.

374   "Families" cover: Ibid.

374   Grenada: Ibid.

INDEX

INDEX

INDEX

INDEX